PRESSURE: is DEFINED Individually...

is ... A MOTIVATOR

is ... A POSITIVE

is ... Attractive ... WANNA Be Around it

Pressure is Attractive =
Motivation
Positive Situation
(Wanna Be Around it)

Do Simple Better....

> CONSTANTLY REDUCE

* Learn it
* Do it.
* Own it

* Mental Mechanics

* Physical Mechanics

* Team Mechanics (Player/Team)

> Game Prep (Video/Data)

> Game Prep (Swings/Throws/Ground Balls)

> Fewer Plays ... Done BETTER

> Just Because We Had the Experience doesn't mean we learned anything

> You only learn from failure if you get cut

The Book of Joe

ALSO BY TOM VERDUCCI

The Cubs Way:
The Zen of Building the Best Team
in Baseball and Breaking the Curse

The Yankee Years

Inside Baseball: The Best of Tom Verducci

Chasing the Dream:
My Lifelong Journey to the World Series

The **Book** *of* **Joe**

Trying Not to Suck at Baseball & Life

JOE MADDON *and* TOM VERDUCCI

TWELVE

NEW YORK   BOSTON

Twelve

Hachette Book Group

1290 Avenue of the Americas, New York, NY 10104

twelvebooks.com

twitter.com/twelvebooks

First Edition: October 2022

Twelve is an imprint of Grand Central Publishing. The Twelve name and logo are trademarks of Hachette Book Group, Inc.

The publisher is not responsible for websites (or their content) that are not owned by the publisher.

The Hachette Speakers Bureau provides a wide range of authors for speaking events. To find out more, go to www.hachettespeakersbureau.com or call (866) 376-6591.

Library of Congress Cataloging-in-Publication Data

Names: Maddon, Joe, author. | Verducci, Tom, author.

Title: The book of Joe : trying not to suck at baseball and life / Joe Maddon and Tom Verducci.

Description: First edition. | New York, N.Y. : Twelve, Hachette Book Group, 2022.

Identifiers: LCCN 2022026037 | ISBN 9781538751794 (hardcover) | ISBN 9781538751787 (ebook)

Subjects: LCSH: Maddon, Joe, 1954– | Baseball—Management. | Baseball managers—United States—Biography.

Classification: LCC GV865.M232 A3 2022 | DDC 796.357092 [B]—dc23/eng/20220701

LC record available at https://lccn.loc.gov/2022026037

ISBN: 9781538751794 (hardcover), 9781538751787 (ebook)

Printed in the United States of America

LSC-C

Printing 1, 2022

For Mom and Dad, who provided guidance and toughness;
Jaye, who created our path;
Sarah and Joey, who give me focus and purpose;
And Bobba Lou and Coach Rute, who provided mentorship

For the Verducci family,
with gratitude for the love and encouragement

Contents

"Get out of the Box"

From his usual perch on the top step of the dugout, Los Angeles Angels manager Joe Maddon watched Shohei Ohtani take his place in the batter's box for an at bat not seen in 118 years.

It was late in the afternoon in Anaheim on April 4, 2021, but early in the game. Shadows covered the field while golden sunshine bathed the outfield seats in the last hour of day. Ohtani had just pitched a scoreless top of the first inning for the Angels against the Chicago White Sox in which three of his pitches had been clocked at 100.1, 100.5 and 100.6 miles per hour respectively. Without time to sit down, here he was batting second in Maddon's lineup. He placed his left foot on the back line of the batter's box, swung his right leg into the box, tapped home plate with his bat, raised his bat parallel to the ground, bounced its barrel once on his shoulder, then tipped the bat upright and high, like a flag bearer announcing his arrival. He took no practice swing. He stood waiting. His leonine posture signaled fearsome readiness. Coiled calm before the pounce.

No Angels pitcher had hit for himself since the implementation of the designated hitter rule in 1973. No pitcher had batted second since September 7, 1903, when Jack Dunleavy did so for St. Louis Cardinals manager Patsy Donovan, who was born in 1865.

The idea had been unthinkable even recently. For three seasons the Angels did not dare allow Ohtani to pitch and hit in the same game. They adhered to the conventional wisdom that the task would be too grueling and subject him to injury. After a discussion with Ohtani in spring training of 2021, however, Maddon blew up such convention. This was the first at bat of the way forward.

"Many people around baseball or in the media were skeptical about it," Maddon says. "It was not fully embraced. Many people were interested, but not with full faith that it would work."

Three years earlier, as manager of the Cubs, Maddon had commissioned paintings by artist Jason Skeldon to raise money for charity, to promote baseball through art, and to provide visual reinforcement of concepts he taught his players about teamwork and winning baseball. In one of those paintings, Albert Einstein is portrayed as a baseball manager emerging from a cardboard box. Superimposed across his jersey in the handwriting of Maddon is a list of baseball conventions Maddon believes should be challenged, such as:

Take BP every day, even day game after night game.
Don't make the 1st out or 3rd out at 3rd Base.
Batting order should remain the same after a win.

Above Einstein are the words "Get out of the Box."

Why Einstein? The greatest scientific mind valued imagination. Einstein personified "out of the box" thinking.

"Accepted beliefs can stifle individuality and instinct," Maddon says. "When you adhere to them, you stifle what the player can become. It's important to be uncomfortable. Getting out of the box spurs growth and denies complacency."

Maddon thought out of the box with Ohtani. Validation took only one pitch.

The Chicago pitcher, Dylan Cease, delivered what he thought was a perfect first offering: a ninety-seven-mile-an-hour fastball at the highest border of the strike zone. Ohtani uncoiled. He smashed the pitch into the sun-washed bleachers in right field 451 feet away. In one inning of baseball Ohtani had thrown three pitches clocked at more than 100 miles per hour and hit one clocked at 115.2, the hardest-hit home run at the time by any Angels player in the seven years of such tracking. The Angels won, 7–4. It was the superhero movie trailer to an extraordinary blockbuster season of pitching and hitting nobody had seen since Babe Ruth.

"My first thought was that it would quiet the naysayers," Maddon says. "The result of one at bat did not matter to me. Shohei and I were committed to this plan. But I knew it gave us some time to prove this was the best approach. By the end of the season, this method of pitching and hitting looked so normal, and, of course, it was the right thing to do.

"To my eyes his swing looked so much better than the year before. More forceful. The sound and carry really stood out. He hits them *loud*. And the way his hands flip at the end really puts the finishing touches on his exit velocity.

"It's weird how the mind jumps in moments like that. I flashed back to Kris Bryant throwing to Anthony Rizzo for the last out of the 2016 World Series. My thought was it took 108 years for the Cubs to win, and now this—a once-in-a-century player. The entire game gave me more confidence we were on the right track."

Joe Maddon never played major league baseball. He logged twenty years in the minors as a player, manager, and instructor before getting a major league job. Despite his late start—or, as he tells it, *because of it*—he joined Joe McCarthy and Jim Leyland, the only other managers with no major league playing experience to manage nineteen seasons and win a World Series. More indelibly, he established himself as one of the great turnaround experts of the modern game. He took over a Tampa Bay team that had never had a winning season and a Chicago team with five straight losing seasons, and within three years at each stop guided them to the World Series. His 2016 Cubs ended the longest championship drought in North American sports.

Maddon gained renown as much for his out-of-the-box methods as for his success. In his first pennant race with the Cubs, for instance, he turned Wrigley Field into a petting zoo for his players, replete with a snow leopard, penguin, armadillo, and flamingo. The flamingo held special resonance for him.

"The flamingo knows balance," Maddon says, "as evidenced by his ability to stand on one leg for prolonged periods of time. Balance is what we seek, especially the balance between data and art."

Like Maddon, what you are reading defies convention. It is not a memoir. It is not an insider's account of how managing has changed. It is not a discourse on leadership. It is not insights into what makes a winning culture and how to manage people, from rookies to superstars. It is not a collection of life lessons from someone who rode in minor league buses for two decades and in the biggest championship parade in American history.

It is all of that. And more. Maddonism by Maddonism, it is a personal guidebook for finding balance as baseball and the world around us are increasingly shaped by data. As with his peripatetic journey, the paths are many, but the starting place is one. Think well.

The Book of Joe

CHAPTER 1

"Whatever You Put Out There Comes Back to You"

Quitting is the easy way. Joe Maddon heard its siren call in the spring of 1991. After fifteen years of service in the minor league system of the California Angels as a player, scout, manager, and instructor, Maddon was done with the organization. If he had to list an official cause for the disillusionment, it would have been easy to sum up in one word: *disrespect*.

The baseball field had always invigorated and inspired him. Yet for the first time in his life, Maddon was miserable on the diamond. Each day at the Angels' minor league camp at Gene Autry Park in Mesa, Arizona, he brooded. His work ethic suffered. Until one day, while walking to the parking lot with pitching instructor Bob Clear, he could take no more.

"Bobba Lou," Maddon said, using the name he gave his good friend, "I've had enough. I'm quitting. I'm leaving the Angels."

"Get in the car," Bobba Lou said. "Let's go for a ride."

Bob Clear was Maddon's baseball father. He was sixty-three years old at the time, twenty-six years older than Maddon. He looked like an honest, properly weathered cowboy from a Louis L'Amour novel, of which Clear had read all eighty-nine. He spoke frankly with language saltier than that of a sailor. He was tougher than the bottom of an old boot. Out of the limelight, Clear spent his life in service of others, sharing his knowledge and wisdom while asking nothing in return. In a word, he was a teacher.

When Clear died in 2010 at age eighty-two, his passing merited little more than a note in most news accounts. The legacy of such a life is found not in its fame but in the ripples of the many lives it touches. Maddon, and the success he has achieved, is one part of Clear's legacy. When Bobba

Lou died, Maddon called him "the best baseball coach who ever lived." Maddon later honored his mentor by naming one of his classic cars after him. The Bobba Lou is a 1972 Chevelle convertible with a 350 V-8, fuel-injected engine, red-and-white interior seats, and the 1908 Chicago Cubs logo on the trunk. Like its namesake, it makes a bold statement.

Elwood Robert Clear was born in Denver in 1927. He entered pro baseball at age seventeen as a five-foot-nine infielder in Class D ball. He could not hit much, so after three years he became a pitcher in hopes of staying in the game. He remained in the minors for thirty-one years as a player, manager, and coach—until the early morning of July 23, 1976.

That morning a not-so-great and cranky California Angels team touched down at Los Angeles International Airport after a flight from Cleveland, carrying among its oversize baggage a three-game losing streak and a 39-57 record. Players had been complaining to general manager Harry Dalton about the authoritative ways of manager Dick Williams, who was in his second year with the team and thought nothing of humiliating his own players under the guise of motivating them. It was the only way he knew. Williams ran his ball clubs with the outsize personality typical of managers in that era who had grown up during the Great Depression. Williams, Earl Weaver, Billy Martin, Gene Mauch, Tommy Lasorda, Whitey Herzog, Don Zimmer, Yogi Berra, and Jim Frey all were born between 1925 and 1931. All became "celebrity" managers whose personas and style became synonymous with the teams they managed. Many were identifiable by just one name. All but Berra had had little to no major league playing time to pave their path to the dugout. All but Williams stood less than six feet tall—he just reached that height.

For most of these men, life was hard and therefore so was the game of baseball. As a child in St. Louis, Williams had been raised by a stern, highly critical father who bore the constant economic stress of the times while working at an insurance company. As a player with the Brooklyn Dodgers, Williams would sit next to manager Charlie Dressen and relentlessly ride opposing players. His incessant bench jockeying earned him a reputation as Dressen's "Designated Jackass." Williams wore it proudly.

As a manager Williams ran even successful teams with a brutally harsh style once captured by Clif Keane in the *Boston Globe*: "He reacts to adversity by going incommunicado. By nature he is as inflexible as uncooked spaghetti. The warmth of his personality would hardly melt a snowflake."

By the time the Angels' plane from Cleveland landed, a revolt was brewing against Williams. The team boarded a bus for Anaheim. Players cranked music from portable stereos in open defiance of Williams, who had banned music while traveling.

"Quiet, all you winners!" Williams snarled from his seat at the front of the bus.

That was enough for third baseman Bill Melton. He jumped from his seat and headed toward Williams. The two men met in the aisle. They were separated before a punch could be thrown.

"You're suspended!" Williams barked at Melton.

Williams was done. Angels owner Gene Autry fired him the next day and replaced him with Norm Sherry, one of the team's coaches. Also gone was bench coach Grover Resinger, Williams's right-hand man. Born in 1914, the son of a St. Louis plasterer, Resinger played and managed in the minors for thirty-two years while often being described as a "pepper pot." He was another Depression-era disciplinarian who grew up admiring the rough-and-tumble Gas House Gang teams of the St. Louis Cardinals.

As a minor league manager, Resinger once refused to leave the dugout after an umpire ejected him. The umpire gave him five minutes to leave. Hearing this, Resinger walked to the umpire. "Can I see your watch?" he asked. The umpire handed it to him. Resinger promptly turned and heaved it over the grandstand.

When Resinger heard Williams had been fired, he resigned, just as he had done as a coach with the 1966 Braves when manager Bobby Bragan was fired and with the 1967 White Sox when manager Eddie Stanky was fired. Resinger believed a manager should pick his own coaches. Often those coaches were the manager's drinking buddies. With Resinger gone and Sherry elevated to manager, the Angels needed another coach. Only then, after thirty-one years in the minors, did Bob Clear finally reach the majors. So respected was Bobba Lou that he lasted eleven years there under five Angels managers.

By the spring of 1991, Clear was in his fifth season after having returned to his role as a minor league instructor. As it turned out, Maddon needed Bobba Lou that day more than any minor league pitcher did. Clear said almost nothing as Maddon drove from Gene Autry Park. Maddon pulled the car into the parking lot of a restaurant, Anzio Landing. He switched off the ignition. Then Maddon unloaded.

He had been stewing for five months. He traced his anger to the Angels' organizational meetings held the previous October at a large ballroom in Arizona. Virtually everyone in baseball operations had been there: scouts, coaches, managers, field coordinators, and front-office executives.

"It was an annual event that has pretty much gone by the wayside," Maddon says, "and I think because quite frankly the front offices don't want that kind of input. They don't feel it's necessary or important.

"They have minimalized information coming from coaches. They're not into as much from coaches. The flow of ideas has turned sharply in the other direction: front offices to coaches. They prefer their own methods, and they would prefer not to go through that process of listening to guys who they have no real confidence in their ability to evaluate. That's just the truth."

It was during that 1990 organizational meeting that the Angels named Bruce "Jeter" Hines as the major league first-base coach, replacing Moose Stubing, who was let go after twenty-two years with the franchise. Hines, then thirty-two, was the roving minor league defense instructor. Maddon, then thirty-six, was the roving minor league hitting and catching instructor. Maddon had nothing against Hines. In fact, they were good friends. He simply could not accept being passed over for a big league job after fifteen years of service in which he'd had a hand in developing players such as Kirk McCaskill, Devon White, Mark McLemore, Bob Kipper, Paul Sorrento, Jack Howell, Lee Stevens, Chad Curtis, Tim Salmon, and Gary DiSarcina.

"A lot of the stuff that we did in Instructional League were my ideas," Maddon says. "There was nobody giving me ideas. They were my ideas. I would sit down and draw out our game plan. I did the scheduling. I sat down and talked to players, and I would go over their strong points and weak points and set goals for them in that particular camp.

"I was the hitting coach, I was the field coordinator, the catching coach, the baserunning coach. I was in close contact with Billy Bavasi, the general manager, all the time. I'm not trying to overstate it. It was true. So when they named Jeter the first-base coach, I was livid."

Maddon thought his being passed over might have something to do with a conflict he'd had with Doug Rader, the Angels' manager. Two years earlier, the Angels had hired Rader as a special adviser, which positioned him as an heir to the managing job, given that he had managed the Texas Rangers from 1983 to 1985 and coached under Tony La Russa with the White Sox in 1986.

Rader was part of a generation of managers hired because they exuded toughness. Rangers general manager Joe Klein had hired Rader in 1983 over Jim Leyland partly because he felt Rader, who stood six foot three and weighed 230 pounds, could physically intimidate players who needed prodding. "I'd like to have him with me in a dark alley," Klein said proudly.

Rader did more than look the part. While a student at Illinois Wesleyan University, Rader had made side money as a professional boxer under the name of Lou D'Bardini and as a semipro hockey player under the name of Dominic Bulganzio. He lost every one of his twenty fights, but not because he lacked confidence.

As a rookie with the Astros in 1968, Rader walked up to a teammate and said, "Are you Bob Aspromonte?" The third baseman replied, "Yes, I am," to which Rader responded, "Well, I'm Doug Rader, and I'm going to take your job." And he did. Aspromonte was traded to Atlanta after the season.

Known as the Red Rooster for his hair, ruddy complexion, and cockiness, Rader also enjoyed playing the role of scoundrel. In an interview with Jim Bouton, he advised kids to eat their baseball cards rather than chew the bubble gum, because the cards were packed with information. He once invited teammate Norm Miller and his wife to his house for dinner, but then decided he was no longer in the mood to entertain. He greeted them at the door stark naked. They left. "Works every time," he said.

Rader began successfully with the 1983 Rangers, but in a short time his intensity created problems. After a fourth straight loss in May in Kansas City, Rader reacted to a reporter's question in his office by smashing an unopened beer can with his fist, throwing his spikes, punching a steel door, and slapping a clothes rack so hard that his pants flew across the room and landed on a reporter's head. The terrified reporter dared not remove the pants from his head until the interview concluded.

A bit later Rader told one of his coaches, Rich Donnelly, "I'm walking back." The team hotel was six miles from the ballpark. He handed Donnelly his boots. "I've got to punish myself," he said. Rader walked the six miles barefoot. By the time he arrived, his feet were covered in blisters.

Rader feuded with reporters, baited umpires, and humiliated his own players. He once answered every question from one reporter with the same two-word expletive. He kept up the profane humiliation for two weeks. The day after losing to Baltimore on a disputed home run call, he handed not only his lineup card to the umpires but also a Baltimore lineup card with four spots left blank. "This," he said, pointing them out to the umpires, "is where you guys fit in." He was promptly ejected.

Rader spoke bluntly without concern for insulting players. As manager at Triple A Hawaii, he would walk into the clubhouse after a loss and bellow, "You guys stink!" After his rookie season managing the 1983 Rangers, Rader blasted popular six-time Gold Glove catcher Jim Sundberg in a radio interview. While acknowledging Sundberg was "a fine human being," Rader said, "I think we need a different kind of human being. I think it is in our best interests and Jim's to go ahead and make a change at the catching position. The thing I want most out of a catcher is some aggressive behavior. I want some leadership capabilities."

A few days later, the Rangers traded Sundberg to Milwaukee, where he made the All-Star team. The next year, 1985, after another trade, Sundberg won the World Series with the Kansas City Royals. The Rangers fired Rader that year with the team off to a 9-23 start. Even Rader understood. "It got to the point where they expected me to act like an ass, and I did," he said. "When I was finally fired, I was actually relieved. I was totally exhausted, and so was everyone around me."

By the time the Angels hired him as an instructor in 1988, Rader had mellowed a bit but still preferred a testosterone-heavy method of leadership. One day that year, Rader and Maddon visited the Angels' Class A team in Bend, Oregon. Rader arranged a white-water rafting trip for the team.

"I think he was testing everybody's courage, probably because he knew he would be the big league manager at some point without us knowing that," Maddon says. "So down the Deschutes River we went, terrified. I did it even though I didn't want to do it."

Rader talked hitting with the players. His philosophies sometimes clashed with those of Maddon, the hitting instructor. Maddon sensed the two men did not click.

"Primarily because of me, honestly," Maddon says. "Doug and I didn't hit it off. I respected him. I thought he was brilliant. He had a tremendous sense of humor and a great mind. But I disagreed with a lot of his concepts.

"Actually, one of my favorite ideas that he brought up to me—and I still utilize it—is that hitting is timing management. I thought that was the best thing he said. But he constantly thought about hitting the outside of the baseball, which means trying to pull the ball a lot. And that's where we went our different directions—from that one thought."

After one year in an advisory role, Rader succeeded Cookie Rojas as Angels manager in 1989. It was after Rader's second season, in the ballroom in Arizona during the organizational meetings, that Hines, not Maddon, was announced as the replacement for Stubing as Rader's first-base coach. Five months later, Maddon still carried the perceived slight like a millstone around his neck.

"It's just wrong," Maddon told Bobba Lou in the parking lot of Anzio Landing. "It's just so unfair. That job belonged to me. I earned it. Nobody else. With all the things I've done for this organization? To be treated like this? It's just wrong on so many levels.

"I've got no choice, Bobba Lou. I'm going to quit the Angels. And you know what I'm going to do? I'm going to go get a job with somebody else and show them just how big of a mistake they made."

Bobba Lou just sat there and listened, the way a good teacher would. He let Maddon vent. Only when it appeared Maddon had exhausted his complaint did Bobba Lou speak, immediately changing the climate in the car with his measured, cool voice.

"Let me tell you something, Joe," he said. "You don't want that job anyway."

Maddon looked at him sideways. Not want that job? Maddon had been plugging away for fifteen years through long bus rides, back fields, decrepit motels, and little money left to save, and Bobba Lou thought he didn't want a major league job? This was *the Show* they were talking about. Sure, the money was better, you could eat at restaurants with tablecloths, and the shower water always ran hot, but a lifelong minor leaguer wanted a big league job for the recognition that he and his work were valued.

"Listen," Bobba Lou continued. "There's not enough for you to do in that job. You'd be bored with it. I know what it's like to coach in the big leagues. And another thing: they're going to be messing with your hitters, the guys you've worked with to help get them to the big leagues, and that's going to drive you nuts. You know you and Doug are not on the same page philosophically when it comes to hitting. Seeing them mess with your hitters will drive you nuts.

"I'm telling you, Joe, you don't want that job. They're doing you a favor."

Because it was Bobba Lou speaking, Maddon listened. It was not just the glacial coolness of Bobba Lou's voice. It was his gift of vision. It was the gift he had to see every side of an issue with astounding clarity.

Most of us look at an issue from our personal perspective, with all the life experiences and biases we've accumulated that have brought us to it. Bobba Lou could see it from many angles. It was the difference between an X-ray and a 3D MRI.

"Bobba Lou taught me—and this was weirdly progressive at the time—when to look the other way," Maddon says. "When I was a young manager and coach, I would get upset about everything. A thousand different little things would set me off.

"For instance, even when earrings became popular, I could not believe guys would wear an earring or have a tattoo. When I was in my late twenties and right around thirty as a young manager and coach, that was not the way you wanted to present yourself in baseball.

"I think Barry Bonds had come out with an earring at that time, and I was kind of offended by it. But Bobba Lou asked me why. Why would I be offended by that? What difference does it make? None. Absolutely no difference whatsoever. The guy played hard, played well, and it made no difference whatsoever. And I knew from then on, I needed to start changing that. He was probably right around sixty years old at that time when I first started working with him more closely in the minor leagues. He taught me that.

"It's true even with some players who may have 'bad body language,' like Jim Edmonds. I love Jimmy. We really had a hard time getting to Jimmy in the minor leagues. We were concerned. His work habits and work ethics weren't that great. I'd get upset. I actually assigned Eddie Rodriguez, a minor league manager, to work out Jimmy at the end of every practice in spring training. I'd sic Eddie Rodriguez on him. And I'd get upset when I thought Jimmy's quote-unquote body language was not good.

"Again, it was Bobba Lou who taught me to look the other way. 'What difference does it make, as long as he plays?' And so to this day there are times when I will look the other way with different guys. So I've learned when it's time to look and stare and other times when to look the other way.

"Players cannot live up to your perception of what they should be 162 games a year, twenty-four hours a day. None of us can do that for anybody. As a manager, you have to realize that. Bobba Lou is the one that got that across to me.

"You'll know when it's time to get in there and put the hammer down, and there are other times when it really doesn't matter and maybe the guy is just having a bad day. Then there are times he's struggling so much you do need to get in there somehow, but more in a way that's going to listen more and try to help as opposed to try to beat them down even further.

"Bobba Lou taught me when to look the other way, and if a player did not run hard to first base, he would tell me to fine him and not take him out of the game because you might need him in the game. There were times I did yank guys. I yanked guys, and Bobba Lou would get pissed off at me for doing that. We used to get in such heated arguments. I mean like yelling at each other in the clubhouse first thing in the morning."

One spring training morning, Maddon saw a picture on the front page of a newspaper of Mark McGwire swinging a bat.

"Look at this!" Maddon shouted. "His hands are in perfect position!"

"That's all wrong," Bobba Lou said.

"What do you mean it's all wrong?"

For the next half hour, the two of them argued about whether McGwire's hands were in perfect or poor position.

"What a great learning ground he created for me," Maddon says, "because either way, nobody ever walked away from these arguments concerned about hurting somebody's feelings or if we said something out of place. Because we weren't attacking each other. We were attacking each other's techniques, philosophy, teaching methods, whatever.

"Bobba Lou is the one guy who showed me the truth in one of my favorite sayings: 'When the student is ready, the teacher will appear.' A corollary to that is, 'I can't teach you anything. I can only make you think.'

"These are things I've read and studied, but Bobba Lou showed me. He would always tell me, 'I'm just trying to make you think,' and that's what he was really good at. He would just make me think. He wouldn't tell me necessarily what to do, but he threw stuff at me all the time."

One day in 1987 in Cedar Rapids, Iowa, Maddon ran a contact hitting drill with the Quad City Angels, the Angels' affiliate in the Class A Midwest League. Maddon showed the hitters how they should move their hands to start the swing. When the drill ended, Bobba Lou fiercely scolded Maddon.

"You can't clone hitters, and you can't clone pitching deliveries," Bobba Lou said. "You've got to let guys be themselves."

"I'm not cloning anybody!" Maddon replied. "I'm teaching them the first move, which I think is important for everybody."

"You can't do that," Bobba Lou said. "Stop trying to clone them. You just can't do that! Don't treat every hitter the same."

Maddon stopped teaching that way, even though he still thought he was right. He stopped because he had that much respect for Bobba Lou.

Three years later, Maddon was working in Instructional League with a strong-armed twenty-one-year-old catcher who'd hit .203 that season in rookie ball. Tim Kelly, the scout who had signed the catcher out of Cal Riverside in the sixth round, believed the kid could hit. Given his own background as a scout, Maddon felt obligated to honor the scout's evaluation. He did everything he could in Instructional League to turn the catcher into a hitter. It wasn't working. The catcher could not hit a lick.

Bobba Lou surveyed the issue in his usual 3D MRI manner. The kid had a great arm. Why not turn him into a relief pitcher? He kept badgering Maddon with the idea. Maddon, in deference to the signing scout, resisted. Finally Maddon gave in. He, Bobba Lou, and the minor league directors decided to try the catcher on the mound. They did so independently, with no input or permission from the general manager, an action that today would be deemed insubordination. They took the catcher to the bullpen mounds between Fields 1 and 2 at Gene Autry Park and said to him, "Throw." The kid had a bit of an unorthodox delivery with a high leg kick, but the ball came out of his hand with velocity and ease.

When the session was over, Bobba Lou told Maddon, "I'm telling you, don't ever let anyone mess with his delivery. Let him wind up and throw the way he wants to and just leave him the hell alone."

Another coach might have polished the delivery—prettied it up. Bobba Lou saw the kid's raw delivery from a hitter's perspective. The kid's leg kick, thick body, and arm swing made it difficult for a hitter to pick up the baseball. The kid threw hard, and the bit of funk in his delivery layered deception upon velocity. The ball would get on hitters even faster because they would pick it up late.

The catcher's name was Troy Percival. From that day at Gene Autry Park when he first climbed the mound to his last pitch nineteen years later for Maddon and the Tampa Bay Rays, Percival threw every pitch with the same delivery. In between, Percival registered 358 saves, secured the last out of the 2002 World Series, and earned $51 million.

"Because of that lesson that day on a mound between fields at Gene Autry Park, I'm really careful when people are trying to alter deliveries of pitchers," Maddon says. "Even with the arm strokes of players I'm careful, because that's pretty much how their body works."

It was only a few months after that Instructional League bullpen session with Percival that Bobba Lou gave a fed-up Maddon career advice of his own in the parking lot of Anzio Landing. And because it was coming from Bobba Lou, Maddon paid heed again.

"Of course, I had bills to pay, too, so I wasn't quitting anything at that time," Maddon says.

He went back to work, but it was not the same. He sulked. He did not see the reward in extra work. His mood darkened.

"I was short and sarcastic around people," he says. "I'm not normally that way. This attitude bled into the season."

Maddon's job involved flying to the Angels' minor league affiliates to work with players on their hitting and catching. He was a teacher. Learning, however, is neither effective nor fun when the teacher is a crank who is bitter about being passed over for his first major league job.

"I just couldn't get over it," Maddon says. "I could not turn the page."

One day Maddon arrived in this dark mood at the Phoenix airport for a flight to Midland, Texas, home to the Angels' Double A team in the Texas League. His mood only worsened when he found out he had been assigned to a middle seat. He boarded the flight and immediately affected the international do-not-disturb posture, putting on the foam-eared headphones of his portable cassette player, pressing "play" on *The Wild, the Innocent & the E Street Shuffle*, crossing his arms, and closing his eyes. A large man took the seat next to him on the aisle. Then a woman took the window seat on the other side, completing the unhappy sandwich.

The woman was not an experienced traveler. She seemed a bit nervous, which she gave away by trying to engage Maddon in small talk that could serve her as a diversion. With polite, clipped responses, Maddon did the best he could to acknowledge her while covertly signaling, "Hey, I'm trying to listen to music here and have no interest in being a lively conversationalist because I'm still feeling sorry for myself about getting passed over for a job I deserved."

This Albee theater production went on for some twenty minutes—the nervous woman seeking the small comfort of idle conversation and the aggrieved baseball coach doing his level best to avoid chitchat without being an absolute jerk. Maddon barely listened to her. Until she spoke these words:

"Whatever you put out there comes back to you."

Suddenly Maddon sat upright and ripped off the headset.

"Whoa!"

For the first time he turned to the woman and looked directly into her eyes with rapt attention.

"Can you repeat that, please?"

"Sure," she said. "Remember one thing: whatever you put out there comes back to you. If you put out positive vibes, you're going to get positive vibes in return. If you put out negative vibes, you're going to get negative vibes in return."

Maddon smiled—for one of the few times in months. The words cut right to his soul.

"Damn, you talk about a moment in your life when the power of words overwhelms you," he says. "Here is this person I never saw before and never saw again after that. I could not have been in a worse mood. And then she said that, and I could not have been in a better mood.

"I got off that airplane, got in my rental car, checked into the hotel, and went to the ballpark at Midland. I walked into that ballpark with all the energy I ever had in my life. I found myself again.

"With me it had always been about a positive message, but I had lost that. I went to the ballpark in Midland that day knowing that if I got back to what I had always been, which was to be a positive influence, that by throwing out positive vibes to everyone around me, that's what I'm going to get in return."

Maddon has been shaped by the lessons and wisdom of great leaders throughout his life, especially in his formative years. It began with his parents.

Along with their father, Carmen Maddon (né Maddonni), Joseph Anthony Maddon and his four brothers operated C. Maddon & Sons Plumbing and Heating in Hazleton, Pennsylvania. Known throughout the blue-collar coal town as Joe the Plumber, Maddon's father kept pipes and furnaces in working condition there for sixty years, always with a smile on his face and a Phillies Cheroot between his teeth. Maddon's mother, Albina, known to everyone as Beanie, worked into her eighties at Hazleton's Third Base Luncheonette, which lived up to its name as "the closest thing to home." From them he learned the value of an honest day's work and how to meet challenges with a smile.

Other leadership influences on Maddon were Richie Rabbitz and Jack Sewell, his midget football coaches, who "taught me how to be tough" by showing him how to take a hit, get up without crying, and not let the group down. There also was Adam Sieminski, his high school football coach, who would wear a short-sleeved shirt even in sleet and snow, and who had one tooth that was always falling out of its socket when he talked, a reminder of a hit he had taken at Michigan State from Alan Ameche of Wisconsin that broke his single-bar face mask so hard it smashed through his mouth and out his cheek. After a loss, Sieminski ran the team as hard and long as marathoners.

"Yeah, I was afraid of him," Maddon says. "Self-discipline and toughness. That's what he taught me."

Another important leadership model was Lafayette freshman football coach Bob Rute, who tutored quarterback Joe Maddon after playing at Duke, serving in the marines in World War II, and retiring from an illustrious career coaching at Easton High School.

"He taught through communication and not through intimidation," Maddon says. "God, did I love him. He was the best. If anybody had the strongest impact on how I am as a coach, it's probably Coach Rute. He is the gold standard because he did a wonderful job explaining things to me and breaking them down without ever yelling. He taught me how important it is to communicate. He was always there for me."

Another model was Lafayette baseball coach Norm Gigon, who had played thirty-four games for the 1967 Cubs, who turned Maddon from an infielder to a catcher and told him, "You might have a chance of playing pro ball, but you ain't ever playing in the big leagues."

"That's so good," Maddon says. "I mean, I laugh now, and I probably laughed back then. I thought it was great. I loved when coaches were straight up with me. It was just fuel to show them they were wrong. He knew I wasn't close to being as good as he thought he was. Loved it.

"The thing about Gig, he was a good teacher of the game fundamentally. He taught me how to catch. He taught me how to run the bases."

Like the rings of a giant oak, teachers, coaches, and mentors tell the story of our accumulated life. They provide layer upon layer of life lessons that shape who we are.

"We're all plagiarists," Maddon says. "Every one of us. We get information that is passed on, whether it's in a classroom, people that coach us, or mentors that teach us. Where it no longer becomes plagiaristic is when you put your own identity to that thought. And that's the difference between a follower and a leader.

"A follower who is in the position of leadership cannot extrapolate independently, 'What do I think? What's the right answer right here?' The follower needs to hear it from somebody else first before he's able to do that.

"Great leaders take the information and act upon it with pure intentions."

In this thick band of teachers, coaches, and mentors who have shaped Maddon and how he manages a baseball team, the one who provided the core foundation of his philosophy remains to this day anonymous. The words forever echo from the woman next to him on the plane from Phoenix to Midland: "Whatever you put out there comes back to you."

"That was exactly what I needed to overcome this particular dark moment in my life," Maddon says. "I was an absolute mess until this woman uttered that phrase to me. And it helps me to this day. I can't tell you how many times I've uttered that phrase to myself and it got me through the day.

"I might be having a hard time with something. I have my moments where I lose that centered feeling. We all do. I'm probably overthinking. Maybe I'm a little bit tired. It's normally a fatigue-based thing.

"OK, what do I do? Two things. One, I think about what she said. 'Remember, jerk, whatever you put out there will come back to you.' If I put positive vibes out there, there is a pretty good shot positive comes back. Put negativity out there, pretty good shot you'll get negative crap in return.

"Think about it. It's true. There's that group of people you just love to be around and there's others that when you see them coming, you definitely try to reverse course, get out of the way as quickly as you possibly can, and hope they won't see you. When the phone rings, you see the caller ID, and it's 'I am not answering that.' Or there are others you cannot wait to pick up the phone. You know there's something good at the end. It so matters. So from that moment on to this point, I think about that.

"We all have our difficult moments. You learn to move on from them. If I'm having a tough moment, it also normally requires a killer stereo, either in the dark or just riding in one of my cars at night to nowhere in particular, with *The Wild, The Innocent & the E Street Shuffle* cranked.

"The conclusion is this: Number one, whenever you're feeling down, realize one thing—whatever you put out there comes back to you.

"Number two, play your favorite music in the dark or at night in your car driving by yourself, and it will get you right every time."

CHAPTER 2

"Be Uncomfortable"

One day in 1871 in the snowbound Swiss Alps, a twenty-three-year-old doctoral geology student lost his footing and fell off a steep cliff. He went hurtling toward his death. In the handful of seconds between going airborne and meeting his expected fate, something very strange happened. Time stretched like an accordion. The student, Albert Heim, had time to think about how he would never get to deliver his scheduled university lecture in five days. He thought about how news of his death would reach his loved ones. In his mind he consoled them. He had time while airborne to consider whether he should let go of his alpenstock and whether to fling away his eyeglasses. Then his entire life played out before him in a series of images. It was like watching a stage production in which he was the main character.

And then Heim heard a thud. He landed in snowpack. He survived the fall. Heim later wrote a paper describing his near-death experience as well as those of other accident survivors he interviewed. They told similar stories about how their lives flashed before their eyes.

At 12:47 p.m. on November 3, 2016, Joe Maddon experienced one of those moments when time slows and a lifetime plays out in the mind. As the throw from Cubs third baseman Kris Bryant perfectly landed hat-high in the first baseman's mitt of Anthony Rizzo on an unusually warm night in Cleveland, ending the longest and most famous championship drought in North American sports, Maddon saw with absolute clarity the people and lessons from his sixty-two-year life that had made the World Series–clinching moment possible. His thoughts began with his late father, Joe, whose favorite hat he had tucked into the waistband of his uniform pants, and his mother, Beanie, who had taught him what it means to persevere. His thoughts moved to the many coaches and mentors who had molded him, through the long bus rides and long hours playing, coaching, and managing in the minor leagues for seventeen years, and through the strife and sweat he'd invested in this baseball life with no guarantees it might ever be so rewarded.

"Here is a question I would ask Phil Jackson or Bill Belichick or any great coach," Maddon says. "If you had the choice to go back to one moment between that first championship in the minor leagues or college or to that big NBA, NFL, or World Series title, which one would you choose? For me the choice is between the Salem Angels winning the Northwest League championship in 1982 and the ground ball to KB and that throw to Rizz.

"On the surface, it appears to be simple. The last out of the World Series is the culmination of this big moment—all the hard work coming together. You're validated in front of a wider group. It's awesome. You always wanted to be in the seventh game of the World Series or win an NBA championship as a head coach, right?

"But think about the choice. Do you choose the struggle or the finished product? What's the preference? For me, the answer is the struggle, which I've always talked to my kids about.

"Every time my kids fell into a rough spot, I would try to remind them that 'Listen, I know this kind of sucks right now and things are bothering you a little bit, but understand one thing: there's nothing better than the struggle if you really go through it in a way knowing you're going to be fine at the other end.'

"In the meantime, that's what really challenges your abilities: the struggle. All the bad days and being able to work through them. The days with no money in your pocket. It's one thing to know when to pull Kyle Hendricks. It's another thing to face how are you going to pay those bills that came in for the last month while attempting to become a coach or manager that eventually is worthy of major league consideration.

"So for me? The choice is simple. It's the struggle. The struggle is why I am here."

Every game that Maddon managed, he stood on the top step of the dugout. He never sat down. With his thickly framed eyeglasses, Maddon resembled a great horned owl on its perch surveying the landscape. The owl is supremely adapted to monitor its environment, given its large eyes containing an abundance of rod cells, its head that can rotate 180 degrees, and the facial disc feathers that direct sound waves to its ears. Maddon stood on the dugout rail because he wanted to "feel" the environment of the game. It informed his thinking. As baseball relies more on algorithms and probabilities to dictate strategy, managers are often hired without the experience of running games in the minor leagues. Maddon was glad he was not one of them.

"The overarching point is that I'm so grateful," Maddon says. "I'm so grateful that it took me so long to get to the big leagues, and I'm so grateful that I hit a lot of roadblocks. So grateful that I had to figure out finances. That I had to figure out what to do with the hitter's hands when he dropped them too much. That I had to figure out when an infielder was too stiff coming at a ground ball and how to get him to soften that up.

"Managing and coaching is an amalgam of skills and experience. Utilize everything you've heard and been told, combine it with your own observation skills, and you actually can *feel* what to do. You have to feel what it is you want to teach because until the player feels what you're talking about, it won't click.

"All the well-intended verbal instruction is wonderful and it's necessary, but it's nothing until you get a guy to do something you want him to do and he immediately says, 'Hey, I just felt that. I get what you're talking about.' *Now* you've got something. Now you get it. That's teaching. That's coaching.

"And wow, when it comes to racism or any social issues, does that not apply in our society right now or what? There's only one way to really get people to change: to somehow get them to feel what you're talking about. Explanations? Words? Anger? No. It won't do it. It's about feel. It's all I ever talk about. It's about feel. How to get somebody to feel what we're talking about here. That's the key."

In spring training after the championship 2016 season, Maddon told his players, "Be uncomfortable.... Get out of the box." Getting out of one's comfort zone, he says, spurs growth and denies complacency.

"If you become a comfortable person, that subtracts growth from the equation," he says. "If you remain somewhat uncomfortable, you'll continue to grow. I think that's a really positive word."

The struggle for Maddon began in Hazleton, Pennsylvania, a town built on coal and a spelling mistake, in that order. Early nineteenth-century railroad developers learned during land surveys that Northeast Pennsylvania sat atop a massive anthracite coal field. Soon the earth was cracked open and the coal industry there boomed. European immigrants arrived in boatloads from across the Atlantic to do the dangerous and dirty work of getting the coal above ground. In 1857 Hazleton became an incorporated town, codifying its unique spelling in perpetuity when a town clerk mistakenly transposed the *e* and the *l* in the official filing.

Among the second wave of European immigrants who arrived to extract the coal from the earth was Carmen Maddonni, a red-haired Italian from Abruzzo, in the mountains east of Rome, though he would soon Americanize his surname to better fit into his new country. Both of Maddon's grandfathers worked in the mines. Beanie's father paid for it with his life. He died from black lung disease. Carmen got out alive. He quit to start C. Maddon & Sons Plumbing and Heating.

Three of Carmen's five sons joined him in the plumbing business, including Joseph Anthony Maddon, Joe's father. The brothers and their families lived in the apartments above the plumbing shop on East Eleventh Street, directly across from the high school. Joseph's eldest son, Joe, was born February 8, 1954. Maddon grew up in the epitome of a blue-collar town. Work, family, and religion formed the pillars of life in Hazleton. "A subdivision of Europe," Maddon calls it for its fusion then of mostly Poles, Italians, and Slovaks. It was a tight-knit, nurturing environment in which Maddon was constantly in the company of siblings, aunts, uncles, cousins, and neighbors. He benefited from the greatest gift a child can receive: the gift of knowing he is loved.

When Joe was a young boy, his father sometimes would take him on plumbing jobs. Joe's father unfailingly kept a smile on his face, even upon answering emergency calls to fix burst pipes in the middle of a frozen Hazleton night. His job was to perpetually solve other people's problems, a life mission his son would embrace. As for the plumbing business itself, however, it was to Joe what the mines were to his grandfather: he saw enough of it to know he wanted no part of it.

Sports fueled him. Friends called him Broad Street Joe—the Hazleton quarterback version of Broadway Joe Namath, his favorite football player—or Termite because he was small and feisty, or Monsignor because of his clean language, a trait that to his parents' chagrin would not last. Maddon was a three-sport standout at Hazleton High School. He went on football recruiting trips to Gettysburg and Brown, but as someone who had never slept outside his own bed on East Eleventh Street, he was uncomfortable at both places. He decided to play football at Lafayette College, about fifty-five miles from home, for coach Neil Putnam. In late summer of 1972, Joseph and Beanie drove their oldest son to Lafayette and dropped him and his footlocker at Room 123 of McKeen Hall.

Only three days later, just after freshman football practice had begun, Maddon walked to the pay phone at the end of the hallway in his dorm. He called his mother.

"Mom, I want to come home," he told her. "I'm going to become a plumber just like Dad."

He was homesick, and the competition he faced for playing time was nothing like what he'd known in little Hazleton.

"No, you are not coming home," Beanie said.

"No, I really want to," Joe told her. "I can't do this. I'm not good enough."

"After a week or so, you're going to be fine," she said. "You're going to get into it and you're going to enjoy yourself. You're staying there."

Maddon hung up. He stayed.

"Of course, after a week or two, she was right," he says. "From that point on, I rarely went home. I had a blast. Best time of my life."

Maddon's backfield coach on the Lafayette freshman football team was a man named Bob Rute who gladly did the job for no pay. Lafayette provided Putnam, the varsity head coach, with only enough funding for five coaches: himself and four assistants. Two retired high school coaches, Rute and Harry Bellis, had volunteered to coach the freshman team.

A former standout at Duke who'd played in the 1942 Rose Bowl, Rute left to serve two years with the marines in World War II and returned to graduate in 1946. He became the coach at Easton High School, where his teams were disciplined, well conditioned, and successful. Easton ran the split T and belly series on offense. Rute gave his quarterbacks the freedom to call the plays and audible. He was a man of few words who was known for his smile and quiet manner. He could effectively convey a message with just the right look, without raising his voice.

"When I looked into Coach Rute's background I found a man who exemplified all the qualities I expected an assistant coach to have," Putnam says. "He was an educator in the classroom and on the football field."

Maddon would play only three months under Rute. As the starting quarterback, Maddon led the freshman football team to a 5-1 record. But in just those three months Rute shaped what would be Maddon's style as a major league manager more than anyone.

"We were raised in such a football culture," Maddon says. "What Vince Lombardi did in the 1960s pretty much established that tough football mentality. Before that, for our parents, it was Knute Rockne. Our dads were raised that way.

"Everybody has always believed that not just discipline but also yelling at people is going to make a difference. I've always had a hard time with that. Coach Bob Rute was the best mentor I had. He's my standard-bearer of what a coach should be."

During the freshman football season, Maddon heard a siren call he could not resist. On an adjacent field, he could hear the baseball team engaged in fall practice. Baseball in the fall? He had never heard of such a thing. The next autumn, as Maddon was preparing to quarterback the varsity team, he decided to switch sports. He joined the baseball team as a shortstop and pitcher, his high school positions.

"My dad didn't talk to me for six months," he says. "But I had to do it."

With that decision Maddon fell under the sway of another mentor, Norm Gigon, the Lafayette baseball coach. Gigon was a learned man.

He had earned an undergraduate degree in history and government from Colby College and a master's degree in history from the University of Rhode Island, where he wrote his thesis on British imperialism in East Africa. Most impressively to Maddon, Gigon had played in the major leagues. (Though one of his managers and a future Maddon mentor, Gene Mauch, summed up Gigon's place in the Phillies organization this way: "He doesn't even look like a ballplayer.")

Maddon made his first two appearances on the mound, losing 6–0 and 3–0 on the team's tour of Florida. Meanwhile Gigon was so disappointed with his starting catcher that he asked for volunteers to catch.

"I had enough of not hitting," Maddon says. "I had caught seven games in Little League for UNICO when I was twelve years old. I would pitch and Danny Matracino would catch, and when Danny pitched, I caught. That was it.

"I raised my hand. 'I can catch.' I had not caught since I was twelve. 'Yeah, I want to catch. Yeah, I can do it. I got it.' So the next day, who's catching? Me. With zero work.

"Gig was a good coach, and he would wear your ass out, man. He would wear you out. I mean, if he didn't like something, he would tell you straight up."

Gigon was never as blunt with Maddon as he was one day when he discussed his chances of playing in the major leagues.

"You know, you're never going to play in the big leagues," Gigon told him. "The only chance you have of playing pro ball is as a backup catcher. But you ain't never playing in the big leagues."

Says Maddon, "I loved when coaches were straight up with me. Gig played in pro ball. He had a good idea of what the standard was. I wasn't close to being as good as what he understood that standard to be."

Maddon knew whatever chance he had of playing pro ball would be enhanced by playing in the Cape Cod Baseball League, where many of the best East Coast college players were seen by scouts.

"If you go back to the struggles that built my baseball career, my first major disappointment was not being able to get into the Cape Cod League when I was at Lafayette," Maddon says. "Coach Gigon, I think he tried very hard to get me in. He talked to different coaches in the Cape. I wanted to play there badly, man.

"I thought it would be a great combination of playing baseball and the opportunity to live there during the summer and all that entailed for an eighteen-, nineteen-year-old male. I couldn't get in. They kept saying no. Now and then I'd hear a maybe. Maybe there was a little bit of a tug at the string, but nothing.

"I ended up going to the Atlantic Collegiate Baseball League for a couple of years. I played for the Scranton Red Sox and that really was the turning point for me. Gary Ruby became my manager. Gary coached me and treated me in a way that brought out the best in me, just like Coach Rute. He let me be me. He let me play. He interfered when he had to, and in the second year, I came real close to winning the batting title there.

"And what happened then? I made the All-Star team. And where do we play? We play at Falmouth against the Cape Cod League All-Stars. I didn't have a big day. I'm not even sure if we won or lost that game, but I was so eager to go play against the Cape Cod League All-Stars because that's where I wanted to be. It's one of those revenge things.

"But that's the struggle. I couldn't get there. Couldn't get to the Cape. But sometimes things line up in a way that is absolutely better for you."

While playing in the ACBL, Maddon earned money digging fence posts one year and serving as a summer playground counselor the next. He worked the installation jobs with Richie Rabbitz, his midget football coach, who owned a fence company. Rabbitz was the kind of good-natured needler known as a ballbuster.

"You know, I could strike you out any time I wanted," Richie would say.

"No, you can't."

"I'll prove it."

Richie always had a bat and a few baseballs in his truck. They would stop at a school and use the brick wall as a backstop. Richie would pace off sixty feet, six inches.

"What would Richie do?" Maddon says. "The intimidation factor. He didn't have a great arm. He'd hit me. He'd throw at me. I'd have to be ducking pitches and hanging in there. And of course, if you don't do it, you're a weakling. So I did it. What a guy."

Every morning Maddon would awaken early, grab a brown-bag lunch Beanie prepared for him, and head with Richie to a giant pile of sand, where they filled ninety-pound bags and heaved them into a rickety dump truck. Then they would head to Sears, where customers filed orders. Richie and Joe would pick up the heavy six-foot metal poles to support the fence, the fence itself, ties, caps, and whatever other supplies they needed.

"The poles had a little edge on the bottom so you can get rocks out," Maddon says. "You had to move the rocks out of the hole because if the hole had to go no more than ten feet—and you're trying to dig a hole that wasn't gargantuan, which would require more cement—if that rock was in your way you've got to get it out with that pole, gloves, your hands, whatever. Oh my God, it hurt. This is the stuff I did before I went and played a game with the Scranton Red Sox. And some nights that would mean a drive to New York City or somewhere over New Jersey.

"Yes, that's the struggle. The next year I worked at the James Street playground. My cousin, Bob Curry, was in charge of the playgrounds. I wanted James Street because James Street was one of the two big basketball playgrounds in the city. Summer league games were huge, and if you're the head male instructor, you get to coach. I'd get my high-top Connies on, go down there in the morning, do my job. And I absolutely loved it because as a kid growing up, man, there was hardly anything better than going to those playgrounds.

"So this is my second year with the Scranton Red Sox. I tore it up that summer. I also was playing fast-pitch softball for the Young Men's Polish Association, YMPA. I'd go to work in the morning knowing I had a game that night. And then I'd drive to it, get there, loosen up, play catch, take a little infield, and the only time you hit is in the game. No batting practice. Maybe that's where my stuff about how so much pregame work is not necessary comes from.

"On the other days I was playing for the YMPA. That's where I learned how to shorten up my swing. Having to hit a ball from forty-five feet helped me get a little further in pro ball. And then we would go to the Young Men's Polish Association Club after the game and drink Pabst Blue Ribbon, and Taylor Mateo, one of the managers or coaches, would sing this song, 'Just Because.'

Just because you think you are something,
Just because you think you're so hot,
Just because you think you've got something that nobody else has got.
You smile and you spend all my money.
You think that I'm old Santa Claus.
I'm telling you, baby, I'm through with you
Just because, just because.

"Every game I pleaded with Taylor to sing that, him and Scrap Iron Fallabel. They were our two coaches.

"The struggle, man. Can you replicate that today? No. Would you give anything to go back to that moment? Absolutely. And then play it out after that the same way. The struggle is beautiful.

"That was my second year in Scranton. Then I go to Boulder. And when you go to Boulder, everything changes."

CHAPTER 3

"Tell Me What You Think, Not What You've Heard"

The telephone at East Eleventh Street rang one night. Maddon answered. It was the summer of 1975, and though Maddon was tearing up the ACBL, he smoldered with disappointment that no major league team had bothered to select this catcher from Lafayette in the draft. The man on the other end of the line identified himself as Bauldie Moschetti. Maddon had never heard of him.

Bauldie would become such an important influence on Maddon that a poster-size photograph of Bauldie hung over Maddon's desk at Wrigley Field when he managed the Cubs. It was as if Bauldie himself were looking over his shoulder. The photograph captured classic Bauldie: the dark, serious, Lombardi-like eyes, his classic coach's windbreaker, and his black wing tips—never spikes—at the bottom of his gray flannel baseball pants.

Bauldie Moschetti was born in Colorado in 1909 to Italian immigrants. At the age of only nine, he followed his father into the coal mines. One day his father did not make it out alive. He died in a mining accident. Bauldie was sixteen years old at the time and already the owner of a trucking company—well, one truck anyway. He turned that one-truck operation into a huge trucking company that made him one of the richest men in Boulder. He seemed to own half the town.

Bauldie's true love was baseball. In 1964, at age fifty-five, he founded the Boulder Collegians, one of the most successful summer collegiate teams in the country. Moschetti was not just the founder, but also the manager, general manager, chief sponsor, and head recruiter. Bauldie Moschetti wanted Maddon on his team.

Moschetti had heard about Maddon from Ralph DiLullo, an East Coast scout from Capracotta, Italy, a village in the mountains east of

Rome not far from Abruzzo, where Maddon's grandfather was born. Based on DiLullo's recommendation, Moschetti invited Maddon to play that summer with the Collegians.

"Quite frankly, I never heard of them before that," Maddon says. "When you're on the East Coast doing your thing, you don't get a lot of that. But yeah, I'll take it. Let's go.

"This is where I started playing against guys from Texas, Oklahoma, Southern California, Miami, the Florida schools, Michigan, Arizona State... everywhere. Now I was out in the real world, man. The real baseball world.

"When you grow up where I did, football was king. And now all of a sudden, you get an opportunity to play in Colorado for the Boulder Collegians. This is the time: either I do it or I don't. This is where I either take my shot and end up today with nineteen years as a major league manager or I don't. And it all happened because Bauldie called me one night and asked me if I wanted to come to Boulder.

"Would I ever want to go back to that moment in time? In a heartbeat. Are you kidding me?"

Maddon flew into Denver's Stapleton International Airport. One of the coaches, Ben Hines, picked him up in Moschetti's 1965 Pontiac. He drove Maddon to Baseline Liquors in Boulder, a store owned by Moschetti. They went to a tiny Mexican restaurant next door.

"What would you like?" Moschetti asked.

"I don't know," Maddon said. "I've never had Mexican food."

It was an educational summer, starting with Maddon's falling in love with the burrito. More important, by venturing out of Northeast Pennsylvania, he was about to find out if he was as good as he imagined he was—good enough to be a pro ballplayer. It took him just one workout to understand how hard it would be. Maddon was one of five catchers on the team. He was fifth on the depth chart. Several of the guys ahead of him were top prospects from California or had been drafted.

"So I said to myself, 'Listen, you have to find out if you can do this. You have to know that you belong,'" Maddon says. "I was happy to be there, hell yeah. But then how the hell do I stay here? How do I survive?

JOE MADDON AND TOM VERDUCCI

How can I possibly survive this with all these catchers? These guys are from such big schools. I'm from little Lafayette. How do I play with these guys? Can I play with these guys?

"Those were real, nightly questions on my mind as I'm trying to fit in. All these other guys were so comfortable. A lot of them had been there before. Bauldie was paying a lot of them under the table at the end of the year. I didn't know about that. They were so comfortable, and I was not. That probably worked in my favor."

For the first week Maddon mostly watched and endured headaches and sinus problems from altitude sickness as his body fought against the strangeness of the light air. Then one night, Moschetti put his number five catcher in a game at Scott Carpenter Park. Maddon played well.

"All of a sudden, I thought, *I'm as good as these guys. I can do this. I belong here,*" Maddon says. "And from that moment on, I became the starting catcher. That is not an exaggeration. That's exactly what happened.

"I went in there just full of doubt, not knowing what I was getting into, the headaches, the light air, guys who had been there and were much more comfortable than me, with greater experience than me. It was tough. But again, that's the struggle. At some point I'm competing and realize I can do this. I'm as good as these guys.

"And the moment I figured that out, I couldn't get a day off. Bauldie started playing me in doubleheaders."

Maddon grew so worn down that late one night he and two teammates flooded the field at Scott Carpenter Park by turning on the sprinklers and letting them spew water on it for hours. The next morning, he told Moschetti that the sprinklers must have malfunctioned.

"Guess there's no game tonight," Maddon said with mock sadness.

He guessed wrong. Moschetti hired a helicopter to air-dry the field. He also had Maddon and his two accomplices burn the water from the infield dirt by raking the dirt into rows, soaking it with gasoline, and lighting it on fire. Bauldie's Collegians, with Maddon behind the plate again, played that night.

The Collegians advanced to the National Baseball Congress World

Series in Kansas. Maddon hit a home run off Arizona State left-hander Floyd Bannister, who would be the first overall pick in the next draft. Maddon caught every inning of every game, even though one night on a play at the plate he was pancaked so badly by a runner that Hines had to take him to a hospital to get his back treated.

"We ended up eating Chinese food at some little dive in Wichita, Kansas, at two in the morning," Maddon says. "Didn't miss a game. Didn't miss anything. But that's also where I hurt my throwing arm for the first time on a strike three. Instead of getting up and throwing to third, I just reached around the hitter and just flipped it to the third baseman and pop, right in my right shoulder. I can still feel exactly where it happened. Dumb. God, I was pissed off at myself, but, of course, you keep playing. The struggle, man."

The Collegians won the World Series. That night an Angels scout named Nick Kamzic visited Maddon at the small, two-twin-bed room Maddon shared with three teammates at the Broadview Hotel, which opened in 1922 with a speakeasy in the basement and a horse-and-buggy station on its northwest side, a nod to the only source of public transportation at the time in western Kansas. Kamzic saw something in Maddon that he liked—probably himself. Kamzic, too, was born in Pennsylvania and had a love for baseball far bigger than his size. A five-foot-eight shortstop, Kamzic played four years of Class D minor league baseball before being drafted into the army in 1942. He came home four years later with bullet wounds from France and shrapnel wounds from Germany. He played two more seasons of minor league ball before becoming a scout. Legend has it that Kamzic was the first employee hired by Angels owner Gene Autry in 1961.

"Nicky Kamzic, my man, had been following me," Maddon says, "and I do believe he loved me for a lot of reasons, especially because I probably reminded him a lot of himself.

"He comes into my room at the Broadview Hotel with a contract offer for absolutely zero signing bonus. It was five hundred bucks a month and an incentive bonus clause. You got a thousand dollars if you spent ninety consecutive days in Double A, fifteen hundred more if you spent ninety consecutive days in Triple A, and five grand if you spent ninety consecutive days in the big leagues. I cannot tell you how I would have killed for that fifteen hundred back then. So I signed for exactly nothing.

"I know for sure I had a bottle of Chivas Regal with me. Not the big seven-fifty. The kind that dudes like to hang out on the street corner in the bag, those little flat things. And that's where it began. I signed that contract. I stayed up all night."

The next morning Maddon, the newly minted pro ballplayer, boarded a plane to Allentown, Pennsylvania, whereupon he headed straight to Jack's, a neighborhood bar near Lafayette. The eponymous owner was a buddy who was so old—around eighty—that he liked to tell Maddon that his favorite player was Hall of Famer Eddie Collins, who was born in 1887 and played his last game in 1930.

Maddon burst through the door of Jack's and shouted to the regulars, "Hey, what's up, everybody?"

"Where have you been, Joey?" Jack asked. "We haven't seen you for a while."

"I just signed a contract with the California Angels," Maddon declared.

The place erupted in cheers.

Says Maddon, "Talk about a thrill for me. Jack told me Eddie Collins was the best baseball player he had ever seen. From Jack's mouth to my ears. Now I'm telling him I just signed with the Angels. God, what a feeling to walk into Jack's and tell my man that.

"The struggle, man. It's a beautiful thing."

It wasn't long before Maddon realized he should not have agreed so quickly to that contract with no bonus money. He called up Walter Shannon, the Angels' scouting director. He tried to get Shannon to throw in a $2,000 bonus.

"Mr. Shannon, I have these school loans I forgot to bring up," Maddon said.

"Sorry, son," Shannon said. "You've already signed."
Click.

Maddon returned to Lafayette that fall while training for his first minor league season. He trained hard, hung out at the College Hill Tavern with fraternity buddies, and ran football betting sheets for a local bookie named Connie to earn some beer money—twenty-five cents for every dollar he took in.

The Angels assigned him in 1976 to Quad Cities, a Class A team in Davenport, Iowa. Players had the choice of flying there from spring training in Holtville, California, or taking a cross-country bus. Wanting to see the country, Maddon opted for the bus. Behind the wheel was Keith Barcus of Ottumwa, Iowa, which also was the home of H. Richard Hornberger, who under the pen name Richard Hooker and with W. C. Heinz had written the 1968 novel *MASH: A Novel about Three Army Doctors*. The book begins, "Radar O'Reilly, just out of high school, left Ottumwa, Iowa." Barcus made sure the bus stopped in Ottumwa on the way to Davenport so Maddon and the boys could get a look-see.

In Davenport, Maddon rented an apartment with Dickie Thon, a talented teenage shortstop signed by Kamzic out of Puerto Rico; Rafael Kelly, a twenty-one-year-old outfielder from the Dominican Republic; and Jerry Brust, a pitcher out of the University of Miami.

Maddon and the other players needed another roommate, so they invited Keith Barcus. Maddon did the cooking and most of the cleaning. "I was raised that way," he says. "I didn't mind it. I gave Dickie one job, one job only: 'Richard, you're in charge of the garbage. Make sure the garbage is taken out.' That's it."

Thon was not diligent about his one chore. Maddon was constantly reminding him, "Richard, take the garbage out. Please." The reminders did not work. Finally, one day Maddon took the garbage can into Thon's room and dumped the contents on his bed.

"You would think that might have injured the relationship at that time, but it didn't because Dickie was such a nice kid," Maddon says. "He got to the point where the garbage was always taken out after that."

The manager of the Quad Cities Angels was the appropriately named Moose Stubing, a large, barrel-chested man who'd passed up a football scholarship from Penn State to sign with the Pittsburgh Pirates. Stubing's first manager in pro ball, at Class D Brunswick Pirates of the

Georgia-Florida League in 1956, was Frank Oceak, who once was suspended for a year by Commissioner Kenesaw Mountain Landis for assaulting a minor league umpire. Born in Pocahontas, Virginia, in 1912, Oceak became a trusted coach of Pittsburgh Pirates manager Danny Murtaugh.

Stubing, then thirty-nine, toiled mostly in the minors. His entire major league career consisted of five hitless pinch-hit appearances for the 1967 Angels. As Stubing liked to say, "Seventeen days of coffee. But I didn't get a doughnut." He later joined the Angels as a scout. The 1976 gig with the Quad Cities Angels was his first as a manager. He insisted his players be on time—players even a minute late for the team bus were left behind—keep a spanking-clean clubhouse, and never forget that he was the boss.

"There's one of me and twenty-five of you," Stubing told his players. "So you better get to know me rather than me get to know you."

Says Maddon, "He told me he heard it from some manager along the way. I absolutely believe that. Don Lyons was my roommate, and he could not believe it, that anybody would actually say that if they're in a leadership position."

Maddon was the third catcher, behind Marty Martinson, a second-round pick out of Lakewood High School in California, and Stan Cliburn, a fifth-round pick out of Southern Mississippi. But by the end of the season, Maddon, who hit .294, earned regular playing time. One day Stubing told Maddon he wanted to see him in his office.

"Things are starting to come together," Maddon says. "I'm hitting and catching really well. So I'm like, 'Damn, this is cool. The manager wants to see me in his office.' I wasn't doing anything wrong. I was pleased to go in there."

The room was as small and spartan as you would imagine the office of a Class A manager might be. Stubing was playing cribbage with Chuck Estrada, the Angels' minor league pitching coordinator, when Maddon walked in with a bounce in his step.

"What's up, Moose?" Maddon says.

"Hey, you're in pretty tight with Dickie Thon, aren't you?"

"Yeah. Good kid."

"You take care of that boy, because he's going to play in the big leagues someday. I want you to keep your eye on him. When you go out at night, make sure you're with him. Make sure he gets home at a good time. Take care of him. He will be a big league shortstop one of these days."

"That's it?"

"That's it."

Maddon walked out shaking his head.

"Nothing about me," Maddon says. "Crickets about me. Not a word. Moose and I, we had a good relationship. I don't want to say love-hate, but...you got to be freakin' kidding me. I loved Richard. That was not the point. But damn it, Moose, give me something. Just give me a crumb to hold on to. Not even 'Hey, nice going. You're catching the ball well. Nice double in the gap last night.' Nothing like that. Nothing. Crickets. So that's what I got out of my manager."

A pattern began to emerge in Maddon's minor league career: he played decently, but with sporadic playing time, and managers did not communicate much with him. Despite his .294 batting average at Quad Cities, Maddon played in only fifty of the 131 games. After the season, a brother of Brust, one of his roommates, invited Maddon to his wedding in Minnesota.

"I starved myself all day so I could kill it at this reception," Maddon says. "As part of the wedding party, I had my tux on, which I couldn't afford but did anyway, and couldn't afford to get there, but I did anyway.

"I get there, and they had all these little finger foods. The groom's wife was Trixie. Very nice. I go, 'Congrats, Trixie. When is the main course coming?' She goes, 'Don't be a smart-ass, Joe.' I started explaining to her about Polish-Italian weddings in Pennsylvania and what they looked like with so much food. So I got screwed there."

The next season, 1977, Maddon was assigned to Salinas in the California League, another Class A league. Stubing, the manager, and Cliburn, the prize catching prospect, followed him there. Maddon played in fifty-eight games, which means he did not play in the other eighty-two. He hit .250.

In one of his rare starts that summer, Maddon rapped four hits as Joseph and Beanie Maddon watched among the 1,044 fans at Salinas Municipal Stadium. The local newspaper, the *Salinas Californian*, took the occasion to laud Maddon's cooking skills, which by then had gained renown among his teammates, not to mention Maddon's confidence.

MADDON TOO HOT FOR FRESNO

The Angels' "designated chef," Joe Maddon, was cooking at the plate last night and led Salinas to a 6-4 victory over the San Jose Giants.

Maddon, a catcher by trade and self-proclaimed master chef of minor league baseball, went 4-for-4 as designated hitter, including a double, and drove in three runs.

The next year, 1978, Maddon was certain he would be promoted to Double A El Paso. Maybe he could even collect that $1,000 bonus. Instead the Angels sent Danny Goodwin there to brush up on his catching after spending the previous season in Triple A. Goodwin was a prized Angels priority; he was the first overall draft pick in 1975. Maddon was sent back to Salinas, this time with Chuck Cottier as his manager.

"Wow, I was upset," Maddon says. "Once I went back to A ball and didn't get in that El Paso door, I had limited opportunity. I was way behind everybody.

"I got to play a little bit at the end of the first half. Then one day we're playing in Bakersfield and Joel Crisler was pitching. Good sinker. Good arm. Good guy. I'm catching. In Bakersfield, the sun sets directly in center field. The ball he was throwing was literally black. It looked like an eclipse. And I'm trying to catch it.

"He throws one of his sinkers and I see it late. I turned the glove the wrong way and it pushes my thumb in the wrong direction. And it blew up so much I could barely get it in my glove. What does that mean? If you can't put your fingers in your glove, you can't catch.

"It was right around draft time. The Angels draft a catcher named Danny Whitmer. They called him the Redlands Rifle because he was from Redlands, California, and he had a great arm. Much better arm than me. He threw out everybody.

"That put me back on the bench. Cottier was my manager, who I really, really liked a lot. But he wouldn't play my ass. I stopped talking to him. I would not talk to him. I could not believe I couldn't get back in there. I don't even know if I played five times the whole second half. I just sat there, brother. That's how this often went. They didn't give a crap about me. I was a nondrafted free agent and I just sat there.

"That's the struggle. Loved it."

Maddon played in only forty-two games. He hit .261. He was better known for his cooking than his hitting. Guys wanted to room with Maddon because, as he says, "I knew my way around a Crock-Pot." Maddon's specialty was homemade lasagna. Players would bring the beer and salad. Before serving the lasagna, Maddon would take a Polaroid picture of the dish. Then he would write the date on it, make a note on it of the people who had come to the apartment, and save it in a scrapbook. Players received only six dollars per day in meal money, so Joe's lasagna was a hit with the 1978 Salinas Angels.

Maddon hit two home runs that year, one of them in Visalia. The next night, while Maddon was taking batting practice, a scout named Loyd Christopher approached him.

"Can I ask you a question?" Christopher asked.

"Shoot."

"When are you going to stop playing and start coaching?"

"What the hell are you talking about? Aren't you paying attention? I just hit a home run last night."

Maddon was angry that Christopher would say such a thing to him. A ballplayer never wants to hear that he cannot play. But Christopher *was* paying attention. He was fifty-eight years old and had been in pro baseball for almost forty years, the past twenty-one years as a scout. He saw that Maddon was a twenty-four-year-old undrafted free agent from Lafayette logging his third consecutive season as a backup catcher in A ball. Christopher knew Maddon's future was brighter as a coach.

It got worse for Maddon that winter. One day a letter arrived. It was from the Angels. Maddon hadn't been expecting one. He opened it. That's how Maddon found out the organization had released him.

"I thought for sure somebody was going to pick me up," Maddon says. "There was a guy in Fresno, with the Giants, John Van Ornum, who loved me. I was so sure the Giants were going to want me.

"Crickets. Nothing."

Desperate to keep playing, Maddon went to spring training with the Bakersfield Outlaws, a dreadful independent team in the California League coming off a 48-92 last-place finish. Maddon never made it to Opening Day. He was living in a rented room in Salinas—"A closet," he corrects—when, toward the end of July, he went to see Joe Gagliardi, who ran the Santa Clara Padres, another independent team in the Cal League, as well as the San Jose Missions. Maddon had heard Santa Clara needed a catcher.

"Joe, listen, we don't need you here," Gagliardi told him. "We could do just fine without you."

"I want to play," Maddon insisted.

"I'll tell you what I'll do. I'll give you two hundred dollars for the month of August. Take it or leave it."

"I'll take it."

Says Maddon, "I'd have done anything to play. Anything."

The California League minimum salary was $600 a month, but the league did not apply it to players who had been previously released.

The 1979 Santa Clara Padres were even worse than the Outlaws. They were a co-op club thrown together just before Opening Day with no spring training together and with a roster of misfit players loaned by the Padres, Angels, Brewers, A's, Cardinals, and Mariners. To fill their roster, the Santa Clara Padres held an open tryout inviting anyone with college or pro experience to show. They listed only one other requirement of prospective players: "Additionally, they must be equipped with gloves and spikes."

The Padres began the season 1-21. They were featured on the ABC News show *20/20* as "the worst team in baseball." They began the season with only seven pitchers. The third baseman, Marty Serrano, worked a landscaping job until 4:00 p.m. each day. The manager, Joe Volpi, thirty-six, was a local high school math teacher who had never played pro ball. Volpi, who also coached the baseball team at Blackford High, was available because he had obtained a two-year leave so he and his wife, who taught French, could explore Europe. When Gagliardi, a friend, called in need of a last-minute manager for the Padres, Volpi had scuttled the European trip. His wife was on board with this choice.

"She understood that this was something I've always wanted to do," Volpi said.

The Santa Clara Padres wore red-green-and-white uniforms: green pants with a red shirt for road games and a white shirt for home games, set off by red caps with a green visor and a gold interlocking "SC." The colors were a tribute to the many Portuguese, Italian, and Mexican families in the area, though opponents' fans took the combination as a cue to taunt them by singing Christmas carols.

The Padres played at Washington Park, a rickety WPA project built in 1935 with a wooden grandstand and seating for about a thousand people. They averaged 285 fans per game, though it was common to see fewer than fifty people there. The ballpark was so bad that the league forced them to play many home games in the afternoon at San Jose Municipal Stadium, home to Gagliardi's other team, the San Jose Missions, a Mariners affiliate.

A twenty-three-year-old pitcher loaned to Santa Clara by the Angels, Mark Wulfemeyer, who had played with Maddon in Salinas in 1979, said two months into the season, "If you had a nightmare that your career was ending, this would be the place you'd end it."

Wulfemeyer went 3-7 with a 7.35 ERA for the Padres. He walked seventy-seven batters in fifty-eight innings. His career ended there. So did Maddon's.

Every day Maddon drove his girlfriend's Volkswagen Beetle the sixty-five miles from Salinas to Santa Clara and then back again. During those drives he learned every word to Meat Loaf's *Bat out of Hell*. He was spending more on gas than he was being paid to play. At twenty-five, Maddon was the oldest player on the team. His only job was to catch Tracy Harris, whom nobody else wanted to catch because Harris threw a knuckleball. The previous season Harris had pitched for the Grays Harbor Loggers, an independent team owned by Bill Murray, the actor, who occasionally put himself into games.

"I was able to catch Tracy for that last month," Maddon says. "Loved the ballpark. Listen, I just wanted to put on a uniform, and I thought I could still do it."

The Padres lost games 22–13 and 24–12 with the Harris-Maddon battery. In his final at bat of the season, playing for Volpi and wearing the Italian colors of red, white, and green, Maddon ripped a double down the left-field line against San Jose at Municipal Stadium. It was his second extra-base hit in his twenty games with Santa Clara, during which he hit a soft .250. It was the last at bat of his professional career.

No team offered Maddon another job. He went home to Hazleton, bought a 1969 Volvo, and took a job as a counselor at the United Charities Children's Home in West Hazleton, a home for foster children and troubled youths. Maddon worked six months there in 1980 until in June he heard again from the impresario who had made his pro career possible, Bauldie Moschetti. Bauldie hired him as a player-coach with the Boulder Collegians and as a clerk at Baseline Liquors. Maddon drove to Boulder in his '69 Volvo, which soon after he arrived would no longer go in reverse. Maddon would have to get out and push it if he wanted to back up. Bauldie paid him $800 a month.

That November, Maddon received an offer to play baseball in Italy.

"Not exactly sure where, but any part of Italy was good enough for me," he says. "Now my future is shifting to another country, and I figured that I would be able to create a new plan, a new vocation to explore while playing the game I loved . . . maybe three times a week. This would allow for much free time to explore the next move. Maybe the restaurant and hotel industry. I always held a fascination with working in the Mediterranean or Caribbean at some first-class resort. Again, my dreams were always grand. My mental escapes were always aiming high. My self-confidence may at times be nicked, but it can be recaptured through relentless pursuits. I know I can do this; just give me a shot. . . .

"So I am considering all of the new adventures awaiting me and I am about ready to tell the Italians, 'Yes, please hold a spot for me.' I still wanted to play baseball, and I could find the area where my grandparents had immigrated from in the early nineteen-hundreds. I had made up my mind to move on, and I felt good about it.

"And then the phone rang on Thanksgiving eve of 1980 at Baseline liquor store."

On other end of the line was Larry Himes, a former player, scout, and minor league manager in the Angels' system who had just been promoted to scouting director. Himes asked Maddon if he would be interested in working as a scout and a minor league manager.

"I know it's a big decision," Himes said. "Think about it. Take your time before you make up your mind."

"Larry," Maddon said, "no considerations necessary. I accept."

Says Maddon, "I never asked how much or where I would have to go. I knew inherently this was the opportunity I was looking for. I was going back to the Angels."

Himes told him he would be paid $1,000 a month. Maddon was thrilled. He hung up the phone. He knew his life had changed.

"I immediately had a thought that has stuck with me from that moment to the present," Maddon says. "If anyone ever attempted to take my uniform away from me again, it would be with me kicking and screaming. Being accountable, and maybe an average self-evaluator at that time, I figured I had done something wrong to put me in this position of being out of the game. I felt my work ethic was always good, but now it would have to become unparalleled. No one is ever going to outwork me as I move forward.

"The 2022 season was the twenty-third season managing, including seventeen of them in the major leagues, for that young man who answered the phone at Baseline Liquors on Thanksgiving eve 1980. I never lost sight of my dreams, and my self-confidence has held up in spite of many obstacles.

"If you know your job, your internal philosophy, the jabs fall rather easily. And you know your job through years of experience. Experience today is being fast-tracked, like everything else in our society. But you can't microwave working in the minor leagues for fourteen years and twenty-six years in the big leagues.

"I was always concerned about not getting anything before it was my time. I was passed over for jobs because there was a part of me not ready. Moving a player too quickly through an organization can injure his mental approach, and you may never see the fully developed player-slash-person. I am very comfortable with my path, and that I did not become a manager until I was fifty-two. Actually, I am grateful. It gave me time to figure out what I think and to make mistakes away from the maddening crowd. All of these steps are vital in developing the self-confidence necessary to do what is correct in the moment and know to have an answer either way and not an excuse."

At the turn of the New Year, 1981, Maddon was due in Anaheim to meet with Himes about his new job. No way the '69 Volvo was going to make it from Boulder to Anaheim. At the time Chrysler, under the restructuring of Lee Iacocca and in the thick of a recession, was practically giving away cars. No money down. Minimal payments. Maddon walked into a Chrysler dealership, did not put a penny down, and drove off in a new Plymouth TC3. He had a little more than one hundred dollars in his pocket, his entire nest egg. No credit card.

"I'm sure my parents were paying for the insurance, and they probably had to cosign for me at that time," he says. "So I head west, going through the Rockies."

The TC3 puttered west on I-70. Somewhere in Utah, the interstate forks. Go north, toward Salt Lake City, and you hit I-80, which takes you to Northern California. Bear left, and you hit I-15, which takes you to Southern California. For Maddon, it was time for a major decision.

"If I go to the right," he says. "I'm going to go to Salinas and ask my on-and-off girlfriend to marry me with no money. But obviously, I was very confident in my future. Always had been. If I go to the left, I go straight to Anaheim.

"I go to the right. I eventually end up sleeping on the side of the highway in the Sierra Nevadas during a snowstorm. I had no money for chains. I spent the whole night pulled off to the side of the road with blankets all over me.

"I get up the next morning and head to Salinas and made a decision that has blessed me with two beautiful kids, my Joey and my Sarah, and my five, count them five, grandchildren.

"So I really was at the proverbial fork in the road. Had I just stayed to the left and gone to Anaheim and got set up to scout, I can't tell you all what would have happened. But because I chose to go to the right, I endured one night on the side of the Sierra Nevadas, drove to Salinas, proposed, and then after that drove to Anaheim to meet up with Larry Himes. That's the beginning part of January. A lot of stuff happened very quickly, and I don't think a lot of guys would have done what I did."

Maddon and the TC3 eventually made it to Anaheim. He had no idea which territory he would be assigned to scout and no idea where and when he would manage.

"Listen, at that point, he could have told me I needed to clean all the toilets in Anaheim Stadium every day and I would have done it if that meant I was back," Maddon says. "You think that's an exaggeration? It's not. I would have done anything to get back in."

Himes assigned Maddon to scout Arizona, Utah, Colorado, and New Mexico until the start of rookie league, when he would manage the Idaho Falls Angels of the Pioneer League.

Maddon's first stop was in Tucson, where Himes arranged for him to meet Lou Cohenour, a fifty-two-year-old scout with tanned skin and ubiquitous cigarettes who could pass for a Rat Pack alum. Lou would teach Maddon about the job. First they went to a college tournament at Hi Corbett Field.

"I just started writing notes," Maddon says. "Do what I was supposed to do. You're supposed to grab a roster and stand there and act like you knew what you were doing because nobody knows you don't. And I didn't."

That night, after the games, Cohenour said to Maddon, "Ever been to the dog track?"

And that's how Maddon, on his first day as a professional scout, with a hundred dollars and no credit card to his name, wound up at a dog track in Tucson. In the gray haze of his cigarette smoke, Cohenour studied the racing form like a seminarian combing through Scripture. Clearly this was not Lou's first night at the track. Maddon was thoroughly impressed by the knowing figure he cut.

"I'm thinking OK, maybe I can make a couple bucks out of this," Maddon says. "I just follow Lou and I can possibly double this stuff.

"And what happened? He lost. Whatever I bet, I lost. It was maybe twenty-five bucks, which might as well have been ten thousand at that point. Then Lou looks at me, puffing on a heater, pulling on it deeply, smoke all around him, and he gives me that smoker's squint and says with that Cohenour giggle, 'Get 'em next time, kid.'

"Cool, man. Looking back on it, being so out of your element and taking a risk, don't you somehow develop balls being in situations like that?"

It reminded Maddon of the time the previous summer when his uncle Eddie, his godfather and a bartender at Susquehanna Valley Country Club, had arranged a golf match for Maddon against three members, one of whom went by the name Cochise. Playing the course for the first time, Maddon was striping the ball and making putts. Cochise, though, was right there with him, shot for shot. Maddon pulled out a win on the last hole.

"Don't ask me how. This guy was good," Maddon says. "I beat him for a couple of bucks. We get back to the clubhouse. There's Uncle Eddie, listening to us tell stories about the round. And then Uncle Eddie goes, 'Yeah, by the way, Cochise is the club champion.'

"I looked at him like, 'Yeah, you've got to be kidding me. You didn't tell me.' Of course, if he had told me that before, I would have gotten my ass kicked. No question. He told me that afterwards.

"It's like being at the dog track with Lou. The point is you put yourself up in these moments and you've got to compete. You learn how to compete.

"As a kid growing up in Hazleton, Pennsylvania, trust me, you've got to be pretty tough to compete. All these experiences conspired to help me as a major league manager in a tough press conference, after a tough loss, after a tough decision that goes awry, confrontations with players where they just don't see it like you do. All these moments. All these moments conspire to make you who you are. I totally believe that."

From Tucson, Cohenour went off to another assignment. Maddon scouted Arizona spring training camps until the end of March, when he left to cover his vast region. He set off in tandem with Jimmy Driscoll, a Baltimore Orioles scout everybody called Bradshaw. Why Driscoll? Driscoll had a bigger car, a 1980 Chrysler, a great sense of humor, and, more important, a credit card.

Then thirty-seven years old, Driscoll was also a rookie scout. On Driscoll's first assignment that spring, the scout who sat down next to him said, "Hi! I'm Joe Maddon. I'm a scout with the California Angels." It was the start of a lifelong friendship in which Driscoll would be the best man at Maddon's first wedding.

Born in Medford, Massachusetts, Driscoll was one of nine children of a train conductor who also worked as an usher at Fenway Park. Driscoll signed with the Milwaukee Braves the same night he graduated from Arlington High School. On his first night in pro ball, in Dublin, Georgia, in Class C in 1962, the eighteen-year-old Driscoll was one of the many Dublin Braves outnumbering the five showerheads after the game when he felt something streaming down his leg. It was not water. He turned to see his naked, potbellied, tobacco-chewing fifty-four-year-old manager, Bill Steinecke, urinating on him. Tobacco juice sprayed toward Driscoll's face as Steinecke spit out, "Welcome to pro ball."

This profane tradition survived in baseball until the 2000s. It was part of the pay-your-dues mentality that passed from one generation to the next. Young players were made to fetch coffee, told to keep their mouths shut, and often hazed like fraternity pledges, including with the golden shower initiation rite. As they gained service time, the aggrieved treated the next wave of young players with similar disrespect. And on and on it went. The "tradition" has largely disappeared from the game, though Maddon saw vestiges of it when he joined the Cubs as manager in 2015. He saw one of his veterans berating a young player.

"So I called the guy over and I said, 'I get where you're coming from with that, but don't you think you're being a little bit harsh, a little bit over the top in your explanation and how you went about it?'" Maddon says. "He agreed. By the end of the season these guys had the best relationship in the world. But you just can't give the veterans a free wheel to act like jerks.

"I don't like when guys get in other guys' heads. Like a veteran, and maybe this guy may be coming at his position and he can see this, he may want to start creating doubt in this young guy's head. I've seen it. That group in Chicago? No. Absolutely not. But I've seen it. Just because a guy is a veteran doesn't mean he's going to have good influence. Just because the back of his baseball card reads well doesn't mean he's a leader.

"That's why as a manager you've got to coach the coaches on top of that and not permit them to carry a message that's not your message."

Being mired in tradition purely for the sake of tradition is limiting. It limits freedom, and only with freedom does a person reach their true potential. That's why one of Maddon's first themes when he took his first major league managing job, with Tampa Bay in 2006, was "Tell me what you think, not what you've heard."

"I want no regurgitation of what you have heard," Maddon says. "We are all originals. So think like an original."

Maddon knew this tenet was crucial to learning the scouting trade. He needed to learn the nuts and bolts of the trade but wanted to avoid the groupthink that can arise in the fraternity of scouts.

Jimmy Driscoll would be his guide. Driscoll had played fourteen pro seasons in which he logged only thirty-six games in the majors before becoming a scout. Maddon and Driscoll worked out a deal. Jimmy would drive everywhere, and Maddon would share his information with him. Jimmy would pay for Maddon's room and meals on his credit card. Maddon would bill the Angels for lodging, meals, and gas mileage and reimburse Driscoll.

"Jimmy, God bless him, his credit card got me through it," Maddon says. "So I would make a couple bucks to get me to the plus side between meals and gas mileage. That was my bonus money, man. Without that I could never have made any of that fly. So that's how I made my first trip through my territory in 1981."

Jimmy was a great storyteller, the funniest guy among the scouts, but Maddon found almost all the scouts to be helpful and kind. There was Eddie Howsam, who was almost as funny as Jimmy, Mickey McDermott, who was part of Billy Martin's coterie, Lee Walls, Gene Thompson, Carl Hubbell, Scotty Reid, Angel Figueroa, Jerry Gardner, Harry Minor, Roger Jongewaard, Eddie Roebuck...

"Those are the guys who raised me," Maddon says.

Driscoll and Maddon rolled the Chrysler through Arizona, into Utah and then Wyoming.

"We spend the night at Laramie and go to some restaurant there," Maddon says. "We spent a bunch of money on Jimmy's credit card. All on the Baltimore Orioles. Great steak dinner. We go to this restaurant and kill it. Man, we killed it. As it ends up, I drafted a pitcher, Brad Withrow, from Gillette, Wyoming."

The Angels took Withrow in the fourteenth round. Withrow pitched that summer at Idaho Falls. It was his only year in pro ball. Thirty-four years later, after a Cubs spring training game in Mesa, Arizona, a police officer on a motorcycle pulled Maddon over. It was Withrow, who had become a Mesa police officer in 1993.

After Driscoll turned in the receipt for a huge meal in Laramie, his boss with the Orioles, Tommy Giordano, called him up, apoplectic.

"When the hell was the last time we signed anybody from *Wyoming*?" Giordano asked Driscoll. "Why would you spend all that dough in Wyoming?"

Driscoll did all he could to stifle a giggling fit.

"Of course, Jimmy was taking care of me, but I don't think T-Bone knew at that time," Maddon says. "And I'm pretty certain even after T-Bone aired him out, as he hung up the phone or turned around he started laughing his ass off because he loved Jimmy, too. And he probably thought it was hysterical."

In the fall of that year, in advance of the January draft and on the order of Himes, Maddon flew from Arizona to Denver, then drove three hours to Trinidad State Junior College to see a pitcher named Danny Jackson. It was Jackson's final game of the season. By the time Maddon arrived, rain was coming down, and the all-dirt infield was a muddy soup. The game looked certain to be canceled.

"I flew all that way," Maddon says. "Larry sent me. I've got to see him. Seriously, I've got to see him."

The Trinidad head coach, Rick Zimmerman, had worked or played for Bauldie Moschetti in Boulder, so Maddon had that connection going for him. He told Zimmerman he had to see Jackson pitch, and he had a plan to make it happen. Zimmerman agreed to it: the Boulder Gasoline Gambit.

Several players grabbed rakes. Others fetched as many gas cans as they could find. Under Maddon's direction, they raked the dirt into long furrows, poured gasoline all over it, and struck a match. The infield burned for half an hour. The field was dry enough for the game. Jackson pitched. Maddon filed his report. The Angels never had a shot at him. The Royals took Jackson with the first overall pick of the January 1982 draft.

"It was just a sense of duty," Maddon says. "I got it done. Checked all the boxes off. And then I flew back.

"And, of course, I wrote my report. We had no chance at him, but I burned the field myself, paid for the gas—of course I expensed it—and had a chance to watch Danny Jackson.

"That was 1981. My first year scouting. My managing is rooted in scouting. It's really an unusual background for managers, especially with what's going on in the game today as experience is valued less. And Larry Himes is responsible for that. Lou Cohenour picked me up first and gave me some direction, and that experience helped me so much because now, when I look at a player, I feel like I can break down their game with confidence and have experience and history to back up my thoughts, whereas a lot of guys today don't. (And I'm here to tell you they don't.)"

Scouting appealed to Maddon's independent streak and need to have his mind challenged. He abhorred the groupthink that some scouts found comfortable. At the end of their spring swing scouting the Western frontier, as they made their way back to Arizona, Maddon and Driscoll drove nine hours from Denver to Gallup, New Mexico, to see Duane Ward, a high school pitcher. By Maddon's calculation they had just enough time to arrive for the one o'clock start of the game. They pulled up just in time to see Ward pitch to the last batter. Maddon and Driscoll had not realized their trip included a one-hour time difference. From that brief look Maddon would need to write a report addressing not just Ward's skill but also a potential signing bonus and in what round of the draft he might be taken. At $1,000 a month plus fifteen cents a mile for gas, Maddon knew a good scout was paid for giving an informed opinion, not repeating the wisdom of the crowd. He valued originality. "Tell me what you think, not what you've heard" became not just a scouting mantra, but a way of life.

"Being in the major leagues all these years, it makes me think about where I come from, what I had to do to get to this particular juncture," Maddon says. "I'm grateful. I'm so grateful when I stood in the corner of the dugout on a nightly basis, there's a lot going on there, brother. There is a lot going on.

"A lot from the past. A lot of learning. A lot of tough moments. A lot of moments lying awake at night because how do you make ends meet, man? How do you pay these bills? And that's where a credit card was absolutely necessary because you could not make ends meet.

"The struggle, man. What's wrong with the struggle? What a blast, right?"

CHAPTER 4

"If It Comes to Your Mind, Do It"

With the score tied in the ninth inning of the seventh game of the 2016 World Series, a voice popped into the head of Joe Maddon. The Chicago Cubs had the potential series-winning, drought-ending, curse-killing run at third base with one out. The voice he heard belonged to a cherubic bald man who had been dead for two years after sixty-six years on professional baseball fields, on which he played, managed, coached, nearly died, and was married. The face qualified as cherubic if cherubs chewed tobacco and had three titanium plugs in their skull thanks to a beaning. A baseball Zelig, Don Zimmer with his echoing wisdom had a way of turning up just about anywhere and anytime.

Zimmer played for the 1955 world champion Brooklyn Dodgers, managed the Padres, Red Sox, Rangers, and Cubs for thirteen seasons with a gambler's bravado—his signature play was the absurdly risky bases-loaded hit-and-run—and practically invented the position of bench coach in the 1990s with the Red Sox, Rockies, and Yankees. Zimmer was Joe Torre's Yoda on the New York Yankees' bench from 1996 to 2003, during which New York won six pennants and four World Series titles.

What Maddon heard in his head in the thickening tension of that Game 7 moment were words of advice that Zimmer had spoken to him many times about managing a game:

"If it comes to your mind, do it."

Zimmer spent the final decade of his life working for the Tampa Bay Rays in a marriage of convenience, seeing that he lived on Treasure Island, Florida, about fifteen minutes from Tropicana Field, where the Rays played their home games. Zimmer served as an adviser who put on a uniform and visited the field during spring training and before home games. His unofficial title was baseball professor emeritus, though "Zim"

50

was an honorarium unto itself. When Maddon was hired by the Rays as their manager in the fall of 2005, Zimmer became a trusted font of wisdom.

One day during spring training, Maddon ambled over to Zimmer on a back field while players engaged in their stretching exercises. Maddon asked him, "Hey, Zim, what was that bunt play you did with Derek Jeter with runners on first and third? We could never stop it. It was an easy run for you guys. What was that play?"

Zimmer chuckled. Then he told Maddon how Jeter and the Yankees executed a very specific kind of squeeze play.

"Runners on first and third," Zimmer said. "The first baseman is holding the runner on. Once the pitcher delivers the pitch, the first baseman's natural reaction is to hop off the bag to his right to fill the hole between him and the second baseman. That takes him away from first base, OK?

"The hitter, he doesn't turn and square around to squeeze like a sacrifice. It's almost like a sacrifice bunt for a base hit. You don't turn or square quite so early. But you square in time to put yourself in position to bunt the ball in that pie-slice area in front of the first baseman.

"Part of the play—and here's the beauty of it—is you don't have to bunt the pitch if you're the hitter. If it's a ball, you can take it. You get to the next pitch. Everything is copacetic, except now the other team has another thought in their head that becomes very confusing to them. So if it's a good pitch, he puts it down in that little pie slice, we score. If not, it's still confusing to the other team.

"The part of the play that's difficult is the runner at third has to be a little more aggressive than normal. He has to get off the bag a little bit and take somewhat of a chance so he can beat a possible throw to the plate. The runner has to take that extra jab and get heavy on his right side, and that makes him vulnerable to the pickoff by the catcher.

"The thing we try to get across to the hitter is you don't have to bunt the ball. If the ball comes out of the pitcher's hand high, the runner can see that, and he knows the bunt is not in play. But if the ball is out of the pitcher's hand and looks like it's on target and the hitter takes it for a strike, that's when you're going to get the runner picked off."

Maddon told Zimmer he wanted him to teach his players how to run the play.

"We would hand Zim the fungo bat, and we'd all stand around and just admire," Maddon says. "It was beautiful, man, because he would totally get into it. Zim would give you that real stern German look. And his voice would start to rise as he wanted to punctuate a point. That chin would jut out a little bit and those cherub cheeks would get a little bit redder in the Florida sun. That's exactly how it came down. It was a beautiful thing. And that all came about because I asked Zim that one question."

Inspired by his Grandmaster of the Jedi Order, Maddon successfully ran the first-and-third "Zim Special" thirty-six times while managing the Rays from 2006 to 2014, more than any other team in baseball. Maddon ran it six times in 2015 and 2016 with the Cubs, though only once in those eleven combined years did Maddon dare run it with two strikes on the batter. In that two-strike count, however, the call was not all that daring because the hitter was a weak-hitting pitcher, Trevor Cahill, a career .103 batter. On August 16, 2016, Maddon initially called for the Zim Special with the count 3 and 1 to Cahill, who fouled off the pitch. Maddon left the play on at 3 and 2, knowing that a fouled bunt attempt with two strikes is a strikeout. This time Cahill dropped a bunt into the pie slice for an easy run in a 4–0 win over Milwaukee.

Two months later, in the World Series, when Maddon heard Zim's voice, the hitter was Javier Báez, who had homered off Cleveland ace Corey Kluber earlier in Game 7. The pitcher was now Bryan Shaw and the count had run full. There was one out. Jason Heyward was the runner at third base. Heyward had arrived there on the previous pitch—a wild swinging strike by Báez—via a stolen base and a throwing error by catcher Yan Gomes. Báez's swing was getting longer. He had swung at five pitches since his home run, whiffing on three of them and fouling off two. With the tiebreaking run ninety feet away, even a modest fly ball could deliver the go-ahead run that could win the World Series for the Cubs. But Maddon was unsure that Báez could put the ball in play against Shaw, especially given that last wild swing.

Cleveland manager Terry Francona gave Maddon time to think. Francona called a time-out to remove left fielder Coco Crisp, whose weak arm he regarded as a liability with the potential go-ahead run at third. Francona put Michael Martínez in right field and moved right fielder Brandon Guyer to left field. (Martínez, a career .197 hitter who had not had a hit in the previous forty-eight days, would make the last out of the World Series while hitting in Crisp's spot in the batting order.)

It was during that delay for the substitution that Maddon heard Zim's voice. He decided to run the Zim Special, even though the count was 3 and 2 and Maddon had never tried it on a two-strike count with a position player in the batter's box. There was no runner at first base at the time, so the first baseman's position did not matter, but everything else about the play would be the same.

"Jason Heyward is on third," Maddon says, "and Jason Heyward is great at this, about getting a jump and a lead. Javy is hitting. Javy already hit a home run in that game, but he's getting real big with his swing."

During the regular season, Báez had struck out in 38 percent of his plate appearances that reached a full count. Báez's proclivity for chasing pitches and Shaw's hard cut fastball that darted out of the zone made contact even less likely. Maddon had just watched Báez chase and miss badly at a cut fastball from Shaw that was well out of the strike zone.

"I knew all this stuff," Maddon says. "I knew too much. But he also was the best bunter we had. The best safety squeezer we had.

"So I'm watching this unfold. There's one out. This would be the second out. And I go back to Zim and what he had told me years ago. If you remember how Zim managed, he was pretty much the antithetical analytical skipper. Zim had told me a couple years prior to that what he learned years ago: 'If it comes to your mind, do it.'

"That's exactly what he told me. And he talked about his own experience with that thinking—how with the bases loaded he called for a hit-and-run with the catcher at bat with one out against a sinker ball pitcher with the pitcher on deck. He wasn't going to sit there and watch the catcher ground into a double play to end the inning.

"That was Zim. Zim had put it in my head, man. 'If it comes to your mind, do it.' This is the World Series! The Cubs! My man Zim up there in the clouds somewhere is sending me a divine revelation. I knew the guy on the mound was going to be tough on Javy regardless.

"I thought the better play, the better chance, was the bunt. If he puts that ball down at all, nobody would have gotten Jason. He would have scored, and we definitely would have burst the game open."

Shaw threw a cut fastball down the middle. Báez bunted it into the ground at Gomes's feet. Foul for a strikeout. The next batter, Dexter Fowler, grounded out to shortstop for the third out.

"You're talking about the World Series and the latter part of the game," Maddon says. "There is all kinds of action going on. But that's your training right there. That's your training taking over.

"It wasn't too quick. I saw it. I saw it in advance. It wasn't just like I pulled it out of my pants right there. I thought about it as that at bat was in progress. So sure enough, he fouls it off and everybody is upset. Had he put the ball down, everybody would have been absolutely effusively happy.

"That was a chance I took in that moment. That chance was born of my conversations with Zim and this particular play. And part of it was having confidence in the guy at the plate and how good he was. And then I thought this was a better opportunity for him to get this job done right now with the right runner on third base and absolutely nobody expecting it.

"This is a classic example of when something works that people consider pure genius and when it doesn't, you're an idiot.

"So maybe Zim was messing with me, man. He was sitting up there messing with me. He knew we were going to win, and he threw that just to remind me, 'If it comes to your mind, do it, brother.' That was my boy Zim."

What is "gut" decision making? Gut is not, to use Maddon's turn of phrase, pulling an idea out of your pants. It is not whim. It is tapping into accumulated life experiences, especially when quick thinking is required rather than the luxury of rumination. Think of deploying information and data as knowledge. Think of deploying gut as wisdom. Gut is not the enemy of information. It is its necessary colleague in good decision-making.

The extreme sabermetrician—the card shark who regards baseball as little more than a series of mathematical probabilities—has little regard for gut feelings in the decision-making process. Former major league pitching coach Rick Peterson had a favorite saying when he worked for Billy Beane's Oakland A's: "In God we trust. All others must show data." One veteran general manager grumbled during a managerial search about a decade ago, "I'll never again hire a manager who manages with his gut."

If you extrapolated to its most extreme outcome how front offices turn the big league manager into a clinical, data-driven decision-maker, the manager of the future would be a machine like Deep Blue, the chess-playing computer master developed by IBM. Or it would be someone like "Elliott," a famous patient of Antonio Damasio, a renowned neuro-scientist and professor of psychology, philosophy, and neuroscience at the University of Southern California, where he leads the Brain and Cre-ativity Institute. Damasio wrote about Elliott in his 1994 book, *Descartes' Error: Emotion, Reason, and the Human Brain.*

Elliott was a successful businessman, husband, and father with an IQ in the 97th percentile when he underwent surgery for the removal of a brain tumor. The surgery damaged his ventromedial prefrontal cortex, which plays a key role in providing emotional cues and stimuli. His IQ remained intact, but Elliott emerged different. He became the extreme extrapolation of the analytic manager: devoid of emotions, the perfectly rational decision-maker.

What happened? His life fell apart. His marriage failed. His busi-nesses collapsed. Without emotion, Elliott was incapable of making good decisions. Damasio described him as "an uninvolved spectator" in his own life—someone who was "always controlled" and without sadness or normal frustration. Small decisions such as where to eat lunch became long, burdensome chores.

Damasio developed the somatic marker hypothesis, which describes how visceral emotion—in the terms of a layman or a baseball manager, listening to your gut—is a necessary component in a good decision-making process. The term *somatic* comes from *soma*, the Greek word for body, and refers to the body and brain signals we read to make decisions. Simple decisions, like stopping at a red light, are easy. But when we face complex decisions, we weigh potential short- and long-term outcomes. The more uncertain those outcomes are, the more we apply emotions and feelings to help us make a good decision. Those emotions can trigger change in our bodies—the somatic connection—such as measurable stress or excitement. Think about sweaty palms, nervously tapping feet, or, yes, a feeling in your gut. The result of that process is an affirmative or negative decision—a green light or a red one. To squeeze bunt or not to squeeze bunt. When Maddon gave the signal to Báez for the Zim Special, he was using his ventromedial prefrontal cortex to perform a body-and-brain process that Elliott could not.

In 1984 Damasio and three other researchers at the University of Iowa devised an experiment known as the Iowa Gambling Task. The subjects were shown four decks of cards on a computer screen. They were told that each deck held cards that either rewarded them or penalized them with play money. Some decks had more reward cards, and some had more penalty cards. The subjects' task was to win as much play money as possible.

After drawing cards from each of the four decks, most people began to understand which decks had the most reward cards. They drew from those favorable decks and avoided the "bad" ones.

Included among the subjects were people who suffered from frontal cortex dysfunction. Those subjects chose differently from the healthy ones. Lacking emotional input, they kept picking through the "bad" decks even though they knew they were losing money. Another disparity was found in feedback from sensors used to measure skin response. The healthy subjects exhibited a stress response with their finger hovering over a bad deck after ten trials, while it should take forty to fifty trials to tell the good and bad decks apart. It was a physiological reaction to the likelihood of punishment—a "red light" from a "gut feeling" to help them make better decisions. The subjects who lacked the emotional component never exhibited any such stress reaction. They kept making bad decisions.

Most people regard emotions as intrusions into the process of good decision-making. To call someone emotional in their decision-making is to suggest irrationality or a lack of preparedness. On the other hand, "cold" and "calculating" are compliments to the shrewd and wise mind in popular culture. Neuroscientists do not think that way—not with their understanding of how the gut and brain are partners—and neither should baseball front-office executives. Gut and analytics are not opposites, as they are typically portrayed in the lazy shorthand of mass media. One needs the other, even in the worst of times.

One of those very dark times occurred on November 14, 1965, in South Vietnam. US Army helicopters transported about 450 troops from the First Battalion, Seventh Cavalry Regiment, to a field known as Landing Zone X-Ray near the Drang River, six miles from the Cambodian border. Their leader was Lieutenant Colonel Harold G. Moore. The troops had no way of knowing it, but they had been dropped into an almost impossible predicament. Three North Vietnamese regular army regiments surrounded them, outnumbering the American soldiers twelve to one. In midafternoon, in punishing 100-degree heat, the first battle between the North Vietnamese and US troops commenced. It turned out to be one of the bloodiest of the entire war.

The Battle of Ia Drang lasted a week. Both sides absorbed such heavy casualties the area would become known as the Valley of Death. In the thick of the fight himself, Moore, commanding the same battalion General Custer once had, somehow held his outnumbered troops together until air support arrived from helicopters, bombers, and howitzers. The North Vietnamese retreated.

Moore served thirty-two years in military service and received the Distinguished Service Cross. His heroism at Ia Drang Valley was the subject of the 2002 film *We Were Soldiers*, starring Mel Gibson.

Moore understood the importance of making gut decisions in those tense times.

"When my head tells me to do one thing and my gut tells me to do another, I always go with my gut," he wrote. "Why? Because my gut, as I've learned, is rarely wrong. Instinct is kind of a caution light, an early warning, or a gut feeling which can on occasion result in a far better decision than one based on a logical process."

Moore was not advocating for gut to replace information. Indeed, like most good leaders, he craved good information, especially when afforded the luxury of time.

"When a quick decision is not required, I get all the information, look into the pros and cons, and then back off from it using two approaches," he wrote. "One approach is to reach a tentative decision at day's end. Do not announce it. Instead, 'sleep on it' during the night and reconsider it early the next morning when your brain is fresh."

Says Maddon, "It is the difference between making in-game decisions and acquisitions in the off-season. The ones in the off-season should absolutely be guided by information and deliberation. Now, you can argue when it comes to the in-game 'blink' moment that you have analyzed the information before the game to prepare for the moment. I agree with that. But there's nothing quite like that moment. The gut process is an entirely different process. Go back to 2016 and the game I thought was the pivotal game in the 2016 playoff run."

It was Game 4 of the National League Championship Series. The Cubs were losing 5–2 on the road against the Giants in the ninth inning. They were three outs away from having to play a winner-take-all Game 5 against San Francisco and its ace, Johnny Cueto, who had dominated them in Game 1 with no walks and ten strikeouts over eight innings.

"We beat them 1–0 in Game 1 with Javy Báez hitting a home run into the wind in the basket in left field," Maddon says. "I did not want to see Cueto again. That's all I could think about in Game 4. And these Giants had been battle tested. They had won three of the past six World Series. You don't want to mess with a Game 5 with these guys.

"Right there—ninth inning, down three, Cueto looming—any decision I'm making has nothing to do with analytics. It has everything to do with what I'm feeling and seeing in the moment."

Giants manager Bruce Bochy, renowned for his mastery in handling bullpens, replaced left-handed starting pitcher Matt Moore with right-hander Derek Law to start the ninth. Moore had zipped through a one-two-three eighth inning with just fourteen pitches. He had thrown 120 pitches in the game.

Kris Bryant greeted Law with a single. Bochy took out Law to have left-hander Javier López pitch to Anthony Rizzo. López walked Rizzo.

Bochy made a third pitching change in a span of three batters. He summoned right-hander Sergio Romo to pitch to Ben Zobrist, a switch-hitter. Zobrist doubled. Bryant scored. The Giants' lead was cut to 5–3.

With right-handed-hitting Addison Russell due next, Maddon sent left-handed Chris Coghlan to pinch-hit. He was laying a trap.

"I knew they were going to come in with a lefty," Maddon says. "And they did."

Bochy made his fourth pitching change in four batters. He removed Romo for left-hander Will Smith. Maddon countered the counter by sending right-handed-hitting Willson Contreras to hit for Coghlan.

"I had Contreras ready right behind him because I liked him on the lefty more than I liked Addison on the righty," he says. "And that's how you have to think it all the way through."

It worked. Contreras tied the game with a two-run single. Jason Heyward bunted into a force play but continued to second base on a throwing error by shortstop Brandon Crawford. Bochy made his fifth pitching change of the inning. He brought in Hunter Strickland to face Báez, the sixth batter of the inning. On an 0-and-2 count, Báez singled to knock in Heyward with the go-ahead run.

"There was nothing analytical about that base decision there whatso-ever," Maddon says about removing Russell to wind up with the matchup he wanted. "Willson gets the hit. We come back and win the game. This is not even patting myself on the back. It's just an illustration.

"Analytic decisions normally come in with starting pitching and not going a third time through the lineup. Another heavy analytic decision would be bullpens and pitching guys in high-leverage moments, which I've been into for years.

"But decisions I made toward the end of that game were all based on what I was seeing and experiencing and having an idea what the other manager would do if I do this. There was no analytical component whatsoever. The analytics before the game to me would be how to pitch somebody based on a volume of information that can be reduced.

"We had two coaches, Tommy Hottovy and Mike Borzello, who were able to take stuff and distill it even further and create game plans out of ingredients such as analytical information and sophisticated video equipment. And if that's analytics, that's fine.

"They would take the numbers—like what a guy hit in a certain count—and reduce it to a specific game plan. What to do and what not to do in certain counts, with pitches, with every hitter, not just certain hitters, throughout the lineup. It was pretty amazing to watch what Borzy did and how he did it."

Teams have long scoured the patterns of the game and of their opponents to find hidden edges. One of the most famous such informational nuggets helped make possible the improbable home run by Kirk Gibson of the Los Angeles Dodgers in Game 1 of the 1988 World Series against Dennis Eckersley of the Oakland A's. On the eve of the game, Dodgers scout Mel Didier gave an oral scouting report to the Dodgers' hitters after watching the A's for more than a month. He ran through the Oakland pitching staff one by one, finishing with Eckersley, the closer. Three Dodgers left-handed hitters, Mike Scioscia, Mike Davis, and Gibson, sat on the floor across from him with their backs against the wall.

Didier pointed at them and said, "Podnuh, let me tell you this: if Eckersley gets you at 3 and 2 and there's a runner at second base or third base and it's the tying or winning run, Eckersley will throw you a backdoor slider on 3 and 2. Don't forget that, because that's what he will do as sure as I am standing here breathing."

Didier later said he had seen Eckersley do it only twice, "But I felt confident enough to tell them."

In fact, Eckersley went to a full count against a left-handed hitter only eight times all year, regardless of game situation. Four of those occasions happened in May, when Didier would not have been scouting

Oakland. Only one of them happened after September 17. In Game 1 of the American League Championship Series, Eckersley had had a full count to a left-handed hitter, Rich Gedman, with the tying run at second base—the exact scenario in which Didier told the Dodgers hitters Eckersley would throw a backdoor slider "as sure as I am standing here breathing."

Eckersley had not thrown a backdoor slider. He had thrown Gedman a fastball away that missed the plate. Didier's "as sure as I am standing here" guarantee actually had little basis in fact.

Davis, aboard via a walk, was on first base when Gibson pinch-hit against Eckersley with two outs. The Dodgers trailed 4–3. Eckersley jumped ahead on the count, 0 and 2, putting Oakland one strike away from a win. But Gibson refused to go away, even as the pain from aching knees and sore legs was visible to all. In their pregame meeting with the pitchers, the Oakland coaches had not spent much time on planning against Gibson because they had not expected him to play. Eckersley would later say he remembered one of the coaches telling him, "Do not throw him anything soft. He'll hit it." But Eckersley did not pay much attention to the report, thinking to himself, *Yeah, but he's not playing.*

So weakened was Gibson that he decided to use one of his previously rejected bats. Whenever Gibson received a shipment of bats, he would weigh them. Those he regarded as too light he would mark with a black X on the knob underneath his uniform number, 23, and hand to the clubhouse manager, Mitch Poole, to put in a storage room. Tired and hurt at the end of the year, Gibson needed a lighter bat. He fished from the storage room one of those rejected bats with the X in black marker on the knob.

By fighting off pitches with four foul balls, Gibson worked the count to 3 and 2, the last pitch being a fastball away on which Davis stole second base. Eckersley had thrown seventeen consecutive fastballs, many of which he'd had unusual difficulty pinpointing to the outside corner.

As Eckersley looked to catcher Ron Hassey for the sign for the next pitch, Gibson suddenly called a time-out. He looked at Eckersley and said to himself in Didier's voice: *Podnuh, sure as I'm standing here breathing, you're going to throw me that 3-and-2 backdoor slider.*

Gibson stepped back in the box. Hassey put down the sign: slider.

"I was tired of throwing fastballs," Eckersley would say later, "so I thought to myself, *If I give him something off speed, maybe he'll pull off it.* It was really stupid, because something off speed is probably the only thing he can get to at this point."

Gibson hit it into the right-field bleachers. As he watched the ball leave the yard, Gibson saw thousands of red brake lights illuminated in the Dodger Stadium parking lot, a visual testament to the many who had abandoned hope. As he rounded third base, Gibson yelled to coach Joey Amalfitano, "Backdoor slider!" Twenty-two years later, Gibson's bat with the black X sold at auction for $575,912, almost one-third of Gibson's annual salary in 1988.

No sport produces more information than baseball. More than a thousand players, more than two thousand games and more than two hundred and fifty thousand pitches every year produce truckloads of granular information, like grains of sand hauled by the Army Corps of Engineers to replenish a beach. What Didier did was find a gold nugget amid all that silt and sand. He distilled his information to one shiny piece of actionable intelligence, even if the original information was somewhat flawed. Since then, the piles of sand have grown so large and the data mining has become so sophisticated that the information can be overwhelming.

"Analytics are a wonderful pregame tool," Maddon says. "Give it to me. Let me look at this information and try to create a game plan—all the while knowing that reality is going to be different.

"The game occurs, and the quickness and rapidity of the way things happen require spur-of-the-moment decisions, and they cannot be analytically blessed all the time. You have to react to what you are seeing as opposed to planning and plotting in advance.

"When you're sitting still, with nothing going on, that's the moment you can actually utilize information. Plan, plan, plan. And then if everything goes to plan, you go this way. But it rarely goes according to plan.

That's what happened in Game 4 against the Giants. There was no plan for that. We ended up winning the game. That game was really, really vital to our championship."

Under Andrew Friedman, Maddon's former boss with the Rays, the Los Angeles Dodgers rely heavily on a data-based, analytical approach to running a game. Friedman hired Dave Roberts as manager in 2016 after a series of exhaustive interviews.

"I didn't know anyone in the organization outside of [vice president] Josh Byrnes," Roberts says. "The process was long and grueling. They wanted to see how you work through problems and grind and keep your focus and attention. The best advice I got was from my wife. She told me, 'Just be yourself.' It's one of those situations where when you don't try too hard for something that you want, you are the better for it. I thought I put my best foot forward."

One of the key questions for Roberts, who had not managed before, was what he thought about "collaboration," which was another way of asking him how he would feel if the front office suggested lineup and pitching options, among other game-related decisions.

"I said I one hundred percent agree on collaboration," Roberts says. "Just because it wasn't done a decade ago doesn't mean it's wrong. It's what successful people do in business now. The CEO has to answer to stockholders. If anyone tells you they're not using data and all the information available to them to make an informed decision, that's not a successful company.

"Early on there was this narrative that Andrew [Friedman] and Farhan [Zaidi] were basically telling me what to do, which is ridiculous and isn't true. I guess people were turned off by collaboration.

"There are times as a manager you can't know how a player's body is affected by workload, like playing six days in a row. When I have that information presented to me, I have to take that into context as well as a conversation with the player. Should he play that seventh day? If a pitcher has pitched two days in a row, now I have information about that, and it may show his stuff isn't the same on the third day.

"Here's the thing: The quick answer is, Do I get information from the front office on a daily basis? Absolutely. Do they tell me who to play? Absolutely not. Have we talked about lineup construction over the years? Absolutely.

"I look at it this way. I hit leadoff my entire career, even when I didn't see Randy Johnson well. I should have been hitting eighth against Randy Johnson. I didn't. I can't preach to my team that our only goal that night is to win the game, whatever it takes, if I don't look long and hard at lineup construction and bullpen use that night.

"The way I look at lineup construction now is completely different from when I first took the job, and it's because I have more information and my players are better. You see the success we've had since 2016, and now the industry has followed in the same manner.

"But I will tell you this: these are athletes, and I still have to trust my gut and my eyes."

Roberts entered 2022 with the best career winning percentage of any manager who has won a World Series (.622). Roberts and the Dodgers won the 2020 World Series after a season-ending loss in the 2019 Division Series swung on a gut decision—in the heat of the moment, when collaboration does not rule decision-making.

The Dodgers were leading the Washington Nationals 3–1, with two outs, in the seventh inning of the decisive Game 5, when Los Angeles pitcher Walker Buehler walked Trea Turner with his 117th pitch. With Adam Eaton, a left-handed hitter, due, Roberts removed Buehler to bring in Clayton Kershaw, his left-handed ace. Friedman and Roberts had collaborated before the game on Kershaw's potential use out of the bullpen. Kershaw had had four days off after pitching in Game 2.

"I knew he was available for potentially three innings," Roberts says.

Kershaw struck out Eaton on three pitches, the last two of which were perfectly executed sliders. That left the Dodgers needing three outs to get the ball to their closer, Kenley Jansen, to close out the series. Roberts's choices for those three outs were to leave Kershaw in the game or hand the ball to right-handed reliever Kenta Maeda, who had pitched in the eighth innings of Los Angeles' wins in Games 1 and 3. The Nationals' two best hitters, Anthony Rendon and Juan Soto, were due to lead off the eighth. That was the moment when collaboration had to give way to gut. In his blink moment, Roberts decided to keep Kershaw in the game.

"The amount of innings, the usage, wasn't in question," Roberts says. "I wanted him to face the first two hitters because of his usage and the way the ball was coming out of his hand that night. I knew I had Kenta behind him. That's when how the game plays out takes over.

"Kersh has obviously done it before—sitting down and coming back out for the next inning. It's not like he had only one day off or pitched the night before. He's fresh. He's ready. The slider is really good. It's all of it . . . the decision encompasses everything. This is not a case of blind faith in a player. I'm going with the information and my eyes and my gut."

Kershaw made an odd choice to start the eighth: he pitched from the stretch with nobody on base rather than his iconic windup. He started Rendon with a curveball. Rendon, on balance, took it for a ball, low.

Catcher Austin Barnes called for a four-seam fastball on the next pitch. He set a low, inside target. The pitch, at eighty-nine miles per hour, seemed almost perfectly placed. In fact, it tracked so far below the low target that Barnes dropped his mitt to the ground to prepare to catch it near the dirt. It never arrived.

When Rendon connected with the fastball, it was only fourteen and a half inches off the ground. It was so low that Rendon, who normally finishes with two hands on the bat, could not keep his top hand on the bat as he reached to hit through it. Somehow he one-handed the pitch out of the park. Home run. In 2019, including the postseason, major league pitchers threw 267,247 four-seam fastballs. Kershaw's fastball to Rendon was the lowest of those 267,247 fastballs to be hit for a home run. A one-in-a-quarter-of-a-million shot.

Hardly a mistake by Kershaw, it could be dismissed as masterful hitting by Rendon. With the lead now 3–2, Roberts left Kershaw in because Soto, the next hitter, was left-handed.

"People are going to think I'm lying," Soto says, "but definitely yes, I said to myself, 'I am going to hit a home run' that at bat."

Soto says he knew it since the sixth inning when Kershaw was warming up behind him in the left-field bullpen. After Soto chased a foul ball, the two stars made eye contact.

"That's when the mind games start going," Soto says. "I turn around to look at the bullpen and Kershaw was looking at me. He stopped his windup halfway when he saw me. I don't know if it was because he was trying to do something, but he stopped halfway. I saw that and I was like, 'He don't want it.' So I was like, 'Well, I've got more confidence now.'

"I knew I was going to hit a home run off him before we got to the dugout after that inning. Ever since he started warming up, I knew I was going to hit a home run off him."

Facing Soto, Kershaw remained oddly in the stretch. Barnes called for a first-pitch slider. He set up down and away. Kershaw was a little too quick with his delivery. He missed badly. The pitch had almost no break to it. It hung belt high on the inner third of the plate. Soto hit it so hard that Kershaw sank to his knees in despair without bothering to turn to watch it. The home run landed halfway up the pavilion in right center field, 449 feet away. Two pitches. Two home runs. The game was tied.

"I think that any manager or any great leader, you know, for you to be successful you have to be diligent and consistent with how you go about things," Roberts says. "It didn't work out the way I envisioned, but I still believed I was very consistent with putting players in what I believed to be the best chance for them to succeed."

Only then did Maeda enter. He struck out three straight batters. After Maeda left for a pinch-hitter, his replacement, Joe Kelly, mowed through three Washington hitters in the ninth with knuckle curveballs on all ten pitches.

The game went to the tenth. Kelly began the inning by walking Eaton. The last errant pitch was his first fastball, a four-seamer, after fifteen straight curves. Rendon followed with a ground-rule double. Roberts ordered Soto intentionally walked to load the bases. He stuck with Kelly rather than turning to Jansen to face Howie Kendrick, a ground-ball hitter. Roberts did so because Kelly threw a two-seam fastball that could induce ground balls. Roberts hoped Kelly could use the two-seamer to get a double play, whereas Jansen, who is more of a fly-ball pitcher, was unlikely to get two outs with one pitch.

With the count 0 and 1, Kelly threw a four-seam fastball, not a two-seamer. Kendrick smashed it over the center-field wall for a grand slam, the elimination blow to the Dodgers' season. Roberts was roasted for his gut decisions on pitching.

"It's not hard to live with because you trust the process," Roberts says. "When the result isn't what you want, every loss hurts, and obviously it hurts more in the postseason. My wife says she sees me in anguish in the dugout sometimes and she asks, 'Would you do it again?' Ninety-nine percent of the time I'd do the same thing. I would do the same.

"I think fans might not understand. But I knew I had gone through the process, and I had my thoughts and information, and this is what I felt.

"I will say early on you take things more personally when it comes to criticism. You learn not to take it personally. You've got to believe in the people around you and the process."

Twenty-one days later, in Game 7 of the World Series, Houston Astros manager A. J. Hinch had his own blink moment blow up on him, and again it was Kendrick who figured prominently. The Astros led Washington, 2–0, in the seventh inning. When pitcher Zack Greinke retired Eaton on a grounder, Houston was eight outs away from its second World Series title in three years. Greinke was dominant. The Nationals had put only two runners on against him, one by way of a single and the other on a walk. Greinke was far better than Hinch expected.

Like the Dodgers, the Astros were a cutting-edge organization when it came to data, especially when it involved defensive shifts and pitch usage. When Hinch was hired by general manager Jeff Luhnow in 2015, he privately worried if game instructions would come with the job—a script from the front office regarding lineups and pitcher use. There were no scripts. Instead, the more Luhnow's staff churned out valuable information, the more of it Hinch wanted. Hinch reserved the right to deviate from the data when his "gut" told him to.

"You'll be shocked—and I give credit to Jeff for this—but he let me do whatever we wanted," Hinch says. "He didn't pressure. He would want to hear the argument for why I might choose to go in a different direction."

The Astros' analytics department turned out stunningly accurate information on defensive shifts. Opponents hit .272 when they put the ball in play against the Astros, the lowest such mark against any team in 2019. But Hinch and his staff occasionally made their own amendments to the shifts recommended by the front office.

"That's where you are challenged intellectually and emotionally, whether you believe the numbers or not," Hinch says. "Conventional wisdom tells you, 'I do not want to open monster holes with runners in scoring position.' You have to ask yourself when you see the numbers, 'When does Joey Gallo, or some extreme shiftable players, take advantage of the holes you open up?' The numbers still come into play, but you still have to be emotionally comfortable enough to believe that in the eighth inning of a tie game, some players may go against those numbers.

"For instance, one of the biggest adjustments that we made was with Robinson Canó in Seattle. He's a very shiftable guy—until he doesn't want to be shifted.

"From an analytics standpoint, I bought in immediately for the most part to the defensive positioning data. I was never presented anything in the way of lineup construction, and there was just a small sample of information presented from the pitch-count perspective. I would get tons of information but was never directly influenced.

"I felt like the more I absorbed the information and the more I learned about the information, the more the front office trusted when I would go away from the exact details. As a manager you must combine what you see with what you know, and then the answer is right there. I felt right about making the decisions because they were well informed.

"For those blink moments—and they mostly involve pitching—the more prepared you are the more comfortable you are making those decisions. I was obsessed with preparation. I went into a game with intricate notes on my card. The more detailed notes I kept, the more I felt I complemented the information with knowledge, and the more those blink moments felt natural to me. I got comfortable not making emotional decisions.

"I wanted on my card things I wanted to do in the game. I didn't want to retain information just for the sake of information. I wanted certain counts I could exploit in the running game. I wanted certain batter-pitcher matchups. I looked at them every half inning.

"I kept score on my lineup card. Once I write it down, I remember it. It's been that way since I was in high school and college. It made me focus on the things I wanted to remember. If I wanted to exploit two-strike counts in the running game, I would write that down. 'This guy has not picked off in three years on a particular count.' Write it down. It was more proactive."

Before Game 7 of the 2017 World Series, for example, Hinch wrote on his 8½-by-11 card that he wanted starting pitcher Lance McCullers Jr. on Cody Bellinger as much as possible because of his curveball; he wanted left-hander Francisco Liriano on the left-handed Corey Seager; he wanted right-hander Brad Peacock on right-handed Yasiel Puig; and he had Charlie Morton available in late relief, with Will Harris and Luke Gregerson behind him. The game played out almost exactly as Hinch wanted. Bellinger, Seager, and Puig were a combined 1 for 11, and Morton was so good that Hinch let him pitch the final four innings to close a 5–1 win. It is the only World Series Game 7 in which a team pulled its starter before three innings, used four relievers, and still won the game—and it happened by design.

Two years later, Hinch formulated another plan for what he wanted to happen in another World Series Game 7. The plan began with Zack Greinke, his starting pitcher.

"If I got five innings out of Greinke I was happy," Hinch says. "I would let him pitch out of one jam. Probably not a second."

Why the short leash? Hinch had watched Greinke struggle in the postseason. In four starts entering Game 7, Greinke had allowed thirty base runners in eighteen and one-third innings with a 5.30 ERA. He averaged four and two-thirds innings and eighty-one pitches per start. His walk rate tripled.

The next part of Hinch's plan was to decide what to do about Gerrit Cole, his best pitcher. Cole had two days of rest after pitching brilliantly in a 7–1 win in Game 5. But Cole had never pitched in relief in his professional career. Moreover, whatever physical risk might be inherent in asking him to fill an unfamiliar role on two days rest was complicated by his contract status. Cole was a free agent after the World Series, meaning his earning power, which was hundreds of millions of dollars, was on the line with his health.

"After his start in Game 5 in Washington, we talked every day," Hinch says. "There was a lot at stake. Either me in particular or the modern manager in general, we are a little closer to the players than they were back in the day. That creates its own set of challenges.

"This isn't from Gerrit. This is coming from me. From a financial standpoint, contracts are available to everyone these days. There's a greater knowledge and acknowledgment of outside influences with the modern-day manager. Managers didn't feel like it was front and center back in the day. Now there's personal responsibility.

"Now people weigh in on every pitching program with all thirty teams, their rehab programs, shoulder exercises, the modern access to information across those topics is multiplying. . . . That influences the manager.

"The way I'm wired is to set a plan and go with it. If Gerrit was an Astro for the next seven years, I would have felt less internal pressure. He would be financially secure. I made a pretty firm promise to myself that when I manage, I make nonemotional decisions. In Game 4, I made a plan that José Urquidy was not going over eighty pitches. [He was pulled after throwing sixty-seven pitches and five shutout innings.] I made that decision without the distractions and stresses of the game. I'm consistent throughout. I didn't think that Game 7 was the time to retreat from that."

Here's what Hinch decided to do with Cole: he would pitch in Game 7 only at the start of an inning and only if the Astros had the lead. That would allow Cole to stick as close as possible to his prestart warmup routine. Under that plan, it was possible that Cole could start the ninth inning to close the World Series, which meant Hinch had to notify his regular closer, Roberto Osuna, to be ready to enter the game in the seventh or eighth inning.

"I think we had a very good understanding of where Gerrit was going into the game," Hinch says. "The difficult part would be navigating the emotions."

As Greinke remained in command in the sixth inning, Cole began to stretch and lightly toss a baseball in the bullpen.

"When he got up to play catch, that was written as if he was warming up and he wasn't," Hinch says. "He got up to play catch because he was in unchartered territory. He got up way before Zack was ever in trouble."

After Eaton grounded out to start the seventh, Greinke hung a 1-and-0 changeup to Rendon in the middle of the plate. It was the worst of his seventy-five pitches. Rendon smashed it for a home run.

"It bothered me in that it shortened the room for error," Hinch says. "Rendon had a nice series and he's a terrific hitter. Zack is not going to shy away from the solo shot. The pitch itself didn't bother me. It was more about the room for error in the equation."

Soto batted next. Greinke missed badly away with his first pitch, a fastball. He came back with a curveball that also was well off the plate, but Soto chased it and missed for a swinging strike. Greinke stayed away from Soto with his third straight pitch, this one a changeup that Soto took for a 2-and-1 count.

Everything that would decide this World Series—Hinch's blink moment, Kendrick's clutch hitting, Cole's lack of use—was set in motion with the next pitch. The cascade of events in which the lead and the World Series title would change hands all started with a 2-and-1 change-up Greinke threw Soto.

Fooled by the pitch, Soto started his swing and abruptly stopped it. The pitch was over the middle of the plate and easily above the bottom of the zone. Home plate umpire Jim Wolf, who had earned the Game 7 home plate assignment by being the highest-graded ball-and-strike umpire during the season, called it a ball.

Sure that he had a strike, Greinke pumped his fist twice, pounded his fist into his glove, and grimaced when he saw Wolf's ball call. Soto gave his trademark shuffle upon taking the pitch. When he saw Greinke react with exasperation at the call, Soto grabbed his crotch and stuck out his tongue at Greinke. The reaction by Greinke unnerved Hinch.

"He showed emotion for the first time," Hinch says. "He barely missed the strike zone and he showed major emotion. That triggered my decision. He threw pitches he thought were dotted pitches. He showed some major emotion, and I was already ready to get him out.

"With the whole planning and managing in the playoffs, the instinct and internal pressure to do something sooner rather than later is multiplied. Every time someone gets on it feels like a rally."

At 3 and 1, Greinke threw Soto a curveball. He had not thrown a 3-and-1 curveball to a left-handed hitter in more than three years, covering III pitches. All III of them had been either a fastball or changeup. The curveball was an indication of how careful he was working Soto. The curveball was not very good. It was well off the plate, making for an easy take for Soto. It was ball four. Hinch walked to the mound to remove Greinke.

Hinch wasn't going to lose the World Series with Greinke on the mound deep into a game, not when Greinke was working in the seventh inning for the first time in thirty-five days.

"We asked him to do more than he had done, and he pitched deeper into the game than he had done in the entire month of October," Hinch said in his postgame comments. "I wanted to take him out an at bat or two early rather than an at bat or two late."

What managers fear most in today's bullpen-heavy game is losing a game by sticking too long with their starting pitcher. Up to that point, the last time a manager lost a postseason game by allowing a starter to give up the deciding run in the late innings was Game 1 of the 2016 National League Division Series, when Bochy rode Cueto to that 1–0 loss on the eighth-inning home run into the Wrigley Field basket by Báez. Entering 2019 World Series Game 7, no manager in 138 postseason games since then had lost a game by sticking that long with his starter.

The next batter due for Washington was Kendrick. What clinched Hinch's decision to remove Greinke in that blink moment was not the presence of Kendrick but rather the on-deck batter, Asdrúbal Cabrera. Greinke had trouble with Cabrera not just in this World Series but also for years. Cabrera was a career .439 hitter versus Greinke over forty-nine plate appearances. In the World Series he was 2 for 4 against him.

"The ironic part of the blink moment with Greinke was the matchup after Kendrick was Asdrúbal Cabrera," Hinch says. "I did not want

Asdrúbal Cabrera to face Greinke again. He had dominated him both games and in his career."

To replace Greinke, Hinch was not going to use Cole. He stuck to his vow not to use the impending free agent in the middle of an inning. Hinch's choices were to use his usual closer, Osuna, with Cole behind him, or Will Harris, his best setup reliever. He chose Harris. For much of the postseason that had been a good option. Harris had not allowed a run in his first ten appearances in October. But then, only the night before, Rendon crushed a home run off one of his cutters. In Game 7, when Hinch brought him in to face Kendrick, Harris was pitching for the twelfth time in twenty-four days, all in high leverage spots. He was wearing down.

"Kendrick was the hitter before Cabrera," Hinch says. "It was relatively neutral: Greinke or Harris on Kendrick. Either way I was fine with breaking balls away from him. You did not have to challenge him in. I went with Will because that gave him more leash to get Cabrera.

"If Kendrick got on or not against Greinke, that was his last hitter no matter what. I'd rather take out a pitcher a batter too early than too late. When I put Will in to face Kendrick it was to give him more runaway to face Cabrera."

It was the third time in seven games Kendrick was getting a look at Harris. The reliever started Kendrick with a big overhand curveball in the zone. Kendrick swung and missed badly. Catcher Robinson Chirinos called for a cut fastball and moved so far to the outside that he set his target off the edge of the plate. The pitch arrived in the strike zone, tucked into its corner down and away.

Kendrick was the best hitter in the National League that year against fastballs, hitting .357. But his power against fastballs throughout his career was entirely against pitches middle to inside. Since 2008, as far as such records go back, Kendrick had seen 403 fastballs in that down-and-away area where Harris threw his cutter. He hit none of them for a home run—until this one.

Kendrick hit it squarely. Harris immediately did a deep knee bend, fearing the worst. Would it stay fair? Would it be deep enough? The ball hit the screen attached to the right-field foul pole. From 2018 through 2021, 418 home runs were hit in the postseason. At 336 feet, Kendrick's home run is the shortest of them all. It put Washington ahead, 3–2.

"I felt the classic tug and pull of decision-making in the eighth inning," Hinch says. "The homer from Harris was not something I was factoring in. A base hit from Kendrick? Yes, base hit. Single. But where Will Harris throws the ball and where Kendrick's homers are, I did not factor that into my thinking."

When Cabrera followed with a single, Hinch removed Harris. He brought in Osuna, who gave up another run in the eighth. Down 4–2 in the ninth, Hinch brought in Urquidy, honoring his commitment not to use Cole if the Astros trailed. Urquidy gave up two more runs. What had been a 2–0 lead with eight outs to go devolved into a 6–2 loss for Houston. The Nationals were world champions. Hinch had a brief conversation with Greinke after the game.

"He just told me, 'You did the best that you could,'" Hinch says. "I had been aggressive taking him out of games. I was careful with him. I wanted five innings. I was not going to let him get beat by Cabrera. It was a one-batter decision.

"I am pretty comfortable with whatever the outcome of a decision is if I was prepared and made it for the right reasons. The coin flip decisions, the Greinke/Harris one, where on paper it's pretty neutral, that's when it's fifty-fifty. Those are the tough ones. A lot of those decisions in a game aren't spelled out perfectly. Those middle ones stay with me for the night. I owe it to my team not to carry it to the next day, just like a player cannot not carry an at bat from one to the next.

"If you make a decision that just didn't work—you bring in a right-handed reliever to face a righty, he throws a slider and the guy hits one off the train tracks—that doesn't bother me. The toss-up decisions are the tough ones. Greinke could have given up the homer and I'd be criticized either way. You have to be okay with that."

The Astros lost the World Series because Game 7 got away from them in the blink moments by the slimmest of margins, much of it apparent only to the one person who must act in the moment on the external cues:

the manager. Greinke's emotional reaction to not getting a 2-and-1 strike call. Concern for Cole's financial future. The shortest postseason home run in four years—on a fly ball that clipped the foul pole, like a metaphor for the thin line between what is fair and what is not.

"Personally, as a manager, only you know how well you were prepared for the decisions you had in front of you," Hinch says. "And if there's nobody else in the building who knows that, you have to be OK with that. That's what makes managing cruel—and at the same time incredibly fulfilling."

CHAPTER 5

"Try Not to Suck"

Javier Báez sat across a desk from Maddon in the tiny manager's office at Wrigley Field. It was September 1, 2015. Báez had just been called up to the Cubs after spending the entire season in the minors. Just twenty-two years old, Báez was blessed with outsize talent—chiefly wicked bat speed and fabulous defensive skills—but he lacked polish. Watching Báez play baseball was like watching a luge or skeleton run: exhilarating, but always with the raw scent of danger in the air. When the Cubs played Báez in fifty-two games the previous season, he had hit nine home runs but batted .169 and struck out in 42 percent of his plate appearances, a staggering rate that was nearly twice the major league average.

Maddon had invited Báez into his office because he sensed the anxiety of a young player getting a second crack at the big leagues. Maddon needed words to relax Báez so that his extraordinary skills could flourish.

"I want you to go out there and play like you're in Little League," Maddon told Báez. "Go out there like we're just a bunch of kids having a good time. Don't worry about making mistakes.

"Look at it this way. We are all professionals. One of the main things you do as a professional athlete on a daily basis is try not to embarrass yourself. So how do you do that? Simple. By trying not to suck."

Báez hit .289 in September and cut his strikeout rate to 30 percent, and when shortstop Addison Russell injured a hamstring in the postseason, he stepped in as the Cubs' starting shortstop in the National League Championship Series.

Three months later, Báez was seated at the "Rock Star Rookies" panel at the annual Cubs Convention at the Sheraton Grand Chicago ballroom. A fan asked him what advice Maddon had given him for his September call-up.

Báez gave a sheepish grin and blurted into the microphone, "'Try not to suck.'"

The ballroom erupted in laughter. A slogan for the 2016 Cubs was born. It wasn't long before "TRY NOT TO SUCK" T-shirts, emblazoned with Maddon's trademark thick-rimmed glasses, flooded not just the Cubs' clubhouse but also the Wrigley Field stands and the hippest bars and restaurants in Chicago.

"Basically, what 'Try not to suck' means is that you go out there and you don't worry about stuff," Maddon says. "You play as hard as you can. When you break it all the way down, all you are doing is trying not to embarrass yourself. That's the essence of professional sports."

"Try not to suck" applies to managers, as well. Shut out the noise and manage as hard as you can, no matter the date or the stakes. Nothing will test a manager's gut decision-making more than a winner-take-all postseason game. Like Roberts in 2019, Maddon received harsh reviews for his blink decisions in Game 7 of the 2016 World Series—and that is despite his *winning* the game. The two-strike squeeze attempt with Báez was just one piece of kindling for the second-guessers' bonfire.

Before Game 7 Maddon told general manager Theo Epstein and assistant general manager Jed Hoyer he wanted to use only three pitchers: Kyle Hendricks to Jon Lester to Aroldis Chapman. Lester's entry would come with two conditions: unaccustomed to relieving, Lester would not enter the game in the middle of an inning, and when he did enter, so would his personal catcher, David Ross.

But then the game unwound with unanticipated pressure points on this script. Hendricks wobbled so badly in the third inning that Maddon told Lester to start warming in the bullpen. Hendricks settled down with an easy fourth inning. But when Hendricks walked Carlos Santana with two outs in the fifth with a 5–1 lead, Maddon pulled Hendricks from the game and contradicted his pregame plan by dropping Lester into a so-called "dirty" inning—with a runner on base.

Several factors pushed Maddon toward the quick hook in that blink moment. One, he was worried Cleveland hitters were seeing Hendricks well.

"I was concerned because it looks like they were on him," Maddon says. "And Kyle is really good, but there's times when if the other team is on him and he's not making his pitches, this could go the wrong way quickly. And we could not afford that on this particular day. This is a real balancing act. This is really threading the needle."

Two, Maddon was worried about Lester throwing so much in the bullpen—getting "hot" twice—that his stuff would deteriorate.

"I had to keep all this stuff in mind," Maddon says, "because I was really concerned about if you keep warming him up and don't get him in the game, whatever utility he has is going to go away, and it's going to be difficult to cover those innings if, in fact, something did happen to Kyle."

Three, Ross had returned to the dugout after catching Lester's first bullpen and told Maddon that Lester looked sharp. "It's jumping. It's alive," Ross had reported about Lester's stuff.

"So that's in my head," Maddon says, adding in a half-joking manner, "Who knows, maybe that's why David told me he's throwing so well, because he knows he's coming in the game with him."

Four, the next two hitters for Cleveland were Jason Kipnis, a dangerous left-handed hitter, and Francisco Lindor, a switch-hitter whom Maddon preferred to face from the right side.

"Because of Kipnis," Maddon says when asked why he pulled Hendricks for Lester. "If it wasn't Kipnis, if it was another righty or a switch-hitter I thought you had a better chance with, I probably would have left him out there. But Kipnis, he's just really good. It could be 5–3 [with a home run], and then it's an entirely different thought. So Jon was ready, they told me he was really good, and Lindor I like hitting right-handed more a lot.

"So I thought even though there's a runner on first base—I had talked about the dirty inning—it was 5–1, Santana was on first, and he wasn't going anywhere. I wasn't worried about any of that. I told Jon, 'Don't worry about it. He's not going anywhere.' So it was Kipnis."

Lester did his job: he induced Kipnis to hit a dribbler in front of the plate, and he struck out Lindor. But somehow in that sequence two runs scored. Ross made a throwing error on Kipnis's dribbler, and Lester bounced a pitch to Lindor that hit Ross's mask and caromed so far away that two runners scored. Lester would pitch without further incident two outs into the eighth, leaving with a 6–3 lead.

"All that decision-making right there, a lot of it was preordained, pre-planned, pre–spoken about in regard to when we got Kyle out of there and go to Jon," Maddon says. "From my perspective, the gut part of it was I cannot permit Jon to keep warming up and anticipate or expect him to pitch well during the course of the game. It was just a bad assumption.

"Bringing him in for Kipnis was one thing. The other thing was Lindor behind him. Again, easy decision to make. Had I let Kyle pitch to Kipnis and something bad happened, I had to bring in Jon at that point to face Lindor because I wanted him right-handed over left-handed, and that would have contributed to a very dirty inning, which also was not great. We didn't want to do that.

"This is all going on in that millisecond, that moment. You've thought about it before the game. Now here it comes during the game. You don't have another game tomorrow. Easy decision to make in the middle of the year: Of course Kyle keeps pitching. Of course Jonny is not in the bullpen then.

"But when it's the seventh game of the World Series, it takes on a different attitude. These are the kind of things that you have to evaluate in your gut in the moment that sometimes—not sometimes, *most of the times*—people don't understand, and the old outcome hits you right in the butt. When things don't work out, well then, of course people want to start pinning it on different things.

"But in that situation, it was first plotted. It was planned. We had Jonny to get in there. He did his job. It was a dribbler and a ball to the catcher's face mask that led to those two moments. But it was all based on gut reaction. On feel. And not analytics."

In the eighth, with Lindor due up, Maddon replaced Lester with Chapman. It was the third time in four days that Maddon had asked Chapman to pitch multiple innings. The previous night, he'd brought Chapman into the seventh inning to face Lindor with a 7–2 lead and two runners on base.

"I had Travis Wood also, but the situation was too big," Maddon says. "And don't forget, it was Game 6 and we're down by a game. We had to win this game to get to Game 7. So I'm not going to trust lightly.

"That's not an analytically written-up this-is-the-way-to-do-it situation. And furthermore, you have to have somebody ready in time to be able to fulfill a plan. It's not like, *OK, this is what's happening, get Chapman up, put him in the game.* This is the stuff you have to read the tea leaves in advance of in order to get Aroldis ready to rock and roll and in there."

When Anthony Rizzo hit a two-run homer in the ninth inning of Game 6 to stretch the lead to 9–2, an unsure Maddon was too slow to get another reliever ready for the bottom of the inning to save Chapman from throwing more pitches with Game 7 looming. He debated so long with pitching coach Chris Bosio about what to do that Chapman had to go back to pitch in a third inning with a seven-run lead.

"The mistake I made there, in retrospect, probably my biggest mistake, was to let him go out and throw four more pitches," Maddon says. "Not that the four pitches were overtly harmful, but they could have been. But what it did to him mentally.

"Once we blew it open, he had already done his job. And that was part of my thought process going into this: *Don't walk away from this moment and save Chappy for the end because that end may never show up in a positive way.* So I got him up at the right time. Got him in at the right time.

"Had I just taken him out right there, that would have been the cleanest way to do it. But at that moment, even with the lead, it wasn't really clear cut. But after he threw four straight balls, I could tell he was not really into it at that moment and probably a little bit fatigued. So I had to get him out because we did have the game coming up the next night.

"He did fulfill what I was thinking about before the game: don't run away from him earlier if, in fact, the game would be on the line before the ninth inning, which I thought it was. Once Rizzo hit that home run, I just was not a hundred percent sold on the full bullpen at that point. So I chose to do that, and, like I said, once I saw his reaction and I knew this was not going to go well with him staying in the game, I got him out with the hope we play the next night, and we did.

"My point is that's all gut. There's nothing written in a book. There's nothing anybody said before the game that could have possibly prepared me for putting him in the game when I did or taking him out when I did or just how do you process what may have occurred that day going into the next day."

Chapman's velocity and command sagged the next night when he entered Game 7 in the eighth inning. Brandon Guyer whacked a double to win a seven-pitch at bat. Rajai Davis also extended Chapman to seven pitches. The last one was a low fastball that Davis drilled for a home run to tie the game.

Says Maddon, "Kyle was really good, Jon was really good, and Aroldis on the home run to Davis had nothing to do with velocity. It was all about location. He just threw the ball into his barrel. If he throws it away or elevates it a little, he can't do that. It wasn't a matter of velocity. It was more a matter of location.

"The idea to use those three pitchers was all laid out before the game, and when it comes down to that game, there's no eighth game, there's no ninth game. It's Game 7. So you've got to try to make your best guess, and you have to be a little more proactive as opposed to being reactive at those moments. And the three pitchers we utilized were pretty good. For me it worked out really well. Save the home run by Davis, everything else I thought was pretty good."

After the Zim Special imploded in the top of the ninth, a fatigued Chapman, relying heavily on sliders that lacked bite, somehow retired Santana, Kipnis, and Lindor—the heart of the Cleveland order—in the bottom of the ninth. Upon the third out, umpire Joe West, the crew chief, ordered the ground crew to cover the infield with the tarpaulin.

"Coming off the field, Joe West said something to me like, 'Oh, they don't think it's going to be that long,' something to that effect," Maddon says. "I think he said, 'Seventeen minutes.' I said, 'Good.'"

Maddon headed toward a flight of stairs behind the visiting dugout to his office at Progressive Field. He wanted to check his weather app.

He also wanted to grab his father's favorite hat, a weathered periwinkle-blue Angels cap that Maddon in 2002 had placed atop the dugout bench, facing the field, during the last inning of World Series Game 7 so that his late father could "see" his son win the World Series. He wanted the same talisman with him for the end of this Game 7. He pulled it from a backpack and stuffed it into the waist of his pants at the small of his back. As Maddon left the dugout, and before he reached the stairs, he looked to his right and saw his players gathered in the visiting weight room.

"I see the guys in the weight room," Maddon says. "OK. I didn't know what was going on. I thought they were just gathering to . . . I didn't know what they were doing. Good. I go upstairs, see Jed, look at my app, grab Dad's hat, stuff it in the back underneath my hoodie, I walk back and here we go."

Maddon did not know that Heyward had called a players-only meeting in that weight room. Heyward reminded the Cubs that they had been the best team in baseball all year and said it was time to show it. The gathering was the perfect manifestation of Maddon's belief in empowering players. From the T-shirts he'd handed out in his first days as Devil Rays manager—which read, "Tell me what you think, not what you've heard"—to the quote from John Wooden that hung in the Rays' clubhouse—"Discipline yourself so that no one else has to"—Madden knew the best version of a player appeared only with freedom, not with rules and fear imposed upon them. When Maddon found out after the game about the meeting, he felt like a proud parent. He had raised them well. They'd remembered the lessons embedded in "Try not to suck."

When play resumed—after a rain delay of exactly seventeen minutes—Maddon felt renewed energy in the Cubs' dugout.

"They were so jacked up," Maddon says. "Seriously, the rain absolutely permitted us to recalculate. There's no doubt about it. If you're talking about a fortuitous moment in the history of time and place as it relates to baseball, that rain delay was the most perfectly timed ever."

Cleveland, meanwhile, passed the delay quietly in the home clubhouse. Lindor took a nap.

"I went to the locker room and I saw the plastic and I said, 'Oh, shit,' "

Lindor says, referring to the sheeting used to protect players' lockers from the anticipated champagne celebration. "So I went down to the weight room and I just laid down for a nap. I was twenty-two. If I was older, we would have won that game. It would have been different.

"Not that I would have gotten the team together, but I would have gone to [Mike] Napoli. 'Hey, Nap. What do you think?' Like, I was just happy to be in the World Series. 'Hey, Nap'—because he was our team leader—'we've got to find a way to do something different.' Or 'Rajai, what you got? Let's do this. Let's do something.'

"I was just happy. Whereas now it's like, 'Damn, the guys saw that [plastic]. Who's the leader of the team? Nap, bro, are we sure we want to bring back Bryan Shaw again? Who we got in the bullpen? Let's find a way.'"

Says Kipnis, "As riveting as any words may have been, I don't think it's that simple. It's not like we let our guard down."

The rejuvenated Cubs immediately scored twice and hung on to win 8–7. What turned out to be the deciding run was knocked in by the third catcher used by Maddon, Miguel Montero. Maddon became the only manager to win a World Series Game 7 in extra innings on the road, the only manager to win a World Series clincher using three catchers, and the only manager to win a World Series clincher while using six position players who were twenty-five years old or younger.

It was a four-hour-and-twenty-eight-minute test of gut thinking—a pop quiz to decide the final grade of how Maddon had affected the Cubs for two years.

Chapman, with his gallant ninth inning working on fumes, was the winning pitcher. Mike Montgomery earned the save, his first in eight years of professional baseball. As Game 7 illuminated, most gut decisions for managers involve pitching.

"Analytically, during the game I think it's primarily preordained pitching, starting pitching primarily, the third time through a lineup," Maddon says. "That is an analytical decision, no question. And I don't believe I've ever done that. I've taken guys out the third time through.

83

Jeremy Hellickson with the Rays was a great example, and that was not based on analytics. That was based on observation. It just went south. There are certain guys, they get to a pitch number and all of a sudden the guy becomes a different pitcher. So not analytics. Just reality. And you have to make a decision.

"The bullpen? Again, before the game, you know there are all these numbers created, matrix numbers, whatever. And of course, when you don't know your guy, or you don't know the guy you're facing, sometimes these do become more important. But if you know your guy and you've seen this other team often enough, you easily could make your decisions pregame and during the game based on what you've been seeing void of any of this kind of information. It doesn't really matter at that point.

"I know what I know. I know what I see. I know who my pitcher is right now. I know what that hitter is like. I know what he's been like more recently because I've researched that. So you then make the decision.

"Now, to me, that's gut. That is not analytics. It's just based on infor-mation. That's normal stuff that's been going on for the last how many years? I don't know. Forever? Managers have been making these kinds of decisions based on that forever, and that's the bullpen.

"There are some bullpens, I think that you'll see, that managers have to replace pitchers at certain points based on whatever has been dictated from upstairs. Again, I have not been dictated in that way, I don't think, ever.

"If there are any close calls based on any of this stuff I just talked about, who to pitch against who and whatever, if there's like a real close call, that's where information, numbers could be beneficial prior to the game. And I wrote my note off of that, but still having to make that determination when the game occured.

"But close calls, I always looked for information, numbers, when it came to something in my mind's eye that was really too close to call. That's where I needed a tiebreaker.

"Listen, I heard voices. Absolutely, you will hear voices in the game based on what different things might have been said to you before the game from front-office people. There's no question. I cannot deny that.

"You'll hear the voice. You'll know the situation. And I promise you, I didn't make it based on the voice. I just knew that if my decision went against the voice, then it better work because otherwise, I was going to have a visitor right after the game in my office that I had to contend with."

Gut thinking by a manager taps into experience and the powers of observation. On August 23, 1996, the Yankees traded outfielder Gerald Williams and pitcher Bob Wickman to the Brewers for left-handed pitcher Graeme Lloyd and infielder Pat Listach. Lloyd was the key to the deal. The Yankees needed a left-handed reliever for the pennant race and postseason.

George Steinbrenner, the late Yankees owner, approached Lloyd as soon as the Australian reported to the team.

"Sorry to hear about that problem you've had back in Australia," Steinbrenner told him in his best empathetic voice.

"What problem?" Lloyd asked.

"The one where all the barbers died."

Lloyd got the message, and a haircut.

In addition to lengthy locks, Lloyd arrived with a sore arm. He struggled. He gave up eleven runs in five and two-thirds innings over thirteen appearances. Fans at Yankee Stadium booed him. Yankees manager Joe Torre surprised people when he put Lloyd on the Yankees' postseason roster.

"It was kind of a gut decision," Torre explained, "though I did go back and read the scouting reports from Gene Michael and Chuck Cottier. Those people's opinions were that he could help us. And I had to listen to that and discount the stuff that was going on when he was on the mound."

Lloyd did not allow a run in his eight postseason appearances, including four in the World Series as the Yankees won their first title in eighteen years. Torre's gut feeling, which leaned on reports from two veteran scouts, was proven right.

In the 2013 American League Wild Card Game, Maddon started right-handed-hitting Delmon Young at designated hitter against Cleveland right-hander Danny Salazar, even though conventional wisdom would be to use left-handed-hitting Matt Joyce as the Tampa Bay DH.

"The decision to use Delmon Young was the antianalytical decision," Maddon says. "You want to call it gut, but I knew Delmon, I knew his swing path, I knew the pitcher, and I knew the other hitter, Matty Joyce. I knew it wasn't going to work the other way and felt very strongly it would work this way."

Young had never faced Salazar. Leading off the third inning, Young hit the first pitch for a home run. The Rays won 4–0.

For an example of how a player uses gut thinking, go back to the famous one-game playoff in 1978 between the Yankees and the Red Sox. With two outs, a full count, and two runners on in the sixth inning, and with the Red Sox leading 2–0, Fred Lynn of Boston pulled a long smash to right field, near the corner of Fenway Park. He was sure it would be an extra-base hit. Two runs would score, and the Red Sox would take a lead of at least 4–0 into the seventh inning. To his astonishment, however, Lynn watched right fielder Lou Piniella make a basket catch on the run.

"What was he doing out of position?" Lynn would say later. "How lucky can he be?"

It was gut, not luck. Ron Guidry was pitching on short rest for a third straight start, those being the only starts he'd made that season with three days of rest instead of the usual four. Piniella noticed that Guidry was not quite as sharp or strong as usual that day. He noticed that left-handed hitters were able to get in front of his fastball. Earlier in the game, Carl Yastrzemski had pulled a home run off a Guidry fastball, tucking it inside the right-field foul pole. Based on his observations, Piniella played Lynn six to eight steps closer to the line than he normally would.

Such observational, intuitive thinking is almost unheard of today. Why? Because players carry analytical laminated cards in their pockets that tell them where to position themselves based on the hitter and the pitcher.

Albert Camus said, "Life is the sum of all your choices." In today's baseball, even as information grows in scale and detail, there remains room for gut-based choice—maybe even a *necessity* for it within a game as stakes rise and blink moments come fast.

In 1988 the USS *Vincennes* shot down a plane over the Strait of

Hormuz that it believed to be a threat. It was an Iran Air passenger jet. All 290 people aboard were killed. In the wake of the tragedy, the US Army and Navy helped fund research into the emerging field of naturalistic decision making, which studies how people make high-stakes decisions in real-life settings, especially under the pressures of time and stress, rather than in theory-based laboratory settings.

NDM researchers studied how firefighters, military commanders, pilots, nurses, and other decision-makers made their choices under real-world conditions. They found that highly experienced decision-makers used a two-layer decision model: first they recognized patterns in situations, and then they imagined how a decision would unfold. Gary Klein, one of the authors of the formative NDM book in 1993, identified this decision model as combining intuition (based on patterns) and analytical thinking (based on running the mental simulations). The combination led to quick, competent decisions, especially as more experience generated a richer repository of patterns on which to draw.

Further research also found decision-makers' certainty in their choices did not necessarily increase with more information. Indeed, it worsened. A 2020 study by a research team at Stevens Institute of Technology, led by Samantha Kleinberg, found that too much information can lead people to make worse decisions. Her team discovered that when people were asked to make decisions on obviously unfamiliar scenarios, such as ones involving mind-reading aliens, they made better decisions than when they were asked about familiar subjects, such as finance or retirement. New information layered on top of prior knowledge and beliefs complicated the decision-making.

When he was a rookie manager with the 2018 Phillies, the decision-making of Gabe Kapler suffered from too much information. With the clinical focus of a card counter, Kapler chased every incremental edge he might gain in probabilities, often without regard for the egos and confidence of players who suffered the consequences. It began Opening Day, when he pulled his ace, Aaron Nola, after just sixty-eight pitches with a 5–0 lead. Philadelphia lost 8–5. He once pinch-hit for rookie shortstop Scott Kingery without letting him take an at bat. He chased platoon-based pitching matchups more than any other manager. He used 138 lineups over 162 games, none more than five times. His team collapsed in September with a record of 8-20.

The next season Kapler admitted, "I believe in chemistry now more than I ever have. You can't play this game on paper, even though it's fun to do. It's not a board game."

Kapler was fired by the Phillies after a second season, after which the Giants hired him. In 2021, a more evolved Kapler, with less zeal for chasing every incremental edge, proved a steady hand who led the Giants to a franchise-record 107 wins.

Card counters operate with the knowledge of finite possibilities. The deck has fifty-two cards. As a card is played, a known number of like ones remain. Baseball is a game played with an unlimited number of decks of cards. Even more unpredictably, it is played by humans. Incremental probabilistic edges based on large-scale mathematical formulas can be overwritten by a person's state of being that day—confidence, health, family issues, etc. It is the manager's job to know the math and understand the player. As with naturalistic decision making—with not life or death but wins and losses at stake—the richness of a manager's experience can lead to better decisions.

Maddon unconventionally put sluggers such as Evan Longoria, Anthony Rizzo, and Willson Contreras in the leadoff spot in the lineup. To get them out of a slump, he changed their perspective. He told his switch-hitters to bat right-handed against Mike Mussina, a right-handed pitcher, and stacked his lineup with right-handed hitters against Shaun Marcum, another right-handed pitcher. He brought in a lefty relief pitcher, J. P. Howell, to face the right-handed slugger Albert Pujols.

"I didn't have anybody analytically tell me to do that," Maddon says about his against-the-grain moves. "It was always something that I saw because, primarily, large sample size, these analytic guys are going to still tell you to play right on left and left on right. But I chose not to in situations because, again, is that gut? Is that paying attention to information? Observation? What is that?

"I've done this for so long and faced so many situations that your gut primarily is the culmination of your experiences coming together in the thick of the moment. That's why I've been better able to trust my gut, because it's well thought out. It is intuitive thinking. Knowing that made me more comfortable making split-second decisions.

"What was going on? What am I feeling? What am I seeing? What am I observing right now? What's happening in this moment? What does this moment require? I'm here to tell you, folks, for the guys that have never had the cache of experiences I've had, it's very difficult for them to make these kinds of decisions in these moments. It just is.

"They have nothing to draw on. There's nothing in the recesses of their mind or their gut that permits them to draw on this and decide these different things in those moments.

"And I promise you, every time I've attempted or utilized a gut reaction, I will give you at least ten reasons why I chose what is perceived to be gut or by the seat of your pants. It's something that has been well thought out. I've probably gone through it in a previous baseball life, and all of a sudden, here it is.

"So the stage is pretty big. Am I supposed to run away from it? Am I supposed to play it safe right here? Am I here to try to do something other than what I think is the right thing to do? Of course not. I'm going to do what I think is the right thing to do."

By drawing on experience and making decisions in the moment, Maddon asked of himself the same ambition he asked of an inexperienced Báez trying to establish a foothold in Major League Baseball: "Try not to suck." Worrying about outcomes and giving thought to the consequences of failure get in the way of the simple execution of the task. Game 7 of the World Series, the biggest stage of all, defined the 2016 team and its manager. At times unorthodox and at times bleak, the game eventually rewarded the belief systems Maddon had spent two years crafting in Chicago.

Seven months earlier, on March 2, the entire team took the field for a spring training workout wearing "TRY NOT TO SUCK" T-shirts. One month later, Maddon was pleased to hear ushers at Busch Stadium in St. Louis, home to the rival Cardinals, had stopped Cubs fans from entering the

JOE MADDON AND TOM VERDUCCI

ballpark if they were wearing the shirts. Regarding them as profane, the ushers forced fans to remove them or turn them inside out.

"It's much better if the fans make a big deal out of it," Maddon said. "Let someone blow your horn, and the sound travels twice as far."

By October, more than a hundred thousand "TRY NOT TO SUCK" T-shirts were sold. The sales generated half a million dollars for the charitable foundations run by Maddon, Ross, and Ben Zobrist. The big payoff from "Try not to suck" came just when it looked as if the Cubs might blow the World Series upon losing a three-run lead with four outs to go. Given the pause of the rain delay to reset, the Cubs remembered to simply play hard.

A few months later, Epstein was the guest speaker at the 2017 commencement at Yale, his alma mater. That World Series Game 7 meeting was the heart of his speech:

After three years of arduous rebuilding, we had a nucleus of young players we believed in who were ready to break into the majors together. Many of these players were twenty-one and twenty-two years old: your peers, your generation. Typically, it takes young players years to adjust to life in the big leagues and to start performing up to their capabilities. Most of the blame for this rests on these ridiculous old baseball norms that say young players are to be seen and not heard. That young players must follow and not lead. That young players must adhere to the established codes—from the dress code that requires them to wear suits and ties to the code that says major league players can't get too excited on the field or look like they are having too much fun.

Thankfully, we hired a manager in Joe Maddon who agreed it was time to turn these conventions on their heads. We asked our young players to be themselves, to show their personalities, to have fun, to be daring, to be bold. The dress code was changed from suit and tie to "If you think you look hot, wear it!" Unburdened and empowered, our young team flourished last season, winning 103 games, the most in baseball, and reached our first World Series since 1945.

After fighting back from a three-games-to-one deficit against the Cleveland Indians, we faced a decisive Game 7 in Cleveland. Still in a bit of a daze, I cut through our clubhouse toward a meeting about the weather. Turning a corner, I saw, through the window of the weight room door, the backs of our players' blue jerseys, shoulder to shoulder and packed tightly, all twenty-five guys squeezed into a space designed for half that many. It was an unusual sight. We hardly ever had meetings and never during a game. I inched closer to the door and saw Aroldis Chapman, the pitcher who had surrendered the tying home run, in tears. I lingered just long enough to hear a few sentences.

"We would not even be here without you," catcher David Ross said as he embraced Chapman. "We are going to win this for you. We are going to win this for each other."

Outfielder Jason Heyward walked to the middle of the room: "We are the best team in baseball," he said. "We've leaned on each other all year. We've still got this. This is only going to make it sweeter."

And then first baseman Anthony Rizzo: "Nobody can take this away from us. We have each other."

Kyle Schwarber stood up with a bat in his hands: "We win this right here!"

I turned away, a big smile on my face, and headed to the weather meeting. I thought immediately of the players' meeting during the rain delay, and how connected they were with each other, how invested they were in each other's fates, how they turned each other's tears into determination. During rain delays players typically come in off the field and head to their own lockers, sit there by themselves, change their wet jerseys, check their phones, think about what has gone right and wrong during the game, and become engrossed in their own worlds. That would have been disastrous for our team during Game 7—twenty-five players sitting alone at their lockers, lamenting the bad breaks, assigning blame, wallowing, wondering. Instead they had the instinct to come together.

Early in my career, I used to think of players as assets, statistics on a spreadsheet I could use to project future performance and measure precisely how much they would impact our team on the field. I used to think of teams as portfolios, diversified collections of player assets paid to produce up to their projections to ensure the organization's success. My head had been down. That narrow approach worked for a while, but it certainly had its limits. I grew, and my team-building philosophy grew as well.

The truth—as our team proved in Cleveland—is that a player's character matters. The heartbeat matters. Fears and aspirations matter. The player's impact on others matters. The tone he sets matters. The willingness to connect matters. Breaking down cliques and overcoming stereotypes in the clubhouse matters. Who you are, how you live among others—that all matters. The youngest team in World Series history, with six starters under the age of twenty-five—they helped me get my head up.

That is why, at the important moments in their lives, I'm going to keep telling my sons about the 2016 Cubs and that rain delay. And I'll remind them—when they are graduating college or starting a new job, heading off to grad school or beginning a new life somewhere foreign—that they have a choice.

CHAPTER 6

"The Process Is Fearless"

Fresh off his scouting adventures, Joe Maddon, twenty-seven years old and bursting with optimism, headed to the manager's office of McDermott Field on the corner of West Elva Street and Blaine Avenue in Idaho Falls, Idaho, for his first day as a manager in professional baseball. It was 1981. His team was the Idaho Falls Angels of the Pioneer League. He was starting in rookie league, the bottom rung of the affiliated baseball ladder, a seventy-game indoctrination for most players and, in this case, for the manager. Larry Himes, the Angels scouting director who had assigned Maddon the gig, had managed Idaho Falls from 1974 to 1977.

"The place is great," Himes had told Maddon. "You will love it."

Maddon opened the door to his new office and gasped. The tiny room was littered with dirt and broken glass. Welcome to the glamorous world of managing in the low minors.

"Here I am going, 'Wow, this is pretty horrible,'" Maddon says. "Finally the general manager shows up. He was in his thirties. He was aloof. It was not professional by any stretch of the imagination. This guy obviously didn't give a crap. That's how it started."

It did not improve much. One month into the season, after the Angels returned from a trip, Maddon was shocked to see clods of dirt over the infield.

"It looked like brown golf balls everywhere," he says.

Maddon found his general manager and unloaded on him.

"What the hell is going on?" Maddon yelled at him. "We've got our number-one pick, Dick Schofield, playing shortstop, and you're going to leave the infield looking like this?"

"Nobody has ever complained about this field before," the GM said.

"Well, it's about friggin' time somebody did, because this is bullshit."

"I know your boss, and I'm going to give him a call and tell him what the hell is going on here and what you're saying. I'll have your ass fired."

"Go ahead. Go call Mike Port. Call him. And if you don't have his number, I'll get it for you!"

The general manager left to call Port.

"Maybe thirty minutes later," Maddon says, "there is a bevy of city workers out at this field trying to get the infield back in shape to play. I called up Mike later, and he said, 'You did the right thing. Thanks for letting me know. If the playing conditions are not right, call me, and we will make sure it gets right.'

"I was twenty-seven years old, managing a rookie league team in Idaho Falls, but it was the big leagues to me. I was also the pitching coach, hitting coach, third-base coach, and English instructor for a bunch of kids from Venezuela. I learned a lot, but this was the most important lesson I learned: back your players."

Scouting is mostly a solitary pursuit—unless you have a trusted wingman with a reliable Chrysler like Jimmy Driscoll. Managing is the ultimate test of leadership in baseball. It requires Dwight Eisenhower's vision of leadership: convincing members of a group to *want* to do something that needs to be done for the benefit of the group, not just the individual. On a micro scale, it's the equivalent of a hitter willingly making an out to the right side to advance the runner at second base. He knows he's lowering his batting average to give the team a better chance of winning.

Eisenhower knew that leaders sometimes must give orders. They make tough decisions that must be followed regardless of what others think. But, he wrote, whenever people "can be persuaded rather than ordered—when they can be made to feel that they have participated in developing the plan—they approach their tasks with understanding and enthusiasm." He referred to the ability to evoke this feeling as the power of persuasion. Churchill, he said, was such a master persuader in how he used words and logic that he would spur Eisenhower to question his own evaluations.

At twenty-seven, the youngest manager in pro ball at the time, Maddon crossed the Rubicon from the narrow responsibilities of playing and scouting into the broad territory of leadership.

"My job," he said then, "is to create pride in the organization and push a winning attitude."

On his Idaho Falls team Maddon had seventeen teenagers, eight players from Latin America who spoke no English, and no full-time coaches. He was only four years older than one of his players, first baseman Mark Bingham, an economics major at Harvard. Maddon and Bingham would sit next to each other at the front of the bus and on long rides engage in deep conversations about American history. Starting in Idaho Falls, Maddon would bring to bear all the lessons from coaches and leaders in his young life and meld them with his own instincts and experiences.

"What is a leader?" Maddon asks. "Churchill was an older man, out of shape, and probably drank too much. And he took that country through World War II in a way that we read about all the time, and we want to read what he said and how he said it.

"It starts with fearlessness. And I love that word. Courage is the quality that permits somebody to be a leader. If you don't have courage—in a sense being fearless—it's impossible to be a leader. Courage is the one quality or trait that permits or allows for all others."

Maddon traces his understanding of the importance of fearlessness to Ken Ravizza, who in the 1980s emerged as one of the leaders in what was then the nascent field of sports psychology. Ravizza was a professor in the kinesiology department at Cal State Fullerton. In 1985, Angels pitching coach Marcel Lachemann invited Ravizza to work with the team's pitchers. Maddon, still a minor league manager in the Angels' system, met Ravizza in spring training. A lifelong friendship was born. Under Maddon's invitation, Ravizza worked with Angels minor league hitters such as Dante Bichette and Damion Easley in a trailer parked alongside a field at Gene Autry Park during Instructional Leagues in the eighties and nineties.

No one affected Maddon more than Ravizza when it came to understanding the mental side of the game. Under Ravizza's guidance, Maddon became an early adopter among uniformed personnel in regarding mental skills as on par with the traditional five physical tools on which players are scouted. Each spring training, he told his players that if they were not working with the mental skills coach, it was no different from ignoring the hitting coach or the pitching coach.

When Maddon was hired by the Cubs in 2015, the club also hired Ravizza as a consultant. Ravizza died of a heart attack three years later at age seventy. Maddon tweeted then, "My brother...your voice and thoughts shall remain in my mind forever...our work continues..."

Ravizza was a big believer in athletes staying in the moment. He helped develop strategies enabling them to do so. Maddon understood the same lessons applied to his job, as well as to any job outside of sports.

"When you get caught up in the future—worrying about the outcome—that's where anxiety lives," Maddon says. "When you're stuck in the past, that's where ego lives, and it's hard to move forward. I tell myself all the time: *Don't miss the present.*"

In 2015 Maddon and Ravizza came up with a slogan to keep the Cubs grounded in the present: "The process is fearless." That season, Maddon's first with the Cubs, his team took out a ninety-eight-win Pittsburgh team in the Wild Card Game and a hundred-win St. Louis team in the Division Series. Chicago's 6–4 win in NLDS Game 4 against the Cardinals marked the first time a Cubs team had won the clinching game of a postseason series at home. After the game, when asked how his young team could handle the pressure of getting to the doorstep of the World Series, Maddon drew from the playbook he and Ravizza had devised to navigate the season.

"I can't emphasize this enough: the process is fearless," Maddon said. "I mean, if you want to go out a little wide eyed and worry about outcomes, you're not going to play nearly as good as you can. You're not. But if you go out there and think, *I'm going to go out there and take ground balls, I'm going to move my feet, make my throws to first base, in BP I'm going to work the whole field, check out your video, game in progress, had a bad at bat, what can I do differently my next at bat?* . . . don't even worry about the score of the game. That will take care of itself. If you take care of these smaller components, that will eventually turn in your favor."

The next spring training, in a scene typical of Maddon's loose camps (Maddon had already hired clowns to visit and staged a dance contest), infielder Munenori Kawasaki belted out an enthusiastic rendition of Aerosmith's "I Don't Want to Miss a Thing." Kawasaki and virtually the entire team wore headbands with Japanese lettering. Maddon was told the words on the headbands translated to "must win."

"I'm digging on it," Maddon said. "Although we don't use the word *winning* here a lot. I'd like to see one that says, 'The Process Is Fearless.' If you're really focusing on outcome and just winning, then you can become fearful. But if you just focus on the process, the process is fearless."

That spring, in what would become a championship season, Maddon defined for his players the four tenets of "The process is fearless":

1. The process lacks emotion.
2. The process is the moment.
3. The process is the mental anchor.
4. The process simplifies the task.

He might as well have been defining the concept for himself. They are the same tenets he used to manage.

"The process is fearless because I don't want to spend time on the outcome," Maddon says. "For me, it's really about staying in the moment and not worrying about the outcome of the game or managing toward the outcome.

" 'The process is fearless' means if you stay with the process you can stay in the present tense, and you won't be fearful of taking chances. It's easy to get out of that and get emotional or get attached to the game. And when I do that, I get really upset with myself internally. That's not helping anybody. Leadership is about being fearless, which is about staying in the moment."

Maddon's version of leadership is built on such fearlessness so that others will follow. The word *leadership* comes from the Indo-European word *leith*, which means to move forward, as in crossing a threshold—even going as far as crossing into death in battle. The threshold is the boundary of your comfort level. Leadership is the courage to extend people's thinking, boundaries, and, ultimately, capabilities so they become the best versions of themselves.

Sports traditionally honored autocrats as leaders—men such as Lombardi, Red Auerbach, and Belichick. As society became more democratic, so did sports. The empowerment of athletes and respect for their individual rights required a more collaborative approach. To lead—to get players to "cross their threshold"—demanded more empathetic leaders. Peter Senge, an American systems scientist and senior lecturer at the MIT Sloan School of Management, argued in his seminal 1990 book, *The Fifth Discipline: The Art and Practice of the Learning Organization*, that such great leaders are never a finished product. They are constantly learning.

"People with a high level of personal mastery are acutely aware of their ignorance, their incompetence, their growth areas," Senge wrote. "And they are deeply self-confident. Paradoxical? Only for those who do not see the 'journey is the reward.'"

The leader has the wisdom to know what he or she does not know. By manner, words, and actions, the leader also conveys a spirit of personality that makes the message worth following, Senge wrote. We often call this power the "it" factor. An even better term for it is *charisma*, a word that derives from the Catholic church as a term for a person's God-given gifts. Charisma is making use of the divine gift of leadership.

"In short, we develop as true charismatic leaders to the extent that we become ourselves," Senge wrote.

Mention charismatic leaders to Maddon and his mind immediately goes to Gene Mauch, a brilliant baseball tactician who managed twenty-six seasons, the last six with the Angels when Maddon was learning the craft of coaching and managing in the Angels' minor league system.

"Professionally, Gene Mauch was the one leader who stands out," Maddon says. "That was primarily based on charisma. This guy, dang, you just felt like he was right all the time, that he knew everything. I absolutely believe that about him. I still do.

"It was a quiet charisma. It wasn't because of great speeches, although it was when he did talk about baseball, and you heard all the common sense and really the pertinent stuff that he was spewing out. But it was never in a grand style. It was never like standing in front of a group and his voice raising and lowering and hands moving. It wasn't any of that. It was Gene talking to you.

"His leadership was a combination of intimidation—no question it was there; he didn't even have to try—and then pure baseball genius."

Ask anyone to name the three most influential people in their lives, outside of immediate family, and the answers are likely to include teachers and coaches. The best of these are about *leith*—they lead us across our threshold. But as Senge wrote, "Leadership is not about role. Management is about role. If you are a manager, you are being paid to be accountable for results produced by others.

"Leadership is different. It's the spirit that animates good management. Good managers can be really good leaders if they have a sense of purpose, and they really care about the people in their group. Leadership is about how we create.... It's more about the spirit of things than the operation of things. Both are important."

It's in the realm of what Senge calls "the spirit of the enterprise" that the change in baseball hierarchal power has changed managing. Front offices, including analytics departments, took evaluative power (building a roster) and expanded it into strategic power (how the game is played), which they usurped from managers. With a diminution of power, the baseball manager's job became more about role (middle management) than leadership. The baseball manager who wants to keep his job does not cross any thresholds set by the front office.

"You want to use the right metrics," Senge wrote, "but you also want to be passionate." Control of the spirit of the enterprise becomes more difficult for the baseball manager when front offices dictate or influence decisions. Players know where the true power resides.

"Great leaders can stand up to opposition and they can stand up to the boss, whoever that might be," Maddon says. "They also can stand up to strong public opinion that's not necessarily true or accurate or right, but it's strong public opinion. And a lot of people cower from that because they won't have to answer to it.

"Typically, in our world right now, social media, like a Twitter feed, is really interesting. It can be distracting. A real leader cannot make decisions based on groupthink only.

"By the same token, the leader will listen to the group. He will ask questions. He will seek other opinions. But in the end, he's just not going to go with the popular decision. He's going to go with what he thinks is right. He should do that in the end. That's where the fearlessness comes in. And if he doesn't, he's probably not going to be there that long, quite frankly.

"I've seen guys ascend to becoming major league managers, as an example, and they become entirely different than what they had been as a coach because they think they have to be different. It's almost like a player when he comes to the big leagues who thinks, *I've got to do something different. I've got to be better in order to be successful here.* And then they fail to be themselves.

"A big part of being a successful leader is the *true you* has to show up, not a book version of you, not a contrived version of you, not somebody else's version of you. Because I've been there with the Cubs where people kind of chip away at your veneer even though you've been successful because they think there's something wrong with your method just based on a temporary lag in performance. It had nothing to do with your way of putting it out there. But that's the perception, and all of a sudden, *chip, chip, chip.*

"It's no different than a coach with a good player where if you coach greatness out of somebody or coach instinct out of somebody, shame on you. And that happens.

"I think there's a chance other guys could have been great leaders, but they permitted too much interference. And then they tried to fulfill somebody else's vision of what they should be like. Again, you listen. You absolutely listen. But in the end, if these other people were so smart, why wouldn't they have this position? Why wouldn't they be successful in it? Or why wouldn't they choose to aspire to it? It's not as easy as people think."

Bruce Bochy was one of the most successful managers in the modern game. He gained renown for his expert touch in running a bullpen and for optimizing veteran role players. Bochy, Joe Torre, and Tony La Russa are the only managers to win three World Series since free agency began in 1976. Beginning in 1995, Bochy managed 4,032 games, the seventh most of all time. By the time he left the San Francisco Giants after the 2019 season, the job had changed in one obvious way.

"I would say it was less fun," Bochy says. "I came up with the more traditional way of managing. I made the calls. I made the lineups. You could see how the game was changing, and that's fine. The information is great, and I wanted it. It made the players better. It made coaching better. Today's managers and coaches have to be somewhat fluent in technology, biomechanics and swing paths and spin rates. But you still love to manage a game and have a feel for it. You need a balance. That's what has gotten lost in the game. That's what takes the fun out as a manager.

"You need a different style of leadership today. A manager has to sell it. You can't just tell a guy what to do. That's why relationships are so important. You have to put your arm around a guy and explain why you pinch-hit for him. You think Earl Weaver would have done that? In some respects, leadership can be a little easier and less stressful because a lot of times the player knows it's not the manager's call. The player can come to him, and he knows this is a front-office decision based on analytics."

As the information boom swept baseball with fiber-optic speed, Bochy discovered a dichotomy that is unique to baseball managers: the more experience you gain, the less your wisdom is valued.

"I'd say more than anything that changed is the decision-making that goes on with managing," Bochy says. "You go back to when I started and just before me, the managers, they drove the bus. You had your checks and balances then. You talked to the owner and the GM. But you drove the bus.

"Now, because of what's going on with analytics, decisions are data driven. That has been the biggest shift I've seen. The front office and their analytics with the coaching staff is more of a collaboration.

"Now the checks and balances are the managers. As a manager you might say, 'Well, I see this or that.' But you're not driving the bus. That is by far the biggest difference.

"But you know what? The world is changing and you're not going to change that. You have to adapt to that style of leadership. You don't have the authoritative type of manager. Now the manager has to change to a different style of leadership. Now it involves a lot of selling. You've got to be the one selling now to get all the players to buy in.

"I think relationships are even more important now with the players because of all the things that are happening, like platooning and using openers as starting pitchers. You have to stay in touch with the team, explain your moves to them, and make sure they are all buying into what the front office wants."

Says Maddon, "In today's game of baseball, front offices say they're looking for leadership qualities, but they don't care if the guy is ready to lead or not as long as he can follow them. So it's almost like in today's baseball world, a good leader has to be a great follower in order to be that. I have absolutely seen that. Absolutely.

"In our game today, if you have to make tough decisions in the latter part of a game—and believe me, I've thought it, but I don't permit it—if you're worried about what the GM might say or the president might say or what writers are going to ask, or what the fan base is going to declare, then you can't do what you're doing. You just can't do it.

"You can't do it because that means you don't know what you think you should do. You don't believe in what you know or think you know. It's just something you've heard and you're kind of just passing it along. You really are.

"Great leaders consider the information and act fearlessly."

Great leaders keep self-assuredness and selflessness in balance. Late in 1943, as the United States prepared for a European invasion the next spring, Franklin Roosevelt needed a commander for the offensive. He asked General George C. Marshall whether he would prefer to keep that assignment or remain in Washington as chief of staff. FDR knew Marshall, like most soldiers, would prefer the more high-profile field command. But Marshall responded, "The decision is yours, Mr. President. My wishes have nothing to do with the matter."

FDR kept Marshall at the Pentagon, where he expertly ran battles on both the European and Pacific fronts. FDR would not have done so without being convinced of Marshall's selflessness.

As Eisenhower wrote in retelling the story and defining what makes a leader, "Perhaps the greatest of these qualities is single-minded and selfless dedication to the task at hand. Any leader worth his salt must of course possess a certain amount of ego, a justifiable pride in his own accomplishments. But if he is a truly great leader, the cause must predominate over self. An old and respected commander of mine used to say, 'Always take your job seriously, never yourself.'"

Says Maddon, "When I think of great leaders, I think of my dad, the quietest guy in the world. He never graduated high school. God, did he lead our family. He taught me how to work. Not by teaching me how to work, but by just watching him work. My mom, same category.

"Being a great leader means being selfless. It means being able to accept a compliment and not have it go to your head. You must be able to accept the compliment and immediately, I mean immediately, say 'Thank you.' And then immediately move on to the next thought because you know if you get stuck on that, those platitudes, whatever you're doing well, you're going to stop doing well in the very near future. I probably got that from my mother. That stands out to me."

From Idaho Falls, it would take Maddon twenty-five years to get a full-time managing gig. When it happened, in 2006 with the Tampa Bay Devil Rays, Maddon was one of only four big league managers at the time who had not played in the majors. The others were Jim Leyland, Grady Little, and Buck Showalter. None of them had waited as long as Maddon.

It is extremely rare for someone to be as successful a big league manager as Maddon without having played in the majors. Twenty-six men have managed 2,500 games and won a World Series. Only four of them never played in the majors: Joe McCarthy, Earl Weaver, Leyland, and Maddon.

If a long education in managing is what Maddon faced, Idaho Falls was a good place to start testing anyone's leadership skills. By virtue of its remote location on the baseball and geographic maps, managing there required plenty of time solving problems and riding buses. Idaho Falls was no closer than a three-hour bus ride to the nearest opponent in the eight-team Pioneer League. The trip to Calgary took ten hours on a good day. One night during a nine-hour trip to Medicine Hat, the bus arrived at the Canadian border only to discover all the agents had gone home for the night. The team slept on the bus until the start of business the next day.

In Billings, Montana, the Angels stayed at the Northern Hotel, a famous western outpost that had been built in 1904, hosted Teddy Roosevelt and Woodrow Wilson, burned to the ground in 1940, and been rebuilt. Maddon was reading a book in the lobby, waiting for the team bus, when a weathered stranger approached him.

"Sir, you have a daring soul," the man said.

"Excuse me?" Maddon said.

"Sir, you've got a daring soul."

"How do you react to that?" Maddon says. "Do you say thank you? Do you say, 'Why do you say that?' I think my answer was, 'Thank you.' And he just walked away. Just like that. I took it as a compliment because I liked the idea of being bold."

The crowds were small in the Pioneer League. The Angels averaged 951 people a game at McDermott Field. It was easy for players and staff to hear individual voices out of the sparse crowd, especially those coming from a motorcycle gang that would pull their bikes along the first base line to heckle players just for the fun of it. One night the motorcycle gang targeted Dick Schofield, if only because the shortstop was a first-round draft pick with a famous baseball name. His father had played in the big leagues.

"They're ragging on Schoey because he signed for all that money and wasn't producing up to their standards—their biking standards," Maddon says.

Maddon had heard enough. In between innings, he told Schofield, "Do me one favor and do yourself a favor: in between innings when you're making practice throws, pick out one of those biker dudes and just nail him from shortstop. Just do it. You've got my blessing. Go for it. We'll all be there for you."

Says Maddon, "Who knew what those biker dudes had in their back pockets? But Schoey is eighteen years old and is the nicest guy in the world and of course he wouldn't do it."

The next night, Maddon went to his second baseman, Craig Gerber, a twenty-two-year-old out of Cal Poly San Luis Obispo who had been a record-setting quarterback in high school and would later become a favored "small ball" scrapper of Mauch's on the Angels.

"Gerbs, do me a favor, please," Maddon said. "If those guys show up again, pick out one of those biker dudes and smoke 'em with one of your throws. Then apologize and just say, 'The throw got away from me' or whatever."

The bikers showed up again. They heckled Schofield again.

"I'm watching them," Maddon says. "I couldn't even watch the game. I just wanted to see one of those guys go down. Gerbs is getting his ground balls. Finally Gerbs overthrows first base. The throw hits the chain-link fence right in front of those guys. It rattled their cage a bit. I was not quite sure what I was looking for, but I think the message was delivered: 'Shut the hell up.' And we were able to move on from there. So thank you, Gerbs. And Schoey, love you, always will."

It was on another trip, in Great Falls, Montana, that Maddon earned his first career ejection. While coaching third base, he waved home Wayne Larker, which was probably a mistake, he says, "because Wayne had about as much speed as me." It would be the first and last season in pro ball for Larker, twenty-three, who returned to school to get his master's degree before embarking on a thirty-five-year college coaching career. His father, Norm, was a former big leaguer who went to Hazleton High.

"It's a close play at the plate and the umpire calls him out," Maddon says. "Of course, every third-base coach thinks he's safe because you feel like crap when you send somebody and he gets thrown out. You feel like crap even if it's the right thing to do to send the guy.

"I went off. I don't know what I said, but the umpire threw me out fast. I go to the clubhouse—and I use that term loosely—and I thought, *OK, that's how you do it. You pretty much cut open a vein and just let it spill out, baby.*

"The only thing I was always upset about is when I called an umpire a certain nasty word. Every time it happened—every time—I got kicked out. The next day I would take the lineup card out to the umpires—making sure I beat the other manager out there—and say to the umpire, 'I'm sorry. I need to learn how to argue in a better way. I shouldn't have said it. So I apologize. But just know that if I get upset again tonight, I'm still coming out. But I'll choose better language.'"

On another night that season, Maddon was awakened by the telephone ringing at three in the morning. It was one of his pitchers, Scott Oliver, from Bellarmine College. Oliver told Maddon that a group of players had been at a party, there was an argument, and the team's trainer punched Butch Dowies, a right-handed pitcher. Dowies suffered a broken jaw.

"Then my trainer calls me and he's apologetic," Maddon says. "Now I have to call Mike Port, the GM of the Angels at that time, in the middle of the night to tell him what had gone on, that my trainer punched one of my pitchers and now he's got a broken jaw. So now you have this twenty-seven-year-old manager with no control over his team whatsoever in his first year of doing this. There were all these different things to contend with there."

One of the seventeen teenagers on Maddon's team was Devon White, a bespectacled third baseman who had been a standout high school basketball player in New York. A raw talent and first-year pro, the Jamaican-born White could neither hit nor play third base. He batted .179 for Idaho Falls. Maddon quickly switched White (who later returned his family name to its original spelling, Whyte) to the outfield, where he would go on to win seven Gold Gloves, make seven All-Star teams, and win three World Series.

As a rookie league manager, Maddon found himself deploying the leadership skills he'd developed as a counselor in West Hazleton the previous year. At Charity House he had learned patience dealing with troubled youths who were away from home or had no home at all. His Idaho Falls rookies were paid $600 a month and given eleven dollars per day in meal money. Counting a few doubleheaders, they played seventy games in seventy days. Idaho Falls finished 27-43, one game out of last place.

The following season, 1982, Himes put Maddon in charge of another rookie league team, the Salem Angels of the Northwest League. Salem played its home games at Chemeketa Community College in Oregon. The season was in its infancy when someone knocked on Maddon's hotel door. It was a seventeen-year-old infielder from San Diego, Mark McLemore. He looked downcast. Maddon told him to come in and sit down.

"What's up?" Maddon asked.

"Joe," McLemore said, "I want to quit. I want to go back to San Diego. I can't do this."

Everybody called McLemore "Fluff" because when he showed up for Salem's spring training camp at Cal State Fullerton he'd had a large, puffy head of hair that could hardly be contained by his cap. He had white spots all over his face from chicken pox, and he laughed easily and often. His sunny outlook changed when the team went to Oregon. He was homesick.

"No, you're not going home," Maddon said. "And let me tell you why."

Maddon told McLemore about the time he'd called Beanie after three days at Lafayette and told her he was going home to be a plumber.

"What you're missing right now, buddy, no longer exists," Maddon told him. "You're missing a memory. What you're missing is no longer there. Your friends are not the same. Your friends are not there. The places are not going to have the same allure to you. It's just not the same. And you're going to go back to something entirely different and you'll be upset with the fact you've done it.

"What your mind is doing is it is not giving you good information. It may have been true before, but it's not true today. I want you to bear down on what we are doing and really get reinvested into just playing here. And know that whatever we miss when we're seventeen, being away from the home for the first time, no longer exists at home.

"Furthermore, listen, you're going to be a very good baseball player and a very good Major League Baseball player down the road. So you have to trust me on this one and you've got to stick it out. You've just got to believe me on this one."

McLemore stayed. He led the team with a .431 on-base percentage.

"He conceded eventually that I was right," Maddon says. "Going back home would have been the worst thing he could possibly have done, and he ended up having a great season. We win the Northwest League championship with him playing second base and Kevin Davis playing shortstop, both seventeen, eighteen years old at the most, and we beat the Medford A's, who were just chock-full of college players at that time.

"Fluff goes on from there. He goes to the Double A Texas League, gets hurt, and we send him to Anaheim to rehab at that time because everybody thought this guy is so important to the organization. It was one of the biggest mistakes the Angels made at that point and something I learned a great lesson from.

"I thought Mark McLemore was absolutely solid, and he was at that time so young in regard to his personality, makeup, and character. But he goes to Anaheim, and he gets caught up in this big league–itis stuff, and after he gets rehab and comes back, my God, he was just a different cat, having participated in this big league rehab and being with the major leaguers and what that was like. It was hard to get him to come back down to earth. He had a regression in his game at that time that took a while for him to get back into.

"The one thing about Fluff that I loved, prior to all this happening, he would come up to hit and he would always look down at the tongue on his shoe. He had the 'Eye of the Tiger' painted on the back of his tongue on his shoe. It would totally motivate him at his at bat. He was one of the worst-batting practice hitters I've ever had, and I never paid attention to that, because the first at bat of the game was probably a line drive up the middle. But that was part of his routine, which I loved. And whenever he got off of it a little bit, I'd remind him, 'Hey, slow things down. Eye of the tiger, brother. Make sure you see that.'

"The guy was so focused. He played such a complete game, and he was dynamic. Then he goes to Anaheim and comes back a different guy.

"It took him a couple years, seriously, a couple years to get beyond it. Once he did, he had a magnificent major league career, eventually became one of the best utility players around."

McLemore played nineteen years in the big leagues, earning $21.9 million. One morning before a Sunday game in the late 1990s at Angel Stadium, while playing for the Texas Rangers, McLemore walked to the Angels' clubhouse and into the coaches' room. He was carrying a large box. He placed it on a table in front of Maddon.

"This is for you," McLemore told Maddon, "and for all the things you've done for me."

In the box was the latest Apple laptop, which went for about $3,500. Maddon started to cry.

"It meant so much to me personally that he would even consider doing that," Maddon says. "He knew how much I was into the computer at that time, and it was fabulous how I was able to do my work so much more efficiently because of that generosity. But that's Fluff."

One of the Angels around that same time was veteran infielder Tony Phillips, a fourteenth-round pick by Montreal who played eighteen years in the majors—and another three after that in independent ball, the last when he was fifty-six years old. Phillips died shortly after that from a heart attack. In 1997, with the Angels, Phillips hit a career-high twenty-seven home runs. One day after that season, Maddon was hanging Christmas lights at home when Phillips called him.

"Thank you for everything you did for me," Phillips told Maddon. "All the drills and all the prep work you put in made me feel more comfortable during the game."

Says Maddon, "Whoa. That beat me up a little bit right there. As a coach or a manager, gratitude is your greatest reward, to know you had an impact on someone. Anthony has since passed, but even in his fifties he was calling me saying, 'Joseph, Joseph. You need a leadoff hitter. I could be your leadoff hitter. Joseph, give me a chance.'"

McLemore's career path had a profound impact on Maddon. Starting the next season on August 1—the beginning of the last month of the minor league season—and every subsequent August 1 in the minors, Maddon would deliver his "McLemore Talk." He would tell his young players, many of whom were away from home for the first time, "Listen, this is a very important month for you and for us. I need you guys to play it right, play it straight and not think about going home or worry about getting home. Everything you're missing is different at home. It's not the same. You're a different person right now, and it's about you and your careers."

Says Maddon, "Young people, we're the same way. There are some outliers, but normally when you break away from home for the first time it's scary, man. It's scary and you're going to find people as good as you are, you think, but maybe not quite. And eventually if you give yourself the opportunity, you rise above."

The other lesson Maddon learned from McLemore is how even the best players can lose focus.

"I'm always aware of that now when it comes to young, really good players, even the guys that are the salt of the earth," Maddon says. "You never think they would change, but I've got Fluff in the back of my mind. He was one of my all-time favorites, still is, but he went through a tough period. He left the Angels and found his footing again later. Fluff was great, but he did go through that moment you fear as a manager.

"I'm always aware when you overindulge on some young players and you just don't know how young people are going to think. You don't know. Don't assume anything. Also, you've got to teach them and coach them. They have to adhere to the policies like everybody else does. When you don't do that, if you set up a scholarship program, it will always bite you in the ass.

"And that's what happened to the Devil Rays before I got there. Eventually we took away the scholarship program. The organization had been just pandering to the youth and putting up with their nonsense and they had way too much power. You cannot permit that."

After the season at Idaho Falls ended in 1981, Maddon returned home to Arizona to manage the Angels' Instructional League team in Mesa. Some of the best young prospects were in his care. In 1983 he would become field coordinator for these camps.

"I would always start out telling them what an honor it was for them to be here," Maddon says. "Remember, this is September fifteenth in Arizona. It is hot, and we would start practice around nine o'clock in the morning and play games at one o'clock in the afternoon. I would tell them what an honor it was for them to be there and how this could accelerate the process to the big leagues. I'd say, 'For those that see it any other way, you're sadly mistaken. If you don't take advantage of this moment, it's really going to injure you, and you are not going to become a major league player.'"

Before each game players lined up on the foul line for inspection.

"Everybody was responsible for shining their own shoes," Maddon says. "Then we'd get together as a group, and I would read off the positives and negatives from yesterday's Instructional League game. When you're teaching baseball, the mental side of it is so important. The physical part is much easier. Redundancy of the mental component was very necessary. I was more into that than I ever knew before, and that was even before I met Ken Ravizza."

It was one reason why Maddon loved putting slogans on T-shirts. Making for much more than a quick laugh or a cool shirt, a slogan tangibly reinforced a mission statement. It was also why he kept hammering away at fundamentals, especially baserunning and two-strike hitting.

Around that same time, before most every game, a jet would be spotted landing at a nearby field. In a few minutes, Angels owner Gene Autry and his wife, Jackie, would arrive at the field and take their seats in two comfy chairs set up behind a protective screen behind home plate. Known as the Singing Cowboy for his country music and acting roles in ninety-three films, Autry was one of the most famous Americans for more than three decades, beginning in the 1930s. His fortune and love of baseball led to him becoming the first owner of the Angels, from 1961 to 1997.

"They would sit there, say hi to everybody, watch the game, and eventually go right back to the airport," Maddon says. "As they flew over the ballpark, they would dip the wing of the plane as if to say, 'See you later.' It was a tremendous moment. It happened a lot in the 1980s as the Angels were really taking off as an organization."

Instructional League ended on October 30. So ended Maddon's first season of his postplaying career. In ten months he had driven from

Boulder to Anaheim to start his new career, crisscrossed five Western states scouting talent, debuted as a manager in Idaho Falls, and run the Angels' Instructional League team in Arizona. He was hooked. There was no doubt in his mind where he was headed. As the season at Idaho Falls neared its end, Maddon told a reporter where that was.

"My first goal was to make it as a player," he said. "But I lost that when my arm went dead. I'd like to stay here another year or two and then move up. That's my plan.

"I'm getting good feedback from my bosses. I hope to move up to the majors eventually."

The process would not just be fearless. It would also be long and punctuated by mistakes.

CHAPTER 7

"Self-Discipline Is the Key to Leadership"

The afternoon of July 5, 1982, was a particularly rotten one for Joe Maddon, skipper of the rookie league Salem Angels. On the heels of a 10–1 defeat the previous day, his team lost 22–3 at Medford, Oregon. The next day would upset him even more.

Maddon picked up the local newspaper to read with his morning coffee. The beat writer covering the Medford A's had had great fun ridiculing the ineptness of Maddon's team. His Angels had made six errors, walked twelve batters, and allowed thirteen runs in the third inning alone. It was only twelve games into the season, and Maddon was trying his young players at various positions. For instance, third baseman Mike Rizzo, who would go on to be general manager of the 2019 World Series champion Washington Nationals, had been taking a stab at first base that day. He made two errors, one on a dropped pop-up. Kris Kline, an infielder who would become Rizzo's assistant general manager, had contributed an error at third base.

"I'm reading the newspaper that day," Maddon says, "and this writer pretty much accuses us of being a circus act and is hypercritical of my first-year players. I did not like it. Didn't like it at all.

"So the dude shows up at the ballpark that day. Shows up in Medford. And I just let him have it. And I threatened him. I said, 'If you ever write anything like that about my guys again, I'll kick your ass! And furthermore, you're not allowed to talk to my guys the rest of the year. You're out. We're not talking to you, so don't even ask questions. When we play you guys, stay out of the locker room. Stay away from everybody. I don't want to see you. I don't want to hear you. Because if I do, I am going to kick your ass.'"

The writer walked away without escalating the issue. "Had he pushed," Maddon says, "I don't know what my career would have looked like." The writer lodged a complaint with the league. Northwest League president Bob Freitas called Maddon and told him he could not threaten writers. He also ordered Maddon to apologize to the writer.

"Well, OK, because I still want to manage," Maddon says. "I don't remember specifically what I said and how I said it, but I probably called him up and apologized. But I still had us on lockdown all year from talking to this guy.

"So we go from this apparent circus act early in the year in Medford to eventually winning the Northwest League title in Medford that same year. After the clinching game, the writer, of course, is around. And I take off the gag order and let the boys know we're good now.

"I learned a lesson. Don't threaten writers. We're all working for the same thing and that's really the entertainment value of the game, and we're here to promote baseball players. But you can attack me all you want. I do get upset once in a while and whenever I do, I go to the source, and I let them know.

"If you attack my guys, that's different. That would get me a little more annoyed and upset, quite frankly."

The minor leagues traditionally provided higher education for managers, not just players. Fans of the eight-team American Association in 1979, for instance, could see five future major league managers honing their craft: Lee Elia, Hal Lanier, Tony La Russa, Jim Leyland, and Jack McKeon. Maddon is part of that disappearing lineage. He managed six years in the minors and logged another seven there as an instructor and coordinator. The most important part of the curriculum was not learning when to pull a pitcher or try a hit-and-run. It was learning how to lead people and solve problems. And in the minor leagues, the problems pile up like cords of wood beside a Maine cabin.

Maddon grew up in the 1960s with the Lombardi model of leadership, which ran as deeply through Northeast Pennsylvania as the coal underground. The model was built on intimidation and toughness, and there was no figure as tough as Adam Sieminski, Maddon's football coach at Hazleton High. He wore only short-sleeved shirts when coaching, even on frigid days, just to exemplify toughness to his players.

"And I mean cold," Maddon says. "I'm trying to talk to him, and his teeth are chattering so much I can't understand him. I'd come over to see him on the sideline, during a time-out, and look in those eyeballs. They were piercing.

"When it comes to toughness, this guy took me to graduate school. He gave me a PhD. Nobody was tougher than Adam Sieminski. Self-discipline and toughness. That's what he taught me."

Toughness that elicited fear was the coin of the realm in that pocket of time and space. But as a minor league manager, Maddon was not leading the sons of coal miners and blue-collar European immigrants into the tumult that was Pennsylvania high school football. His charges were far more diverse and older. His PhD in toughness from Sieminski would always serve him well, but Maddon needed to develop more reasoned methods.

"There was a lot of fear involved in that motivation when you're growing up back in Pennsylvania, especially in football," Maddon says. "Those are the things you feel when you become a coach you never want to attempt to get your point across via fear.

"I still believe I could have been a football coach, a very high-level one, too. I mean a head coach. I think what I believe and how I do it could have worked there, too. No doubt in my mind. Zero doubt. Just teaching different things. Mechanics, fundamentals, but teaching the same mindset. No doubt.

"I do believe I could run a large company. I still believe I could, based again on the same principles I've utilized. Building relationships. Creating trust. Exchanging ideas. And then being able to be constructively critical. Hell, I believe I can do that with any company right now. And I hope that doesn't sound pretentious in any way, but I just feel that. I do."

The minors afforded Maddon time to make mistakes and learn lessons out of the spotlight as he crafted his leadership style. For instance,

Maddon was managing a second season at Salem in 1983 when his roster included a player he did not think was good enough for pro ball. Marty Cain was a seventeen-year-old third baseman and an eighteenth-round pick out of Anadarko High in Oklahoma, where he had been the school's most outstanding athlete. He had been co-captain of the football team and hit .400 and thrown three no-hitters for the baseball team. Pro baseball proved another and much more challenging story. Maddon found his skills to be so raw and lacking that he did not want to use him.

"He was signed by Lou Snipp and of course with the OK of Larry Himes," Maddon says. "So I've got to play him, but I don't know when. I don't know how. Not because I was afraid of us losing, but because I was afraid for embarrassing Marty.

"As a manager, I'm maybe twenty-nine years old and just learning my craft. But as a scout, I knew one thing for sure: this guy was not ready. He's one of those guys that should have never been signed. But if it makes a good story for him and his grandkids, I'll take it because he was a great, great guy."

The day Maddon finally decided to play Cain was a game at Eugene, where the Emeralds led the league in attendance.

"I played him," Maddon says. "I don't even know why. This is my fault, too, by not evaluating the whole situation. I played him in Eugene, third base, packed house, and, of course, he made some errors and punched out. You could see how overmatched he was. It was like watching a high school kid in a major league game, and not even an above-average high school kid. I took him out in the middle of the game.

"The next day I apologized to him. I did. I don't know how that went over with him. He was such a nice, quiet kid. I don't know because he never came back at me angry, never came back at me at all.

"So yeah, I felt really bad. That was one of my worst moments as a minor league manager, when I read the situation wrong. I did not put enough thought into it. Did not look at all the potentialities, and, of course, it's forty years later, whatever it is, and Marty is fine. But I just knew it was the wrong thing to do. I tried to do it to ameliorate other people and it didn't work. And I embarrassed the kid and felt horribly for it. Absolutely horribly."

Cain played in only five games that season. He went 0 for 8 with seven strikeouts. He made two errors on his five chances at third base. He never returned to pro ball. Cain enrolled at Oklahoma State that fall. He obtained a law degree and eventually established a law firm with his wife.

The next season, 1984, Maddon was promoted to manage the Peoria Chiefs of the Midwest League for his first season managing at the full-season Class A level. One of the players was Jay Lewis, a twenty-year-old third-year pro out of Eastern Oklahoma State who played the outfield and enjoyed Van Halen, not necessarily in that order.

"Jay was just a fun guy," Maddon says. "Good guy, fun guy. I don't know that he ever thought he could be a major league player. I think he just liked to play baseball and have a good time. Nothing wrong with that, either. I advocate that. Of course I think that's great."

On June 29, 1984, Maddon's pitching coach, Aurelio Monteagudo, gave Maddon a heads-up about Lewis. Van Halen was playing the Peoria Civic Center that night. Monteagudo had picked up chatter among the players that Lewis planned to skip the Chiefs game that night to see Van Halen. It was not unusual for Monteagudo to ferret out such information.

Then forty years old, Monteagudo was a beloved, savvy resource. Born in Cuba and known to all as Monty, Monteagudo had been a screwball pitcher for seven years in the major leagues and many years in Venezuela and Mexico before joining the Angels as a minor league coach. Monty would throw batting practice in spikes. If a player hit the ball too well off him in batting practice, Monteagudo would bear down and throw them his famously hard-to-hit spitball.

"I'd say, 'Monty, they're supposed to hit you good in batting practice,'" Maddon says. "He couldn't stand it. All the players didn't care because they loved him so much.

"Monty was a free spirit. He laughed easily. In a good way, he taught me the Latino concept of it's OK if it gets done tomorrow. It's OK to live for today. It's OK to have a good time. It's OK to make a mistake once in a while as long as your heart is in the right place and your effort is there. He didn't sweat it. He didn't sweat the small stuff.

"We came from different worlds, but we did love each other. And he made me laugh. He was a sharp dresser. Real tight clothes. You know, the gold chains everywhere, visible on his chest. Gold bracelets. Big rings. And the clutch. One of the first dudes I knew that carried a purse around with him, like a woman's clutch.

"His pitchers loved him. He wasn't a mechanically strong coach. His strength was being Monty. That was his strength. And being a friend. And being an ear. And being loyal. And being funny. And you know what? Sometimes that goes way overlooked. Everybody wants the most brilliant. I'll take the C student with the good personality. And that's probably what Monty was. Loved the guy. Absolutely loved him."

Seven years later, Maddon would be visiting a friend in Ciudad Obregón during the Mexican Pacific League season when he asked someone how he might reconnect with Monty. That same night, Monteagudo was killed in a car accident in Ramos Arizpe. It was the first in a triad of eerie coincidences. Only three men named Aurelio have played in the major leagues. All of them—Monteagudo, Rodriguez, and López—died in car accidents between ages forty-four and fifty-two, within a ten-year period.

It was Monteagudo's easy rapport with the players that led to his hearing about Lewis's plans to skip the ball game that night in Peoria for a concert. Sure enough, Lewis called in sick to the Chiefs' trainer, Richard Zalesky. The trainer passed the information to Maddon that Lewis was feeling ill.

"Call him back at seven o'clock, right at game time," Maddon told Zalesky. The trainer did as instructed. There was no answer. Maddon knew Lewis could later claim he had been asleep or had felt so ill that he did not hear the phone ring, so he ordered Zalesky to check Lewis's apartment.

"Think about that: I'm asking the trainer to leave the ballpark in the beginning of a game to go find out what Jay's up to," Maddon says.

Zalesky knocked on the door several times. Nobody answered.

"That's all I needed to know," Maddon says, "and pretty much convicted him right there internally. The next day Jay comes in and he's feeling great. I called him into my office."

"Jay, what's up, man? How are you doing?" Maddon asked. "Feeling a lot better than last night?"

"Yeah, I am," Lewis said.

"Great. Great to hear that. I'm glad you're feeling better. Just one thing, Jay. I had Richard call your apartment. No answer."

"Yeah, I must have been asleep. I felt pretty bad, so I probably had fallen asleep."

"Then I sent Richard over and he knocked on the door and nobody answered. So that's not good, obviously, Jaybird. What's the deal?"

"What time was it? I might have gone out to get some medicine."

"Come on, Jay. You weren't there. We called. You weren't there. We came to see you and then now you're telling me you went out for medicine. I know that's not true. Just tell me one thing: How was the concert?"

Lewis had a wisp of a mustache. He raised it slightly as a sly smile came over his face and a glint appeared in his eye.

"Best one I've ever been to."

Says Maddon, "Had I been a little bit more experienced, I'd have laughed my ass off right there, given him credit for telling me the truth, and fined him or covered for him somehow. But my next thirty-year-old thought was, *That's it. You're done.* So I called in and I'm pretty sure the Angels released him, sent him home. I don't remember ever hearing from him again. It was a pretty unilateral time. There were no agents or anybody else to plead anybody's case, and he's an A-ball player.

"I was right, based on my guy Monteagudo being right. And then we had the conversation, and the guy was being honest, and I still followed through, which I wish I had not, quite frankly. I think it was right to get him in there, right to confront him, right to nail him down on it, but I don't think it was right to release him, retrospectively.

"That's one thing you do as a young manager without a whole lot of experience and you really are just a company guy. We had so many rules and regulations back then right down to your pants had to be pulled up and bloused and an inch of red from your stirrups had to be showing at the top. If [farm director] Larry Himes came into town and somebody did not have an inch of red, it was my ass, not the player's ass. And it happened.

"This is a formal apology to Jay—whatever that did to him and his career."

Lewis left Peoria with a .223 batting average and no home runs in forty-eight games with the Chiefs. He played the next season with the independent Miami Marlins and hit .183. It was his last year in baseball. But that night in 1984, he did see Van Halen kill twenty songs at the Peoria Civic Center, starting with "Unchained" and closing with "Ain't Talkin' 'bout Love."

Maddon's closer on that Peoria team was a hard-throwing right-hander named Paul Cozzolino. The Dodgers had originally signed Cozzolino as an undrafted free agent out of Mount Vernon, New York, in 1979, four years after Cozzolino's father died. They released him after two seasons in Class A. "That should have set off alarms," Maddon says. After a year out of baseball, Cozzolino signed with the Angels, who assigned him to Peoria.

One night, playing in Clinton, Iowa, the Chiefs were up 6–1 late in the game in what looked like the end to a losing streak.

"No time to screw around," Maddon says. "Just bring in Coz. Let him rock and roll. I felt good about it. He threw ninety-five miles an hour.

"That night he comes out throwing in the mid-eighties. All of a sudden, they start kicking his ass. By the time I was able to get somebody up and in—this is A ball, not the sixth game of the World Series—we wind up losing the game.

"He went about his business like he didn't give a damn, or that he should not have been in the game based on the score. We had lost several in a row and needed this badly to get going again. It had the feeling of insubordination to it. The rest of the team all wanted a piece of him. I may have told some guys, 'I got this.'

"I call him into my room, because in Clinton, Iowa, we dressed at the hotel. I'm on the second floor, corner room. I call him in there, shut the door, and I just start cursing at him up and down. 'Everyone is busting their ass. You come out there throwing eighty-five. You've had plenty of rest. There's no excuse for it!'

"To his credit, if there is any to be given, he didn't yell or argue. This entire event took maybe two minutes. I was pissed."

One day during three o'clock batting practice that season, Monteagudo spotted two strangers in the bleachers who caused him to tell Maddon, "I don't like the looks of it. Could be criminals. Maybe drugs." Monty was right again. Two of Maddon's players were eventually arrested on drug charges. First baseman Steve Lusby was arrested after the season for setting up a $120,000 cocaine deal in Clearwater, Florida, with a dealer who was a government informant. Cozzolino was arrested in Peoria in May 1987 along with two other men from New York for selling cocaine to an undercover cop.

The next season, 1985, Maddon was promoted to the Midland Angels of the Texas League, his first Double A assignment. One of his relief pitchers was a five-foot-seven left-hander who weighed 133 pounds and had had one of the quirkiest paths to Midland among the usual assortment of lottery tickets, projects, and retreads that can populate a Double A roster. Eddie Delzer was a military brat who was born in Birkenhead, England, when his father, Edwin, was stationed there in the air force. He attended Lennox High School in Los Angeles County, where he wrestled and ran cross-country, before following his father into the air force.

Stationed near Sacramento, Delzer was out running one day when he happened upon a summer league baseball team practicing. He joined the team and quickly found he had a knack for pitching. So good was little Eddie Delzer that he signed to pitch at Sacramento City College, then at Sacramento State, where he went 20-2, and then at Cal State Fullerton, a college baseball power.

On December 1, 1982, Delzer's father was shot and killed at a holiday party in Los Angeles. Eddie was devastated by the loss of the man he called "my number one fan." He exhibited emotional and behavioral problems. In 1983 he was arrested and jailed on auto theft charges in Eureka, California, leading to a suspended two-year sentence and six hundred hours of community service. But Eddie and the world around him seemed just right whenever he was on a pitchers' mound. In 1984, just after receiving his suspended sentence, Delzer was 5-1 with a 1.34 ERA for Fullerton. He set a school record with eighteen strikeouts against La Verne. Fullerton reached the College World Series final, where it was to face Texas and future big league star Greg Swindell.

Thirty minutes before the game, Fullerton head coach Augie Garrido told Delzer he was starting. Delzer pitched a gem. He allowed two hits over seven innings. Fullerton won the title with a 3–1 victory. Delzer broke down sobbing in front of the dugout after the last out.

The Angels drafted Delzer in the twenty-first round. He continued to flummox hitters with his command and craftiness. He posted a 1.31 ERA in Class A in 1984, after which the Angels assigned him to Midland in 1985.

"He was a media darling because this little guy had been dominating these big hitters," Maddon says. "The year before I get him, he had around thirty consecutive scoreless innings out of the bullpen in Peoria.

"Eddie was a fun guy. He was great to be around. Big balls for a little guy. Never afraid of anything. Pitched out of all kinds of situations. When you watched him pitch, standing off to the side, you realize he had to throw the ball farther than a lot of these other guys because he had short limbs."

Maddon quickly discovered that Delzer had outstanding legal issues.

"While Eddie was at Cal State Fullerton, he was arrested for stealing tape players out of cars," Maddon says. "That was Eddie. He gets arrested on that. And now, the next year, I have him in Midland. And of course, he's still good, but now he has to do community service. And listen, I supported this guy. He's so likable. Could not have been more likable.

"So he has to do community service at this local junior college. In order to do that, I permitted him while we were at home to come to the ballpark later—just to make sure he takes care of everything, gets everything done. He was a relief pitcher. I told him, 'Don't worry about it. Come a little bit later. We're good.'

"I would periodically check in with Eddie. 'How's it going? How are we doing?' He'd say, 'Great. Everything is going well. Doing good. I like the people. I get my hours in. I'm staying in touch with my probation officer. Everything is good. Great.' I'd say, 'That's outstanding, buddy. Good to hear that.'

"I was just calling him into the office from time to time. I'm supporting him. There were no checks and balances like there are now. I mean, nobody from the front office was calling your junior college in Midland or Odessa to find out if Eddie was doing his community service."

Then one day in mid-June, Maddon received a phone call. It was from Delzer's probation officer.

"I'm checking about Eddie Delzer," the probation officer said.

"Great," Maddon replied. "I check with him all the time. I know he is doing really well. Really proud of him. I—"

"Stop." The probation officer cut off Maddon. "Eddie has not gone there one time."

"I call BS on that. I checked with Eddie. I believe him. You're wrong."

"No, I checked in with the school. I spoke to the people he's supposed to be checking in with, and not one time has he checked in with these people. Not once."

Says Maddon, "Wow, I felt like such an idiot. The biggest part was I defended him so vehemently."

After Maddon hung up the phone, he called Delzer into his office.

"Eddie, I just talked to your probation guy, and he said you have not been there one time."

"Aw, bullshit, I've gone . . ."

"He said you have not been there one time."

"Uh, oh, OK. You're right. I haven't gone. It's my fault. I should have."

The Angels promptly demoted Delzer to the Redwood Pioneers in the Class A California League. He pitched well there, with a 1.93 ERA, until one day he was picked up for a probation violation. He spent a week at the Humboldt County jail and was ordered to finish one hundred hours of community service. Delzer never pitched in affiliated baseball again. He became a baseball consultant, especially related to the mental side of the game, and a batting practice pitcher for the Dodgers and A's.

"He was another guy I really liked, like Jay Wright," Maddon says. "Both were in the early twenties. Both were mischievous. Not bad guys by any means, just a little bit of a different beat. I ran into him when he was throwing batting practice with the Dodgers at Dodger Stadium. No hard feelings. But just lesson learned.

"These young guys like that, when they get to you face-to-face and tell you one thing, it's maybe not always so. That's just no different than the rest of society, but in this situation, it hurt these guys to the point where they lost their ability to play baseball."

While managing those 1985 Midland Angels, Maddon ran into multiple problems in Little Rock, home of the Arkansas Travelers, who were managed by Jim Riggleman, another future big league manager. Before the first game of a five-game series, the Arkansas general manager, Bill Valentine, told Maddon that because of a threat of rain the Angels could not take pregame batting practice the next day. Valentine was a Little Rock native and a former major league umpire who was the first umpire to eject Mickey Mantle. Maddon did not object, seeing that his team had taken a ten-hour bus ride to get to Little Rock and could use the rest.

It did not rain. After the game, the batboy said to Maddon, "Mr. Valentine said it's going to rain tomorrow. They're putting the tarp on the field. No batting practice tomorrow."

Says Maddon, "I thought, *Seriously?* Because I really don't remember any rain."

After the third game—and again, no rain—the batboy delivered another message to Maddon: no batting practice tomorrow again.

"No, that's not going to work," Maddon said. "Where is Mr. Valentine?"

Maddon bolted from his office. He found Valentine in one of the portals of the grandstand. They jumped into a nose-to-nose argument as heated as anything on the diamond between a manager and an umpire.

"We're going to hit tomorrow, I don't care what you say," Maddon said.

"No, you're not!"

"Yes, we are!"

"I'm telling you, you are not!"

"Yes, we are!"

"You're not, and I'm calling your boss!"

"Go ahead! Call my boss."

A big man, Valentine spun away and started lumbering through a breezeway toward his office. Maddon followed him stride for stride, the argument gathering steam. When Valentine reached his office, he hurriedly closed the door to keep out Maddon. But Maddon stuck his foot in the doorway to keep it wedged open.

"I was actually almost fighting him," Maddon says. "I mean, it was that close. If he had stopped in front of his office door, it would have been me and Joey Tempest in the Lady of Grace schoolyard all over again."

A standoff ensued in which Valentine was pushing on his office door to close it and Maddon, with his foot in the doorway, was pushing on it to open it.

"Listen, you put that tarp down tomorrow, fine!" Maddon shouted. "But I promise you one thing: we're hitting tomorrow! We're taking batting practice, and we're taking it with spikes on. So if you want your tarp full of holes, you leave it down there, and you're going to have to deal with it. But I promise you, we are hitting tomorrow with our spikes on, just so you know."

Just then, Maddon looked up to see that a small crowd had gathered to see what the commotion was about. The crowd included players' wives and children. He pulled his foot from the doorway and let the door slam shut.

"God, what a jerk," Maddon said softly.

Valentine called the farm directors of the Cardinals and Angels. When Maddon arrived the next day, the tarp was not on the field. The batting cage and protective screens were set up for batting practice.

"I found out later the Cardinals' players were happy, too, with what I did," Maddon says. "Because if we weren't hitting, they weren't, either. It was on that same trip that I found out how racist it was in Little Rock."

Maddon was coaching third base. He was waving home Reggie Montgomery, one of his Black players, when he heard someone yell from the box seats near him, "Look at that monkey bouncing on his tail."

"Wow, that was nasty stuff I had never experienced," Maddon says. "I got pissed. I didn't do anything at the moment, but I found Valentine after the game. I said, 'I want more security there tomorrow because this is bullshit. This should never freakin' happen.'

"He looked at me and said, 'Ah, the boys are just having a little fun.' That was his response. Unbelievable.

"The next year we're playing in Beaumont. I had a guy named Greg Key, a bright kid, sharp wit, funny, and had some tools. He was wiry strong. So we're playing in Beaumont and I don't know what exactly was said, but it was nasty, and Keymo looked at the guy who said something and grabbed his crotch. Under the circumstances, I thought it was a pretty fair exchange based on a racist and derogatory comment from the fan."

The fan rose from his seat and started walking quickly toward an exit. Monteagudo was watching from the bullpen. The street-savvy pitching coach alerted Maddon and ballpark security that the man might be going to his car to get a gun. A security official stopped the fan at the gate as he tried to reenter. Sure enough, the man was armed with a gun.

"Monty picked up on all this," Maddon says. "The man was denied access and we never heard anything more about it. So this was the Texas League in 1985 and 1986. I saw firsthand what I only had read about and how ugly it can be."

At least twice as a major league manager Maddon has intervened to stop racist comments from fans, once with the Rays in Port Charlotte, Florida, during spring training and once with the Cubs in Pittsburgh.

"Dude gets up in Port Charlotte and uses the N-word," Maddon says. "Man, I couldn't believe it. And the sad part is when you turn around and get upset, not everybody's immediately on your side.

"In 2020, during the lockdown, we had the staff and players together on Zoom calls, and some of our most honest discussions were about the Black Lives Matter movement. I wanted to have an Angels way or a method of dealing with any topic so that we are comfortably uncomfortable talking about it in front of one another.

"The thing that I find curious is how some people, if others speak contrary to their belief system, immediately go into attack mode. That baffles me. It does. It absolutely blows me away. I so love when people want to go in the other direction from me. Wow. It's absolutely the time to open the ears, eyes and shut the mouth. See if I can learn something here.

"It's no different than having to back up Reggie Montgomery, Devon White, Mark McLemore and Donny Timberlake in Little Rock, Arkansas."

Maddon's next season at Midland, 1986, proved especially taxing. One night he wound up in a shouting match in his office with Raul Tovar, a catcher and outfielder who was on his third organization, all because Tovar's wife had said something about Monty's wife within earshot of Monty's wife and Maddon's wife.

Another time he invited Midland teammates Glen Walker and Vinicio Cedeno into his hotel room in Beaumont to quell a simmering feud between the two. Walker liked to needle players, and Cedeno did not take kindly to it. Instead of reaching a détente, the two of them came to blows in the manager's room.

The entire season seemed to be a cascade of confrontations and frustrations. One night several of Maddon's players stormed into the stands at El Paso after a walk-off loss, trying to confront fans who had been heckling them all night with what Maddon called "vile language" due to "a few too many beers."

Two months later, Midland lost at El Paso by the astonishing score of 31–5, causing a weary Maddon to observe that he had not seen such bad baseball since he was eight years old and lost 22–8 in the first game of his first season playing baseball in Hazleton.

"I made five errors at shortstop and felt like my world had ended," Maddon said. "That was the only thing close."

The day after another particularly bad loss, Maddon decided he needed to do something to rouse his team. He remembered a motivational stunt recounted to him by Dennis Rogers, the manager of the rival Medford team that Maddon's Salem Angels beat for the 1982 Northwest League title. "And I took it to another level," Maddon says.

Maddon dashed to every newsstand and every newspaper box he could find to round up a thick stack of various newspapers. Then he pulled the classified section from each one and taped the broadsheets over the walls in the clubhouse bathroom, including above the urinals and behind the doors of the toilet stalls. In case his players did not get the message, Maddon translated it for them in his loudest, strongest voice: "Shape up or start looking for another job!"

"I thought this was a great idea because I was so upset over what I perceived to be a lack of caring and a lack of effort," he says. "I did not have a good team, and I resorted to my lowest level ever. It was just the wrong way to go about it. It was based purely on the fact that we weren't playing well, and I was taking it personally. That was a mistake.

"You never teach or lead through intimidation or in a punitive way. That's a mistake. My generation was all based on what we thought of Lombardi. Everybody wanted to be angry. But to me self-discipline is the key to leadership. Discipline does not have to come through with how loud your voice is. Discipline comes through with consistency."

Lessons from the minors propelled Maddon toward being a confident, more consistent leader. Many of those lessons emerged from that long, turbulent summer of 1986 in Midland, Texas. With three weeks left in the season, an angry and worn Maddon sat down with a pen and unlined sheets of paper with a Midlands Angels letterhead. He dated the letter, August 7, 1986, and opened it with the salutation "To Whom It May Concern." He composed a letter to himself. It began:

Where to begin? Following, I want to make an attempt to cleanse my soul as well as my mind. I am basically in an angry mood and maybe

I need to be in order to be justifiably negative. I'll begin with the negatives and reinforce the many positives. I also may have to rewrite this letter in an attempt to develop the correct pecking order with B following A, C following B, et cetera.

Legendary sports columnist Red Smith gave a classic response when somebody asked him in 1946 if it was difficult to crank out columns: "Why, no. You simply sit down at the typewriter, open your veins, and bleed." Maddon opened his veins with his Midlands manifesto.

He complained about organizational leaks in which players learned about impending promotions before they were announced or even decided on. He complained about how roving instructors made "snap judgments" about his players' talent and character. He complained that Midland's home park was a wind-aided hitters' haven that made pitching evaluations difficult and advised the Angels to either get out of Midland or "stop criticizing the instruction" the pitchers were getting there. He complained it was "sort of ridiculous" that the Angels instituted a curfew on the road when one did not exist at home. His idea: hand out the day's meal money at 10:30 a.m., which should keep guys from staying out too late. He complained the Angels were running "a halfway house" by signing minor league free agents with questionable character. He wrote:

Finally, we must keep a consistent goal of development over winning-type attitude. Camaraderie plays a part in both these areas. This has been a trying experience in terms of re-orienting a bunch of players to the workings of our organization.

The 1986 Midland Angels finished 62-71, twenty-two games out of first place in the West Division of the Texas League. Their pitchers gave up 5.76 runs per game, the most in the league. When the season ended, Angels farm director Billy Bavasi told Maddon he would not be returning to manage Midland in 1987. In fact, Maddon would not be returning the next season as a manager anywhere. Bavasi told him he was pulling him

from the dugout after six years of managing to be the organization's roving minor league defense instructor.

"It probably took until the next year for me to realize how bad it was
in Midland," Maddon says. "I think Bavasi knew. Billy knew because he
got me out of managing. He got me into roving because I was probably
getting too intense. And the best thing that ever happened was I became
a rover because I got to see everybody. I'd go to town for five or six days.
You saw both teams' styles—your team, the other team—and you learn
what you like, and you really learn what you didn't like. I loved that. Roving is the best minor league job."

Over the next seven seasons, Maddon served the Angels as an instructor and minor league coordinator. He was in the business of fortifying
dreams—and occasionally snuffing them out. New players enter professional baseball every year, which means about the same number leave
it—and usually not voluntarily.

"You get really close to these guys," Maddon says. "When you're
releasing a minor league player, it's totally different than sending a major
league guy back to Triple A or talking to a major league player kind of at
the end of his string when you may have to say, 'We're going to let you go
right now.' But he's probably pretty much at that point where he accepts
that. He gets it. He understands the drill by then. That conversation is
straightforward, matter of fact.

"But when you talk to Kenny Grant in the offices at Gene Autry
Park . . . just reliving that right now gets to me."

Grant was born in South Carolina and played baseball at Paterson
Eastside High School in New Jersey. Grant hit .466 and pitched to a 1.46
ERA as a senior. A New Jersey newspaper called him one of the twenty-
five best high school players in the country. Oklahoma State offered him
a scholarship. Ed Ford, a scout for the Angels, watched Grant play on a
field that was in terrible shape. He wrote in his report that the Angels
should draft anyone who could look that good on such a lousy field. The
Angels drafted Grant in the tenth round.

Grant's high school coach recommended that Grant sign because he could suffer an injury and never get the same opportunity to play ball. Grant agreed, while acknowledging he was not as interested in his studies as he was in baseball. He entered pro ball.

Playing second and third base, Grant showed occasional pop at the plate and, though he was a career .253 hitter, excelled at getting on base, mostly with walks—a skill that was not valued then nearly as much as it is today. For six years he never advanced out of Class A ball. The Angels traded him to the Minnesota Twins after the 1987 season, then repurchased Grant midway through the 1988 season. His on-base percentages from 1986 through 1988 were stellar: .426, .406, and .380 respectively.

"I was the one holding on to him and eventually had to relent to the herd opinion," Maddon says.

In spring training of 1989, Maddon called Grant into his office at Gene Autry Park in Mesa. Maddon knew Grant well. Over the previous two seasons he had worked with Grant as the Angels' minor league hitting instructor.

"Kenny comes in and sits down," Maddon says. "And I see his little face right now. 'Kenny, that's it. We're going to have to release you.' And then you try to explain to him why.

"He's just looking at me. He's not complaining. He's not crying. He's not blaming anybody. None of that stuff. He just took it. He took it like I would have expected him to. That's just who he was. So he pretty much said, 'All right.' Stood up. Shook his hand. Gave him a big old hug, and I was crying, I don't know how noticeably to him, but I was."

Maddon had released players before, but none before or since hit him as hard as this one.

"At times you can question his ability to retain things, but never question his heart and never question his laugh and what a great teammate he was and how hard he played," Maddon says. "He did all that stuff. He had ability. Don't get me wrong. He had tools. He had physical tools.

"I don't know how many hours I put in with this guy. But I do know I really loved Kenny Grant. Guys like him, you keep working, keep working. You try to get him over the top. You see it, but there's always that level of inconsistency physically or the level of inconsistency mentally that doesn't permit the player to arrive at his dreams and what you're dreaming for him. It just doesn't match up.

"You have to understand that was tough. I'm reliving it right now. Calling Kenny in the office there and telling him that was it. You're crushing his dreams. You're letting him go. It's a guy that trusted you. Believed in you, too, because you worked with him doggedly.

"Of course I cried. This one hurt. Normally I'm really good at maintaining an emotional separation, but sometimes you just can't. And there is this great line I love: 'Honesty without compassion equals cruelty.' So you're honest, but you never beat up or blow anybody up because you're honest. And you pretty much know your students, your pupil. You know what he can deal with and what he cannot. So to what level you want to go to regarding total honesty, go for it. And if you can't, be aware of that, too. But he's got to know the straight up and what level you can present it to him.

"And I did. And I told him about pretty much they just weren't getting there. And that's it. We shake hands. He walks out the door. And you sit there and you ask yourself, 'Where did I screw up? Where did I fail in this process?'

"It's tough. It's tough because I was that guy when I was released. It happened in the wintertime. I was in Salinas, and I got that letter in the mail that the Angels were letting me go. Apparently they were dropping a full club. I guess twenty-five or thirty of us were just lopped off immediately. I think Mike Port was the purveyor of the bad news, and, of course, I hated Michael at that time. I wish I had an opportunity to be in the same room with him. I mean, I had that kind of a fire. I don't think I would have done anything, but you think you would. You get that letter and then your dreams are absolutely crushed.

"That was winter of 1978. Of course I was going to be a player in the major leagues with the California Angels. And Kenny probably thought the same thing. It's a tremendous blow to your confidence and your ego.

And you've got to go through that moment, and who do you talk to? Who do you call? Are you embarrassed? You're probably embarrassed. You don't want to talk to your parents. You don't want to let anybody down.

"That's the beauty of my past. My professional baseball life was anything but glamorous. I can empathize with anybody. When your ultimate dream is crushed, that's tough. And when you're the purveyor of or the crusher of it, wow, that is really hard.

"And as I'm talking about it right now, I've got to catch my breath a couple of times only because I felt it and still feel it. I know Kenny turned out fine. But that was the one that obviously impacted me heavily early on in my coaching career because I still think of it.

"How do you learn how to end someone's career? Wow. There's so much instinct involved in everything that we do. And that's also why people that pooh-pooh high school athletics, collegiate athletics, Little League athletics, whatever, should know that being part of a group, part of a team, and then assuming a leadership role, even at that point on those levels, it all comes to bear.

"There's training going on without you even knowing it. You are becoming more of a leader just by being a leader when you're ten, eleven, and twelve on UNICO; ten and twelve and thirteen on the State Trooper Eagles; thirteen, fourteen on the Molly Maguires Teener Leagues All-Star team; the Hazleton American Legion; and then, of course, going to Lafayette and eventually being named team captain on the baseball team with Artie Fischetti, and would have been easily that had I stayed with football.

"So it matters. It matters. It truly matters regarding how you process all that. I had a sense of sincere humility because my mom would not permit otherwise. I know there were times, even as a kid, I might have shown a little bit of ego, and she would absolutely put me down very quickly.

"And I guess that's why it's so important where colleges like to see a track record of success with individuals with regard to fitting them into their program. If I'm part of an admissions board, yeah, I like grades. Yeah, I like brilliance. Love intelligence. Love it.

"But you also have to have a feel for what you're doing and have leadership qualities. Where do you get them from? You don't get them from a book, brother. You just don't."

Thirty-one years after releasing Grant, Maddon stood in front of his Angels team in March of 2020, just three weeks into spring training, just as he was establishing the culture with his new team, to tell them they were all going home, at least temporarily. Major League Baseball had put the season on hold because of the coronavirus pandemic.

"There is another great line I like to follow: 'Never deny the truth of bad news,'" Maddon says. "At that meeting we understood we were going to have to be flexible. The key for me was to communicate accurately and keep them informed. I knew the more I could keep my players calm, the better we would be when we did return."

In 2021 it was more common for teams to hire major league managers with no minor league experience than those like Maddon who had learned there. Eighteen of the thirty major league managers in 2021 had never managed in the minors.

"When you face a manager in the major leagues who had to learn in the minors, wow, what a difference," Maddon says. "I saw it in Buck Showalter, Jimmy Leyland, Tony La Russa, Jim Riggleman, Mike Shildt. It stands out. I know the guys who managed in the minor leagues and the guys who did not. And the guys that did? Believe me, you're not going to pull any wool over their eyes anywhere. Anywhere. And I'm always trying to pull the wool over yours.

"There are definitely advantages to be gained in different moments based on experience in the dugout, where I've tried so many different things, from Idaho Falls to Salem to Midland to Peoria to stuff on the back fields of Gene Autry Park. You try stuff. You listen. You learn.

"One time in Midland my best hitter is up, James Randall, 'Sap.' We had a runner at first base. Two outs. They played behind him. I let the guy on first base run, and so then they walked Sap. With the wind blowing out in a small park, he never got to swing the bat because of a mental mistake I made there by sending the runner. Guys have been trying to get me to do that ever since.

"When you do what we did in the minors, there was a lot of growing up very fast and a lot of different situations that you had to react to. We were taught to be so independent—independent thinkers. A bad thing? I don't think so.

"The way I was raised in baseball, a lot of decisions were left to me. But it's really important that you permit your people to work—you permit your people to take what's given to them and create. That's identity. That's culture."

In May of 1994, Maddon, then the Angels' director of minor league development, was called to a pay phone outside the clubhouse in Vancouver, home to the franchise's Triple A team. On the line was Billy Bavasi, who was three months into his new role as the Angels' general manager. Bavasi had just decided to fire the team's manager, Buck Rodgers. He replaced Rodgers with Marcel Lachemann, the Marlins pitching coach who had worked with Bavasi as a coach in the Angels' system. First-base coach Bobby Knoop became Lachemann's bench coach, which meant bullpen coach Max Olivares replaced Knoop as the first-base coach, which meant Bavasi needed a bullpen coach.

That was why he was calling Maddon. In his fourteenth season playing, managing, coaching, and supervising in the minor leagues, Maddon finally was a major leaguer. Even before he hung up the phone, Maddon cried.

"Then I called my mom," he says. "I cried. My dad was still alive, but I called Beanie. What was happening? I rushed to the airport. I got on the plane. I flew to Orange County, John Wayne Airport. I get there. They had a car for me. Hertz rental car counter. Pick up my car. Get in. Drive to the hotel. That's when two thoughts came to mind. The first was, *Where's my jacket?*"

Maddon had left Vancouver with his favorite leather bomber jacket, a Christmas gift from only the previous year. He realized it was gone.

"I loved it," he says. "And I promise you, had I not screwed up, I'd still have that thing. It was that timeless. I left it at the counter at Hertz, John

Wayne Airport, May 1994. Anybody have it? Please, name your price—as long as it's not too nuts.

"So that was my first thought. *Why? How could I possibly do that?* And for whatever reason, I came up with another thought: *I'm just happy to be here, man.*

"Happy to be here" would gain meaning to Maddon over the years. It helped inform what became his fundamental concept for building a winning team: The Five Levels of Being a Professional.

CHAPTER 8

"The Five Levels of Being a Professional"

Joe Maddon pulled into the parking lot of the Under Armour Performance Center at Sloan Park in Mesa, Arizona, on the dank morning of February 18, 2019. His windshield wipers strained to keep up with the cold, hard rain, and his headlights illuminated sheaths of the gray gloom. He looked at the outside temperature on the car's thermometer: forty-five degrees. An ominous chill was in the air around the Chicago Cubs, a chill that would prove prescient. As was his wont, Maddon chose to interpret the digital readout optimistically.

That's about right for an April game at Wrigley Field or a postseason game, he thought. *So maybe that's not so bad.*

Maddon had not slept soundly. Every year he gave great consideration to the address he gave his team before the first full-squad spring training workout. This one seemed especially heavy with import. In his four years as manager of the Cubs, Maddon had led the team to the best record in baseball (387-261, a .597 winning percentage), four straight seasons with at least 92 wins for the first time for the franchise since 1911, and its first World Series Championship since 1908. Despite that run of success, he knew the ground underneath his feet was unsteady. Maddon was in the last year of his contract. Cubs president Theo Epstein had made it clear to him after the previous season, which had ended with a Wild Card loss at home to the Colorado Rockies, that there would be no extension, nor even a discussion about one.

"Believe me, I put a lot of thought into it the last couple days and nights before it," Maddon says. "It's a bit of a nerve-racking experience because even though you do this often, this audience is different. For this audience, you have got to make sure you put out the right message and it's received properly. The night before, I probably tossed and turned more than normal, still thinking about it. Even though I spoke to the pitchers and catchers five days before, it's on my mind. I've got to do this right."

Starting at 8:00 a.m., Maddon held the final preseason evaluation meetings with three pitchers, then met with his coaches to review the day's schedule. At 9:00 a.m., all Cubs personnel filed into the large theater-like room off the main clubhouse in the five-year-old Performance Center. Players, coaches, trainers, analysts, executives...everybody associated with the major league team filled every seat in the auditorium, which ran about fifteen rows deep and ten seats across.

Maddon ran the program. He started by introducing the owner, Tom Ricketts, who gave a short speech welcoming everyone to another season and pledging his best efforts to support them. Next up was Crane Kenney, president of business operations.

"Crane did a wonderful job of explaining things," Maddon says. "When you feel like you have some kind of contact with the ownership and the president of the ball club on the business side, it makes a difference."

Next to speak were Vijay Tekchandani, director of travel and clubhouse operations; Peter Chase, director of media relations; and Tim Buss, director of strength and conditioning and unofficial director of laughter. Bussey showed a five-minute video worthy of *Saturday Night Live* on the dos and don'ts of weight room and clubhouse protocol. Think Emily Post meets John Belushi. Players laughed so hard they cried. Next up was Epstein.

"He recapped last year very well," Maddon says. "I thought the guys got a great picture from him about what was expected.

"And then it's my turn."

The very setting of the annual opening address spoke volumes about how baseball, and the job of the manager, were changing. Front offices were expanding rapidly, especially the analytics departments. Titles were inflating. Training staffs were expanding with nutritionists, therapists, scientists, and "performance coaches." Training complexes were being upgraded. Where once batting cages and bullpens had sufficed—Earl

Weaver would hold his Orioles' spring training entirely on one and a half fields at Bobby Maduro Miami Stadium—the Cubs had built high-tech pitching and hitting "labs" where hitters could measure ground forces from their legs and pitchers could tweak the spin axes of their sliders. The theater had the look of an MIT lecture or an all-hands corporate meeting.

In the days of Gene Mauch, the manager would gather his team in the outfield, lean on his fungo bat, and give his brief but pointed my-way-or-the-highway speech, peppered with rules about dress codes and curfews. No questions were entertained. Even as recently as 2006, when Maddon started with the Devil Rays, and 2015, when he started with the Cubs, he had held his opening address in the outfield, without the excessive rules and always with humor sprinkled in. In the Performance Center theater—the name alone is a giveaway to the change— those days when the game seemed smaller and the audience more intimate were over.

"My job now is to address everybody," Maddon says. "Everybody's there. They're in this one big room. This theater. They can see you and hear you really well and you're totally exposed."

Maddon decided to build on the theme of his opening remarks to the pitchers and catchers five days earlier. It was the root of how Maddon wanted his team to play unselfish, championship baseball. It also was the root of his career arc in professional baseball.

"Let me tell you about the Five Levels of Being a Professional," he began.

The Five Levels date to an epiphany Maddon had late one night in 1995. It was one o'clock in the morning after a difficult loss in Anaheim. Maddon was in his second season in the majors, having moved from Angels bullpen coach to first-base coach, with occasional duties as hitting coach in the stead of Rod Carew when Carew needed to attend to a family matter. Maddon and the other coaches were grinding away on their notes from that game and preparation for the next. Manager Marcel Lachemann somberly studied how the game had been lost, asking himself what he could have done differently to assure a different outcome.

"Marcel took every game that we lost as though it was his fault,"

Maddon says. "Of course that's not true, but that's just who he is. He is just one of the most accountable people you've ever met in your life. You talk about somebody who always had your back? That's the man. A beautiful man. Tough guy, too. Don't mess with him. He's a sweetheart, but if you go in the wrong direction, if you're not appreciative, he will let you know."

Something overcame Maddon in that moment. It arrived in the form of questions.

"I asked myself, *What am I seeing here? What are the big leagues all about?*" Maddon says. "And I answered that question myself."

For the first time, he knew he belonged in the major leagues. He realized the deference, doubt, and subjugation he'd allowed himself up to that point in his time in the majors. The epiphany came to him with perfect clarity: there is a natural arc of growth for most people when they arrive at the highest level of baseball. It so energized him that he could not wait to get home—actually, he was living at his uncle Rick's place in Long Beach—and preserve it in writing.

He drove the 22 until it merged with the 405 by the Seal Beach Boulevard exit. He took the exit. On the left, toward Second Street and Studebaker Road, stood a power plant with smokestacks that stood like sentries, lit from below by flood lamps and topped with blinking red lights to warn low-flying aircraft of their presence. In the dark and quiet of the night, the plant and smokestacks radiated a golden glow. There was something serene, even magical, about the tableau, especially after victories. Maddon had come to equate it with the pleasing coda of an honest day's work.

It wasn't long before he turned on East Garner Street in Long Beach, on the border of Los Alamitos and Rossmoor. Uncle Rick loved his VO, and he would pour a shot for the two of them to celebrate a win. Uncle Rick would usually put his drink down on a counter about twelve feet away from where he sat. That way, whenever he wanted a sip, he would have to get up, walk to the counter, take his drink, walk back, and continue to watch *The Rockford Files* and smoke his Lucky Strikes. It was the over-seventy Uncle Rick workout.

After the VO, Uncle Rick would move on to his beloved Coors, and

Maddon would needle him for choosing a "fake" beer not worthy of their Pennsylvania roots. Uncle Rick and Maddon drew energy from one another, like college roommates. Uncle Rick had received undergraduate and medical degrees from Harvard, served in Vietnam, and worked at Strategic Air Command in Omaha, but was more than happy to have little more than this house on East Garner, his comfy chair, his VO workout, and good conversation.

"An absolute hermit," Maddon says. "A latter-day Howard Hughes."

Maddon told him that if he bought an old Dodge pickup, Maddon would drive him all the way back to West Reading, Pennsylvania, to see his family.

"Go shit in your hat," Uncle Rick said.

Says Maddon, "When Uncle Rick and I got to that point, it was pretty fun."

Uncle Rick is gone now, but today Maddon, taking the same exit, still sees the glow of the stacks as he drives to his new home in Long Beach.

"The warm, fuzzy feeling is absolutely still there," he says.

On this night at Uncle Rick's in 1995, with a headful of thoughts on making it in the major leagues, Maddon began writing. He decided right then that these are the Five Levels of Being a Professional.

LEVEL ONE: HAPPY TO BE HERE

With one phone call from Billy Bavasi in May of 1994, Maddon went not just from Vancouver to Anaheim but also from running the entire minor league organization to running six bullpen guys.

"When I first got there, I felt useless," Maddon says. "Here I was running the whole minor league system, A to Z. I felt on top of the world. Smart. I knew what I was doing. Knew how to do it. Knew how to implement new ideas. How to talk to people. Everything.

"All of a sudden I'm in charge of the bullpen and I don't know squat. How does that happen? I'm not kidding. That's exactly how I felt.

"And there's a lot of tossing and turning at night that came from not being sure. You questioned yourself. *Was I wrong? Am I good enough to do this?* And there was the vitriol from other coaches that had played in the big leagues toward me because I did not. I think a lot of my teachings were frowned upon because of that reason and that one alone. That's just the way the world evolved back then."

Maddon would sit in on preseries meetings and feel disconnected. The information came fast: how to attack opposing pitchers, how to defend opposing hitters, pickoff moves, pitchers' times to the plate...in the minors Maddon had had all this information. But this was different. He wasn't familiar with the teams. The level of detail was greater. And the consequences were greater.

"How could I possibly be helpful in these meetings?" Maddon says. "It's impossible to be helpful because I didn't know anything about these other teams.

"I'm here to tell you folks, it is the same sixty feet, six inches from the mound to the plate and the same ninety feet to the bases. It's the same 330 down the line and 375 to the power alley. But the game could not be more different. And that's because of what happens between the ears."

LEVEL TWO: SURVIVAL

"I felt worthless and helpless, but boy, did I like being there, right?" Maddon says. "Survival happens after you get over the shock of not knowing anything and after you get over the shock of how the major leagues are just so different. The day is different. The egos are different. The interactions are different. Everything's different.

"Now it becomes, *Listen, I like this. I want to stay here.* That is known as survival. Stage two is survival. So that's what came to me next. And level two is dangerous. It's dangerous because you're not focused on helping the team win that night. You're focused on *How do I stay here? How do I not screw up? What's the right thing to say in this moment?*

"You just get out of your normal patterns. Your lane changes. Everything changes. It's just true. It is one of the more dangerous of the five levels.

"When you are in 'happy to be here,' you can still do some things because you're not afraid about making a mistake. You're just out there running on adrenaline and instinct, and you might throw a nugget out there now and then. But once you get in the survival mode, you start overthinking stuff. Your pure intentions leave you, and it's not a good coaching method or a playing method.

"I went through this, and I'd love to give you exact timelines. I can't. But I do know in that second year, 1995, we had the real good year. I was learning a lot of different things including picking up hitting coach duties when Rod Carew had to leave. So from the manager right down to the last bench player, a lot of guys were coming to me for different things and I was able to help."

Level two is where many players see their careers come to a halt.

"A lot of guys you hear a lot about who are supposed to be very good languish at this level because they're just not sure enough of their abilities and of themselves," Maddon says. "They just aren't. Why? I don't know. Could be that their dad yelled at them all the time. Could be the coach always tried to correct them and wouldn't leave them alone. There are tough coaches. More players have been ruined by being overcoached than undercoached.

"Could be that one tough moment that will stick. It will stick like the stickiest Velcro you ever met in your life, and it won't go away. That one thought sticks in your cranium, and it will constantly come back and prevent you from moving forward."

LEVEL THREE: I BELONG HERE

"Finally," Maddon says, "one day, I arrived at that point where I said, 'God, I belong here. I can do this.' That's level three. For all of us in every occupation, until you arrive at that spot, it's hard to bring forth your best you.

"Dan O'Brien said that one time in a meeting years before I got there. He was the general manager, and I was in a meeting with him, and he mentioned something about 'you have to feel as though you belong.' I never processed it. I don't know how many times I've said it, and finally, in my last year with the Cubs, it resonated with the guys after they heard it for four years. It goes back to that old line: 'When the student is ready, the teacher will appear.'

"It was that night in 1995 when I finally felt like I belonged there. I finally felt like I had a contribution to make. I finally had something to say. I understood the meetings. I started to understand the league. I understood what was going on.

"That's the whole thing, man. Same game, but totally different game. You don't know what's going on. You don't know the other team. You don't know pitchers. You don't know hitters. You don't know defense. You don't know nuance. You don't know. But by the middle of my second year, I began to know. And that's where I felt like I could help and make a difference. *I belong here. I can do this.*

"That's where the mind you operated with for fifteen years in the minor leagues finally grabs a cab from John Wayne Airport where you left it and arrives at Anaheim Stadium and finds you in the clubhouse and jumps into your head and becomes your brain again. Because you go for a while without it. I'm telling you, it's true. It's absolutely true. It took me halfway through my second year for my brain to arrive.

"Level three is a great moment. It's me in Boulder, Colorado, a week or ten days into playing there and we've got all these catchers from all over the country and finally one evening it just clicked. *Man, I'm as good as these guys.*

LEVEL FOUR: MAKE AS MUCH MONEY AS YOU CAN

"OK, once you know you belong here and you know it's normally not that long of a career, what would be your next motivating factor?" Maddon says. "And that's where I thought, *Make as much money as you possibly can.* From a coach's perspective, we were always just wanting that next contract. The minor league jobs and major league coaching were never going to get you rich."

After the Angels won the 2002 World Series, Maddon asked general manager Bill Stoneman for a raise. Maddon said he deserved to be paid as much as Yankees bench coach Don Zimmer, seeing that Maddon considered himself and Zimmer the best bench coaches in baseball.

"I think Stoney probably laughed pretty heartily inside," Maddon says.

Stoneman offered him a $5,000 raise.

"That's five thousand dollars from the previous year, the non–World Series–winning Angels," Maddon says. "Wow. I'm sitting there in his office thinking, *You have got to be freakin' kidding me*. I have no abilities here at all to argue for myself. None. Zero."

Stoneman offered him a two-year deal with a $10,000 raise spread over the two years. Of course Maddon accepted.

"From a coach's perspective, it's really hard, although they are getting better recognition and better pay now than back then," Maddon says. "But a player, he has much more leverage. He needs to make some dough before that opportunity goes. Injuries and poor performance could occur at any point, and all of a sudden that window is gone.

"Make as much money as you can, and not for a second would I denigrate anybody in that stage based on what it took to get there, the amount of money you made prior to that, how you were treated . . . everything. The minor leagues, brother, are not even close to being glamorous.

"So what you're seeing today with the players and their fight, just understand, yeah, a lot of them make a lot of money right now and there is a lot of money. Absolutely. But they've got to get it while they can, and there were all those lean years when you put in all that extra work in an attempt to get to this point."

LEVEL FIVE: ALL I WANT TO DO IS WIN

"Nirvana. You want a bunch of these guys," Maddon says. "We all do, in every occupation. It means you have gotten through levels one, two, and three, and you are satiated with four. And that permits your mind to shift to the altruistic component of 'all I want to do is win.' In any sport. In any business. That's the pinnacle.

"The level-five player thinks, *I want to do well for myself, for my team-mates, for my community, for my city*...all of it. *All I want to do is win. I feel like all those other needs had to be satisfied first.*

"It is the rare cat that sees through all those different phases and arrives as a level-five player. That's not normal. Derek Jeter. Michael Jordan. Ken Griffey Jr. Mike Trout. They are the real confident ones who know they belong here real fast. Wally Joyner stands out to me; Wallace Keith from the beginning thought, *I belong here*, and he absolutely showed it.

"Javy Báez had to go through level two, survival, but he got there fast. Evan Longoria skirted through level two very fast. He thought he belonged here quickly.

"You get a bunch of level fives on your team, it runs so smoothly, and you do have a much better chance to win. Those are the guys taking the risks necessary in situations to be successful, not playing it carefully. They are out there uninhibited. They know they belong there. They made some money. And now all they want to do is win. The key is to get guys from one to three to five as quickly as possible. If you can get guys in and out of two and four as quickly as possible, it is just outstanding. If you can accomplish that, you got something.

"Everybody is different. Never, ever denigrate the young man or lady in level one who is just being happy to be there after all their hard work. It could be school, graduate school, A ball, Double A, Triple A, winter ball. You've got to be happy to be there, man. If you're not, you don't have a heartbeat. You're a cyborg of some kind.

"But it's only one stage. What matters is you get to the point where you know you belong, and if you're confident in your work and what you believe in and you put it in your requisite numbers prior to that, it doesn't matter what anybody may challenge you on. It doesn't because you *know*. You know in your heart of hearts what's going on, and you know what you think and feel, and you know it wasn't by the seat of your pants, and you know it can work.

"There are so many times when we as managers have to talk to the press. There are times where what you say is not going to be universally accepted. You're always going to get somebody that's going to interpret and put a different spin on it. And sometimes, I don't know if it's legit or if it's just an attempt to create controversy knowing whoever the speaker is, they don't have any ill intent. And if they're misinformed in your mind, inform them. Don't act like a jack-off and start talking smack about them because that happens way too often.

"Teach me, then. If I'm wrong, teach me. Inform me. Instruct me. Just like I try to do with you."

Maddon personalized his speech to his players that day.

"I tried to be very specific," he says, "about where it came from, how I thought of it. I tried to make the story more relatable in the sense of what I've learned in the past. When you can put dates and times and situations in the story and paint the picture, there's a much better chance it plays, and the guys remember it."

Maddon was not quite done. He had another message to drive home, knowing that his players were surrounded with every state-of-the-art technological tool to help them in their training.

"Let's all be working off the same sheet of music," Maddon told them. "At this point, please do not forget to compete. When you're in high school, when you're in college, junior college, the minors, whatever, that's what you did. Just compete.

"Before you got to the point of being so mechanically concerned, all you ever tried to do is beat somebody. You tried to win. You didn't know enough about mechanics to be worried about them. You made adjustments on the fly. Don't forget to purely, plainly compete. Compete.

"It really comes down to the basic stuff, who wants to win more on a nightly basis. That's attitudinal. That comes from within. That is everybody in the dugout during the game, guys not filtering up to the clubhouse. It's teammates supporting teammates all the time.

"I really want that to be part of our structure. I'm not saying it hasn't been in the past, but having been eliminated as early as we did last year and teams getting better this year, I think it's really important with everybody working off the same sheet of analytical music that we now become even more in tune to playing this game right and well. And that will be the difference maker on a nightly basis."

It would be only the next year that the professional golfer Jordan Spieth touched a similar theme. Spieth won three majors before he was twenty-three years old, then largely disappeared from leaderboards. His game deteriorated. The more he tried to fix it, the more it foundered. In 2020, as he launched a comeback to regain his place among the best golfers in the world, Spieth rediscovered the spirit of why he had been successful in the first place.

Reminiscing about his own junior college days, Spieth said, "Honestly, I wish I'd played with the mentality I had back then. You overthink the game the more you're out. You just want to play like a kid and just freewheel it and have fun. So I'd tell myself to just keep my head down; focus on why you love the game. Try and hit the cart picker on the range. Try and hit that flop-slice five-iron. Try and punch it and hit the flagstick. Just don't take it too seriously. Because I didn't back then, and the only times the game has been difficult to me is when I take it too seriously."

Maddon spoke for about twenty minutes. The program ended at 10:00 a.m.

The feedback from the players was positive. They liked the five-levels concept so much that Maddon quickly thought about reinforcing it with T-shirts. He imagined T-shirts with "Level Five" on the front and "All I Want to Do Is Win" on the back. In any other year he would have jumped at the opportunity to drive home his message and generate money for charity at the same time. In 2018, for instance, he commissioned works by the artist Jason Skeldon in which many of Maddon's themes were superimposed on modernistic portraits of Muhammad Ali, Albert Einstein, and the *Mona Lisa*. One piece sold for $50,000 and benefited his Respect 90 Foundation. Another went for $25,000 and benefited Anthony Rizzo's foundation, which helps families dealing with pediatric cancer.

This time, however, something gnawed at Maddon. He had learned from Epstein after the previous season that some players had complained about the artwork and T-shirts. They saw them as grandstanding by Maddon.

"I kind of gleaned from our conversation that it was seen sometimes as self-promoting on my part, which bothered me if that's what they saw,"

Maddon says. "I tried to really be introspective and understand why. I concluded that if you know me, I'd like to believe you wouldn't believe that.

"I was kind of gun-shy a little bit and wanted to make sure that people understood it's coming from pure intentions. It was purely to give guys something to think about—a cool shirt to wear while raising money for a foundation."

The tone was set for 2019. It wasn't just the rain and cold in Mesa. It was that Maddon, with his instincts checked and his methods questioned, could no longer manage the Cubs with the freedom that for four years had produced the best record in baseball. He was on borrowed time. It did not take long for him not just to suspect it, but to know it.

CHAPTER 9

"Attitude Is a Decision"

Joe Maddon began the first day of his major league managerial life with an emphasis on fundamentals. He told the forty pitchers and catchers of the Tampa Bay Devil Rays before their first spring training workout on February 17, 2006, that he wanted them to be the most fundamentally sound team in baseball.

"All these things matter," Maddon explained to the press about his attention to detail. "You emphasize them here, and here comes the regular season and they get caught up in other things and they stop working on it. I want those little things to make a difference at the end of the season, and they will.

"Hey, if you can't believe in hard work, what can you believe in? So for me, we're going to believe in hard work."

Less than an hour later, a rookie pitcher named Carlos Hines blacked out in the middle of a drill, collapsed, and was carted off the field. Hines turned out to be OK. He had given blood that morning and had not eaten. But the sight of a man down on day one served as an appropriate metaphor for what Maddon inherited. The Devil Rays had been nothing but down in their existence. Every one of their eight seasons had been a losing one with at least ninety-one losses. In every season but one they'd finished in last place.

The Devil Rays had no history of success. They had no identity. They had no expectations.

They were a blank canvas, which made them ideal for an artist like Maddon.

Maddon was a major league managerial rookie at age fifty-two. He had interviewed five previous times for managing jobs and gone 0 for 5. His first two interviews had both been with the Angels—one after the

1996 season, when Terry Collins was hired, and another after the 1999 season, when Mike Scioscia got the job. Both interviews seemed like courtesies based on his years of service in the organization.

"In 1996 and when Sciosh got it, I truly thought those were right decisions," Maddon says. "I wasn't ready. I just wasn't ready to pretty much say screw it to everybody else and just do what I thought was right. I didn't have that firmly established. It wasn't on a major league level, you know."

Four years later, in 2003, the Boston Red Sox interviewed Maddon after they fired Grady Little after coming up one win short of the World Series. Owner Larry Lucchino, General Manager Theo Epstein, and Assistant General Manager Jed Hoyer ultimately preferred someone with experience. They hired former Philadelphia Phillies manager Terry Francona to manage what was a ready-to-win team.

"The big opportunity was with the Red Sox, and that would have been the hugest mistake ever for me," Maddon says. "I would never have had a chance to go to the Cubs, never been a World Series champ there, never had a chance to be a part of the first one in a hundred and eight years. Wouldn't have happened.

"There's no question, had Theo and Jed decided to take that chance in 2003, retrospectively, I know that things would have soured at some point, and I'd have been gone.

"The interviews with Larry Lucchino, I can tell you I didn't really want to do that. My interview with him was on the phone, driving from Arizona to California to see Jaye, my future wife.

"I'm on the phone, I don't know how long. I just talked, being very honest with him.

"And either Theo or Jed really indicated Larry didn't think I was ready for it. He was right. I wasn't ready for it. Again, they made a good decision by picking Tito there. Tito had enough experience to develop the right proving ground. I had none. I had no proving ground. I did not belong there, at that time, at that moment in baseball time, the way things were for me."

The Seattle Mariners and Arizona Diamondbacks both came calling the next year, after Francona's Red Sox won the 2004 World Series. Maddon was one of five candidates for the Seattle job. The other four all had previous managing experience: Don Baylor, Terry Collins, Mike Hargrove, and Little. The Seattle general manager was Maddon's friend Bill Bavasi, who had been hired a year earlier. The two shared roots working in the Angels' farm system that went back to 1981.

"I was making twelve thousand bucks a year and married, and I was extremely poor," Maddon says. "He was making ten thousand a year and single and felt extremely rich. He later came up with the phrase, 'Thank God we didn't know then what we know now because we would have been paralyzed.' When you're twenty-one years old, if you are being wise and well thought out, my God, all the crazy stuff you did you would have never done. That was me and him."

Owing to their friendship, Bavasi told Maddon he would skip the usual face-to-face get-to-know-you job interview. They talked on the phone. Maddon was hesitant about the job.

"I might have been a decent candidate there," Maddon says. "I was getting ready to manage. I was coming out the other side of a divorce and getting my personal stuff in order. I did feel confident in what was going on. I had had enough major league experience as a coach. I was ready."

But Bavasi hired Hargrove. Then the Diamondbacks called. They interviewed Maddon and Manny Acta, Wally Backman, Mark Grace, DeMarlo Hale, Bob Melvin, Al Pedrique, and Jamie Quirk.

"The interview went really well—really well," Maddon says. "But there was a lot of stuff going on in my life at that point. I called up Joe Garagiola Jr., the general manager. I asked him if I could respectfully have my name withdrawn from consideration because I had things going on personally—my relationship with my son and also the recent divorce. It just wasn't the proper time. And so I asked out and Joe was great."

Arizona hired Backman, only to fire him four days later over alleged domestic incidents. The Diamondbacks replaced Backman with Melvin, who had been fired by Bavasi in Seattle.

Two years later, the Devil Rays called. This time Maddon was ready and eager.

"The Red Sox job would not have been nearly as attractive as it was working in Tampa," Maddon says. "In Boston, my first opportunity would have been where everything was already in place—most of the players, the organizational dynamics, the organizational identity. There was nothing in place with the Devil Rays. Nothing.

"When I was starting out with the Angels in the 1980s in the minor league system, honestly, I was the guy who helped create the identity in the system. I was not told what to do. The workouts, the training, the drills . . . along with Billy Bavasi and in the early going with Larry Himes, I pretty much pulled this together. There was no interference. A lot of times I was left to my own devices."

Maddon wanted the same opportunity to make a difference, this time with a big league team. He knew the Devil Rays were in transition. Stuart Sternberg, a Wall Street investor, became managing general partner in October 2005. He had put two twenty-eight-year-olds in charge: team president Matt Silverman, whom he'd first met at the investment banking firm Goldman Sachs, and head of baseball operations Andrew Friedman, who also came from Wall Street and who had played baseball at Tulane.

The new Devil Rays front office considered at least six other candidates to replace Lou Piniella as manager: Joe Girardi, John McLaren, Terry Pendleton, Mike Schmidt, Alan Trammell, and Bobby Valentine. Girardi ended talks with the Devil Rays to take the Florida Marlins job, saying the Marlins were closer to winning. Friedman and Silverman interviewed Maddon at a hotel in Houston during the 2005 World Series. Maddon walked into the room carrying a thick binder.

"I brought stat sheets, normal sheets from the Elias Sports Bureau," Maddon says. "From that I wanted to know how well or how badly the Devil Rays had done in their division. I wanted to see how far we needed to ascend in the division.

"I also brought information on the players. I looked at the hitters in my unique way based on the numbers. I looked at walks versus strike-outs. I looked at on-base percentage—I wasn't into slugging at the time. I wanted to know, 'How does he balance his walks and strikeouts?'

"I looked at batting average. If I thought the walks-to-strikeout ratio was in a good balance, then I looked at batting average, and that pretty much tells you who he is as a hitter.

"I had seen the Rays play and was impressed with their athleticism. I also knew who was coming up in the minor leagues. They had a glut of many interesting prospects. I used *Baseball America* and any kind of source that talked about their minor league system, and I included that in the binder so I could speak intelligently about the Rays system.

"I talked about my own cocktail of how to take raw numbers and create my own analytics number. That was all within the binder. I had been keeping track of these things for years. I looked at starting pitchers' times to the plate, whether there were any keys in their delivery that allowed you to run, any action counts, grading outfield arms, trying to get signs of other teams, knowing who could hit and run and who couldn't...I don't know if anybody else was doing it at the time, but I was keeping track of those things for years."

For instance, as Angels bench coach Maddon compiled finely detailed "opposition action sheets" on every opponent. He took note of when teams ran, when they bunted, and the signs and tendencies of the manager and third-base coach. He drew up detailed spray charts of opposing hitters against both right- and left-handed pitchers. He kept track of delivery times to the plate by pitchers and the quality of their pickoff moves. He graded the strength of outfield arms. Some of it was handwritten, though Maddon had been using a computer to assist in the preparation since the early 1990s. It took four hours of preparation, often done into the late hours of a night upon arriving in the next city, accompanied by a tall beer and headphones filling his ears with classical music.

"I was killing myself," he says of the grind. "That stuff I did in the mid-nineties, it was labor intensive. You had no idea. There was one year we had like twenty-five two-game series. When we were on the road I had like a big anvil box, with my printer in it and my laptop. I'd get in at two o'clock in the morning and I'd do all this before I went to bed so I could have it ready in time the next day. I don't know how many times I did that.

"You talk about learning your craft. All this stuff we can talk about now, it's about all the stuff I did to prepare myself for those moments, the labor-intensive work, the ten thousand hours. My God, it had to be way more than ten thousand hours."

The work yielded results. In 1998, for instance, Maddon's "opposition action sheets" were rich with intelligence on the New York Yankees, the legendary team that would win a record 125 games, postseason included, on its way to the World Series title. Maddon noted that New York manager Joe Torre would cover the "NY" on his hat as a sign the steal was on. If he covered the back of his hat, it meant no go. Right ear to right leg meant a green light for the runner. Torre was most active starting runners in the first inning. He tried to manufacture runs late with a lead to add on. Third-base coach Willie Randolph used a touch to his left ear as an indicator. Nose to left ear to chest meant a steal or hit-and-run.

Paul O'Neill took a bigger lead and ran on first move when he was stealing. Chad Curtis tipped off when he was running by lowering his left knee and turning it inward as he took his lead. Reliever Mike Stanton would not look at first base when he attempted a pickoff. "Glove will push out to 1B when coming over," Maddon's report said. Hideki Irabu would "push his glove back to get started from the stretch"—a key tip-off for a runner. David Wells took between 3.6 and 3.8 seconds in the windup with a runner at third base. "Possible steal of home," Maddon wrote.

O'Neill had the best outfield arm. Tim Raines and Bernie Williams had the weakest ones. Derek Jeter hit many ground balls against left-handers into the hole between third base and shortstop; the third baseman should play him off the line and toward that hole. Against right-handers, Jeter hit fly balls from the left-field line to straightaway right field, but not down the right-field line. Williams, a switch-hitter, was a pull hitter from the right side, prompting Maddon to write, "90% of action occurs from middle to pull side." From the left side, Williams had "more action in air to left center." O'Neill rarely pulled the ball in the air down the right-field line. His ground balls were clustered "from hole to hole. Bunch infield."

The 1998 Yankees were one of the greatest teams of all time. They steamrolled opponents. They scored the most runs in baseball and allowed the fewest while outscoring their opponents by 309 runs.

Only one team managed a winning record against them: the Angels (6-5).

The Yankees won four World Series in the five years between 1996 and 2000. Only one team managed a winning record against them in that dynastic run: the Angels (28-27), buoyed by the intelligence from Maddon's "opposition action sheets."

When he interviewed for the Boston job in 2003, Maddon said, "I used to be made fun of for carrying a computer. Now everyone on the [team] airplane has one. It was met with a lot of resistance at first. Like anything new, it takes a while to catch on.

"You're talking about information and people. They are two separate issues. The person is always going to count more. When it comes right down to it, you can only give [data] to the players in handfuls. Once you get it and disperse it, you have to determine who can handle what and how much and if it's going to be productive or counterproductive."

Years of such detail-oriented work prepared Maddon well for the interview with the Devil Rays.

"I knew what it took to manage a major league team," Maddon says. "That's what I brought to bear. It was twentysomething years of preparation. I had all this stuff spread out in front of me and I just talked to these two guys, and I thought it went really well. I remember sitting there, I knew immediately—I knew before, really—but I knew this was the right thing to do."

After the interview ended, Silverman and Friedman walked with Maddon to the elevator, where they boarded together for the ride to the lobby.

"Oh, one more thing," Maddon said.

"What's that?" Friedman asked.

"My girlfriend, Jaye, is in law school, and she's graduating next May. Would it be OK for me to take two days off to fly back for her graduation?"

Friedman and Silverman didn't flinch. They laughed and assured him it would not be a problem. Hearing their casual response, Maddon thought to himself, *This really is the right place for me.*

"I don't know if that indicated cockiness or a good kind of a family guy or loyalty," Maddon says. "I think they took it the right way."

The Rays asked Maddon back for a second interview, this time during the general managers' meetings at a hotel in Indian Wells, California, with Friedman and his most trusted and most veteran adviser, Gerry Hunsicker.

"Of all the interviews that I've been through, that was the only one I really wanted," Maddon says. "I didn't think the other ones were realistic. The time was right on this one. Why? Having gone through a divorce, making sure my kids were good, being a bench coach long enough, and I felt the Devil Rays were still an expansion team. I thought the opportunity was wide open.

"That would have been the first job, had I not gotten it, I would have been disappointed."

Friedman and Hunsicker were blown away. On November 15 they hired Maddon with a two-year contract with two option years.

"I've been through a lot of manager interviews, and this was the most impressive interview that I have ever been through in my career," Hunsicker said. "This guy is a diamond in the rough. From the short time I've been around him, I think he is one of the best-kept secrets in the game."

The press at the introductory news conference ran with the narrative that Maddon was a "new age" manager who wielded a computer keyboard as well as he did a fungo bat. Maddon cautioned that they were overplaying that angle.

"I like numbers. I like instincts. I like trusting your gut," he told them. "I think you think with your brain, your heart, and your stomach."

The woeful Devil Rays quickly would test all three. Maddon has managed three major league franchises. Each time, the team he took over was a ball club accustomed to losing. The Devil Rays had eight straight losing seasons when he was hired, the Cubs five straight losing seasons, and the Angels four straight losing seasons. Maddon brought Tampa Bay to the World Series in his third year, and he won the World Series with the Cubs in his second year. The Angels improved each season under Maddon until he was dismissed fifty-six games into his third season.

"Changing the culture" has become a sports cliché. It is summoned with most every new hire of a manager or head coach by a losing team. But what does it mean in practice? How do you overcome serial losing by creating a winning attitude—before the winning begins? Maddon is the rare proven expert in the field. He is one of only nine managers to win a pennant in both leagues. He and Jim Leyland, with the Marlins and Tigers, are the only ones to do so within three years of inheriting a losing team each time.

Maddon used the same three building blocks to change the culture in all three franchises. In order of flow, they are:

1. Build relationships.
2. Establish trust.
3. Exchange ideas.

Everything builds from that foundation. On the eve of his first day managing the Devil Rays in that 2006 spring training, Maddon was asked if the responsibilities of being a first-time major league manager concerned him.

"I've done it before, even if it was on an interim basis," Maddon said. "So that's not my biggest concern. I think the biggest thing is getting the relationships going.

"I really didn't plan on doing anything different. Hopefully everything I've done in the past has suited me well. I think the worst thing you can do is change. I think you have to be yourself. I think the people respond to that."

Building relationships. To announce it as the bedrock of the job was a new concept in managing. In another era—the one we think of as more gilded when it comes to managerial powers—Gene Mauch, the Little General, who was one of Maddon's inspirations, rarely spoke to his players, unless it was to scold them or shout at them as he flipped a postgame spread of food after a bad loss. He brooded quietly. Relationships did not matter. He was omnipotent. His players needed only to listen to him, not the other way around.

"I'm not the manager because I'm always right," Mauch once said, "but I'm always right because I'm the manager."

Likewise, Hall of Famer Earl Weaver believed the rare times he spoke to players were those calling for negative motivation.

"His idea of being positive," pitcher Jim Palmer says, "was to give you everything possible that could go wrong. I'd have a one-run lead against Boston in the eighth with Yaz, Rice, and Fisk coming up, and as soon as my foot hit the cinders of the warning track at Memorial Stadium coming out of the dugout I'd hear, 'Can't get beat until you walk somebody!' That's a pretty negative thought, but to Earl it meant, 'I just told you to be aggressive.'"

Weaver wanted nothing to do with emotion or friendship, because, as Palmer says, "I don't think Earl ever wanted anything to do with anything that interfered with him winning baseball games."

"Back then," says Houston Astros manager Dusty Baker, who played in the 1970s and 1980s, "negative motivation was more of a factor than it is now."

Baker's father, Johnnie B. Baker Sr., worked on air force radar equipment by day and earned a few more bucks at night at Sears in the Sacramento area. He was so strict he was known around town as "Mr. Baker," and thought nothing of chastising townspeople if he deemed they had done something wrong. Managing was done the same way through the twentieth century.

"With negative motivation you wanted to say, 'I'll show you,'" Baker says. "You can't use negative motivation today with players because they'll quit on you. Everything has to be positive."

Strong communication skills were one bullet point Friedman wanted in a manager. Maddon knew it was the key to building relationships, his cornerstone for "changing the culture."

"I wanted to set this method of self-discipline on their part, which means permitting them freedom," he says. "I always believed the game needs to be played hard—to prepare hard. But when the game is not being played, there has to be this close connection between people. There has to be a great sense of humor, a feeling of wanting to hang out with one another.

"With the Devil Rays this was going to be communication like they had not seen before. We had spring training meetings with individuals where they knew exactly where they stood. We told them exactly what we had in mind for them. There was no gray area. When you do that, you're not walking on the field for guys who don't know you. You know them and they know you.

"There are no hidden agendas when you try to interact with them in an open and honest way. If you don't have a meeting with them, the player will always fear the worst, and trust is dead.

"How do you do it? It's just a lot of conversations. The most important thing is having one-on-one evaluation meetings with the players. My pitching coach, Mike Butcher, who I had in the minors, asked me one day, 'Do you still do those meetings we had in Instructional League?' I said, 'No, I haven't been their manager with the Angels. I've been the bench coach.' But Butch's input coming back to me was important. So I brought it back with the Devil Rays.

"It's about full disclosure. It's about how you view the guy right now, and you create this plan moving forward. It's an open method of communication that permits building trust, which permits an exchange of ideas, which permits feedback.

"It's not just talking to people. It's not being afraid to look somebody in the eye and ask them an honest question. I think it's about honesty more than anything."

On his very first day as a big league manager, Maddon asked the clubhouse manager, Chris Westmoreland, to order and hang signs that said in several languages, "Attitude Is a Decision." When Maddon gathered those 2006 Devil Rays for the first full-squad workout, he revealed another key building block for changing the culture: unbridled, unqualified, and, as some might have viewed it, unbelievable optimism. Maddon stood before a group that had lost ninety-five games and given up the most runs in baseball the previous season and announced the goal: to make the playoffs.

"I'm not going to talk about seventy wins," he told them. The Devil Rays never had won more than that in any season in their existence.

"Seventy is not a goal. Eighty-one is not a goal. Our goal is to play the game properly every night. I'm going to keep telling you that, and I know it sounds like a cliché, but it's not. We're going to aim high."

The way Maddon saw it, change required nothing short of a full buy-in, which meant striking the right attitude with the right expectations from the start.

"When you're a professional and you walk into a situation, whether it's baseball or any industry, why would you go into there with low expectations and kind of tentatively create your mark within the organization?" Maddon says. "Why not go in there boldly and create the vision you really want to occur?

"If I had gone in there less than bold, I don't know that it would turn as quickly as it did. When players hear that, they're going to start believing that. When the front office, the coaches, and the scouts hear that, that means an expectation of a high level of mental performance and preparedness, and then the physical performance will follow.

"Why aim low? Where is the threat when you aim low? The threat is that you're going to hit your mark, which is less than what you want to be. I had been successful everywhere I had been—from midget football to high school baseball to collegiate football and baseball to minor league instructor. As a player I was on a lot of championship teams. In 1986 and 1987 we had one of the best minor league systems in baseball, and we did so because I believed in what I said and what I taught. And of course, we won the 2002 World Series with the Angels. I'm used to this stuff. I'm used to aiming high and getting there."

He also took to heart a piece of advice in *Coaching the Mental Game: Leadership Philosophies and Strategies for Peak Performance in Sports and Everyday Life*, written by Harvey Dorfman in 2003: goals have to be specific to be effective. The "Attitude Is a Decision" signs could not be missed. Maddon also handed out T-shirts in his first camp as a major league manager that said, "Tell me what you think, not what you've heard."

"There are so many people in this game and in business in general that only mimic what they've heard," he says. "I don't want conventional thinkers. I want the freethinker. I want the elastic mind, not the inflexible one."

To help instill his new attitude, Maddon also brought to camp as a special instructor Dave Martinez, who had played for the Devil Rays in his sixteen-year-playing career and was known as a clubhouse leader.

Maddon had four future managers in his first camp: players Rocco Baldelli and Kevin Cash, coach Charlie Montoyo, and Martinez, a special instructor. It was clear from day one that the Devil Rays under Maddon would operate differently. Maddon held a thirty-minute drill with pitchers and catchers without a baseball. The pitchers, most of whom were young, stood across from the catchers and explained how they liked them to set up for each pitch. Catchers asked questions of pitchers about their stuff and how they liked to use it.

"When a pitcher walks out there, I want him to know every catcher," Maddon explained. "There's no way we're going to win games unless our pitching does a good job and catching is an extension of the job. Let's see if it works."

Maddon loved the vibe he felt in that first workout.

"It's beautiful. It's amazing," he said. "There's a lot of enthusiasm among the coaching staff also. Everybody's excited about it big-time. The players have been fantastic. They make it fun. They make it easy. It's all about the players.

"We've got to make sure it stays fresh. You're going to be with the same people every day. Sometimes it gets kind of tough. You've got to keep it open and fresh. If you can do that, you have a chance."

Truth be told, it was not all beautiful. It did not take long for Maddon to also see how difficult the job would be. The lone potential impact player the Devil Rays added for 2006 was Japanese reliever Shinji Mori. He hurt his throwing shoulder in spring training and never pitched in the majors.

Elijah Dukes, a twenty-year-old outfield prospect, nearly came to blows on the field with outfielder Carl Crawford, a teammate. Dukes had endured a troubled childhood growing up in the Tampa area. He had been arrested five times since he was thirteen, including one occasion after which he underwent court-ordered anger management counseling.

"We're going through drills, running first to third," Maddon says. "Just arcs around the infield because we weren't quite ready to cut the bases yet. All of a sudden, he and Carl go after each other right in front of me. I don't know who initiated it, but it was a scary moment. Everybody jumped in and broke it up quickly. But right there you saw a part of what Elijah was going through."

Another top prospect, Delmon Young, also twenty, came to camp in a sour mood. The number one pick in the 2003 draft, Young seethed because he had not been called up to the majors the previous September. He had yet to play a day in the big leagues but already was looking forward to getting out of Tampa Bay. He said then, "As soon as I'm a free agent I'll bounce out of there."

Maddon called him over the winter.

"For me and you, it's a new beginning," he told him.

Maddon invested time with Young throughout spring training.

"I needed to start establishing that relationship sooner, or there were going to be some issues later," Maddon says. "I wanted to get to know him, and I wanted him to get to know me. I asked questions about his family. I told him I liked his brother a lot, Dmitri. Delmon was a very impressive hitter, and we started talking about that. The whole point was just to establish a normal conversation."

Midway through spring training, however, Maddon had to have a difficult conversation with Young. The Rays were sending him back to Triple A Durham for more seasoning.

"I can still see it," Maddon says. "He comes into the manager's office at Al Lang Stadium. He could not have been more difficult with the way he took the news. I can still see him saying, 'You're sending me back to that Little League?'

"That's when as a manager you have to hold it together. I didn't know him well enough yet. I just told him, 'We think it's wise for you to go back. There are other things you can work on.' Delmon wasn't an analytical kind of hitter. He was a hacker. But he could hit. He was just abrasive, so it was difficult for people to like him. It was the right thing to do at the time, to send him back."

Both Dukes and Young ran into trouble at Durham. Dukes was suspended indefinitely midway through the season for violent confrontations, including one with the team's hitting coach and another with a teammate. Young was suspended fifty games for throwing a bat that hit an umpire. Young made his major league debut later that year, on August 29. On the first pitch of his first at bat, Young was hit by White Sox veteran right-hander Freddy García. Maddon interpreted it as old-school justice meted out by the White Sox and their manager, Ozzie Guillén, over Young's minor league misbehavior.

"I was livid," Maddon says. "Of course there were denials from the other side. All I said was, 'Listen, we'll take care of our own discipline. We don't need the White Sox to take care of discipline with Delmon.'

"To me, there was no doubt they were throwing at him. Between Elijah and Delmon and a really controversial article about them in *Baseball America*, it seemed like Major League Baseball was going to take it upon themselves to hand out more discipline. I couldn't have that. So I defended him in Chicago. I think that led to a great relationship between Delmon and me and Ozzie and me."

Issues with Young resumed in 2007. At least three times that season, Maddon warned Young about his lack of hustle. When it happened again, on a sixth-inning groundout on September 29 in the penultimate game of the season, Maddon had enough. He pulled him from the game.

"That was a blatant disrespect for the game and what we're all about," Maddon says. "I've had several conversations regarding that, and that was it.

"I don't want to do it. I don't like doing that. But it's to the point where you're made to do it. And the word for me is *disappointing*."

Young complained he was unfairly being singled out. Then he came up with a novel response to getting pulled from the game: he told reporters he would boycott the season finale the next day.

"I'll see you guys next year," Young said.

It was one example of how Maddon was not always successful at building relationships. He had known mostly the collegial Angels minor league system. With the Devil Rays, he quickly found a snake pit, where players and coaches often were out for themselves, not the good of the organization.

"That first spring training, wow!" Maddon says. "You talk about having a lot of work ahead of us. When I saw the minor league staff and how everybody was pretty much pulling in different directions, I knew it would be a lot of work. Everybody wanted somebody else's job. There was little pride in being part of an organization.

"I was an outsider coming in, so I could see it. There was also this comfort level in the minor league system because there weren't any expectations."

Maddon took mental notes throughout spring training. He watched coaches with the same eye he used to evaluate players. Some, he knew, would have to go.

"For some guys, it only takes five minutes to know," Maddon says. "I always want to be fair and to give guys an opportunity. As an Angels lifer in the minor leagues, I knew what that meant. So I wanted this group to show me they deserved the opportunity.

"Some guys reveal themselves quickly. Maybe they're not competitive. Maybe they are too political. Maybe some guys need time to show you what they're all about. There was a lot of thin slicing going on."

Attempts to change the culture will inevitably meet with doubters. Human nature more readily accepts status quo over change. Maddon calls these people "resisters." And the most poisonous of the resisters are coaches.

"Resisters start with coaches," he says. "Where I came from and what I learned, my methods were maybe a bit looser than the previous regime. I thought the methods we brought were totally antithetical to some of the coaches that were there. As I said, you want to make sure you give an opportunity to everyone. But when it becomes apparent that you have a resister, you have to cut out the cancer. You have to eradicate it, like with chemo. There is no other option.

"Why? Even one resister can bring down an entire group. Once you identify that negative influence, you must cut it out. You have to get rid of coaches who don't belong there. Players will seek allies when things aren't working in their favor. If they think management is unfair, they will go to other players for support. More important, if they can find a coach they can find sympathy with, then that can really blossom into negativity. The coach may curry favor and tell the player, 'Yeah, you're getting screwed.' Now the negativity starts to spread.

"That's why the message from the staff and coaches has to be consistent. If a coach chooses not to do that, and aligns with one or two bad ballplayers, it can bring a whole team down."

Another corrosive element emerged to Maddon that spring training: player entitlement. The meritocracy and work ethic of the Angels' Instructional League camp were irrelevant to many of the Devil Rays.

"That place was a total scholarship program," Maddon says. "Entitlement? It was everywhere you looked. This was the furthest thing from a major league group of players. They thought that if they had one good month in the minors they should be in the majors on merit. That was all they were concerned about.

"I wanted Davey Martinez there to set a different tone. A more professional tone. He was a great example of a smart team player. And that led to Fred McGriff and Wade Boggs and Roberto Hernández showing up—prominent guys who knew what it meant to be a professional.

"Again, it gets back to establishing relationships. Once you do that, everyone is working off the same sheet of music."

It took two years for Maddon's plan to change the culture to take root. When it did, the result shocked the baseball world.

CHAPTER 10

"Aim High"

The Devil Rays lost 101 games in Maddon's first year there and ninety-six the next. By the time they assembled for spring training in 2008, they had a new name—just the Rays—and a stunning new look. Of the twenty-five players on the 2006 Opening Day roster, twenty-two were no longer in the organization. Dukes and Young had both been traded. Professionals in the mold of Davey Martinez had been brought in: outfielder Cliff Floyd, first baseman Carlos Peña, infielder Eric Hinske, pitcher Edwin Jackson, and, by way of Minnesota in the deal for Young, shortstop Jason Bartlett and pitcher Matt Garza. First-round picks Evan Longoria, a third baseman, and David Price, a pitcher, were major leagues ready without the earmarks of an entitlement program that had marked the Devil Rays system.

The Rays, Maddon believed, were ready to smash conventional wisdom. That is, if his players believed they could do it. A few weeks before spring training began, he composed a letter to them. In part it read:

> We accept conventional wisdom as true, especially if it blends with what we already think. It is the "raft" that supports the world as we see it. We are in, we agree. Who will benefit the most with the acceptance of this "conventional wisdom?" Does it in fact stand up? Is it actually true and worthy of our support? Do we really know, or are we repeating what we have heard?
>
> Our view of the baseball world is different than say, the Yankees, the Red Sox, etc. We play by the same rules, but at the same time, we do not. The sameness occurs on the field, and that is up to us to make sure that we stand toe to toe with them in the execution of the game. The preparation. The desire to be the best. The will to win.

Conventional wisdom tells us that we have no chance based on their economic base. They have the ability to spend countless dollars to arrive at the top. We need to find another path. A path that lies below the surface.

We have to do all the little things better than anyone else. We are in the process of creating the "Ray Way" of doing things. Conventional Wisdom be damned. We are in the process of creating our own little world. Our way of doing things. The Ray Way. To those of you who feel as though this sounds "corny" wait a couple of years and you will see how corny turns into "cool" and everyone stands in line to copy our methods.

Shortly after sending that letter, Maddon was riding his bike on his usual jaunt along Birch, Rose, and Bastanchury in Brea and Fullerton, California, when a particularly clear thought floated to the top of his mind: *Nine equals eight.*

If nine players played hard for nine innings every night, he thought, then the Rays could be one of eight teams in the playoffs in 2008. And maybe even the World Series.

It made sense to Maddon. It sounded like lunacy to everybody else. Tampa Bay was coming off a ninety-six-loss season. Two hundred and twenty-nine teams in baseball history had lost ninety-six games or more. Only one of those previous 228 losers had gone to the World Series the next year, the 1991 Atlanta Braves.

Maddon liked the combination of power and simplicity in his equation. He rolled it around his head some more.

Nine more wins from the offense, nine more wins from the defense, and nine more wins from the pitching staff equal twenty-seven more wins, which should be enough to get in the postseason. Add the digits of twenty-seven and you get nine. And nine equals eight.

Neanderthals used cave walls. Ancient Egyptians used papyrus. Jackson Pollock turned household alkyd paints into eternal art. Maddon's medium is the T-shirt.

Maddon has a sloganeering tradition that dates to the Angels' minor league system in the 1980s, when he handed out T-shirts that read, "Every Day Counts." As manager, starting in 2006 with "Tell me what you think, not what you've heard," every year Maddon likes to come up with a slogan that eventually finds its way onto your basic cotton T. In 2008 the slogan was "9=8," which the Rays began sporting early in the season. Much more than a gimmick, such themes are mortar to Maddon.

"When you are with an organization like the Rays, where there is no established identity, this kind of repeated language helps that identity that you want to form," he says.

Maddon stood before his players before the spring games started and told them, "I want you to play the same game. I don't care if it's March fifteenth or June fifteenth or, yes, October fifteenth. Play hard. We will play hard in spring training and take it into the season."

The Rays took his message to heart—and to the New York Yankees. On March 8 at George M. Steinbrenner Field in Tampa, a Rays utility player named Elliot Johnson broke from first base for home on a ninth-inning double with Tampa Bay leading 3–1. As New York catcher Francisco Cervelli caught the throw from the outfield, blocking the plate, Johnson lowered his shoulder into Cervelli.

"Boom!" Maddon says. "He absolutely pancakes Cervelli. The ball flies out. Run scores. We win the game. Cervelli breaks his wrist."

Word reached Maddon after the game that Yankees manager Joe Girardi was incensed over Johnson plowing into Cervelli.

"I'm in the manager's office, and I'm getting word from the press that Girardi's upset," Maddon says. "I thought I needed to know why he's upset. Did he consider it a dirty play, or did he think you shouldn't do it in spring training? I needed that answer. There's a big difference, and there would be a big difference in how I would respond.

"If he thinks it's dirty, well, that's just his interpretation. We can disagree. But if it's the other thing..."

One of the writers in the room explained to Maddon that Girardi said the play was "uncalled for" in a spring training setting.

"The moment he said that—that you shouldn't do it in spring training because you don't want to get anybody hurt—man, that opened up a whole can of worms for me," Maddon says. "I went off. We're trying to ascend in this division. This idea that it's OK if the game is played in the regular season but not in spring training didn't sit well with me. Not at all."

Told of Girardi's view that spring training should be played with less effort and intensity, Maddon shot back, "I never read that rule before.... We play it hard, and we play it right every day."

"A few days later, we're playing the Yankees again," Maddon says. "Jerry Crawford, the home plate umpire, has a meeting before the game at home plate with Girardi and me. I go, 'We're good, man. We just want to play baseball.' I could tell Joe was upset.

"Jerry goes, 'We can't have it. I'm telling you, we can't have it.' I go, 'Jerry, you've got nothing to worry about.' But I knew Joe was not pleased.

"Game starts. Shelley Duncan of the Yankees hits a line drive off somebody's glove and tries to stretch it into a double. There is no way any runner is going to go to second under those circumstances—no way—but Shelley knew this was his opportunity to get revenge. Shelley comes in spikes high into our second baseman, Akinori Iwamura, at second base. He spikes him in the right thigh and knocks him down. It was a dirty play and I said so. All hell breaks loose. Jonny Gomes is in the middle of the melee just picking guys off the pile—I mean picking them up and tossing them away.

"Now I will tell you this: those two moments—the play by Elliot Johnson and the way we came together after the Shelley Duncan slide—accelerated us out of the chute. Icing on the cake was a fight we had later with Boston. But when Shelley came in spikes high and when those writers told me Girardi said you shouldn't play like that in spring training, we were on our way. It was validation. Everything I had been telling them, they were putting into practice.

"We knew the Yankees had had their way with us. We knew we were going to have to take it from them. They weren't just going to give it to us. But that day at Al Lang Stadium was like Bizarro World. It was turned upside down. We were taking it from them. Had the Yankees chosen not to go after us, then nothing at all would have happened. I am absolutely convinced that set us on our way."

The Rays finished spring training 18-8, a club record for wins and the best record among all thirty teams. They went 15-12 in April, followed by 19-10 in May. By July 6 the Rays led the American League East by five games. But suddenly they collapsed. They lost seven straight games heading into the All-Star break, getting outscored 45–13 and falling into second place.

On July 18, before the first game after the All-Star break, a home game against Toronto, Maddon called a team meeting. This was one of the three planned meetings Maddon will hold during a season, all to reinforce a positive message. The first meeting is held as spring training begins. His second meeting is held just before or after the All-Star break to refresh the message to his team. The third takes place before the start of the postseason. Otherwise, Maddon hates team meetings.

"How does the line go? 'The beatings shall continue until morale improves,'" Maddon says. "In the big leagues, I've been around managers like Scioscia and Marcel and Terry Collins who have had meetings. Even one time Billy Bavasi, the GM, came down during a bad moment, and, if I remember correctly, he was airing us out.

"And it's really hard. You have to understand, it sounds like it's such a good idea in your head before you do it, but it's rare that it actually has the impact you're looking for.

"And I would sit there on the floor during major league team meetings by the manager and I would shake my head because hey, I played in the minor leagues, at least, but I'm an athlete. I played a lot of games, for a lot of teams. And some really bad teams like the Scranton Red Sox, my first year up there, I think we won, I don't know, 8 and 32, something horrible. So I've been on that side—rarely—but I've been there.

"So when a coach sits you down and wants to start beating you up verbally, it rarely works. It makes the coach feel better. It makes the deliverer of the message feel better and getting it off his chest. Not necessarily the players.

"I'm here to tell you, it was rare that I was involved in a meeting that there was any kind of substantial boost to our morale, our play. It's just a venting procedure for the guy that's doing the yelling. I really believe that.

"The other thing is, usually with a team that's losing there probably has been a lot of negative backlash about the team, negative things said about you as a manager. Most of the time it's not true, but it's something you've got to wear it. You got to wear it.

"That's another reason why I don't like team meetings: because it always sounds like you're making an excuse.

"Most meetings, I'd say ninety-seven percent of them, are not necessary."

On the Rays' first day back from the 2008 All-Star break, Maddon gathered his team for a meeting in right field at Tropicana Field. It is his policy not to conduct team meetings in his team's home clubhouse. Why?

"It poisons the room," Maddon says. "To show up at home every day and then have it be this negative room and a lot of yelling and screaming and throwing of things and name calling? Not good.

"The other part about that, the thing I learned from in the past, all these other major league meetings I was in? A lot of them were in a home clubhouse. Home clubhouse after a loss. Two things about that: You just lost. You feel like crap already.

"And two, you're at home. This is your living room. This is supposed to be the warm fuzzy you need to go to when things are bad to get your act straightened out. If it's going to be a blowup, folks, if at all possible, remember two factors: do it on the road, and do it after a win. That's the best time to make your point."

Gathered in the outfield, Maddon told his players a story about the 1983 Baltimore Orioles. They had two seven-game losing streaks, one in May and one in August. Each one knocked them out of first place.

"Do you know what they did?" Maddon told them. "They won the World Series.

"Do you really think we're going to roll through this without hitting some bumps? Treat this moment with respect because this doesn't happen every year—the chance to win the World Series. For you young guys, it's happening for the very first time, so treat it with respect because it doesn't often come along. For you veterans that maybe have been through this before, treat it with respect because it might be your last chance."

That night the Rays trailed Toronto, 1–0, two outs into the seventh inning. Hinske drew a six-pitch walk from Blue Jays right-hander A. J. Burnett. Ben Zobrist hit the next pitch for a home run. Tampa Bay won, 2–1, and regained first place. The team held first place the rest of the season, though not without Maddon calling one of those rare fire-and-brimstone meetings that he detests.

The Rays were in Kansas City. It was a Saturday night, and only eight days after Maddon's inspirational 1983 Orioles speech. Tampa Bay had beaten the Royals, 5–3, but Maddon seethed about how they'd played. The baserunning had been lethargic. Second baseman Akinori Iwamura, for instance, had jogged from first base on a bloop double by B. J. Upton, costing himself a chance to score.

"We made all kinds of mistakes," Maddon says. "We weren't running hard, mental errors…we were doing well, so we thought we were hot stuff. I went off."

As a steamed Maddon walked back to the clubhouse, he said to bench coach Dave Martinez, "Get 'em in here. Right now."

The meeting was brief, but hot. For the first time in three years, Maddon ripped his team for not hustling.

"I've seen teams miss the playoffs by one game!" Maddon told them. "And here you are up by one game and you're not playing hard!

"We haven't done shit yet, and if we keep doing this, then this wonderful beginning we've had to this year is going to end up hollow. So for those of you who think you're hot shit, know one thing: you're not! And if we don't get our shit together from here on out, it ain't going to happen."

Says Maddon, "It was one of those times when you talk and cry at the same time a little bit. You're crying because you can't control your emotions. I was a little bit out of control. I was really loud. I don't think my message was long or elegant, by any means. I'm screaming. I mean, it's to the point where I'm yelling, crying, and running out of breath at the same time. I don't think it took more than three or four minutes, but

I did find out—I didn't ask, but I found out, you always do—that a lot of guys thought that was perfect. We needed that kind of a thing."

As reliever J. P. Howell said, "From then on, every game was important to us. We weren't going to give anything away. I think that's when we realized we could really do this."

The Rays went 36-23 after that meeting. They finished 97-65 and won the division by just two games.

Maddon had succeeded in changing the culture. The Rays played hard, they expected to win, and they did not reek of entitlement. It had happened not because Maddon forced discipline upon the team but because of the relationships he'd built and how he trusted his players to be guided by self-discipline. Anybody who walked into the Rays' clubhouse not only felt that vibe but also could read about it in giant letters plastered on the walls there, courtesy of placards that Maddon ordered:

DISCIPLINE YOURSELF SO THAT NO ONE ELSE HAS TO

—JOHN WOODEN

INTEGRITY HAS NO NEED OF RULES

—ALBERT CAMUS

RULES CANNOT TAKE THE PLACE OF CHARACTER

—ALAN GREENSPAN

Not posted, but at the root of the same philosophy, was this pearl from Maddon to his Rays: "The more freedom given, the greater respect and discipline returned."

Maddon also knew he had to step in if the self-discipline broke down. On August 5, B. J. Upton did not hustle down the line when he hit a grounder back to the pitcher in the eighth inning with the Rays up 8–4. Maddon benched him the next game.

"I didn't run it out," Upton said. "But it's over, done with, you move on. Learned a lesson."

Eight days later in Texas, Upton failed to run hard again on a double-play grounder that ended the sixth inning. *So much for Camus.* Maddon motioned for Upton to return to the bench rather than to his position in center field. He pulled Upton from the game and replaced him with Justin Ruggiano.

"If we're going to be a really good organization, it has to permeate the entire group," Maddon said. "I'm not just talking about the major league team. I'm talking from rookie ball all the way up to Triple A. So I hope that our minor leaguers read about all this also, because I want that message sent to them, too. That's how we play."

Upton sat out one game. He returned August 17, the night Maddon ordered an intentional walk to Josh Hamilton with the bases loaded. The Rays were leading, 7–3, with two outs in the ninth inning when Maddon told pitcher Grant Balfour to walk Hamilton, choosing to give up one run rather than risk a game-tying grand slam. Maddon then replaced Balfour with Dan Wheeler, who promptly struck out Marlon Byrd to seal the win. (Maddon reprised the gambit in 2022 with the Angels. He intentionally walked Corey Seager of Texas with the bases loaded while trailing—and won the game. No other manager in the previous twenty-four seasons ordered a bases-loaded intentional walk once.)

Maddon managed the Rays unconventionally. He used a four-man outfield and a five-man infield. He brought in left-handed relievers to face right-handed batters, and vice versa.

His team stole more bases and bunted the least of any team in the majors. His players ran into more outs on the bases than all but one team. It was not because his players were reckless. It was because Maddon encouraged them to be bold. Maddon never liked the bromide "Don't make the first out at first base or third base" because that is a negative thought that encourages conservatism on the bases.

"The proper mindset is, 'Get to third base with less than two outs as often as possible,'" Maddon says.

The Rays ran all the way to the World Series, where a loaded Philadelphia Phillies team stopped them in five games. Maddon responded to the World Series defeat in a thoroughly Maddonian way: with optimism and a paraphrase of a quote from an 1858 collection of essays by the poet and polymath Oliver Wendell Holmes Sr.

"The mind, once expanded to the dimensions of larger ideas, never returns to its original size," Maddon said.

He knew his players were better for the experience. They had expectations now of success. The culture was changed. The Rays had an identity. From that formative season of 2008 through 2021, during which time Maddon and Kevin Cash, his former player, each managed seven seasons, the Rays posted the fourth-best winning percentage in the majors, behind only blue blood franchises the Dodgers, Yankees, and Cardinals.

Maddon helped launch one of the most shocking turnarounds in baseball history. A franchise that had never had a winning record, that had never won more than seventy games, suddenly won ninety-seven games in 2008—a thirty-one-win improvement over the previous year—and did so with the second-lowest payroll in baseball. The Rays finished eight games ahead of the Yankees with a payroll that was one-fifth of what New York spent.

Less than a month after the World Series, Maddon was honeymooning in Rome with Jaye when his phone rang. It was nine o'clock on an oil painting of an Italian evening, and the two of them were well into a bottle of red at a restaurant not far from the Spanish Steps. There was good news on the line: Maddon had been voted American League Manager of the Year—and by the largest margin ever. He'd received twenty-seven of the twenty-eight first-place votes.

On their trip Maddon and Jaye also sampled Florence, Prague, and London. The highlight for Maddon was being in the presence of two of the greatest works of Michelangelo, the ceiling of the Sistine Chapel and his sculpture *David*.

"Those may be the two most religious moments you can have as a human being," Maddon says.

So inspired by Michelangelo's work and life was Maddon that he sat down to write a letter to his newly crowned American League champion Rays:

The greatest danger
For most of us
Is not that our aim is
Too high

And we miss it,
But that it is
Too low
And we reach it.

MICHELANGELO (1475–1564)

Maddon then liberally quoted from *Wisdom of the Ages* by motivational speaker and author Wayne W. Dyer, a book he had read recently. Maddon was so impressed by Dyer's insights that in a 2009 interview he included Dyer among his three ideal dinner guests. The other two were Branch Rickey and Mark Twain. Rickey, the innovative baseball executive with the Cardinals, Dodgers, and Pirates, is Maddon's "administrative idol." And Twain? Maddon admires Twain's "zest for life." He regards Twain as an especially keen observer of human nature who captured our complexities and nuances with a razor-sharp wit and the simple turn of a phrase.

Michelangelo is one of sixty intellectuals whose teachings Dyer explores in *Wisdom of the Ages*. Fresh off his trip to Italy, Maddon quoted from the book to his players:

> The world is full of people who have aimed low and thought small who want to impose this diminutive thinking on any who will listen. The real danger is the act of giving up or setting standards of smallness for ourselves with low expectations. Listen carefully to Michelangelo, the man who many consider the greatest artist of all time.
>
> Michelangelo's advice is just as applicable today in your life as it was in his, over five hundred years ago. Never listen to those who try to influence you with their pessimism. Have complete faith in your own capacity to influence others with your attitude of aiming high and achieving it.
>
> Aim high, refuse to choose small thinking and low expectations, and above all, do not be seduced by the absurd idea that there is danger in having too much belief. In fact, your high expectations will guide you to heal your life and to produce your own masterpieces.

It was one of Maddon's core tenets for changing the culture in Tampa Bay. Concluding his letter, Maddon continued to aim high and asked his players to do likewise. He wrote:

I have been to Italy and have seen both the Sistine Chapel and the statue David. Michelangelo's level of skill and talent were indescribable then and now.

I believe you are all artists in an athletic sense. Very few people are able to perform daily with your level of skill and consistency. There are different levels of success within our profession. My wish is that you all understand to participate is merely the first goal, and one to be passed very quickly. The ultimate goal is to play the last game of the year which is more the result of teamwork over individual achievement. This requires dedication above and beyond. Kind of like walking through the Vatican for four-plus years and spending much of the day lying on your back while painting a ceiling that you had no idea would be talked about for the rest of time.

Hopefully this piece will stir a bit of thought within you. We all have to apply total dedication to our goals. We may not cause people to talk about us for the rest of time, but I would settle for this next century.

Joe

THE FOUR BASIC HUMAN NEEDS:
1. *to live*
2. *to love*
3. *to learn*
4. *to leave a legacy (let's leave ours)*

Years later, Joe Maddon would give a similar look to umpires. *Courtesy of Joe Maddon's personal collection.*

A proud and loving mother, Beanie taught Joe about empathy and fairness. *Courtesy of Joe Maddon's personal collection.*

His father, Joe, was his strongest role model who taught him hard work and a smile could go hand in hand. *Courtesy of Joe Maddon's personal collection.*

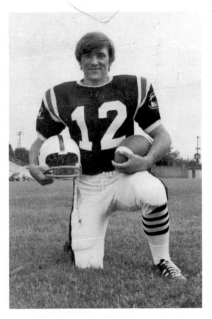

Friends referred to Hazleton High star quarterback Joe Maddon as "Broad Street Joe." *Courtesy of Joe Maddon's personal collection.*

Joe (second from right, back row) with the fast-pitch softball team of the Young Men's Polish Association of Hazleton, Pennsylvania. *Courtesy of Joe Maddon's personal collection.*

Joe Maddon with another hit for Lafayette College. *Courtesy of Joe Maddon's personal collection.*

First-time manager Joe Maddon with the Idaho Falls Angels in Butte, Montana, 1981. Then 27, he was the youngest manager in pro baseball. *Courtesy of Joe Maddon's personal collection.*

Joe Maddon (far right) with Angels owner Gene Autry (middle) and minor league coach Gary Ruby at spring training in Palm Springs, California, 1988. *Courtesy of Joe Maddon's personal collection.*

The managerial training of Joe Maddon, here in 1998, included 12 years as a coach with the Angels. *Courtesy of Joe Maddon's personal collection.*

Gene Mauch in full-throated, silver-haired glory at Yankee Stadium, 1982. Renowned for his baseball smarts, the Little General personified the last generation when managers wielded autonomy over how teams played. *Permission and credit go to Getty Images / Focus on Sport.*

BOB CLEAR COACH

Known as Bobba Lou, Angels coach Bob Clear was a mentor and close friend to Maddon. *Courtesy of Trading Card Database.*

Impresario of the Boulder Collegians, Bauldie Moschetti occupied a special place in Maddon's Wrigley Field office. *Courtesy of Joe Maddon's personal collection.*

Twelve years after minor league catcher Troy Percival converted to pitcher under Bob Clear and Joe Maddon, Percival (with back arched) celebrates the last out of the Angels' 2002 World Series championship. *Permission and credit go to Getty Images / John Biever.*

Soon to be 52 years old, Joe Maddon becomes a full-time MLB manager for the first time. Introducing him as Tampa Bay Devil Rays manager is general manager Andrew Friedman. *Courtesy of Joe Maddon's personal collection.*

Two former catchers with a way with words, Yogi Berra and Joe Maddon. *Courtesy of Joe Maddon's personal collection.*

One year after they posted the worst record in MLB, the Rays and Joe Maddon reached Game 5 of the 2008 World Series, where their run came to a soggy end. *Permission and credit go to Getty Images / Damian Strohmeyer.*

Sports psychologist Ken Ravizza, a mentor and close friend. *Courtesy of Joe Maddon's personal collection.*

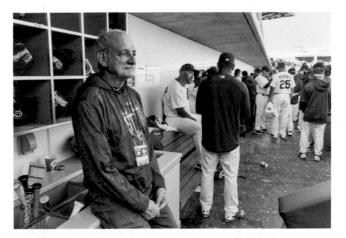

One of Maddon's many themed trips, this one was a "onesie" trip for the Cubs leaving Los Angeles. *Courtesy of Joe Maddon's personal collection.*

Beanie rocking one of the most popular T-shirts from a deep closet full of Maddonisms. *Courtesy of Joe Maddon's personal collection.*

Joe Maddon heard the voice of the late Don Zimmer when he asked Javier Báez to bunt with two strikes in the ninth inning of Game 7 of the 2016 World Series. It didn't work. *Permission and credit go to Getty Images / Ezra Shaw.*

The moment of a lifetime. First baseman Anthony Rizzo catches a throw from third baseman Kris Bryant (in foreground) for the final out of the Cubs' first World Series championship since 1908. *Permission and credit go to Getty Images / Al Tielemans.*

World Series trophy in hand, Joe Maddon celebrates with his Cubs players and staff after winning the rain-delayed Game 7 in extra innings. *Permission and credit go to Getty Images / Stephen Green.*

Cubs fans celebrated their team's first championship in 108 years with impromptu notes of gratitude on a wall outside Wrigley Field. The writings included words of advice from the Cubs' bespectacled manager. *Permission and credit go to Getty Images / Scott Olson.*

An estimated five million people attended the 2016 Cubs' victory parade and rally, making it the largest gathering of humanity in Western Hemisphere history. *Courtesy of Joe Maddon's personal collection.*

From Hazleton to the White House. Joe holds court at the White House after President Obama honored the 2016 Cubs. *Courtesy of Joe Maddon's personal collection.*

The home team, Jaye and Joe, at Wrigley Field. *Courtesy of Joe Maddon's personal collection.*

Spring training 2018 team meeting, emphasizing "Putting the Art Back in the Game." Intended as a team-building exercise and charitable endeavor, the artwork would turn sour with his players. *Courtesy of Joe Maddon's personal collection.*

The 1976 Dodge Tradesman van, aka the "Cal State Fullerton" or the "Shaggin' Wagon." *Courtesy of Joe Maddon's personal collection.*

The Winnebago, aka the "Cousin Eddie." *Courtesy of Joe Maddon's personal collection.*

Through his Respect 90 Foundation and his Hazleton Integration Project, Maddon has supported several initiatives, including a boxing card to benefit the boxing program of the Hazleton Area Recreation Program. *Courtesy of Joe Maddon's personal collection.*

Joe Maddon considers only a few players to be baseball geniuses. One of them is Shohei Ohtani, who in 2021 posted the greatest two-way season since Babe Ruth. *Permission and credit go to Getty Images / Kyodo News.*

A man at work. With all the information he needs on his lineup card, Joe Maddon always manages from the rail of the dugout so he can best gauge the flow of the game. *Permission and credit go to Getty Images / Jayne Kamin-Oncea.*

CHAPTER 11

"Never Forget the Heartbeat"

Fog crept over Los Rodeos Airport on the Spanish island of Tenerife like the opening motif of Beethoven's Fifth Symphony, the *Fate* Symphony. Portent, allegro con brio, hung in the air on the afternoon of March 27, 1977. It already had been a very bad day.

Seventy-three miles to the east, a bomb had exploded at 1:15 p.m. in a flower shop at Gran Canaria Airport in the Canary Islands. The leader of a Canary Islands separatist group claimed responsibility. Air traffic was diverted to Tenerife. Los Rodeos Airport quickly grew so crowded that some aircraft had to park on the taxiway, leaving the 11,155-foot runway to double as the taxiway—the equivalent of a one-lane bridge.

Among the diverted planes parked on the taxiway were KLM Flight 4805, a charter flight from the Netherlands with 248 people aboard, and Pan Am Flight 1736, a commercial flight that had originated in Los Angeles and stopped in New York. It carried 396 people. Both airplanes were Boeing 747s.

The Pan Am 747 was the same one that seven years earlier had taken the maiden flight of the 747, the first jumbo jet, the iconic airliner that began the era of wide-body aircraft that opened air travel to more middle-class consumers. Eight months after the maiden flight, that same 747 also became the first such airplane to be hijacked.

The fog was thickening at 4:30 p.m. when air traffic control instructed the KLM plane to prepare for takeoff. Visibility was down to about sixty feet. ATC told the KLM aircraft to taxi the length of the runway to its end, where it was to turn around and prepare for takeoff.

ATC also instructed the Pan Am plane to taxi behind the KLM plane and leave the runway via the third exit on the left. Both aircraft began to carry out their instructions. In the thickness of the fog, the pilots of the

Pan Am plane struggled to find the third exit, which had no visible markings. They slowed the plane to a stop to find their bearings.

By then the KLM plane had reached the end of the runway and had turned around. It was now facing the Pan Am plane, though neither plane could see the other through the soupy mist. The captain of the KLM plane advanced the throttles and moved forward.

"Wait," the first officer said to the captain. "We don't have clearance."

"No, I know that," the captain said. "Go ahead. Ask."

The first officer radioed the tower.

"We are ready for takeoff," he said to the tower.

The tower responded with instructions for their route after takeoff.

The first officer read back those instructions and added, "We are now at takeoff."

The captain interjected, "We are going."

The controller in the tower, responding to the first officer's description that the plane was "at takeoff," and thinking the plane was merely *in position* to take off, radioed, "OK." But after a brief pause, sensing an urgent need for clarity upon second thought, the controller added, "Stand by for takeoff. I will call you."

The KLM first officer and captain never heard those words. Just as the controller issued the standby command, the Pan Am cockpit sent out a radio call to alert the tower it still was on the runway. The dual announcements created interference. Instead of hearing the standby directive, the KLM crew heard only a three-second shrill noise.

The KLM aircraft started its takeoff. As it began to gather speed, its flight engineer suddenly heard chatter between the Pan Am flight and the tower.

"Is he not clear, that Pan American?" the engineer asked.

"Oh yes," the KLM pilot responded confidently.

The KLM pilot continued his takeoff. As the KLM flight sped down the runway, the Pan Am captain suddenly caught sight of the jumbo jet emerging from the fog and heading straight for him.

"Goddamn, that son of a bitch is coming!" he shouted.

The Pan Am captain applied full throttle to the wide-body beast to get out of the way. It was too late.

The giant KLM, weighing more than 735,000 pounds, was traveling at 160 miles per hour when it left the ground only a hundred feet in front of the Pan Am. The nose cleared the Pan Am, but the left and right engines and fuselage smashed into the fellow jumbo jet, ripping it apart. The KLM jet exploded in a fireball.

All 248 people aboard the KLM flight died. Only sixty-one from the Pan Am flight survived. In all, 583 people died. It was the worst aviation disaster in history.

The subsequent investigation left little doubt about the cause of such a massive loss of life: misinterpretations and false assumptions. It was one of the first accident investigations to highlight "human factors" as a cause.

In short, it was a catastrophic case of poor decision-making of a specific kind: heuristics.

The word *heuristics* comes from the Greek for *to find*. With heuristics we are looking to find a correct solution to a complex problem, but we don't have enough time or information, so we deploy approximate strategies, or mental shortcuts. The shortcuts allow us to make quick decisions. Examples of these strategies include rules of thumb and process of elimination. Psychologists Amos Tversky and Daniel Kahneman are credited with first exploring this method of decision-making in the 1970s.

Because of limited time and information, heuristics don't get us to the perfect solution, but they are used to get us closer to one. We use them all the time. Think of how a grandmother makes her Sunday pasta sauce: without a recipe and using rules of thumb to "know" the proper amount of ingredients. "Measure twice, cut once" is a familiar heuristic for people who work with lumber.

Heuristics are handy, but fallible. The deadliest accident in aviation history was selected as an example of heuristics gone horribly wrong in *Practical Human Factors for Pilots*, a 2015 book by David Moriarty. The KLM pilot was never told that the Pan Am airplane was off the runway.

Yet he was certain that it was not there. Why? He used heuristics, or the mental shortcuts of decision-making, to make that determination.

The pilot was KLM's chief flight instructor, a highly respected veteran flier with 11,700 flight hours. Into his many years of what he knew from takeoffs, he folded the visual and auditory clues available to him, including no sight of the Pan Am jumbo jet and the "OK" response from the tower when his officer radioed that the KLM flight was "now at takeoff."

As a result of the investigation, communication protocols were changed. The word *takeoff* is spoken between tower and aircraft only when the actual takeoff is cleared or canceled. The change came too late to save 583 lives.

In the heat of the moment, cooks, carpenters, pilots, and, yes, baseball managers use heuristics, though thankfully on a baseball diamond without human lives at stake. The proliferation of analytics has produced heuristics that have reshaped how baseball is played. "A sacrifice bunt is a waste of an out." "Stolen bases and hit-and-run plays are poor risks." "Sinkers get hit." "Strikeouts are just another out."

Those modern rules of thumb are based on huge amounts of data used to determine the likeliest outcome—a generic outcome, not a specific one. Managers are so schooled in these analytically based heuristics that they become their go-to shortcuts. The 2020 World Series famously was decided on one of those modern heuristics gone wrong: "Don't allow the starting pitcher to face the opposing lineup a third time."

The Tampa Bay Rays were eleven outs away from sending the World Series to a seventh game against the Los Angeles Dodgers when Rays manager Kevin Cash removed starting pitcher Blake Snell as the lineup turned over a third time. Snell was dominant. Since Cy Young of the Boston Americans threw the first pitch of the 1903 World Series, there had been 1,356 starts by pitchers in the Fall Classic. Snell was the first of those pitchers to strike out nine batters while allowing just two baserunners. He had thrown just seventy-three pitches and had struck out the next three hitters due, Mookie Betts, Corey Seager, and Justin Turner, all six times he'd faced them.

"I'm not exactly sure why," Betts said when asked about Cash remov-ing Snell. "I'm not going to ask any questions, but he was pitching a great game. It was kind of a sigh of relief. Had he stayed in the game he might have pitched a complete game. It was the Cy Young Snell that pitched tonight."

"We were all just excited that Snell was out of the game," said Dodg-ers manager Dave Roberts.

The Dodgers immediately rallied to win, 3–1. Cash had simply man-aged the same way he had for years. He'd deployed a heuristic that had worked well for the Rays. Since Cash had begun managing the Rays in 2015, no team had allowed its starters to face a batter a third time less often.

"My motive," Cash said after the game, "was the lineup the Dodgers feature is as potent as any team in the league. Personally, I felt Blake had done his job and then some. Mookie around for the third time, though, I really value that.

"I totally respect and understand the questions that come with it. Blake gave us every opportunity to win. He was outstanding. They are not easy decisions. I felt it was best after the guy got on base—Barnes got the single—[I] didn't want Mookie or Seager seeing Blake a third time."

Taking out a pitcher as the lineup turns over a third time is a recent trend that has spread quickly. Large-sample data has shown that a hitter seeing a relief pitcher for the first time has less success than a hitter facing a starting pitcher a third time. In 1970, a starter who pitched two times around the lineup remained to pitch to 91 percent of hitters in his third time around. Because starters were allowed to win and lose games them-selves, they became stars. Drawing cards. "Probable pitchers" listed daily in the morning newspapers were come-ons to buy tickets.

There have been only six seasons in baseball history when at least twelve future Hall of Fame pitchers pitched enough innings to qualify for the ERA title. Four of them happened in the 1970s: 1970, 1972, 1973, and 1976.

By 1980, as relief pitching began to take root, the percentage of hitters that pitchers faced a third time had dropped slightly to 80 percent. It remained stable for the next quarter of a century, hovering between 75 and 79 percent from 1990 through 2014.

The 2015 season began a precipitous decline as the new gospel of "third time around" spread. The 76 percent rate of 2014 fell to 50 percent in 2021.

"When I first started with the Rays in 2006 in the big leagues, Andrew Friedman, the GM, was really into it, man," Maddon says. "He was up my butt all the time. I used to keep track of pitches per game, the stuff that I was always into. Right around one hundred to 105 is not going to hurt anybody. Not only that, just who's the guy? Scott Kazmir would take a hundred pitches to get to the fifth inning. So then you were forced to use your bullpen more than you'd want to.

"But I think the new system is based on front offices. It's based on data and information. The third time through the batting order. All this stuff that they're actually nurturing in the minor leagues because they don't let guys pitch through issues. By the time they get to the big leagues, they're looking at their pitch count, not just if we're winning or losing. They want to know where they're at. 'Am I going to pitch another inning? Do I have another in me? I don't even know. How many pitches have I thrown?' Really not a good method, not at all.

"That's the one we're incorporating. It starts at the top, right from the moment they're drafted, signed, money put into them. Investment. Investment from the agent's perspective. Investment from the player's perspective. He wants to do this longer, make more money. All this stuff plays in. I'm not saying there's anything wrong with that. I'm just saying that's a big part of it."

Analytics is built on mining patterns and information from the huge samples of data baseball seasons produce. Oakland A's president Billy Beane compared the guided-by-numbers approach in baseball to actuarial work. When his teams kept faltering in the playoffs, Beane dismissed it as the vagaries of small samples inherit to postseason play. Maddon's experience is that front offices become *more* hands on in the postseason as the sample size gets smaller.

"All the information sent down from front offices now is for you to set the stuff up based on what they're telling you, regardless of what they may say publicly and how they may want to be perceived," Maddon says. "And the closer you get to or once you get in the playoffs, they really want to interfere and really want to take over."

Maddon, Joe McCarthy, and Jim Leyland are the only managers to make eight or more trips to the postseason after never playing in the big leagues. Maddon managed sixty-seven postseason games (32-35). Only eight men have managed more. He won three clinching games by one run, including the only such World Series Game 7 win on the road in extra innings.

"From the players' perspective, I didn't want them to do anything differently in the postseason, not a thing," Maddon says. "Everybody talks about 'emptying the tank' or 'leaving it on the field,' all that kind of stuff. But I anticipated my guys were going to do that anyway without me having to tell them that because all year, starting from the time we got to spring training, I talked about not playing anything differently.

"I wanted the same kind of effort, same kind of prep, same kind of everything so that when you come to the ballpark, you have this comfort, this baseball rocking chair to sit in. Your routine, your mindset, everything about it puts you in a mental arena where this is comfortable and familiar.

"That's one thing I really tried to constantly talk about was don't add any more weight to any game. I wanted them to all weigh the same. Theoretically, the seventh game of the World Series obviously doesn't weigh the same. Any elimination game doesn't. It just doesn't. Anything but those games, I wanted them to weigh the same.

"From my perspective as a manager in the postseason, I wanted less and not more information. That's definitely true for the players, too. There were a lot of times in Tampa and in Chicago where you get later in the year and the games get tighter, bigger, whatever, and the playoffs occur, and now the front office just wants to feed you more and more information. And for me, it was exactly the opposite.

"Give me the nuggets. Give me something that's different... compared to what we saw during the regular season.

"But man, in Tampa Bay, Andrew would just start piling it on. And it's not necessary. What was necessary was what we needed to know.

What's different? What are the couple of things that we need to be aware of? Something that can make a difference in tonight's game.

"Here's an example. Over my last two or three years in Chicago when we were playing the Cardinals and Yadier Molina was batting with a guy on first, we were not going to cover second if the runner is running, including the playoffs. Why? Because we pretty much believe he's going to make contact on a hit-and-run. He's not going to swing and miss. So the ball can be put in play. That was our bet. That wasn't something from analysis. This was ours.

"What happened? In those two or three years they did not put one hit-and-run on with Yadier. There was not one moment where somebody went with him hitting. I'm talking less than full count. It didn't happen. Unbelievable. So that's just an idea we talked about in the scouting report. To me, that's germane."

Before the 2015 ALCS, Kansas City Royals scouts noticed that with a runner at first, Toronto right fielder José Bautista would throw to second base on a ball hit down the line (defending the batter/runner) rather than throwing toward home (defending the runner taking off from first). When this exact scenario occurred in the eighth inning of Game 6 in a 3–3 tie, a properly alerted Lorenzo Cain scored from first base on a single by Eric Hosmer as Bautista's throw went to second. It was the run that put the Royals in the World Series.

As in baseball, the amount of intelligence processed by the military has proliferated exponentially in the past two decades. Data collection has expanded through drones, satellites, and other systems. The ballplayer or soldier, however, can process only a finite amount of information. All that data becomes useless and even counterproductive unless it is distilled to the right information at the right time in the right context to let a person make a timely, correct decision. The military calls this distilled information "actionable intelligence." Similar winnowing of information is important in baseball, especially in postseason play as scouting reports grow more intricate.

"When you start talking about 'This guy throws a pitch x percentage of the time when he comes out of the bullpen,' you don't know how he sees you in that moment," Maddon says. "You don't know how he's feeling. You just don't know. And you don't know the hitters, truly, either. You just don't know.

"That's why the large sample size to me is beautiful when it comes to acquisition, sure. I want to buy certain bonds or stocks; how did they perform over the last two or three years? Makes sense. But in the playoff situation, there's no such thing as a large sample size. It is small.

"In this little microcosm of the baseball season, things can change. Again, this is where hot and cold does matter. Absolutely it does.

"This is where in pitching, guys step up or good guys get their ass kicked. It has nothing to do with a report; has everything to do with the players. Think about it. All of a sudden, you're going to try to understand a different group of numbers or incorporate more information into your decision-making in that moment? Best out of five, maybe wild card, one game? That's unreasonable.

"If it's a Wild Card Game, if there are three major points that the group has been able to extract that they think these could be difference makers, give me those three points. And I promise you, we will remember them during the game, your players will remember them, and we will be able to be on the top step of the dugout to remind them.

"But if you're trying to give me fifteen things to think about going into that real hot moment in a Wild Card Game, that is absolute insanity, brother. Insanity.

"The bottom line is when you're trying to manipulate thought there, add layers of information to a postseason game, I'm telling you, it's a mistake. It's a mistake."

In Game 7 of the 2008 ALCS against Boston, the Rays held a 3–1 lead in the eighth inning when the Red Sox loaded the bases with two outs. The Rays had reached one of those switching posts that change history. They were four outs away from the World Series and one hit away from blowing it. With left-handed hitting J. D. Drew at the plate, Maddon had a decision to make. He turned to his pitching coach, Jim Hickey, and said, "Are we OK? Can we do this?"

"If you want to see David Price standing on the mound in the ninth inning," Hickey said. "If you're OK with that."

"Yeah, I am," said Maddon, who promptly walked to the mound and signaled for Price to come out of the bullpen. Price was a twenty-three-year-old rookie with just seven major league games under his belt. He was a starting pitcher who had never closed a game in his professional life. Why ask Price to get the last four outs with the American League pennant on the line? Price was a talented young left-hander. But it was a conversation Maddon had had in the outfield during batting practice that day that had convinced Maddon he could trust him.

"I looked him in the eyeballs and said, 'How we doing?'" Maddon says. "And he looked right back at me. 'I'm fine. I'm good.' Nothing wordy. Not 'Well, you know, if...' No. No hesitation. 'I'm good. I'm ready.' The fire coming out of his eyes indicated to me, *I'm fine, I'm good, stop asking me the question, put me in the game when you want to.*

"So if you're trying to make a decision in the dugout, how much easier is it with that kind of input from the guy you're considering in the moment? The confidence putting him in the game was greater based on that moment."

Price struck out Drew to end the inning. Maddon sent him back for the ninth. Price walked the leadoff batter, Jason Bay, bringing the tying run to the plate.

"People would ask, 'Why didn't you take him out?'" Maddon says. "Because you know the situation. The question you have to ask yourself is, Who's better? Who would you rather see? Seventh game. You have to win it. There's no other game tomorrow. You must win it.

"Those are the kind of things you can never totally get unless you're doing it yourself, unless you're there with the crowd, the noise, the input coming from the pitching coach, the way the pitcher answers when you ask him how he feels...there's so much to ponder. But when a David Price says to you, 'I'm fine, I'm good,' that's it. What do you do? You put David in there and you ride it."

Price struck out the next two batters and obtained a ground ball, sending the Rays to their first World Series. They became the first team to win the American League pennant the year after posting the worst record in baseball.

Eight years later, with the Cubs, in Game 1 of the 2016 NLCS against the Dodgers, Maddon made another risky call with a postseason game on the line. He brought in Aroldis Chapman, his closer, with the bases loaded and no outs in the eighth inning with a 3–1 lead. Chapman struck out two batters before yielding a game-tying single. In the bottom of the inning, knowing Chapman was due up with two on and two out, Roberts ordered an intentional walk. Maddon responded by pulling Chapman for a pinch-hitter, Miguel Montero. On an 0-and-2 count, Montero smashed a grand slam. The Cubs won, 8–4.

"Just imagine, had that broken down and he doesn't hit the home run, all of a sudden the game is tied and there is no Chapman," Maddon says. "What kind of narrative is created over something like that? Outcome bias, boys, outcome bias."

Maddon was an early adopter of the use of computers in baseball. He welcomed analytical input from Friedman in his early days managing the Rays. His comfort with numbers was one of the reasons he had been hired. Back then, Maddon feared instinct in the dugout was irrational. But the more he managed, the more he understood instinct to be "thinking in advance." He began to regard it as deep-rooted knowledge that surfaces as instinct. In the hottest moments of a postseason game, he learned to trust it, not fear it.

"Unless you've actually sat in that dugout in that spot and felt what it feels like, there's no way you could, with any assuredness, say what you would have done in those spots," Maddon says. "I absolutely, positively, unequivocally believe that to be true. You had to have sat there to be able to say that.

"And that's the point I appreciated about my job and why I'm not hypercritical about my peers, my colleagues. People want to beat up on them. A lot of times when they get hammered in the press, I'll text them and assure them I get what they did. I understand why they did it and tell them Good for you for sticking to it. And that's that. I did that with Mickey Callaway, Gabe Kapler, Dave Roberts . . . I would text them and just try to get them to know, Hey, continue to be who you are.

"Somebody had done the same thing for me way back in the day. I'm sitting in my office in St. Petersburg one day and a bottle of wine comes in—a real nice bottle of wine—with a note from Joe Torre welcoming me to the fraternity and saying if I need anything, just give him a call. How about that? Don't think that doesn't make a huge impression."

With Tampa Bay, Maddon trusted Erik Neander as a reliable source of targeted information. A native of central New York who had last played baseball in high school, Neander enrolled at Virginia Tech in 2001 to study engineering. But after three semesters he changed his major to the science of food, nutrition, and exercise. He wanted to work in medical or athletic training. Upon graduating in December 2005, he was hired at Baseball Info Solutions, a company that supplies statistical data to many major league teams. In 2007 the Rays hired him as an intern in their baseball operations department, the start of a meteoric rise in the organization. Neander was hired to a full-time entry-level job in baseball ops in 2008, then promoted to research and development manager in 2009, director of baseball operations in 2012, general manager in 2016, and senior vice president of baseball operations in 2018.

Maddon would use Neander to test and challenge his observations. For instance, when Rays pitcher Erik Bedard was struggling early in the 2014 season, Maddon emailed Neander:

> Can we do some work on how often and in what counts he was very successful with Baltimore?…He loves his change and FB and I believe he needs to be less predictable and pitch backwards more….Would love to see first pitch curve strikes, behind in count curve strike or change….Bury the curve with 2 strikes when appropriate…and save FB for proper moments….Think it is time to either re-invent himself, or live in the past.…
>
> This is what i think i saw regarding the curve.…i believe for him to be very successful he should throw it more often.…Is this something we can dig up….Would love for him and the catchers to know how to approach Yankees.

Maddon also gave Neander a list of situations from the previous night in which he had given the green light to a hitter on 3-and-0 counts,

THE BOOK OF JOE

including one time when Evan Longoria took the pitch and eventually struck out.

Neander responded:

> The K was better than a ground into double play with Longo v Cueto. Just saying. Love that you are keeping notes on 3-0. Keep them coming and let's all continue to discuss.
>
> Got it on Bedard. We will do a ton of work to think through the best way(s) for him to have success.

Neander added later that night:

> Based on the work we've done on Bedard so far, while his velo is down about 1 mph, the one thing that checks me up on recommending any changes to his approach is that we had him as the 23rd most valuable SP in the AL last year; very comparable to Arch and Cobb. He just happened to play in front of an incredibly terrible defense. His usage/approach was very similar to what he's shown us so far.
>
> That said, his CB was still his best pitch last year, especially when he was even or behind in the count, so I think recommending more CBs is very justifiable as long as his arm can take it. Again, will share more info with you asap, likely tomorrow.

Says Maddon, "The information I got from the Rays was very good. Always very good."

Front offices don't typically outright tell a manager what to do. They present evidence that creates preferred strategies. In the blink moments of a game, a manager's choice is to follow the preferred strategy or to defy it by recalculating the situation based on real-time evidence.

"When you've got a pitcher that's not necessarily an established guy, those execs upstairs, when it gets third time through, they cannot be more antsy," Maddon says. "They're fidgety. They cannot wait until the manager gets to the bullpen. And I promise you, it's true. If they don't, they'll hear about it.

"I'm telling you, that's exactly how this works. I'm thinking, *Hey, we might get another inning out of him. I think we can. I think he's throwing that well. They're not getting good swings.* Why would I take him out? Why? Alec Mills in Chicago is a perfect example of a guy that would be absolutely out of the game the third time through.

"I ran into that issue with Jeremy Hellickson in Tampa. But Helly deserved it. Helly got to the point where he would not want to throw the ball to the plate, build up a big pitch count, and then it would get guys on base and one swing and it's a bad moment. There are certain guys that have earned the right to really be careful with the third time through."

Hellickson, who debuted in 2010 with the Rays, proved time and again he was one of those guys with a quick expiration date in a game. In his career he held batters to a .679 OPS—a measurement of on-base percentage plus slugging percentage—first time through and a .729 OPS the second time. His mark the third time through soared to .846, the worst third-time-around OPS since he debuted other than Mike Pelfrey (.847).

"Then there are other guys who are trying to become guys that can handle the third time through, and you got to know when that moment arrives," Maddon says. "There's no blanket rule for this. If you see your guy get out easily, lots of bad swings and bad takes, why are you taking him out?

"Then you train the player to believe it's the right thing to do. If you do it often enough, the player thinks it's right and he acquiesces and that's what you got. You got yourself a seventy-five-to-eighty-five-pitch pitcher—four, maybe five innings on a good day, and he's out.

"So on that day, you've got to match up four innings of bullpen. Damn, that's not easy to do often unless you've got yourself a dynamite bullpen with a bunch of guys you trust when the game is even or you're ahead. It's all part of it. When you're putting your team together and if that's the approach you want to take, yeah, I'd spend a lot of money on a bullpen. I would pay closers to pitch in the seventh and eighth inning. Absolutely I would. If your starters are only able to go five because that's what you nurtured, you better find those dudes."

In 2021, managers made 3.4 pitching changes per game, almost double the rate in 1986 (1.8), when Mauch was running the Angels. From 2005 to 2021, starting pitchers' workloads dropped from 67 percent of all innings to 57 percent. The 2021 postseason was a showcase for the decline of starting pitchers. It turned upside down the traditional structure of the game. Relief pitchers threw more innings (55 percent) than starters.

"And that's part of the game that really has a large disconnect to how the math is ruling over experience," Maddon says. "I love math *incorporated* with experience. You should not have math void of experience. You should not have experience void of math. There's a balance to be had.

"When I talked to my managerial brethren, it was rare to find a manager that said, 'I love the way my analytics guy does it. I love the fact they don't interfere. I love the fact they let me make my lineup and they don't tell me who to put in the game or when.' I didn't hear that very often because a lot of guys confided in me. That's not what I heard.

"More often, the execs want to be involved, and it's not based on experience. It's based on numbers and math. And you know what? For the most part, I would say ninety percent of the time, the manager would have come to the same conclusion that the math wants him to do. But it's one of those things where you felt constantly interfered with."

Maddon remembered one time when an opposing manager handed him a lineup showing one of his bench players oddly hitting third that day. The look on the manager's face told him the lineup was the result of front-office input based on the matchup. Many front offices are being truthful when they say they do not make out the lineup. Influence is another matter.

"The man with the largest stick matters. I get it," Maddon says, referring to front offices wielding more power than managers. "And I'm totally into it because I've been the advocate to coaches in my generation, saying, 'Listen, you'd better attempt to stop and listen and understand how this works because if you don't, you're going to become unemployable.' If you fail to remain contemporary, you become unemployable.

"That leads to a good question: What is contemporary right now? What is contemporary baseball? From the front-office perspective, is that eighty percent math, twenty percent experience? Seventy-five–twenty-five? What is contemporary right now?

"When I first started with the Rays with this with Andrew, I thought it was pretty much fifty-fifty. And sometimes sixty-forty in my favor. He was great at listening. He's one of the best young scouts I've ever met, so what you're seeing with the Dodgers is no surprise. He's real good.

"But what is the contemporary flow of things right now? Who is in charge and how much responsibility goes to the front office and everybody associated with that? How much responsibility should go to the manager and the coaches, really?"

In his back pocket Maddon managed a game with a lineup card "dripping with numbers." Yet he thought of his experience—the art of reading the moment—as another tool that could be just as valuable. When Maddon was introduced as manager of the Angels on October 30, 2019, he held forth with a forty-minute graduate-level lecture on his roots in the Angels organization and a philosophical tension that exists in the game.

"Data versus art," he said. "That's what it came down to for me."

Data guides strategy. Art is belief in the human element, or, as Maddon told his teams, "Never forget the heartbeat." In his Angels introduction he emphasized the balance of data versus art, not the tension.

"You can use both of these things to your advantage," Maddon said. "You should never, ever disassociate one or the other. To just be all analytically inclined or heartbeat inclined, you are going to lose. You are not going to be the best version of yourself. You are not."

CHAPTER 12

"Don't Interfere with Greatness"

Before there were the 2008 Tampa Bay Rays and before there were the 2016 Chicago Cubs, there were the 1982 Salem Angels, the original Cinderella story authored by Joe Maddon. Playing in the Northwest League, a rookie league, Salem finished the regular season 34-36, which was good enough to win the North Division and a date in the championship series against the mighty Medford A's, who not only won the South Division but also had the best record in professional baseball (53-17).

The Angels were the youngest team in the league, with an average age of 20.0. Populated with more former college players, the A's were the oldest at 21.6. Medford led the league in hitting and had been shut out once in seventy games. Maddon prepared his team for the best-of-three series by resting most of his starters in the regular season finale. The Angels absorbed a 15–5 loss to Bellingham in which his pitchers walked eleven batters and hit two more.

"We'll just see what happens," said Maddon, then twenty-eight and in his second year managing in the minors. "I think we can beat them in spite of our record, in spite of everything that's happened, and in spite of what everyone thinks."

In Game 1 at Salem, Maddon gave the ball to Kirk McCaskill, a twenty-one-year-old right-hander who had been a baseball and hockey star at the University of Vermont. Al Goldis, the Angels' scouting supervisor, had seen McCaskill pitch at Vermont and turned in an enthusiastic report. Goldis, forty years old at the time, had learned the tricks of the scouting trade from Nick Kamzic, the veteran scout who was born in 1918 and had signed Maddon. Kamzic was one tough, battle-tested scout. He would drive fifty thousand miles a year to see ballplayers, all the while selling car wax or shoes or working in factories to supplement his meager scout's income. From Kamzic, Goldis learned how to scout players. It was not just about the physical tools. Goldis paid particular attention to a prospect's self-esteem.

Goldis's favorite line when it came to scouting players was, "When the cat looks in the mirror, he sees a lion." McCaskill passed muster.

Just before the June draft, McCaskill was pitching in a beer league game at Phoenix College. Goldis wanted a second opinion on McCaskill. He asked Maddon, whose scouting territory included Arizona, to see him there.

"I go there and see a low-nineties fastball with a nasty, nasty curveball," Maddon says. "Wow. So of course I'm on board."

The Angels drafted McCaskill in the fourth round. They offered him two contract options. One option would allow McCaskill to max out the bonus money by giving up hockey. His other option was to take less money and continue playing both sports. McCaskill took the second option. The Angels sent McCaskill to Salem. He made eleven starts in which he was 5-5 and averaged six innings per start.

McCaskill found himself locked in a pitcher's duel against Medford. The Angels scored a run in the second inning on a wild pitch. No other runs scored. No others were needed for Salem. The Angels won, 1–0. Maddon let McCaskill throw a complete game. McCaskill allowed only two hits, both ground-ball singles that were the only balls hit out of the infield against him. He walked none and struck out twelve.

Today a minor league manager might be making a fireable offense by allowing a twenty-one-year-old pitcher in his first pro season to throw a complete game with twelve strikeouts. McCaskill retired the last fourteen batters he faced.

"I usually start to lose it by the fourth or fifth," McCaskill said that night. "But I didn't tonight. I don't know why. I guess I was pumped up."

Maddon believed McCaskill could become a better pitcher without artificial boundaries placed on him.

"Rookie ball, first-year guy, from Vermont, hockey guy…and I let him go," Maddon says. "You know what that does to his self-confidence? That's why I say, 'Don't interfere with genius' and 'Don't interfere with greatness.'"

"You don't know what someone is capable of when you start putting restrictions on people based on what you think. You think if you let him do this he's going to get hurt? You think if he throws ten extra pitches tonight he's going to go on the injured list?

"Wow. That's the kind of thinking that really bothers me. Not a little bit. A lot. When guys get hung up on that pitch-count number, it bothers me a lot."

McCaskill made his major league debut three years later. He pitched twelve years in the big leagues.

The night after McCaskill's two-hit shutout, Maddon gave the ball in Game 2 at Medford to Urbano Lugo, a first-year pro out of Venezuela who had just turned twenty. Lugo also threw a complete game, beating Medford 6–0 with a five-hitter to clinch the Northwest League championship. Lugo would pitch six years in the major leagues.

Ringo Starr once said there was no thrill for the Beatles quite like the release of their first album, *Please Please Me*, in 1963. The bandmates would stop the car whenever they heard a track play on the radio and have a celebratory dinner whenever a track rose on the charts. This was before worldwide fame and before the screaming grew so loud at their gigs that they could not hear themselves play. The simple joy of their first success was incomparable. And so it was for Maddon in Salem, Oregon, in the summer of 1982. Maddon would go on to win many more games and bigger championships, but none held the same sweetness as the Northwest League championship, clinched with 1,835 people in the stands at Miles Field in Medford, Oregon.

Maddon and the Angels repaired to the Rodeway Inn in Medford to celebrate.

"We did not go to sleep that night," Maddon says. "There was like all kinds of nonsense at the pool, guys jumping in the pool. I'm in the pool. A lot of adult beverages."

Whatever beer and cheap champagne remained were consumed for breakfast the next morning on the four-hour bus ride back to Salem. When the bus pulled in to Chemeketa Field, seventy-five people were there to greet their unlikely champions. The gathering included local news reporters. As McCaskill was about to step off the bus, Maddon stopped him and handed him his sunglasses.

"Here. Wear these," Maddon said. "You cannot go out there looking like that, brother."

Says Maddon, "He definitely had those stayed-up-drinking-all-night eyeballs and probably some wrinkles from being in the swimming pool most of the night.

"We get off the bus and are greeted as Northwest League champions by two cameras, maybe. And I'm telling you what, it's all relative. That was the greatest feeling in the world in my life up until then. And still one of the highlights of my managing career, taking a team that was 34 and 36 and giving up no runs to this juggernaut of a Medford team, beating them two in a row. Really, really cool stuff. Lesson learned there. You're never out of it. You're never out of it."

Maddon was named Northwest League manager of the year. Salem's *Statesman Journal* saluted him by writing, "His easy-going manner and rapport with players and fans made him a crowd favorite."

"I want to come back here," said Maddon, who would get his wish. "I'm in no hurry to move up yet. I need to get three or four years of experience."

Including the playoff starts by McCaskill and Lugo, Maddon's rookie league team threw eleven complete games, more than any major league team in any season from 2016 through 2021.

"When I ran the minor league teams," Maddon says, "I was a big proponent that if you could get a kid through a complete game, it would almost always catapult him. Almost one hundred percent of the time."

Bob Kipper also pitched for Maddon on the 1982 Salem Angels. He was a first-round draft pick who had reported straight out of high school in Illinois. Kipper made thirteen starts, including one complete game, and averaged 5.9 innings per start. In his fourth start, one week after he turned eighteen years old, on twenty-five-cent beer night at Chemeketa Field, Kipper threw 145 pitches before Maddon removed him with two outs in the ninth inning of a 9–2 win. Kipper pitched eight years in the majors.

In 2019, the Pittsburgh Pirates also drafted a high school pitcher in the first round out of an Illinois high school, Quinn Priester. In his first year in pro ball, Priester made eight starts, averaged 4.1 innings per start, and never threw more than thirty-eight pitches. The baseball industry puts governors on young pitchers to guard against overuse injuries, then puts governors on them in the big leagues based on analytics such as the third-time-around heuristic.

Braves pitcher Ian Anderson, for instance, was the third overall pick in 2016 out of high school in Clifton Park, New York. He reached the major leagues in 2020 without ever throwing eight innings in eighty minor league starts. He threw one hundred or more pitches only nine times in his first 122 professional games through 2021, with a high of 110.

In Game 3 of the 2021 World Series, Atlanta manager Brian Snitker pulled Anderson after five innings and just seventy-six pitches with a no-hitter intact. Snitker had so many good options in his bullpen that he was eager to get to them. As training methods have improved, the universe of pitchers who throw hard has expanded. The population increase in hard-to-hit power-throwing relievers permits teams to maintain and even expand the governors on starting pitchers. Snitker, a baseball lifer who was born a year after Maddon, in 1955, admitted his decision to remove Anderson reflected the recent changes in the game.

"The me of old, probably a couple of years ago, would be, 'How the hell am I doing this?' quite honestly," Snitker said after the game. "But the pitch count was such that he wasn't going nine innings. So it wasn't about that.

"It could have backfired, I guess. I just thought at that point in time, in a game of this magnitude and all, that he had done his job. And we had a bullpen that all the guys we use had two days off, and they were only going to pitch an inning apiece, and that made them available for the next two games after if it went south."

Snitker also mentioned a factor in his decision was that the Houston lineup was turning over for a third time against Anderson. How long could Anderson have flirted with a World Series no-hitter? Could Blake Snell have pitched a legendary World Series game? The modern game does not allow such questions to be answered. Probability and all those hard-throwing relievers have curtailed what starting pitchers are permitted to do.

"Don't interfere with greatness," Maddon says. "One time with the Rays, Edwin Jackson threw a no-hitter against us with one hundred and forty-nine pitches. I think his manager, A. J. Hinch, got in some trouble for that. But you've got to let the guy go, man. Sorry, new wave thinking, you've got to let the guy go.

"Never interfere with the player's potential to be great. Never. I get it. I know there are times you've got to be smart and pull the plug. I get it. But in moments that apply to greatness, you really try to stay out of the way.

"Javy Báez is a perfect example of that. I recognized that early on with Javy, not to interfere with this man's genius and his potential greatness because he was just that good. He would make mistakes, aggressive mistakes. He didn't have the experience yet to know when to keep going or throttle back, whether it's on the bases, trying to hit a home run, when a base hit to right field would have been fine, making the throw when there's no play, whether it's from in the hole or cutoff, the relay, all this stuff.

"But there's a genius about him. When you coach or manage a guy like that, you do have to create a higher level of discipline and decision-making, but if you ever interfered with the genius of an instinctive player, I don't care what the sport is, shame on you. That to me is the most fireable offense, when guys do that stuff, and I've seen it."

The historic 2021 season of Shohei Ohtani is a testament to not interfering with greatness. Ohtani signed with the Angels in December of 2017 because he wanted to try his skills as a pitcher and a designated hitter in the majors. No one had successfully pulled off such full-time duty since Babe Ruth. The Angels proceeded with caution. They used complex data to monitor his energy level, sleep, soreness, and nutrition—right down to tracking how many times he dove back to first base on a pick-off attempt—to decide when he should play and when he needed a day off. A deviation of as little as 5 percent in his energy level would cause the Angels to issue a "yellow light" of caution on his use. In the name of proactive "load management," Ohtani typically did not hit the day he pitched, or the day before or the day after. Ohtani won the American League Rookie of the Year Award in 2018 but played in only 104 games and blew out his elbow. The next season, 2019, he was troubled by a chronic knee condition that required off-season surgery. His slugging percentage dropped 59 points.

When Ohtani returned to the mound in 2020, his left knee was not fully recovered. He started slowly. Maddon, new to the Angels, was getting his first extended look at Ohtani in summer camp after the pandemic had delayed the season.

After Ohtani pitched twice, Maddon said, "I think the way to get the best out of this guy is to not baby him. Because I really see him as an overanalyzer. He thinks too much, and it's understandable. He's always being videoed. The attention he garners is just incredible. I'd love for him to make sure he gets out of his own head and just plays the game. He's so good. He doesn't need to overthink anything. So that's my first impression.

"Right now, the way he's pitching is very reminiscent [of] when I first saw Yu Darvish with the Cubs. He's very careful, trying to not make mistakes, pitching around the zone, trying to trick everybody. I'd like him to be less careful and not think so much. I'd like every baseball player to be that guy."

Ohtani made his 2020 pitching debut against Oakland on July 26. He was so bad that Maddon had to pull him after he did not retire any of the first six batters. Maddon saw a great athlete who needed to be unlocked.

"Ohtani right now is way off in all facets of the game," Maddon said two days after the start. "Not only was his stuff way down, he was not throwing strikes. Right now, it's a very passive mindset. I'm starting to wonder if all the publicity is getting to him a little bit, even though he's been on that train ride since the beginning. I don't know if that's bothering him because at the plate he looks awful, too. There's no refuge for him right now.

"In my opinion the solution to all this is let him play. Just let him go. Let him play the field, let him pitch, don't be restrictive, let him be a baseball player because when he's not, his mind has way too much stuff to think about. And I do believe that might be getting in the way. That's my impression.

"Since he's been here, he's been handled with kid gloves. I was thinking about that and the Joba Chamberlain rules from years ago when he was with the Yankees and how he was so restricted in the beginning. If you need to be restrictive, do you need to be vocal? Is this because there's so many methods of information now and the people are clamoring for it that we deem it to be wise to give it to them?"

Maddon spoke to his general manager, Billy Eppler, about loosening the governors on Ohtani. He asked Eppler if Ohtani could also bat when he pitched—essentially playing by National League rules, without a designated hitter.

"I think he needs more rather than less right now," Maddon said. "I think he needs to be an athlete. I think whatever he can do to prevent him from having idle time to think about everything would be wise right now. That's what I'm seeing. That's what I believe."

On July 28 the Angels faced Seattle left-hander Justus Sheffield. Ohtani was hitting .111 after four games.

"I seriously considered two things: not playing him or put him lower in the batting order," Maddon said before the game. "But both would be an affront, and the last thing I want to do is have him having to explain even more. So sometimes you think you're doing the right thing by making a good baseball decision. And in this situation, the good baseball decision is to stick with the guy that you've called a generational player even though you're pretty certain he can have another tough night. So we will see how it plays out. I hope I'm absolutely wrong."

Ohtani went 1 for 5. The Angels won, 10–2. Five days later, Ohtani was shut down from pitching with a forearm strain. He continued as a DH. His swing was compromised by a lack of full strength in his surgically repaired knee. He hit .190.

Maddon knew the next season for Ohtani, 2021, would have to be played by different rules. The Angels needed a new plan that would not interfere with his greatness. Early in spring training Maddon sat down with Ohtani, his interpreter, Ippei Mizuhara, and new Angels general manager Perry Minasian. All governors were to be removed, Maddon said. No more yellow caution lights.

"It's a very easy method," Maddon told Ohtani. "You are in charge of this. I want your absolute honesty, and in return you will have mine. There are no specific limitations to your pitching and hitting. You are in charge. When you feel like you need rest, you tell us. That's it. It's that simple."

Ohtani agreed. He looked and felt stronger. He told Maddon he would let him know when his legs felt tired, which for Ohtani was the signal that his body needed a break.

"There are no controls," Maddon said. "You own the joystick."

Freed from limitations, Ohtani put together the most amazing season in baseball history. He became the first player with forty-six homers, twenty-six stolen bases, and the most triples in the league. On the mound he went 9-2 with a 3.18 ERA in twenty-three starts. He was named Most Valuable Player. Not once did Ohtani say his legs were so tired he needed a day off.

"They broke the glass house," Angels coach Mike Gallego says. "They let him go play baseball and not hold him back in any manner. Because of that, he *feels* the game."

Says Maddon, "It was all based on that spring conversation, starting with pitching and hitting in the same game. We first had to work through the mental adhesions where everybody was comfortable.

"Compared to the previous year, it was night and day. In 2020 he was not enjoying himself. He always appeared to be somewhat stressed. This was exactly the opposite in 2021. There is a joy about his game.

"He's got a great sense of humor and is always laughing and joking easily. The guys on the team love him. They really appreciate his abilities. But it's also because he is so respectful and humble. He does it in the right way. He's easy to like. Nothing about him is contrived. He's got that high-pitched giggle, and whenever you hear it, everything is right with the world."

Ohtani ranks among players Maddon calls "baseball geniuses," an honor reserved for players who see the game at a different level. Mike Trout, Ohtani's teammate, is another one of those baseball geniuses. It is easy to see that the Angels center fielder is an outlier when it comes to raw skills, especially the combination of speed and power that ranks him among the greatest ever to play the game. Through his age-twenty-nine season in 2021, Trout compiled the sixth-most wins above replacement at that age (76.1) and a higher WAR than the *career* totals of 72 percent of the hitters in the Hall of Fame. But as his manager, Maddon found the true genius of Trout is in what motivates the three-time MVP from Millville, New Jersey, even with $524 million in guaranteed contracts.

"I recognize where he comes from matters . . . a lot," Maddon says. "It is so easy for me to identify with this part of him. He has been influenced by growing up in a small town in New Jersey with nurturing parents who he wants to please and he respects in the same manner he did when he was seven years old.

"His entire family and friends are involved in his life, and he will drop anything at any time to be there for them. He has a strong sense of loyalty, sincerity and authenticity. He can't help it. Millville bred it in him. He cannot abandon that even if he tried.

"This speaks to him being the ultimate teammate and clubhouse guy. He is very inquisitive, knowing he doesn't have all the answers. Don't get me wrong, when it comes to our game, he has a very high baseball IQ. When he does seek answers, he is not asking just anyone. He will ask those he respects. Otherwise, he will lay in the weeds and observe until he knows his next move.

"He also has a great sense of humor. He's got a great laugh and a sharp wit. He can be a bit of a practical joker, but not without considering the target. He will play the tape out in advance. If he believes no one will be hurt, he will go for it. Otherwise he will pull back and move on.

"I feel like I've known him forever. He could have grown up on Alter Street in Hazleton. He'd be the guy who still returns to Bellhops for a steak-and-cheese hoagie on Italian bread with a mix of hot and mild peppers. He is all of that."

Another Angels center fielder, the former All-Star Jim Edmonds, ranks among the baseball geniuses Maddon has coached or managed. Edmonds was a seventh-round draft pick by the Angels in 1988 out of Diamond Bar High School in California. He hit one home run in his first two years in pro ball in the late 1980s. He went on to hit 393 home runs and win eight Gold Gloves over a seventeen-year major league career.

"The thing I loved about Jimmy, you never saw his first step in the outfield," Maddon says. "He was already on the move. To me that's genius. He swears he could see the catcher's signs from center field. He actually knows what pitch is being thrown. On the bases and on the bench, him and Eddie Pérez were the best I saw at picking something up if the pitcher was tipping. Jimmy had that innate instinct and genius for the game."

In August of 1998, the Angels were flying to New York to play a five-game series against a loaded Yankees team that would win a record 125 games, postseason included. Preston Gómez, a former player, manager, and coach who served as a consultant, was sitting next to Maddon on the plane.

"Hey, you better talk to your boy," Gómez said. "We need him in this series."

Maddon knew exactly who he was talking about. As soon as the Angels checked into their hotel rooms, Maddon called Edmonds into his room.

"Quite frankly, this is a pretty big series and we need you," Maddon told Edmonds. "I know you have an on-and-off switch. I'd prefer it being a dimmer switch, but you have an on-and-off switch, and right now, we need you to put that bitch on straight up. Just flip that bitch on."

Edmonds didn't deny he had an on-and-off switch. He nodded at Maddon and told him, "I got you. I understand."

In the next five games at Yankee Stadium, Edmonds was 8 for 17 with two homers, a double, and several outstanding catches in the outfield. The Angels took three of the five games, becoming the first road team to win a series at Yankee Stadium that year.

"He played his ass off," Maddon says. "He turned it on. He turned it on, and that's my boy. With Jimmy, honestly, weirdly, he was that good at this game just naturally. So I don't want to say he got bored at times, but he needed to be challenged in order to really get the most out of him.

"So maybe that was inadvertently a challenge. I mean, that was not my intention. My intention was to do something that Preston recognized and make sure I didn't let Preston down.

"Jimmy is a unique young man, but among all baseball players I've ever had, he's a genius. Even his slides, the way he could avoid a tag, were genius. Like Javy."

Former Angels and Cardinals shortstop David Eckstein was another baseball genius to Maddon. It wasn't because of his physical tools. The undersize Eckstein was known among scouts as Just Enough because his hitting, throwing, and running were just enough to keep a major league job.

"The thing I loved about David was the communication between us," Maddon says. "I was the bench coach working with the defense. The middle infielder's attention has to be greater than any corner guy. Anybody who plays in the middle of the field: center fielder, middle infielder, catcher. That's what the great scout Gene Thompson taught me from scouting. 'Whenever you go to a ball game, the first thing you look at every time, I don't care whether it's high school, junior college, or college, first thing, you look straight up the middle. You look up the middle, and that's the first place in the ballpark you scout.'

"Eck would look in to me from shortstop. We had talked about something maybe before the game and, again, it was hand signs and gestures. Eck was pretty big on a little head nod. He would see things, and sometimes he was looking for validation or sometimes he might be missing something that I may have been able to pick up on."

Eckstein's awareness and slyness at shortstop reminded Maddon of another genius at the position, Cal Ripken.

"Ripken called pitches from shortstop for many years," Maddon says. "Cal relayed the sign to the catcher to give to the pitcher. I mean, what shortstop has time to do that? What shortstop could process the game in advance in order to do that? That is pure baseball genius.

"I was the first-base coach, and I tried so hard to figure out Ripken's signals. What I saw was he would bite the string of his glove. He would kind of kick his foot right or left like a punter with a low leg, but he wouldn't pick it up in the air, but he would like kick to the right or the left. He would turn his head to the right or left. He would pick his hands up and like hunch his shoulders over his head.

"And again, there had to be a key to the whole thing, and there was a method to transmit the signs. Genius.

"But there are other guys that I think the genius lies in their ability more than in the mental component, the natural movement of their bodies, the tension-free method with which they play, the fact that they've just taken what they had done in Little League or high school and transmitted it to the major leagues.

"I saw Barry Bonds in college at Arizona State. I saw Bonds hit a grand slam one night to dead center when he was a freshman, I think it was against Darrel Akerfelds to the right of the batter's eye in center field. Absolute rocket. The only thing he didn't do well then was throw. And believe it or not, there was a lot of old-time scouts that were concerned about that because they loved all the tools, baby. 'If you're going to pay that kind of dough, the guy better do everything.'

"Another kind: Derek Jeter. I think his genius was in his heart. The guy just competed. Is competing at another level, a Michael Jordan–esque kind of level, is that genius? A combination of ability and competitive nature, what does that equal? Is that another method of genius? I think so.

"And maybe it's God given in a sense that it's pure talent combined with the work ethic or competitive nature that exceeds everybody else. Bill Bradley. What was Bill Bradley? Genius. Why? I read something he once said that he would never permit anyone to outwork him. That was the genius of Bill Bradley."

Others Maddon considers baseball geniuses include Yadier Molina, because of how he runs a game from behind the plate; Kyle Hendricks, because of how he can outthink a hitter; Evan Longoria, because of his grittiness; Ben Zobrist, because of his work ethic; Jason Bartlett, because he was taught so well coming up in the Minnesota Twins system; and Anthony Rizzo, because of how he makes adjustments at the plate and because his acumen at first base permits a manager to play aggressively with bunt defenses.

On normal bunt situations with runners at first and second, the pitcher will shade toward covering the third-base side while the first baseman covers the first base side. But Rizzo suggested to Maddon that the pitcher should loop behind him, toward first base, while he fielded bunts in the middle or third-base side.

"So that just permitted him to be more aggressive coming across the middle in front of the pitcher's mound," Maddon says. "The one problem with that is pitchers haven't been doing that. And it's hard for them to think in the moment to do that because naturally, they're going to want to break to the third-base line, but Anthony came up with that thought. Genius."

For genius to flourish, a great leader creates an atmosphere where such dialogue in the unit or team is unencumbered. The word *dialogue* comes from the Greek words *dia* (through) and *logos* (word or meaning). Dialogue is "a flow of meaning." It is not two sides—that is a debate, a lecture, or an argument—but a shared center. It was only because Maddon fostered dialogue with his players that Rizzo was empowered to create a new bunt defense and share it with his manager. That is flow.

"A big part of genius is the permission to be a genius," Maddon says. "When you get people interfering with your mental flow, your ability to think and create, when you feel as though you have no, for lack of a better term, power to be creative or come up with your own thoughts, you won't do it. You won't do it. Coaches won't do it. Managers won't do it. Players definitely won't do it.

"But if a player feels open and that he's going to be heard and listened to, that's where genius can flourish and that's where greatness occurs. So again, I'm not patting myself on the back. I'm just telling you a lot of guys I've worked with could arrive at that point because I never interfered with their genius. I never wanted to get in the way of them being great. I think our game for many years would prohibit that, and guys would be afraid to take chances, do different things."

One night during Tampa Bay's run through the 2008 playoffs, Fernando Perez, a Rays rookie outfielder from Columbia University, shouted during a game, "We err on the side of aggressiveness!"

"Oh my God, did I fall in love with that," Maddon says. "'We err on the side of aggressiveness.' How incredibly cool is that? But again, a player won't say that out loud—a player won't even go to that thought—if he doesn't feel like he can. If he's restricted, he won't do it. If there are no restrictor plates, no governors on him, then he has a chance to do that.

"That's what I think. If I've done anything right or well, where some of the things I did come into dispute, I think what I've done or permitted is not getting in the way of greatness, not getting in the way of genius—letting it flourish.

"When you are heavy-handed as a teacher or coach, you will prevent that from occurring. Not intentionally. I think a lot of times people who are working from that end, they are working from good intentions. Not necessarily pure intentions, but good intentions because they think that's the way it's got to be based on what they've been told growing up. But again: tell me what you think, not what you've heard. Because the worst reason to do anything is because that's the way it was done before."

The third-time-around heuristic is the restrictor plate of starting pitchers. It gets in the way of their greatness. Between them, Greg Maddux and David Wells pitched forty-four seasons and won 594 games. One day in 2007, as teammates with the San Diego Padres, Maddux and Wells were in the clubhouse telling stories to young pitchers about how often they had thrown complete games in the minor leagues. Maddux had thrown nine complete games in the minors one season when he was twenty years old. Wells had thrown five complete games at the same age in the minors. The young pitchers looked at Maddux and Wells as if they were Walter Johnson and Carl Hubbell, relics from an ancient era. In 2019 the entire Cubs minor league system threw four complete games out of 882 combined starts.

On the night of June 21, 2015, Maddon gave the ball to Jake Arrieta, a talented power pitcher for the Cubs whose career record in the big leagues, 40-37 with a 4.34 ERA, did not match the quality of his stuff.

Arrieta had spent his first eight seasons of pro baseball in the Baltimore Orioles system. He often clashed with pitching coaches and organizational philosophy about pitching mechanics and strategy. In the worst of those turbulent times, in 2013, the Orioles demoted Arrieta to Triple A just two starts after he was the team's Opening Day pitcher. He was twenty-seven years old, owned the worst ERA in franchise history of any pitcher who had made at least sixty starts (5.46), and found himself stuck in Norfolk, Virginia, for two months with his wife and infant son. He thought about quitting and going back to Texas Christian University to finish his degree in communications.

That's when the Cubs rescued him. They traded for Arrieta. Buoyed by the change of scenery and encouraged by Chicago pitching coach Chris Bosio to return to his natural cross-fire delivery, Arrieta began developing into a valuable starting pitcher.

On that night in 2015 in Minnesota, Arrieta was 6-5 with a 3.40 ERA through his first thirteen starts of the season. He had been good, but on this night he was great. The game was a pitchers' duel through seven innings. The Cubs held a 2–0 lead until they blew open the game with six runs in the top of the eighth.

Arrieta had thrown ninety-two pitches to that point. With the Cubs holding an 8–0 lead with six outs to go, the rote move in today's game would have been to remove Arrieta rather than "waste" more pitches from him in a one-sided game. Maddon sent Arrieta back for the eighth. Arrieta threw eighteen more pitches in another shutout inning. Maddon sent him back for the ninth with 110 pitches. Arrieta pitched a one-two-three ninth with another twelve pitches, finishing a four-hit, no-walk shutout.

Cubs president Theo Epstein could not believe it. He was angry. How could Maddon allow his starting pitcher to run up 122 pitches with an 8–0 lead? He called out Maddon for being cavalier.

"He couldn't understand why I would let him go all the way," Maddon says. "I explained it to him. I said, 'Theo, let me explain it to you right now.'"

The answer traced all the way to 1982. Maddon told Epstein about the lesson of McCaskill and the 1982 Salem Angels. "Don't interfere with greatness," Maddon told him. He had been banking on the confidence from throwing a shutout, not just seven strong innings, catapulting Arrieta. It did. It began one of the greatest pitching runs of all time. Starting with that game, Arrieta went 16-1 with a 0.86 ERA in twenty starts. When Maddon gave him the ball for a winner-take-all Wild Card Game at Pittsburgh, Arrieta delivered one of the greatest pitching performances in postseason history. Never looking for bullpen help, Arrieta threw what remains the only postseason shutout with no walks and double-digit strikeouts. (He fanned eleven Pirates.) Arrieta won the National League Cy Young Award.

How could any set of data account for what that game did for Arrieta? It could not.

"The proliferation of the bullpen is derived from the proliferation of analytics," Maddon says, "and indicating the third time through is not a good time to leave the starter in. I have known so many good starters on the other team where I'm going, 'Please, please, please take him out third time through.' That's like David Ortiz, where you put the shift on and you're saying, 'Please bunt.' You're doing something that makes the other team happy.

"Those are the kinds of things that if you're sitting upstairs, yes, or if you're playing fantasy baseball, yes, and if you're purely working off percentages and you think by the end of the year it will work out in your favor because it's the large sample size, yes.

"But there is momentum to be attained or lost—momentum individually for the pitcher and momentum for the team. And when you don't win that game because the percentages said to get him out, you lose more than the game."

Maddon wants the data to inform decisions, not to dictate them, and especially not to interfere with greatness. "The disconnect," he says, "happens when math rules over experience." There must be room, he says, to allow players to become the best versions of themselves. As happened with McCaskill and Arrieta, the benefits can accrue beyond the moment. "It's just a big, big part of what we do in baseball, and it's not calculable," Maddon says. "It's definitely not calculable but it's absolutely there. It's *feel*, man."

The English wit and writer G. K. Chesterton more than one hundred years ago defined with his usual cleverness the peril of relying too much on data. Chesterton, the creator of the priest/detective Father Brown, was known as "the prince of paradox," and as a gentle soul who stood six foot four and weighed over twenty stone (about 286 pounds), he was something of a walking paradox himself. Chesterton observed that chess players and mathematicians go mad but poets and creative artists seldom do so. The danger, he explained, lies not in imagination but in logic.

"Science must not impose any philosophy," he wrote, "any more than the telephone must tell us what to say."

CHAPTER 13

"Let the Lead Bulls Run"

Joe Maddon learned a key lesson about leading a baseball team from James A. Michener, by way of Uncle Chuck. It was 1974, when Maddon was a student at Lafayette and devouring novels from writers such as Kurt Vonnegut and Joseph Heller. One day Chuck, one of his father's brothers, told Maddon about Michener and his new novel, *Centennial*.

"You need to read this guy," Uncle Chuck said. "It's a great book."

Says Maddon, "That's where I fell in love with James Michener and could not get enough of him."

Centennial traces the history of a fictional town of that name in the high plains of northeast Colorado. One of the lines from the book Maddon vividly remembers is, "Only the rocks live forever." "Great line," Maddon says. "When you're in your twenties, it doesn't have much meaning. When you're in your sixties, you think about it."

What did resonate immediately with Maddon was Michener's description of how the Native Americans hunted buffalo, their main source of sustenance. The hunters understood each herd tended to follow the lead of a certain alpha buffalo. The hunters would identify that alpha buffalo and chase it so that it was running toward a cliff. The rest of the herd followed. By the time the lead buffalo realized it was approaching a cliff, it was too late to stop. The momentum and weight of the thundering herd carried the buffalo off the cliff and to their demise in a ravine below, where other Native American hunters were waiting with their knives.

"Their food, clothing, and shelter were all attended to just by getting the lead bull running in the right direction," Maddon says. "Brilliant."

The image stuck. Embedded in this method, he decided, was how to be a good leader of a baseball team. Starting in 1999, when he was named interim Angels manager, Maddon annually gathered about ten of the most influential players on his team to decide club policy. This was his Meeting of the Lead Bulls.

"I just tried to use the analogy if I get the lead bulls running in the right direction, they will absolutely monitor the herd and take care of any of our issues that may arise," Maddon says. "Furthermore, they're in charge of the policy making."

That 1999 meeting included veterans such as Mo Vaughn and Tim Salmon.

"I remember I called these guys into the meeting room at Anaheim Stadium right next to Diego's video room," Maddon says. "Nice conference table. Probably ten guys sitting around it. I'm certain I used the line, 'Listen, guys, I'm not into rules, but I want us to create policy here.' Policy is methods and thoughts that aren't so hard and fast that can have latitude attached to it. There is common sense attached to it.

"The point was to create policy among the team, within the team, that is borne of the thoughts of the most influential guys on the team—veteran guys with a nice history, well established, guys that have been around. These are the guys I want to hear from.

"I remember Tim and Mo sitting there, and they probably thought, *What the hell is he doing?* They've never seen anything like that before, I'm certain of it. I mean, *The manager is going to call us in and ask us what we think?* And they think we're going to create rules. But I'm thinking policies. How are we going to act here?

"I said, 'What's important to you guys? Because I'm going to tell you right now what is important to me is going to be so minimal, you're not going to believe it. What's important to me is that you run hard to first base. What's important to me is pitchers work on their defense. What's important to me is that you're in the right position on a cutoff and relay. Pitchers, that you back up bases after a bad pitch. That's what's important to me.'

"Being that I come from the Land of Rules Are Overrated, there has to be things in place. I also know a lot of laws are based on the explanation of 'because it's always been done that way.' To me that is the absolute worst reason to do anything. The worst. Everything else comes in second behind that one as the worst. I hate that reason.

"With my Lead Bulls, I explained the difference between rules and policy. They didn't want anything so hard and fast that later on they couldn't come in and ask for some kind of an extension, some kind of a different interpretation. Happened all the time. So why do you want to establish something so hard and fast that there is no latitude whatsoever? That's called a rule. That's called a law."

With the Rays and Cubs, Maddon would draw up a tentative list of Lead Bulls, who typically numbered between eight and twelve. He would run the list by his coaches, asking for additions or deletions. After getting their input, Maddon would submit the updated version of the list to Andrew Friedman in Tampa Bay or Theo Epstein in Chicago for any of their suggestions. The same process took place with the Angels with GMs Billy Eppler and Perry Minasian. "It was very inclusive," Maddon says.

The Lead Bulls meeting typically occurred in a spring training conference room. Maddon was the moderator. He started by explaining the Lead Bulls' *Centennial* origin story and the philosophy behind it. "And then we went," he says. He worked off a sheet of paper listing topics for the Lead Bulls to decide policy on, including:

CLUBHOUSE ACCESS

" 'It's your clubhouse,' " Maddon says he told them. " 'I want you to understand that. I am not here to legislate your clubhouse. So within that clubhouse, when do you allow kids in there? Do you allow dads in there? Do you allow uncles in there? And if you do, at what time are they allowed in and what time do they have to get out?

" 'And then postgame, how much downtime before anybody is allowed in? Go.'

"And I just sat back. Off that comment or that one thought, others were born of that. I know many managers that would sit there and tell them, 'Well, kids are allowed in. They can show up at two thirty. They have to be out of the clubhouse by four thirty. And your dad, same thing. After the game, you got a half-hour moratorium because you have to respect the guys that both played well and poorly.' And on and on."

ENTOURAGES

"I understand guys wanting to show off the clubhouse—bring in some of their boys in there," Maddon says. "Fine. But they generally make sure it's when nobody else is there. Bring them in real early, then have your boys get out.

"An offshoot of that also would be the parking lot after the game, when they congregate outside, and it makes it more difficult for the players to access. And on top of that, believe me, man, game over, good or bad, you don't want to walk out there, take selfies and autographs for an hour. This is where they've got to rein in their friends.

"Good teammates take care of that. They think of their other guys. And especially stars on the team. They get impacted under the circumstances. And trust me, when you play that often every day, that includes like hotel lobbies and stuff, wow. That's what can wear you out."

PLANE RIDES

One Sunday morning when he was a coach with the Angels, Maddon was leaving the team hotel in Chicago to go to Comiskey Park when he saw one of the Angels players helping his wife and children into a taxi to the airport. It was the last day of a road trip.

"I thought, *Wow, how incongruent is that?*" Maddon says. "How wrong is that where we get to sit on this airplane—and I know we're the team. But being as protective as I am, and these guys are about their brood, I did not like that. That always stuck with me."

As manager, Maddon introduced a new policy: families got to ride on the team plane on the last flight home, one trip per half.

"And that would be something that was up for discussion among the Lead Bulls," Maddon says. "I didn't just say it, although I would have definitely steered the conversation in that direction if there was resistance. Anytime you get one of your real stars having children, all of this stuff becomes a lot easier."

PLAYOFF TRAVEL

"The Lead Bulls would decide on how we travel in the playoffs," Maddon says. "We did it really well with the Cubs. I'm pretty sure it was Dexter Fowler's idea to have two planes so that we could fly out separately— players can stick to their normal patterns getting out to where we're going, and the next day, wives and kids fly out on a separate airplane. And when it's all over, we get a bigger plane, come back together. Wow. Perfect. Could not be more perfect. And it worked really well.

"So that's pretty much it. You talk to the Lead Bulls. You sit down, and we discuss these things. The person that was most interested in it was the traveling secretary, Jeff Ziegler with the Rays and Vijay Tekchandani with the Cubs. Those guys were great. I'm telling you, man, I've been spoiled. Those two guys rock. Vijay took care of me like I was a member of the family. Ziggy was the one that made me laugh."

Maddon once mistakenly sent a text to Ziegler that he'd intended for his wife. It contained content a husband would send only to his wife.

Ziegler texted back, Gee, skip, sounds great, but I think I'll pass.

"Bring that up now and we'd still laugh like a couple of tenth graders," Maddon says.

The Meeting of the Lead Bulls is a departure from how Maddon was raised in the game. Mauch, for instance, insisted that players wear ties on the road. Transgressions were met with a hundred-dollar fine. Pitcher Mike Marshall rebelled against Mauch's dress code on the 1979 Minnesota Twins by wearing the same clip-on tie every trip. Marshall intended the clip-on tie as a mockery of the idea of telling grown men how to dress. Nobody in management complained about his stunt.

"I guess it went over their heads," the pitcher said. "Once again, they were oblivious to the obvious."

Marshall took his protest a step further the next year. He wore leisure suits with the fashionable open collar—no tie. Mauch fined him a hundred dollars after each of the first three flights of the season. Marshall didn't budge. Neither did Mauch. He released Marshall with a year left on his contract.

Another of Maddon's mentors, Larry Himes, believed in strict dress codes. Under the edict of Himes as Angels farm director, Maddon and other minor league managers were charged with enforcing the rule that players were required to show one inch of their stirrups. As general manager of the White Sox in 1987, Himes handed his players a dress code manual. It ran to thirty-two pages. It also was enforced. After games, Himes would check his players to see if anyone was not wearing socks with their street clothes. Violators were fined a hundred dollars on the first offense, two hundred on the second.

"I've never been from the dress-to-impress segment of society," Maddon says. "I much prefer my guys running hard to first base and make good turns as opposed to wearing a tie on an airplane.

"As a manager, you must be strong and know what you believe in so you don't leave your authentic self in an attempt to ameliorate others in tough moments like that. As opposed to making things tighter, my thing has always been to make things looser."

In 2008, the worst-to-first fairy tale of Maddon's Rays was in danger of falling apart in September. After losing a series at home to the New York Yankees, with their first-place lead cut to three and a half games, the young Rays headed on a nine-game trip to Toronto, Boston, and New York. That's when Maddon invented what would become a staple of his teams: the themed road trip. Outfielder Cliff Floyd purchased more than three dozen fashion T-shirts from the artist Ed Hardy, which sold for between $150 and $200 apiece.

Maddon explained why he'd done it: "I told them this was the most important road trip in this franchise's history. I saw it as a way to relate to the guys. Look, I'm fifty-four, but you have to remain contemporary in your thinking. I don't agree that you have to accept and say, 'This is who I am, and I can't go any further, and I can't relate to the next group of guys coming up.' I think that's wrong."

The Rays traveled in their jeans and their trendy Ed Hardy T-shirts.

"The best part of the Ed Hardy road trip that I can still visualize is seventy-seven-year-old Don Zimmer," Maddon says. "Zim is sitting next to me on the airplane, to my right. My seat is in the last seat on the left aisle, first class.

Zim is right across. And here he is with his Ed Hardy T-shirt on, and I mean, his boiler was at its absolute zenith. It was a big league boiler. It had been paid for, nurtured, earned, everything. God, did we love it. The fact that he was game and did that and bought into the team, that stuff is magic."

The Rays went 3-6 on the trip, and with their next loss fell into a virtual tie for first place with Boston, the defending world champions, with fourteen games to play. The Rays rebounded to win nine of those fourteen games and win the AL East by two games.

A tradition was born. Maddon annually organized theme trips, as many as five per year. The *Miami Vice* trip to Miami. A Jimi Hendrix trip to Seattle. Beach Boys to Southern California. *Anchorman* to San Diego. *Urban Cowboy* to Denver, followed by *Midnight Cowboy* to New York. Camouflage, all white, lettermen's sweaters, grunge, Johnny Cash, hockey, football, soccer…the theme trips mostly were big hits, even if the players did not realize the philosophy behind them.

"A lot of guys that ended up having the most fun were guys who at first weren't comfortable," Maddon says. "It's something they would have never done on their own. They would have been too embarrassed. 'No way. I look like a jerk.' All that kind of stuff.

"But put them in this moment, put them in this situation, stretch their mind a little bit, and all of a sudden they had a pretty good time out of it. They start laughing a little bit and don't take themselves so seriously, and they figure out it's pretty cool.

"And I believe this could have an impact with what they're doing on the field because they're not so hesitant, not so self-involved and concerned about what other people are thinking. I think it all plays in. And that's a big part of why I wanted to do that—the opposite effect of the dress code.

"There were guys that did not do it because they didn't consider it professional. Kelly Shoppach with the Rays didn't think it was professional so he wouldn't do it based on that, I'm pretty sure. Kyle Farnsworth might not do it because he's already got his gig going on. He's the perfect guy for all of this because when he was comfortable, he was dressing in his camo walking on that airplane, strutting his stuff, no doubt.

"It's part of the leap from not being confident in yourself to self-confidence and what that means. I know that because I've done that I don't know how many times. Probably the biggest thing for me was public speaking, that I did not want to do it. I mean, it normally ended up well, but it's always the prep and the angst leading into it, the travel, all the different things you have to do to do that. It's uncomfortable. It's scary.

"The longer you live in your comfort zone, the more difficult it is to be as successful as you like. Feel the fear, and do it anyway."

In 2020, after Maddon rejoined the Angels as manager, he held his Lead Bulls meeting over Zoom after the pandemic put the season on hold. Eppler joined the meeting because MLB safety protocols trumped policy decided by players. The clubhouse, for instance, was closed to anyone outside of team personnel. Maddon used the occasion to engage the players in a discussion about what the team's identity would be. The result was a collaboration with his Lead Bulls on the team they wanted to be. Maddon took their ideas and commissioned an artist to create an "Identity Wall" in the Angels' clubhouse. "What better way to reinforce your culture than putting it on the wall where you have to walk by it every day?" Maddon says. The artwork included:

- "Flying High with the Angels at Wrigley Field," an old logo from the Pacific Coast League, because Maddon digs history.
- Maddon's trademark eyeglasses with "2020" in the lenses. "I wanted something to indicate the year," he says.
- "Dominate K2." It refers to winning two-strike counts. "Whoever dominates the two-strike counts wins, both on offense and defense, especially when it comes to full counts," he says.
- "Pound The Zone." The 2019 Angels pitchers yielded the ninth-most walks in MLB. "The big thing is make the other team earn it. You can't catch a walk."
- "We R 1st to 3rd." Running the bases aggressively has long been a Maddon point of emphasis. "Every Instructional League I did, I would talk to the position players [about] how important base-running was for us," he says. "It's a difference maker."

- "Engage." Says Maddon, "That came to mind the day we were doing bunt defense. We were on Field 2 with Brian Butterfield. I don't know how many times he used *engage* on bunt defense. If we are engaged, everything on this wall would be in the present tense and within our grasp on a daily basis."
- "Relentless." Says Maddon, "I love that word. Our 2002 World Series team defined that word on offense."
- "Edge." "There's a level of fearlessness about that," he says. "Courageousness. Individuality. Things that never need to be sanded off. If you play relentless with an edge, people are going to see you coming."
- "*Una Familia.*" "One Family." "Every championship team talks about being *una familia*," he says.
- "Attitude is a Decision." Written in English, Spanish, and Japanese, it is a nod to Ken Ravizza, the late sports psychologist and Maddon's friend. "I had that on my fridge when my kids were growing up," Maddon says. "We always have the ability to change our attitude as we walk in the door."
- "Big Innings" with a red slash through the words. As long ago as 1908, in a publication called *American Physical Education Review*, in an article titled "Baseball Technique," it was written that the winning team usually scores more runs in one inning than the losing team does in the entire game. It is still true. "What's a big inning? For me, it's three runs," Maddon says. "I want to stay away from allowing three or more. Mentally, as a pitching staff and on defense, lock in to prevent the big inning."
- "Tough," with the number six substituted for the *g*. Maddon asked third baseman Anthony Rendon what he wanted the Angels to be. "Tough," said Rendon, who wears number six.
- "Believe It and You'll See It." Maddon drew this concept from Wayne Dyer, the author and motivational speaker. "As opposed to you see it and then you believe in it, which is a reactionary thing," Maddon says.

A group has its hierarchy. In baseball it is typically defined by service time. The better seats on the airplane, the better lockers in the clubhouse, the better parking spots in the players' lot, and such tend to go to the players who have been in the big leagues the longest. That Maddon chose to designate Lead Bulls to define policy and identity was proof that "Everybody is treated the same" is a managerial fallacy.

"I had Mike Trout, Shohei Ohtani, Anthony Rendon," Maddon says. "Superstars. There is more latitude for these guys, not in the sense that you're easier on them or you bend over backward for them. That's not the point. It's that they get more latitude because they might have more demands.

"And the big thing with that is to definitely make sure communication is good, that you do speak to one another comfortably. Not that you have to do it every day, but he can come to you, or you can go to him. I've had some loquacious stars and I've had some that are rather silent, like Jonny Lester, although for Jonny it became easier and easier for him."

Maddon was an Angels coach in 1997 when the team signed Eddie Murray, then forty-one years old and the proud owner of more than three thousand hits and five hundred home runs. Murray struggled. He was hitting .219 and injured in June when the *Los Angeles Times* ran the story "Here's How Murray Can Help Angels." The answer, columnist Mike Downey said, was for Murray to quit. Downey wrote, "Murray's tools are shot." The Angels released Murray two months later.

"Eddie and I would talk a lot, and I liked him," Maddon says. "I've always been a pretty good observer. And one day by the bat rack in the dugout, it just came to me. It was just from watching how people reacted to him, how tough the season was going, and how his talents had diminished. And how we had to answer for him in spite of all the wonderful things he had done. And I just said to Eddie, 'Hey, it's not easy being you, is it?' And he looked at me and cocked his head a little bit, like an acknowledgment. He appreciated that."

Maddon would have similar moments with Albert Pujols as his career with the team withered. Pujols hit .214 over the 2020 and 2021 seasons before the Angels released him. In 2020 Maddon told Pujols about his conversation with Murray.

"The more I sat with this guy, the more I got an appreciation for him," Maddon says. "It goes well beyond the field how he's grown. In one of my conversations with Albert, I just drew the parallel with Eddie. Both are Hall of Famers. Obviously Albert's career is even more substantial than Eddie's, but with all the things that Albert went through—the age he's playing in, the decline in his abilities, and the assault he gets either from the media or sometimes from within—at times he feels contradictory messaging, where people are nice to him but then may not be so nice behind his back.

"That's when I said, 'Listen, brother, it's not easy being you. I get that. But you've got my respect, and I will keep you informed. And at the end of the day, if there's something that from me comes across weirdly or unexpectedly that you need more clarification on, I really want you to call me on it. I would appreciate that.' I said, 'I will try to avoid that, because my job is to be frank and honest with you.' And he will deal with that a lot better than the sweet, warm fuzzies to his face and then the disastrous conversations behind his back.

"This big epiphany came to me watching the games early in 2020. And this is how I operated sometimes. I kind of saw everything. I went out to make a pitching change. When I did that, I asked the infielders always to come to the dirt of the mound so we can talk if we have to or if they had to say something to me or the pitcher. So I went out, and all the guys are circled around the mound, and Albert was at best halfway between the mound and first base. And I'm not saying there's anything malicious about that. All I'm saying is it's not a total buy-in from the point that I promise if he had gotten a couple, three hits, if he was hot, he would have been right there. But I think there's a level of professional embarrassment. He has such pride. And I can only say I think I probably would feel the same way."

Maddon had several long conversations with Pujols.

"Nothing held back," Maddon says. "He was great. He said, 'Play me like you want to.' I promised him I would communicate with him, which I did, but I knew if we were going to get better, it would be without him. Albert is not a vocal leader. He was very liberal with his hitting advice to a lot of young guys, which is great. Whenever he does speak up, he always took the team route, which is outstanding, but he was holding back young players from getting at bats, like Jo Adell, Jared Walsh, and Brandon Marsh.

"He was not a negative voice. That's not it. But to walk in and people feel your presence because of who you are and that you're not that player anymore is tough. And he comes from a different generation with the way to do things, a little bit more serious than my way or what I think is required.

"And on top of that, the aisle had to be absolutely swept clean for Trout to assume the leadership role he needed with the Angels, so he didn't even have to even think in the back of his mind. Mike does a great job of getting out there, but he's used to being cautious in what he says."

Lead Bulls don't just set policy in an annual preseason meeting. Lead Bulls drive the herd all season. They are level-five players—all they want to do is win—who put team above self. They become adjuncts of the manager, if only because some players respond better to peer-to-peer communication than the imbalance of the manager-player power structure. Joe Torre, for instance, was a great communicator as manager of the Yankees, but he also benefited from having Derek Jeter be a level-five player from the moment he stepped on a major league field. Teammates watched not only how Jeter played, especially in the big moments, but also how he carried himself.

"Never before had I seen anything like that," Torre says about how a veteran team relied so heavily on a rookie. "I may have made a comment about a guy or two in the past, but this guy was there every single day to really stand up—not only to stand up to the pressure of being a rookie, but toward the end of the year guys were counting on him to get something started or knock in a run. It was so unusual.

"And the cherry on top was this was New York. You've seen guys melt away from the pressure and expectations in New York. He had a good upbringing. His parents did a wonderful job. They raised him to be ready for this situation."

Says pitcher David Cone, "As veterans, you look for reasons to get on young players to make sure they stay humble. Believe me, we looked for anything to get on Derek about. The way he carried himself, the way he dressed, the way he spoke... and we found nothing. It was truly remarkable how at twenty-one, twenty-two he was so completely ready to be a major leaguer and a star."

When Maddon was hired by the Devil Rays in 2006, he had no such Lead Bulls to influence the herd. The Devil Rays were loaded with level-two players—players concerned with just trying to survive in the major leagues, not winning. That changed in 2008, when the Rays signed free-agent veterans Cliff Floyd, Carlos Peña, and Troy Percival, and in 2009, when they added Gabe Kapler.

"As we morphed into a good team, Carlos Peña, Gabe Kapler, definitely Percival, Cliff Floyd... I would mosey up to them or ask them to come to the office, and I would run something by them," Maddon says. "Or I would ask them to take a message to a particular player or to the group.

"If I thought a player was getting away from what he should be doing or just pissing me off, you call one of those guys in and you talk to them about it and ask if they would do a flyby with the player and just approach them on the subject.

"Gabe Kapler, I thought, was really good at it. I felt really strong about that with Kap, and I'd say, 'Come in the office. Listen, this is what I'm seeing. So-and-so has not been running. Maybe he does not run hard to first base a couple times and we've talked to him. Davey Martinez, one of the coaches, mentioned it to him. Would you do a flyby, make sure that he's well? Make sure he's healthy? From what I understand he is, but could you impress upon him why that's important, as an example?'

"Kap did it in a way that I thought was as good as it got. That's the point where I thought I'd like him to be my bench coach someday and then, from there, maybe a major league manager, which he has become.

"Cliff Floyd just had everybody's attention and respect. He was at the latter end of his career, but there was just something about the way he carried himself.

"Percy was primarily the guy with pitchers, bullpen guys or even starters who were young then, guys like James Shields and Scott Kazmir, and Percy was definitely not shy about saying what was on his mind."

JOE MADDON AND TOM VERDUCCI

When Maddon joined the Cubs in 2015, he quickly found he had several level-five players who could provide peer-to-peer counseling, including Anthony Rizzo, Dexter Fowler, Jon Lester, and David Ross.

"And there was no BS. It was just for real. And that comes with time. It has to be organically grown. And that's why my Lead Bulls meeting at the beginning of the year was so important," Maddon says.

Kris Bryant developed into another Lead Bull with the Cubs during a storybook beginning to his career. Bryant was the 2013 college player of the year, the 2014 minor league player of the year, the 2015 NL Rookie of the Year, the 2016 NL Most Valuable Player, and a world champion. Bryant had so much success so quickly that Maddon wanted to make sure he stayed in the moment rather than chasing the high standards he'd set.

"With KB, it's all about he's got to be supported and it's all about self-confidence regardless of all he's accomplished coming up, maybe *because* of all he's accomplished coming up," Maddon says. "Maybe he always felt a certain level of angst or pressure on him to perform and be perfect. Look at his track record of success. Pretty incredible. When you do it that young, think about it, what do you do for the encore, right?

"I know Mike Trout annually is in the MVP mix, but he's living in the LA Angel fishbowl where KB was living in the Chicago Cub fishbowl. I mean, incredible expectations from the moment he got drafted. So how do I deal with KB? KB loved the phrase 'Never permit the pressure to exceed the pleasure.'

"He and I had a lot of one-on-ones. He would sit in my office, and I would say to him, 'KB, how old are you?' And he'd say twentysomething. I'd go, 'Wow. Do you realize you're one of the best players in the world? On the face of the Earth, you are among the best on the face of the Earth right now at that age.

" 'Do me one favor, KB. I want you to go out there today and enjoy every friggin' second. There's only one thing as a manager I really would ask you to do. Just one thing, and I know you can do it. And that would be to compete. Just go compete. All I want you to do is compete against that pitcher, compete when you're on the bases, compete when you're on defense. That's all I want you to do. Stay in the moment. Don't permit the pressure to exceed the pleasure. Stay right there.' "

Lead Bulls are not always the most talented on the team. Role players Maddon has managed such as Orlando Palmeiro, Jon Jay, and Ben Zobrist stand out as leaders for their unselfishness. Yu Darvish is one of the most talented pitchers Maddon has ever managed, but their time together with the Cubs provided Maddon with a unique lesson about the importance of listening to players.

In February of 2018 the Cubs signed Darvish to a six-year contract worth $126 million. He was a four-time All-Star who had averaged eleven strikeouts per nine innings the previous season but made two poor starts in the World Series for the Dodgers against the Astros. There was speculation that Darvish had been hit so hard because he was tipping his pitches. It also came out two years later that the Astros had been using cameras and a video monitor to steal signs that year.

"From the beginning, he was one of the nicest young men I've ever met," Maddon says. "Tremendous. Looked you right in the eyeballs. Speaks very slowly and clearly. So we get him. He gets this big contract. And there's all this scuttlebutt about the last couple years and particularly in the playoffs, when he got his ass kicked a little bit. As part of the ass kicking, there was a tipping angle to it, and that scarred him pretty good. It may have left him gun-shy about throwing the ball over the plate.

"Now, this guy had great stuff. And he has the ability to manipulate a baseball, as I found out, as good as anybody I've ever been around ever. Ever. Incredible. But when he first came in that door, he was searching. Big contract. Big city. High expectations.

"He's thinking, 'I don't know if I'm tipping my pitches. Does the other team know what I'm throwing? Here's the catcher's sign. OK, I'm going to throw that pitch, but I'm not sure if they know I'm throwing this pitch or not. I really want to throw it for a strike, but should I just miss so even if they know it's coming, they won't hit it?' I totally believe that was part of it.

"And I think the Dodgers did not want him to throw certain pitches. So then his repertoire is culled down, and on top of that, these guys are pretty convinced they know exactly what's happening. Wow. That is not easy. He starts the season and it's not going that good. He gets hurt."

Darvish made only eight starts before he was shut down with a sore arm. His rate of walks, 4.7 per nine innings, was the worst of his career. It took three months for the Cubs to provide a diagnosis: a stress reaction in his right elbow and a strained triceps. In the interim, before the Cubs pinpointed the injury, Maddon grew concerned about Darvish's future as a pitcher.

"I'm sitting with him and I'm trying to figure him out," Maddon says. "He talks to me. He's talking about coming back, when is he going to come back, how is he going to come back, what is it going to take for him to come back... and I just listened. And I was concerned there was more than the injury, right down to the expectations and maybe the different methods of training that were imparted on him with the Cubs versus what he had done in the past. While this is all going on, I'm trying to figure out what can I do to help him.

"You have to maintain contact. He has to know that you actually liked him and believed in him even though he wasn't able to pitch. If he thought you were talking about him behind his back or lost confidence in him, you were done. It would be really hard to recapture that friendship.

"While all this is going on, his son, Shoei, came to the ballpark a lot. This kid, I thought, was outstanding. What a kid. Really athletic. Everybody, I mean everybody, loved this kid. We would be out there taking BP and it would be like thirty-five degrees and he's out there in short sleeves in center field running stuff down, goes out to take a couple hacks. Really good swing.

"Brandon Hyde's son Colton was there. Him and Colton became good friends, and they played Little League together, and Hyder would tell me, 'My God, this kid's good.' But beyond all that athleticism, when you spoke with him, wow, he was a really, really nice kid. He looked you right in the eyeballs. Spoke well. Smiled so easily. Nothing pretentious. Just wonderful.

"So one day, not unlike my moment with Eddie Murray, I walked up to him and I said, 'Yu, let me talk to you a second. I just want you to know, I've been watching you and your son. And I talked to your son, watched him interact with people. I just want you to know the way your kid behaves, he is an absolute reflection on you and your wife and what great parents you are. I just want to commend you on that.'

"He appreciated that. My intent was not to try to sway him to like me. My intent was for him to know that I noticed what a great kid his kid is and how responsible he was for that. If it helped his confidence at all, if it helped my relationship, I'll take it. But I would have said that to anybody, and I did say it to other people with their kids when they show up and how impressed I would be with their kids and how the kids would act and how it reflected upon them as a parent."

Darvish did not pitch again in 2018.

"I thought from what I'd been seeing, and from listening to him, and what was really bothering him, he may be done, and I was prepared for that," Maddon says. "Then he comes to camp in 2019 and he lights it up. He looked great. His body was different. He got real strong looking. He started on a different program. He liked lifting heavier weights. When he came to camp, he was different.

"Here comes the season. He kept building and building, and, all of a sudden, he just starts to take off."

In thirteen starts after July 12, Darvish posted a 2.76 ERA while becoming one of the best strike throwers in baseball. In eighty-one and two-thirds innings he walked only seven batters.

"I've never seen anybody command the slider like him," Maddon says. "Back door to lefties and then straight up to righties. Virtually unhittable. And with that came his confidence and his delivery, and now, all of a sudden, the fastball was a strike when he wanted it to be. And then the part about him that's so unique is his feel for what he does. When he's confident and he's breathing properly, and he feels as though he belongs, that people like him, that he's accepted, wow. We took the wraps off. Tommy Hotovy, the pitching coach, didn't hold him back with regard to the pitches he was throwing.

"It got to the point where he would watch guys. He would watch Kyle Hendricks with his changeup and, all of a sudden, take it to the bullpen before the game, walk out into the game and sure as rain, here comes a two-two count, he drops it on a hitter. Awful swing, strike three. Kyle Hendricks–style changeup.

"Or he would come out of there and Tommy would say his splitter was filthy in the bullpen. Here comes a couple good left-handed hitters. *Wham, wham, wham!* He dropped that split fork on them. No chance. From a baseball perspective, I think what happened is he started to dominate lefties because of the backdoor slider and the split came back into play. His confidence permitted his command, which then permitted his fastball to be thrown for a strike, which then gave hitters difficulty on his breaking ball, and that split was ridiculous.

"So the thing with him, which stands out to me, is something I did with all my guys: listen. A lot of times they will answer their own questions, their own problems. They will answer them to themselves. That's Yu Darvish. Never met anybody like him before. The lesson there is, 'Listen.'"

CHAPTER 14

"Don't Ever Permit the Pressure to Exceed the Pleasure"

The oldest line in managing is that managers are hired to be fired. Or, as Hall of Fame manager Leo Durocher put it, "If you don't win, you're going to be fired. If you do win, you've only put off the day you're going to be fired."

Managing is overwhelmingly a losing, short-term proposition. Baseball Reference lists 828 managers in major league history. Only 273 of them, or about one-third, have a winning record. The median number of games managed in a career is 270—less than two seasons' worth of games until you're done for good. Maddon is an outlier. He is one of only twenty-three managers to last in the job nineteen or more years and win a World Series.

The first manager was a British-born high school dropout, Harry Wright, a cricketer in New York City who fell in love with this new game of baseball. Born in 1835, Wright formed the first professional baseball team, the Cincinnati Red Stockings, in 1869 from former cricket players. They were so good they needed to go on tour to seek good competition. They had a hard time finding it. The Red Stockings went 83-0-1 over two seasons before they lost a game. Wright played center field and pitched. The role of "manager" in the nineteenth century meant not what it does today but was more like that of a captain and business manager.

Early managers often were player-managers like Wright who were valued for their skills as field leaders, instructors, and, in the manner of college basketball coaches, recruiters. They signed and traded players. The running of a game was unimportant because almost no strategy existed. Starting players generally played the whole game, including the pitcher.

As bunting, relief pitching, and pinch-hitting grew in the early years of the twentieth century, the manager also became a strategist. Think five-foot-seven John McGraw of the New York Giants, whose nicknames—Muggsy and Little Napoleon—reflected how he ran a team. Managers picked, traded, fined, and ordered players as they wished.

"With my team I am absolute czar," McGraw said. "I order plays and they obey. If they don't, I fine them."

As strategy increased, more teams hired these "professional managers" rather than allowing a captain-type player to run the show. Managers reached the height of their czarist powers in the early part of the twentieth century. Half the managers in 1919 wound up in the Hall of Fame: Ed Barrow, Clark Griffith, Miller Huggins, Hughie Jennings, Connie Mack, McGraw, Branch Rickey, and Wilbert Robinson.

The scope of the job began to narrow in 1925, when Rickey, relieved of his managerial duties at age forty-three, moved to the St. Louis Cardinals' front office as "business manager," or the equivalent of today's president of baseball operations. Rickey built a system of minor league affiliates to develop players for the major league club. With the rise of player development systems, the responsibility of talent acquisition shifted from the manager to the front office and its network of coaches and scouts.

Rickey was a 1911 graduate of Michigan Law School, where he met and befriended Larry MacPhail, the son of a Michigan banker. MacPhail followed Rickey as the next great influence in shifting some of the manager's power to the front office. From 1934 until he quit in 1937, MacPhail served as general manager of the Cincinnati Reds, long enough to stage the first Major League Baseball game at night, introduce air travel for teams, and, owing to his hard-living ways, get into a fistfight with a police detective in a hotel elevator.

MacPhail dressed the way he drank: noticeably. With Cincinnati and later in similar capacities with the Brooklyn Dodgers and New York Yankees, MacPhail brought showmanship and impetuousness to what had been a staid job. He also seized control of major league player acquisition and movement from managers. When he quit the Reds, for instance, the press marveled at how in 1937 he flew twelve thousand miles and spent more than $100,000 scouring the country for ballplayers. As they had with Rickey's player development model, other general managers followed MacPhail's lead in the 1940s and took more control of putting teams together.

The 1970s saw the next major change to the powers of a manager with the rise of the Major League Baseball Players Association. Free agency, the death of the reserve clause, multiyear contracts, and the right to file grievances empowered players like never before. The 1990s saw a rise in the popularity of coolheaded "players' managers" such as Bruce Bochy, Bobby Cox, and Joe Torre, who eschewed czarist rule for a more empathetic approach. From 1991 through 2014, Bochy, Cox, and Torre accounted for almost one-third of all pennants, fifteen of forty-six.

Over a century of change, one area of control for managers remained sacrosanct: running a game. Teams played baseball the way the manager decided they would play, which to some skippers seemed practically a divine right.

"I believe if God had ever managed," Billy Martin once said, "he would have been very aggressive—the way I manage."

Asked what it took to be a good manager, Alvin Dark replied, "A fellow has to have faith in God above, and Rollie Fingers in the bullpen."

The next reduction in managers' authority came from the growth of analytics, and this time it went straight for that last refuge of absolute power for a manager: how the game is played.

The beginning of the modern shift in such power from the dugout to the front office can be traced to one hire in November of 1995. Oakland Athletics general manager Sandy Alderson needed a manager after Tony La Russa left to take a job with the St. Louis Cardinals. Like Rickey and MacPhail before him, Alderson was a lawyer who looked at the game differently from the baseball establishment, which is to say as an outsider not bound by the game's traditions.

Alderson had served in the marines in Vietnam, was a Dartmouth and Harvard Law School grad, and at age thirty-three in 1980 was practicing law in San Francisco. One of the firm's partners, Roy Eisenhardt, also was a Dartmouth grad who had served in the marines. When Eisenhardt's father-in-law, Walter A. Haas Jr., bought the distressed Oakland A's from owner Charlie Finley in 1980, Eisenhardt became team president. Eisenhardt hired Alderson to be the club's legal counsel. A year later he named Alderson executive vice president of baseball operations, a fancy title then that gave him many of the duties of a general manager.

One of Alderson's first orders of business, in conjunction with Eisenhardt, was to fire Martin after the 1982 season, even though Martin still had three years on his contract and a house the A's had bought him. They simply could not take any more of him.

The phrase "Managers are hired to be fired" was never truer than in the career of Martin. Finley had hired Martin just days before spring training of 1980 began. He was available only because the Yankees had fired him a few months earlier for punching a marshmallow salesman at a Minneapolis hotel. The hard-drinking Martin had become a literal punch line. It was the fifth time out of a record nine occasions that Martin would be fired.

Martin had inherited the worst, dullest team in the history of the Oakland franchise. So bad were the 1979 Oakland A's that one night only about 250 people showed at the Oakland Coliseum to watch them play the Seattle Mariners. Officially, 653 tickets were sold. Catcher Jeff Newman stopped a couple of writers before the game and pleaded, "Do me a favor, will you? Sit in the stands tonight."

The A's averaged only 3,787 tickets sold per game in the fifty-thousand-seat stadium—worst in the league. Finley was running a bare-bones operation while trying to sell the team, first to a group from Denver and then to one from New Orleans before Haas came along. He fired just about everybody in the front office except six people, one of whom was a local teenager named Stanley Burrell, who would go on to bigger fame as the entertainer MC Hammer. The 1979 A's lost 108 games, still the most by the franchise since 1916, when it had played in Philadelphia.

Then Martin arrived and everything changed. It usually did with Martin. He was a tornado on the horizon. You could see trouble coming and knew there would be hell to pay. You just didn't know how soon or how much.

Martin was typical of the smallish, domineering managers raised through the hardships of the Depression who were ready to fight anybody who challenged them or their style of baseball. Martin was born in Berkeley, California, in 1928. His father abandoned the family when he was eight months old, leaving his mother, Jenny Salvini Pesano, to raise him. She later married a nightclub singer. Billy grew up playing sandlot ball and boxing, which honed skills he used throughout his life, especially when he had too much to drink. Nobody was going to tell Martin how to manage a game, not even Finley, the parsimonious and loudmouthed owner of the A's.

"Charlie is the owner and general manager," Martin declared at his introductory news conference. "He's certainly entitled to his say-so, and I'm always open to constructive criticism—off the field.

"But on the field, the game is mine. Charlie and I know exactly where we stand."

With Martin running his game, Oakland improved from fifty-four wins to eighty-three wins in 1980. This happened mainly because Martin, as he would tell it, managed the way God Almighty would have managed—aggressively. The A's finished second in the league in stolen bases and sacrifice hits. They stole home seven times. The rest of the American League combined did so only eight times. So influential was Martin that Oakland built its marketing campaign around him and adopted the eponym of "Billyball" to sell its style of play. Martin had spoken the truth when he said in front of the owner, "The game is mine."

After his initial success, and after Finley sold the team to Haas, Martin lapsed into his usual self-destructive ways. The tornado hit. He destroyed furniture in his office after a loss to Milwaukee in August 1982, apparently in a dispute with the club about a contract extension Martin sought to help cover a debt of $100,000 in back taxes. Alderson and Eisenhardt tired of Martin's rashness in handling players. Martin played favorites and ran off those he disliked. Fed up with Rob Picciolo, Martin traded the infielder and called up from the minors Tony Phillips, who wasn't ready for the big leagues and had to be returned to the minors, while Fred Stanley, a thirty-four-year-old Martin favorite hitting .193 for a second straight year, held down the starting shortstop job.

Alderson and Eisenhardt vowed they needed a more stable manager who would run the team according to the needs of the organization, not his own hard-drinking whims. They fired Martin after a ninety-four-loss season in 1982. They replaced him with the antithesis of Martin: Steve Boros, a genial first-base coach for the Montreal Expos, a University of Michigan man who read history books and classic literature and aspired to be a professor and—*gasp!*—used a computer. Boros brought an Apple II computer into the Athletics' clubhouse and hired a data analyst to record pitch information and input it into a mainframe computer in Philadelphia.

"The first manager we hired was Steve Boros, and we got our list of candidates from a writer," Alderson says. "True story. Back then a national baseball writer would come across a lot of interesting names, which was helpful, especially in 1983, when Roy and I were new to the game."

Boros didn't last two years. He was fired two months into his second season, with the baseball press delighting in the failure of what in the wake of "Billyball" (winning percentage .497) it mockingly called "Computerball" (winning percentage .456). Alderson hired Jackie Moore as what turned out to be a placeholder manager before snapping up La Russa midway through 1986 after the Chicago White Sox fired him after a nine-year run.

Because of La Russa's unquestioned bona fides in the game, Alderson allowed him to run games as he saw fit. La Russa pioneered modern bullpen usage when he developed layers of left- and right-handed relief pitchers to set up his closer, Dennis Eckersley. Under La Russa, the A's won three straight pennants starting in 1988 and one World Series. As the run fizzled, and on the heels of a last-place finish in 1995, La Russa left to manage the Cardinals.

Alderson's next hire was the one that changed modern managing. Alderson always had leaned toward analytics, and now with fifteen years in the game he had the footing and opening to hire his kind of manager: someone who would manage the way the front office wanted, not the way managers had done for a century by putting their own wisdom and observations to work. His next manager would never even think about telling Alderson, "The game is mine."

Alderson considered ten candidates. One of them wanted the job so badly he called Alderson himself looking for it. It had been two years since Art Howe was fired after a thoroughly unremarkable five-year run as manager of the Houston Astros, in which he had never finished higher than third place and had accumulated a losing record. Nobody had called him about another managing job for those two years, during which time he'd scouted for the Los Angeles Dodgers and coached for the Colorado Rockies. Wanting another chance, and knowing the job was open, Howe called Alderson.

He got the job. He was the perfect man for Alderson. When Alderson hired Howe, he made clear why he was hiring him. With these words to Howe in November of 1995, Alderson altered the course of managerial history:

"We're not hiring you for your philosophy. We are hiring you to implement *our* philosophy."

Nothing was implied. Alderson dictated to Howe how it would be, and Howe, needing the job, and having none of Martin's lusts for drink and power, was fine with it. Alderson hadn't said that to Boros or Moore and certainly not to La Russa. But with Howe, Alderson had arrived at a time and place where he could impose the will of the front office on the manager, reversing baseball history when it came to how the game was played.

"Go back to 1986 with Tony La Russa, and we went in a different direction with the hire," Alderson says. "By 1986 we already had hired an analyst to work with material for us. Around 1984–85 we hired Eric Walker to do that. We were already dabbling in analytics, but it was different in those days. There wasn't a lot of data to analyze. It had grown by 1996.

"What I said to Art Howe I would not have said to Tony La Russa, in part because of his résumé and cachet but also in part because of our lack of credentials. When we hired Art Howe, it marked a transition in some ways. Not so much a transition itself as much as it was the culmination of a larger transition."

Two months before Alderson hired Howe, Haas died. The new owners, Stephen Schott and Ken Hofmann, ordered Alderson to slash the payroll. Alderson would have to rely on analytics to find cheap players who were undervalued, such as those with high on-base percentages at a time when batting average retained its traditional value as the coin of the realm. He wanted players to get on base. Whether they could run well, play the kind of "small ball" Martin loved, or make consistent contact was immaterial.

It was easy for Alderson to buck tradition. He was an outsider who had not entered baseball until he was thirty-three. In that way he was like MacPhail, another lawyer who had also served in combat (he rose to the rank of captain in World War I), had dabbled in the business world, and had first entered baseball at age forty when he bought a minor league team in Columbus, Ohio.

Under Howe, and at the direction of Alderson, the A's struck out with abandon and stopped running. The 1996 A's struck out more times than any previous team in the franchise's ninety-six-year history. They dropped from third in the league in stolen bases to next to last. It began a stretch in which Oakland would finish in the bottom five in stolen bases in eleven of twelve seasons. One opposing player said it was easy to defend Oakland in those years because the A's often did not even bother with the theater of signs from the third-base coach, such was their disregard for bunting, running, and playing hit-and-run.

After three losing seasons with Howe and under tighter payroll restraints, Alderson left to take a job with the commissioner's office. His handpicked successor was Billy Beane, a former player he had hired in 1990 to work in the team's player development department. Beane took all of Alderson's philosophies and ran with them. He fielded eight straight winning teams, including the 2002 team that Michael Lewis chronicled in his book *Moneyball: The Art of Winning an Unfair Game*. That 103-win team lost in the first round of the playoffs to a ninety-four-win Minnesota Twins team. In what would become a familiar song he sang as his teams went 1-11 in postseason matchups, Beane said dismissively, "You can't prepare for the playoffs. There's a certain randomness there." Translation: Analytics-based baseball relies on the power of mining truth from large sets of data. A postseason series is its small-sample-size nightmare.

Lewis had visited the Boston Red Sox in the summer of 2002. Boston, Cleveland, and Toronto were among the few teams that relied on data as much as Oakland, if not more so. Unlike Beane and the A's, the Red Sox were not interested in sharing their ideas with the world. One of the bright young minds in the Boston front office who were not happy about the book, which was published in 2003, was Theo Epstein.

"No," Epstein said later. "We heard what he was working on. At the time there were a handful of clubs that were fully bought in. It just seemed like it would take an idea—while not a secret, because Branch Rickey was using a lot of it a half-century ago and Bill James had been writing about it for decades—it would take a nuanced idea and make it mainstream pretty quickly.

"The book hit the *New York Times* bestseller list. People who own baseball teams tend to read the *New York Times* bestseller list. So they read the book and they started asking questions about the processes their front offices were using, and it changed things really quickly.

"We went from a lot of teams who had one stat guy who was marginalized, who was in the front office and contributed ideas but wasn't always listened to...let's just say at the time you had five teams really using it, using data in a sophisticated way, fifteen were using it to a certain degree, and the rest were giving it lip service. Those numbers flipped within five years.

"That was a sea change very quickly in the game. It changed the competitive environment. It forced teams to look for new competitive advantages. It made trades more difficult because teams valued prospects more. It impacted every area of the game. The draft, for example. In the years following *Moneyball*, the industry all of a sudden began to focus disproportionately on college players. So there was an opening for teams that still valued high school players."

The publication of *Moneyball* had another profound effect on baseball: it validated, even glorified, the number sharks who once had been marginalized, if not dismissed, by the baseball establishment. It gave them a seat at the table—and sometimes the chance to sit at the head of the table. Those with no playing experience now saw a path to influence how baseball teams were built and even how they played.

Says Alderson, "I wouldn't describe it as power that the modern front office took from the manager as much as I'd call it influence. People got into the game because they recognized they can have influence. People get involved because they love it. They learn they can have influence without being on top of the organizational chart.

"I think baseball has to embrace the influx of intelligent, curious, motivated minds. The question is, How do we reshape the game so that this kind of influence doesn't influence what the game looks like? Because ultimately baseball is entertainment. There are aspects other than probability and efficiency that make it fun to watch."

One of the many quants inspired by *Moneyball* was a brilliant student in the behavioral economics PhD program at UC Berkeley. The student happened upon a job posting for a baseball operations assistant with the A's, of which one requirement was fluency in four coding languages. More than a thousand people applied for the gig. Farhan Zaidi got it. The salary: $32,000. He is now president of baseball operations for the San Francisco Giants. His team set a franchise record for wins in 2021 with 107.

Fully empowered, and no longer confined to back rooms, next-gen number sharks like Zaidi challenged the conventions of the game, many of which had remained in place for generations out of sheer inertia. Baseball men honored the wisdom of the elders who had taught them the game, who had learned from their elders…and so on all the way back to John McGraw. The sharks asked questions that began with a word few people in baseball had bothered to use before: *Why?* Why are sacrifice bunts, stolen-base attempts, and hit-and-run plays regarded as "smart" baseball? Why is batting average so exalted when it treats a single and a home run equally? Why is the leadoff hitter a smallish, fast guy, even if he doesn't reach base at a premier rate?

From 1979 to 1982, for instance, no player in the major leagues took more plate appearances from the leadoff position than Pittsburgh Pirates center fielder Omar Moreno. Batting order is important because it should optimize a team's ability to score runs (which is why the first inning traditionally is the highest-scoring inning of a game) and because it should get a team's better hitters to the plate more often than its weaker hitters. Over the course of a season, each spot in the batting order is worth fifteen to eighteen more plate appearances than the one below it. That means the leadoff hitter will get almost 150 more plate appearances over the season than the number nine hitter.

Moreno was a bad offensive player. From 1979 to 1982 his adjusted OPS was 80, with 100 being average. Moreno was about 20 percent worse than the average player. Yet the Pittsburgh manager, Chuck Tanner, kept giving Moreno more at bats than anybody else on his team by batting him leadoff. He even won a World Series in 1979 despite it.

The son of a railroad conductor, Tanner grew up in New Castle, Pennsylvania, in a house with no electricity, only a potbellied stove for heat, and an outhouse. The Tanners considered themselves lucky: their outhouse had two holes, not the usual one. As a player Tanner learned his baseball from managers such as Charlie Grimm, who was born in 1898, and Jimmy Dykes, who was born in 1896. Moreno was a leadoff hitter because he was fast and he could steal bases. That was the tradition Tanner had learned from his elders. Moreno *looked* the part rather than *played* the most important part: getting on base. In those years, for instance, by batting Moreno leadoff Tanner gave him 553 more plate appearances than third baseman Bill Madlock, who had an adjusted OPS of 123.

Tanner was not alone in putting a bad hitter at the top of his lineup. In only four of the ten seasons in the 1980s did the leadoff position in the major leagues produce an adjusted OPS better than 100. By the 2010s, when all clubs were applying data to help fill lineup cards, the leadoff spot registered better-than-average production in eight of the ten years.

Data-driven front offices started hacking the game in this way in the late 1990s. As computational power, technology, and the size of analytics departments burgeoned, the game changed. Teams stocked their front offices with their pick of quants like Zaidi with advanced degrees from America's premier institutions, the kind of brainpower that otherwise would be working on PhDs or on Wall Street or in Silicon Valley. They pioneered brutally efficient strategies not unlike a card-counting system in Las Vegas. If everybody was following the numbers, and everybody was, because mathematics allowed little room for creativity, everyone would wind up in the same place. Baseball wasn't a game with a Mauch style and a Weaver style and a Martin style, but a game with one style—a risk-averse game like the one Alderson and Beane cultivated in Oakland.

"Everybody," Maddon says, "reading from the same sheet of music."

Former Atlanta Braves shortstop Jeff Blauser liked to tell the story about one night in the 1990s when he and some teammates went to a bar to unwind after a game. Pitcher Greg Maddux, one of his teammates, was with them. Maddux is the son of a Vegas card dealer who inherited from his father a quick mind when it comes to understanding risk and game theory. The bar had one of those early electronic card games as an amusement.

"Hey, who wants to play?" somebody asked.

"Don't bother," said Maddux, who had just given the machine a quick once-over. "The odds of winning are no good."

"Here we were just looking to have fun and kill time," Blauser said, "and he figures out in the blink of an eye it's not worth it."

Savvy, number-crunching front offices figured out the odds of baseball down to the smallest increments. Quite often, like Maddux sizing up a mindless video game, that effort conspired against anybody who might be in it for the actual fun.

Take Martin, the exciting 1980s A's, and his compulsion for the stolen base as an example. Fans loved Billyball. Attendance shot up 175 percent. Had card-counting analysts run games then, they would have hated it. (Whether they would have deigned to risk the wrath and fists of Billy the Kid by telling him so is another risk-reward proposition altogether.)

Martin's 1980 A's were successful on 68 percent of their stolen-base attempts, only slightly better than the league average of 67 percent. Those percentages are nails across a chalkboard to a front-office quant today. The data miner in baseball hates outs on the basepaths because they severely depreciate the run-scoring potential of an inning and thus reduce the odds of winning the game. Their algorithm includes no accommodation for the paying customers included in the 175 percent attendance increase who were drawn by Martin's team's playing a daring style of baseball. Entertainment value is not measurable, so it does not register with the quant.

Beane likes to say that general managers follow probabilities and risk management like actuaries. As true as that observation may be, so is this: people do not consider actuarial science a spectator sport. The baseball quant begins to consider a stolen-base attempt worthwhile only when the odds are about three in four that the runner will be safe. In 2021, for instance, teams were successful on 75.7 percent of their stolen-base attempts. But, paralyzed by the fear of being thrown out, they stole less than one base per game for a third straight season, marking the first time that had happened in half a century. It is the opposite of Billyball: risk averse instead of risk taking.

Counterintuitively, as managers have lost power and the game has come to include less strategy, the job has become more difficult. All the czars are dead. To manage now requires squeezing adroitly and diplomatically into the narrow space between a front office that controls the roster and playing style and the players who need explanations and support and who know their real boss is not the manager. The difficulty is mastering that "different style of leadership" Bruce Bochy came to recognize in the modern game—to "sell" to players, as Bochy put it, without being a salesman. It is the tightrope act of a circus: the simplicity and difficulty of the task are one and the same.

In November of 2015, Epstein, then the Chicago Cubs president, wanted the coaches, managers, and decision-makers in his player development system to understand what this "different style of leadership" required. Epstein gathered them in a ballroom at the team's annual Instructional League meetings. The lights dimmed. A video began to play. White lettering upon a black background appeared over soft music: "Great Lessons About Leadership."

Three people addressed leadership in the video. The first person to appear was Jason Garrett, then the Dallas Cowboys head coach and a 1989 Princeton graduate. Garrett was addressing the Princeton Varsity Club. He told a story about the last preseason game as he was trying to make the Cowboys' roster as a journeyman quarterback. The Cowboys had the ball past midfield late in the game. A time-out was called. Garrett met with the coaches on the sideline. He returned to the huddle to call the next play.

"All right, guys, what snap count do you want to go on?" Garrett asked his teammates. "Do you want to go on a quick count? Hard two? What do you think?"

Kevin Gogan, a six-foot-seven, 311-pound lineman, threw a piercing look at Garrett and addressed him by his nickname.

"Hey, Redball," Gogan said. "You're the quarterback. You decide what snap count we're going on."

Garrett absorbed his lesson in leadership right there.

"Dagger. Right through my heart," he said. "I am the quarterback. I'm a leader. I'm the guy in charge. When you're the leader, grasp the mantle of leadership. That's rule one of being a leader. As the quarterback, you get in the huddle, you call the play, and you tell them what the damn snap count is."

The next to appear on the Cubs' video was former United Kingdom prime minister Tony Blair. He was delivering the 2008 Yale commencement address.

"Leadership is about wanting the responsibility to be on your shoulders," Blair said. "Not ignoring its weight, but knowing someone has to carry it, and reaching out for that person...to be you. Leaders are heat seekers, not heat deflectors."

The third person to appear was Maddon. He was seated at a table in front of a microphone at the press conference to introduce him as manager of the Cubs, a franchise that had not won the World Series since 1908 and had finished in last place five years in a row under four managers. It was November 3, 2014. Maddon, looking professorial with his black-framed eyeglasses set off by his tousle of white hair, wore his Cubs jersey unbuttoned over a windowpane dress shirt.

"Joe Maddon. Our Guy," the title on the video read.

The press wanted to know what leadership style he intended to bring to the Cubs.

"The selling point are the people," Maddon said, as inspirational orchestral music played underneath his words. "You have to be aligned with people you want to be aligned with. You have to want to show up every day and work with a certain group of people. That matters more than anything. There's not enough money in the world to make you want to work in a place or a situation where you don't want to be and be productive or good.

"To me it's about getting to spring training, getting to know everybody, building relationships, developing trust. . . . You get all that stuff working, man, then really magical things can happen. So that's where I'm at with this whole thing.

"It's more about people and connections. The other stuff is going to take care of itself. Because if you have talented players, which we do, and you put them in the right environment, you set up a situation to me where they are not afraid of making mistakes. That's the most important thing I want any player who plays for me or for us: to never be concerned or afraid about making mistakes. That's the worst thing you can do. To coach aggressiveness out of a player, to coach fear into a player, those are the two worst things you can possibly do.

"So I'm going to get to know all that stuff, but I'm telling you succinctly that's my overarching philosophy when it comes to managing or teaching or coaching. Those two really big components, and combine them with really good people.

"When you're doing something like we're doing here, the trust has to go both ways. It has to flow from both sides. I'm here to tell the players who might be listening, you've got my trust already. I have to earn the trust of the players on the field. Once you establish the trust and they believe in what we're talking about, and they know that we think that they're good, really special things can occur.

"We can sit here and talk mechanics, hitting mechanics, base-running, whatever you want, but it really comes down to personal relationships and trust. And because what happens then, when you get to that point, now you can really have constructive criticism flowing back and forth. And when you get to that point, that's when really good things can occur.

"You have to have thick skin to play this game. You cannot be thin skinned and play this game and be successful. Once you establish trust and open lines of communication, anything is possible.

"Me? I'm going to be talking playoffs next year. I'm going to tell you that right now. Because I can't go to spring training and say any other thing. I'm just incapable of doing that. Why would you even report? It's all about setting your standards, your goals, high, because the problem is that if you don't set your goals high enough, you might actually hit your mark. That's not a good thing.

"We're going to set our mark high. Absolutely. I'm going to talk play-offs. I'm going to talk World Series. This year. I promise you. I am. And I'm going to believe it. And I'm going to see how all of this is going to play out. And it's within our future. There's no question about that. But I don't know exactly when that's going to happen, but in my mind's eye we're going to make the playoffs next year."

What, a reporter wondered, made him think he could turn the Cubs into a championship team?

"Don't ever permit the pressure to exceed the pleasure. Don't ever permit the pressure to exceed the pleasure. That's on the top of my lineup card every night. I've been wanting to do this since I was six. Everybody who played in the big leagues has been wanting to do it since they were six, seven, eight years of age. Don't ever forget that. Don't forget why we're here. This is baseball. This is a game and it's entertainment."

The video transitioned to white letters over a black background, music still playing underneath:

"Build Trust. Focus on Relationships. Communicate Well."
"Never Permit the Pressure to Exceed the Pleasure."

The words eventually faded to a Cubs logo, which then faded to black.

What the video did not include was how Maddon's introductory news conference had ended that day. With Wrigley Field closed for renovations, the event was held at a bar across the street from the ballpark. As it ended, Maddon announced he was buying a shot and a beer for everyone in attendance.

"The Hazleton way," he said.

CHAPTER 15

"See It with First-Time Eyes"

Instructional League is the blast furnace of baseball. Raw talents are honed. Necessary and unglamorous is the work. And sometimes it is just as hot.

So it was at midday of another triple-digit scorcher in October of 1984 at Gene Autry Park in Mesa, Arizona. Fresh off managing the Class A Peoria Chiefs, Maddon was throwing batting practice in an outdoor cage between Fields 1 and 2. Coaches in Instructional League threw batting practice constantly. Hitter after hitter, basket after basket of baseballs, on fields and in cages...you threw until your shoulder ached in protest. And then you threw some more. Every time Maddon's arm came around with the next pitch, a miniature shower of sweat flew from his hand along with the baseball.

Suddenly Maddon felt a silent presence to his left. He turned. There stood one of the smartest baseball men who'd ever lived. The man spent every waking moment studying angles and details to be one step ahead of the competition, if not always one run. Bobby Fischer in spikes. Managerial royalty, with the visage to match. The tanned, perfectly proportioned face set off by the polished steel-gray eyes and the immaculately groomed, Brylcreemed helmet of snowy white hair. The Ban-Lon polo shirt. The polyester slacks that dared not wrinkle. The pristine white loafers. The faint mixture of Aqua Velva and Marlboros that atomized the oven-like air around him.

The man had *presence.* It was said of Gene Mauch that you knew he was in the room before you saw him. Players felt his stare even when their backs were turned to him. Mauch had once played for the minor league Hollywood Stars, and nobody looked the part better than he. He could have stood in for George Peppard in *Breakfast at Tiffany's.*

248

Maddon was thirty years old. He had just completed his fourth season of managing in the minors, all of them in rookie ball or Class A of the California Angels organization. Mauch was soon to turn fifty-nine years old and set to begin his twenty-fourth season managing in the major leagues. Known as the Little General, Mauch was a man fully in command at five foot ten. He had just been renamed manager of the Angels, two years after a disastrous end to the Angels' 1982 season had sent him into a self-ordered Napoleonic exile.

"Hey. Come here a minute," Mauch said softly, tilting his white head for Maddon to approach him with only the netting of the cage between them. Maddon leaned in to listen to the wizard.

"You've created a wonderful atmosphere around here," Mauch said.

"Thank you."

Then Mauch promptly turned on his white loafers and left.

"*Poof!* He disappears," Maddon remembers. "He said that to me that day and I thought, *Wow, what is he talking about?* I had no idea what he was talking about. Sincerely did not.

"So that kind of made me pause. I go home that night and in subsequent nights, I'm trying to think, *What is he talking about here?* Finally I concluded I needed to figure it out because I wanted to be able to do this next year again, and I might need to intentionally get it done. It's not going to happen organically all the time.

"So what is it? What is it that we're doing here? And I concluded it was about how we dealt with the players, the relationships we built, the communication that we had. There was a lot of trust involved, and it was definitely openness both ways, especially from the staff to the players.

"We also had fun. We had *fun*. We bought these used, big old column speakers, and every day we would roll them out when BP would start. We'd kill some music all over the complex. Nobody was doing that at that time. We had music blasting everywhere. We would have rock and roll one day, country the next, Latin music the day after that. It was wonderful. It was all of that."

There was another important element to the charged atmosphere: winning. Instructional League is a boot camp of fundamentals. It is primarily a player development mechanism to shorten as much as possible the repetition-based learning curve for a ballplayer on the way to the big leagues. Maddon understood that the requirements of team baseball were part of that learning curve, even when the games were played on practice fields in stifling heat surrounded by chain-link fences and no fans.

"I wanted the players to play to win always," Maddon says. "I never wanted players to think they were being developed. I thought that was an excuse for trying to get it tomorrow or the next day or the next day, and it was never that thought that I really have to get it done today. It's always 'I could put it off.'

"So players were there to play to win, and coaches and managers were there to develop."

As a minor league manager and later as a field coordinator, Maddon prioritized development over winning for the first four months of a season. In May, for instance, if a young left-handed hitting prospect out of high school was due to bat in the ninth inning of a close game against a tough left-handed pitcher, the kid would get the at bat, even if the manager had a better option on the bench in an older right-handed hitter out of college. But in August, the final month? Maddon put the greater priority on winning and sent the more seasoned right-handed hitter to take the at bat.

"August was the only time we took the wraps off the managers," Maddon says. "That's when we would say, 'Go ahead and play to win. You have April, May, June, and July to develop guys, and now you do things in order to win.' We permitted them to do more things as a manager in August.

"It was important to learn how to win on a minor league level to win on a major league level, but coaches and managers are always there to make decisions based on development.

"And I still like that method. I think it's a good method because some players just have got to deal with it and think, *Listen, if I'm not doing well enough, maybe somebody is going to take my place.* You just can't always put people on scholarship and expect a good result."

Maddon brought the same philosophy to Instructional League.

"Part of the allure of our Instructional League was we wanted to win games," he says. "We made no bones about it. Instructional League is a developmental situation, absolutely. We had specifics we wanted guys to work on every day in the game, even if it caused them to not do as well, they were there to work on it. But while you're within this framework of working on new things, we wanted you to win."

Mauch's compliment inspired Maddon. Maddon had managed for four years using the best practices he knew. But because of what Mauch said—and because it came from Mauch, the renowned baseball acharya—Maddon reflected on why and how those methods created a productive, inspiring atmosphere. The key, he decided, was creating a foundation of mutual trust.

"Gene, by just saying that to me that one day, made me mindful what we were doing," Maddon says. "And for me it came down to the way we interacted with the players—to make sure that we had meetings with the guys. They knew where they stood, so that [when] we were on the field they would have fun and know we would not just beat them into the ground in a hundred-degree weather from the middle of September to Halloween.

"The energy in that Instructional League camp was palpable, and Gene picked up on that. I was starting out, and so were the players. He made me aware of what we were creating. There was a lesson in there, too, that I never forgot. In fact, it becomes more important the longer you do something: See it with first-time eyes. Feel it with first-time passion.

"Your mind and heart are never as far open as they are when you encounter a place or an opportunity for the first time. I used that lesson with my teams often. Familiarity can dull your edge. Make every day count by seeing it with first-time eyes.

"Gene taught me that atmosphere matters."

Gene Mauch would do anything to win a baseball game. The best evidence of his all-consuming drive was a can of peach nectar. As a benchwarming infielder with the 1949 Chicago Cubs, Mauch used binoculars from the center-field clubhouse at the Polo Grounds to steal signs from New York Giants catcher Walker Cooper. Mauch would signal to teammates what pitch was coming by placing a brightly colored can of peach nectar on the windowsill for a fastball and removing it for an off-speed pitch. Mauch had learned such espionage the previous season from Hank Schenz, a five-foot-nine Cubs infielder who would steal signs using binoculars from inside the center-field scoreboard at Wrigley Field.

Mauch and Schenz came from the same baseball genus: *Scrappus*. Each was a scrappy infielder with "future manager" written all over him. They compensated for limited size and skill with a mastery of extra-curricular talents, such as bench jockeying, pugilism, and espionage, all valued assets in those rough-and-tumble days of baseball. (Years later, in 1954, before both became managers, Mauch and Schenz pummeled each other in the infield dirt of Edmonds Field in Sacramento in the middle of a Pacific Coast League game, Mauch playing for the Los Angeles Angels and Schenz playing for the Sacramento Solons.)

Both Mauch and Schenz had their baseball careers interrupted by military service in World War II. The war created a boom in the tools of surveillance. Service members relied on binoculars and telescopes, including those made by the Wollensak company of Rochester, New York. As the servicemen and -women returned home, sales of binoculars and telescopes exploded. One of the many veterans who purchased a Wollensak telescope was Schenz, who would make use of it not just with the 1948 Cubs but more famously with the 1951 Giants.

Giants manager Leo Durocher, the archetype of *Scrappus*, picked up Schenz on a waiver claim midway through the season. The infielder was hitting just .213 in little playing time for the Pittsburgh Pirates, who had proudly dubbed him Mouthpiece in honor of his world-class bench jockeying. Durocher did not want Schenz for his bat or glove. He wanted him for his mouth—and, in short time, for his Wollensak.

The Giants used Schenz's Wollensak to steal signs from their center-field clubhouse. They went 24-6 at the Polo Grounds with it to erase a thirteen-and-a-half-game deficit to the Brooklyn Dodgers, the run culminating in "The Shot Heard 'Round the World," a pennant-winning home run by Bobby Thomson off Ralph Branca.

Exactly two months after Thomson hit the home run, the Giants said goodbye to Schenz. They sold his rights to the Oakland Oaks of the Pacific Coast League. Schenz never batted for the Giants, never appeared in a home game after he told Durocher about his Wollensak, and never again appeared in a major league game, yet the $10,000 waiver claim had been money well spent by the Giants. To commemorate the extraordinary "good luck" Schenz had brought the Giants, a photographer posed him late in the season for a seated portrait in his home uniform. On his right knee was the infielder's glove he'd never used in a game for the Giants. Schenz raised both hands and crossed his fingers. Schenz smiled, though not broadly. It was the smile of someone who knows a secret.

"It was with a pang of regret that they let him go," wrote Arch Murray in the *Sporting News*, "because all hands at the Polo Grounds believe he played a vital role in the spiritual life that enabled the Giants to make their tremendous drive down the stretch."

"The spiritual life." Like Schenz, Durocher, Eddie Stanky—who played second base on those 1951 Giants—and so many other ballplayers-turned-managers of their generation, Mauch was a staunch devotee of this "spiritual life" style of baseball, a euphemism for "by any means necessary." These were baseball men made hungry, in literal and figurative ways, by the Depression and war. They brought an iron will—a desperation, even—to ball fields and then to dugouts. That force of will, which flourished under absolute authority in running a ball club, came to define the traditional view of a baseball manager. No will ran hotter than the one that burned inside Mauch.

Gene William Mauch was born in 1925 in Salina, Kansas, where railroad tracks crisscrossed the plains, flour mills belched steam relentlessly, and fields of golden wheat stretched to the horizon outside a rapidly expanding city. His father, George, was a former boxer who by age twenty-six owned a successful bakery in Salina. His mother, Mamie, worked there as one of the bakers.

Then the stock market crashed. George Mauch was ruined. His bakery went out of business. Gene was four years old. His sister, Jolene, was a baby. The Mauchs eventually moved to California to seek work and a

better life. In 1943, just after Mauch turned seventeen years old, Branch
Rickey personally signed him to a contract with the Dodgers organiza-
tion. Just one year later, Mauch was playing for Durocher in Brooklyn.
Rickey knew right away he was looking at a future manager, the next
Durocher.

"Look at him and you think he's sixteen," Rickey said. "Talk to him
and you think he's twenty-six. Talk baseball with him and you think he's
thirty-six."

With rosters depleted due to the war, the Opening Day double-play
combination for the 1944 Dodgers was set to be the eighteen-year-old
Mauch at shortstop and the thirty-eight-year-old Durocher at second
base as player-manager. Those plans ended April 9, an Easter Sunday
at Ebbets Field, when Brooklyn played an exhibition game against the
Boston Red Sox. With a runner at first, the teenage Mauch fumbled a
ground ball. In his haste to get the out at second base, Mauch threw hard
and errantly toward Durocher. Leo reached with his bare hand to corral
it. The force of the baseball broke his hand in two places, ending any
plans of playing time for Durocher.

Durocher was not mad at the kid about his broken hand. Far from it.
Durocher had not been keen on coming out of retirement as a player. It
had been Rickey's idea. The next day Durocher showed his gratitude to
Mauch by buying the kid a tweed topcoat. Besides, like Rickey, Durocher
saw much to like in Mauch. It was not so much his skill. It was his brains
and desire. The admiration was mutual. From the moment Mauch met
Durocher he saw what he wanted to become: not just a big league manager, but a manager in full control of his team who would cut your heart
out to win a baseball game.

From 1943, when Rickey signed him, to 1995, when he quit as bench
coach for Kansas City Royals manager Bob Boone, Mauch pursued winning with an intensity that was unsurpassed, part of a life mission that
went unfulfilled to his grave. Mauch played for, managed, or coached
the Dodgers (twice), Cubs (twice), Braves (twice), Angels (twice), Pirates,
Yankees, Cardinals, Red Sox, Phillies, Expos, Twins, and Royals. Not
once did the roulette ball that is a major league life land on his number.

He never made it to the World Series. Mauch managed 3,942 games, the ninth most in history. No manager ever tried longer or harder without ever getting to the World Series.

His managing career began in the minors in 1952, when Boston Braves general manager John Quinn asked Mauch to be player-manager for the team's Double A farm team, the Atlanta Crackers. Mauch was an angry dynamo who baited opposing players, ordered pitchers to throw at hitters, openly stewed over his players' failures, played games under protest, routinely argued with umpires, and found his way into fistfights. He was so worn out by the job that he quit after one year.

Mauch returned to managing in 1958, this time as a player-manager with the Minneapolis Millers, the Triple A affiliate of the Boston Red Sox. He led them to the Junior World Series Championship. Mauch and the Millers returned the next year to defend their title against the Havana Sugar Kings, the Cincinnati Reds' Triple A affiliate.

Games 3 through 7 were played in Havana, Cuba, where a revolutionary movement led by Fidel Castro had recently overthrown dictator Fulgencio Batista. Machine gun–toting soldiers who had fought with Castro in the mountains stood at the ready in the dugouts. The crowd included about three thousand soldiers, most of them bearded, almost all brandishing rifles with bayonets, and some as young as fourteen. Many lined the field.

There was no doubt about what the series meant to Cuba. "After the triumph of the revolution," Castro told the crowd before Game 5, "we should also win the World Series!" During one game, Millers center fielder Tom Umphlett robbed a Sugar Kings player of a hit with an outstanding catch. As he returned to the dugout, Umphlett's gaze caught the hostile stare of one of Castro's armed soldiers. With his right hand, the rebel made a slashing motion across his throat.

The series went to a seventh and deciding game. Castro made his usual grand entrance from the center-field gate. This time as he made his way toward his box seat in the grandstand, Castro suddenly stopped in front of the Minneapolis bullpen. Staring at the Millers, he placed his hand on a large revolver holstered at his hip.

"Tonight," he told them, "we win."

The Sugar Kings won, 3–2, on a walk-off single in the bottom of the ninth. Many in the crowd rushed to Castro's box to crowd around the premier. "Fidel! Fidel! Fidel!" they shouted. The Millers did not mind the defeat. It may have been the only time that Mauch lost a game and was the happier for it.

Mauch's big break came in 1960, when Eddie Sawyer quit as Philadelphia Phillies manager the day after an Opening Day loss. Someone asked Sawyer why anybody would quit one game into a season. Sawyer provided a classic line that spoke timelessly to the demands of being a major league manager.

"I'm forty-nine," he said, "and I'd like to live to be fifty."

Quinn, now the Phillies' general manager, hired Mauch, the same manager he had hired seven years earlier to manage the Atlanta Crackers.

"Let's go. I'm ready," Mauch announced. "My ambition isn't to be just a big league manager. It's to be the best big league manager in the business."

It took Mauch only twenty-six games to show his *Scrappus* bona fides in what must have been an unprecedented display of rage by a major league manager: he charged the mound from the dugout after three of his batters were hit by the Reds. A twelve-minute brawl ensued that involved Frank Robinson, Billy Martin, and six-foot-eight Gene Conley.

"How much of that stuff can you take?" Mauch said, explaining why he'd charged the mound.

Over that and twenty-six more seasons as manager, the Little General would chase in vain his white whale, the World Series. Forged by his father's Depression-era work ethic (and, when he deemed it necessary, the boxing skills he'd also inherited from him) and by Durocher's maniacal will to win, Mauch fit the role of the classic genius. He read the rule book with the zest of a monk studying the Bible. He looked for ways to win a baseball game with the painstaking thoroughness of an archeologist on a dig.

Mauch popularized the five-man infield as a last-gasp defensive gambit. If he did not actually invent the double switch, he popularized it.

One day Mauch visited the pitching mound to remove a Phillies pitcher who had just given up a home run. He pointed to shortstop Bobby Wine and said, "You, too. You're out."

"Why me?" said a stunned Wine. "I didn't give up the home run."

It was the first time Wine had been involved in a double switch, in which a manager replaces two players to move the pitcher's batting spot.

Mauch was one of the first managers to defend the running game with signals from the dugout. He obsessed about pitchers getting rid of the pitch quickly with a stolen-base threat at first base. Mauch would signal to the catcher when he wanted his pitcher to throw with a slide step, an abbreviated delivery in which the front foot barely rises off the ground.

"Gene was very much into that," Maddon says. "Controlling the running game from the dugout and signs to the catcher was something I watched and really got into as a young minor league manager. I thought, *If my pitchers are going to get to the big leagues, they're going to have to do this because that's what Gene wants there.*"

Mauch looked everywhere for edges and took every opportunity to exploit them. On July 4, 1966, New York Mets catcher Jerry Grote reached into the Phillies dugout to catch a foul pop-up. Mauch smacked Grote across the arms, making sure he could not secure what otherwise would have been an out. Grote protested, but to no avail. Mauch knew there was no rule preventing a manager from such an action. His shenanigans prompted baseball to adopt one.

In Detroit one day in 1987, Mauch, then managing the Angels, noticed Tigers catcher Mike Heath use his mask to gently scoop the baseball back to him after it bounced in the dirt with runners at first and second. None of the umpires noticed that Heath had violated Rule 7.05, Paragraph (D), which calls for an automatic two-base error when a player uses any piece of equipment other than his glove to control the baseball. Mauch noticed. He walked to home-plate umpire Durwood Merrill and explained what had happened and the rule. Merrill agreed. He waved home the runner from second and placed the runner at first on third. Mauch's Angels were losing 5–0 at the time, on their way to a 15–2 loss.

"No one knows the rules better than Gene Mauch," said Sparky Anderson, then the Detroit manager. "He could teach a seminar on it."

Mauch was the manager's manager. He garnered enormous professional respect from his peers. Hall of Fame manager Dick Williams, a crusty sort known for throwing compliments around like manhole covers, once said, "If they were to hold a managerial clinic, and just have managers there, Gene Mauch should run the clinic. That's how good a manager he was."

Anderson, in the book *The Man in the Dugout: Fifteen Big League Managers Speak Their Minds*, wrote, "If you had the best club, you had a chance to beat him. If he had the best club, you had no chance. If the clubs were even, he had the advantage."

In 1980 Anderson said of Mauch, "There's no way to prove it, but he might be the best manager who ever lived. He's given twenty-one years of everything he's had, and he never cheated this business for one minute. He's number one on my list."

Mauch once said, "The worst day is when you realize you want to win more than the players." The problem with that outlook was that it would be almost impossible to find anyone who wanted to win as much as Mauch.

On September 22, 1963, the Phillies lost 2–1 in Houston to the Colt .45s on a walk-off hit by five-foot-nine second baseman Joe Morgan, who three days earlier had turned twenty and was playing in only his second major league game. Mauch's team had already been eliminated from contention. His Phillies were fourteen games out with one week left. Not even four thousand fans had bothered to show up for the game. It was, in the framework of a long season, a classic meaningless game. But no such game ever existed for Mauch. When Mauch saw his Phillies lined up around the postgame spread of food in the clubhouse, he could not understand their lack of anger at losing. The thought enraged him.

"You just got beat by a guy who looks like a Little Leaguer!" Mauch shouted, whereupon he swiped his arm clear across the postgame spread, sending barbecued ribs, watermelon, and potato salad flying across the room. Much of the food landed on Wes Covington and Tony González, who had already showered and dressed. The next day Mauch bought them new suits.

It was not Mauch's lone episode of turning over the clubhouse catering. His postgame table-turning furies grew so infamous that when the Angels hired him midway through the 1981 season, designated hitter Don Baylor greeted him with a question: "Will the food be served on the floor?"

Three times the Little General pushed and cajoled his team to the precipice of the World Series: with the 1964 Phillies, the 1982 Angels, and the 1986 Angels. Three times his team fell. Three times Mauch, the master strategist, bore blame for it because of how he'd managed.

The last one eventually drove Mauch to his exile. "For a few weeks after that," Mauch would say later, "every morning when I woke up, I felt it in my stomach like a hot dagger in my belly button."

It was his last, best chance. His 1987 Angels sank to last place. The years, the losses, and the cigarettes were taking a toll on him. Mauch smoked when he was happy with a win, and he smoked when he wanted to dull the pain of a loss. He smoked when he was playing golf, and he smoked when he was playing bridge. He smoked nearly every waking moment. He smoked three packs a day, which works out to one every eighteen minutes for someone who gets six hours of sleep. And often he smoked more than that.

Mauch told the story of how he once fired up a cigarette on every tee and every green while playing a round of golf with friends in Palm Springs: thirty-six cigarettes in four hours.

"I read in some journal that in the business world cigarette smokers tend to be more effective than nonsmokers," he told his playing partners.

"Yeah," rasped one of them, who'd had surgery for larynx cancer, "but not for long."

In spring training of 1988, Mauch was sick, exhausted, and wheezing when he submitted to his first checkup in forty years. Doctors thought they found cancer in his lungs, though it would turn out to be bronchitis. Mauch left the team for fifteen days to rest. When he returned, he shocked the team by quitting. He was sixty-one years old and looked much older. He said he wasn't quitting for health reasons. It was the losing he could not take.

"Unfortunately, even when you win championships, there are a certain number of games that you're going to lose—sixty or more, probably," he said. "As I've gotten a little older, I have developed an inability to cope with those inevitable losses. You'd think when a guy's been around...as long as I have, that tolerance would develop. It hasn't been that way. It hasn't been that way at all."

In 2002, fifteen years after he managed his last game, Mauch watched on television as the Angels, with Maddon as bench coach, won the World Series. Maddon watched proudly as Troy Percival, the former no-hit catcher whom Bobba Lou and Maddon had converted to a pitcher on a side mound in Instructional League in 1990, secured the final out by getting Kenny Lofton on a fly ball to center fielder Darin Erstad. Maddon and manager Mike Scioscia embraced in the dugout in the same spot where Mauch had watched the Red Sox rip a World Series berth from his hands in 1986.

"They've always said about this game that you can't get too high or low," Mauch said during the 2002 World Series, when he was about to turn seventy-seven. "I mastered the high part, but I could never master not getting low. I couldn't get over bad losses. I've always known that wasn't one of my strong points, coming right back after a tough loss.

"I never wanted players to see my eyes after a tough loss because I knew they could see how hurt I was. Because I did hurt, very badly. And the players could see it in my eyes just how much I hurt.

"Mike does some things I wish I had understood better. He has an ability to get over things."

Maddon's first major league managing gig was a twenty-two-game trial with the 1996 Angels as an interim replacement for John McNamara, who was ill. McNamara had replaced Marcel Lachemann, who had quit that year. Maddon took over a team that was dead in the water at 62-77. It played nothing like a Gene Mauch team. The Angels were last in stolen bases, last in walks, and last in sacrifice bunts.

"We were just static," Maddon says. "I thought we needed to get moving. We were facing a lot of sinker ball pitchers, so I thought, *Let's get the guys going.*"

Maddon called for a rash of hit-and-run plays. They did not always work. One call gnawed at him, even though it was meaningless in the outcome of the game: a hit-and-run play with Randy Velarde at the plate early in a game, when he should have let Velarde swing away. At 8-14, the Angels were not much better under Maddon, but he thought his little trial went well because the club did play more aggressively. But there was only one way he would know for sure how he had done.

"I only wanted to be critiqued by one person," Maddon says. "The only guy I needed to hear from was Gene Mauch. I just wanted to know what Gene thought."

He needed feedback on his twenty-two-game interim managing gig, and only the judgment of the smartest baseball man he ever knew would suffice. Maddon telephoned Mauch. Having returned to his Rancho Mirage routine of golf, cocktails, and incessant watching of televised baseball, the Little General was more than a bit familiar with Maddon's work.

"He was very complimentary," Maddon says. "He liked the way I ran the games—and thought that I had done a good job with the pitching staff and, again, the game itself, the different things I attempted to do during the game, putting players in motion, et cetera."

The praise meant the world to Maddon. If Gene Mauch thought you did a good job managing, nothing else mattered.

"But...," Mauch said.

"Yes?"

"But there was one time when you had a hit-and-run with Velarde early in the game. It was too early. I didn't like that. I would not have done that there."

Maddon laughed quietly to himself. The Little General missed nothing.

"You're right! It was not a good time."

For the next half hour, the two of them discussed in exhaustive detail the merits and timing of hit-and-run plays.

In many ways, Mauch represented a managerial ideal for Maddon. His baseball intellect, mastery of the rule book, teaching of fundamentals, and grand-master stratagems made Mauch an exalted wizard of the dug-out. But in an equal number of ways, Mauch represented to Maddon how *not* to do the job. His spirit is a Jacob Marley in spikes, remind-ing Maddon from his purgatory that the raging fire within a *Scrappus* is destructive to the manager and his team.

Mauch never wanted players to see his eyes after a tough loss because he knew they could see how much he hurt. Maddon prides himself on his equanimity. He *wants* players to see the consistency of his emotions and approach through the ups and downs of a season.

"When I walk in, they should see the same person every day, not based on whether we won or lost the last game," he says. "I've had that guy be my manager or coach. Not good. That will infiltrate the psyche of the team. Like it or not, players are always looking at you and how you react."

Mauch once compared baseball to malaria: "Once it gets in your sys-tem, it may let up for a while, but it's always there." He had energy only for baseball when he was managing, admitting, "I've often wished that I could do things more casually. But when I'm doing it, it doesn't seem like anything but the right way to do it." He never learned to cope with losing, conceding at the end of his career, "Losing still hurts me like it always did. The best way for it not to hurt is not to lose." He drank, played cards, and smoked with a ferocity that harmed his health.

Maddon embraces a more holistic approach. Among many his pur-suits in season and out, he meditates, reads, bikes, golfs, cooks, owns a restaurant, runs a charitable foundation, and collects classic cars. What he calls a "liberal arts approach" to managing games and his life has its roots in his curriculum at Lafayette.

"We all want levelheadedness," he says. "Sleep, diet, exercise, and meditation all help promote it. It's amazing how a fifteen- or twenty-minute meditation slows everything down. If you want to take care of the big moment when it comes along, you start by taking care of yourself."

Maddon so respected Mauch that one of the early highlights of his career was when Mauch asked him to run the Angels' bunt defense drills in spring training. It was 1985. Maddon was a thirty-one-year-old minor league instructor—younger than Angels infielders Rod Carew, Doug DeCinces, and Bobby Grich. That Mauch trusted him sent his confidence soaring. It happened only a few months after the Little General had complimented him on the atmosphere he'd created in Instructional League.

Mauch helped develop Maddon into a full-time major league manager, though he did not live long enough to see it. On August 8, 2005, with Maddon still an Angels coach, twice having been passed over for the team's managing job and four times having interviewed for jobs without getting them, his old friend and managerial touchstone took his last breath in a hospital bed at Eisenhower Medical Center in Rancho Mirage. Gene Mauch was seventy-nine years old. The official cause of death was lung cancer. Losing was a contributing factor.

CHAPTER 16

"Do Simple Better"

Earl Weaver became a Hall of Fame manager while hardly speaking to his Baltimore Orioles players for seventeen years. He was another one of those *Scrappus* autocratic managers raised in the Depression. He never shook his winning pitcher's hand after a game. He would walk through the clubhouse only to get to his office or the field, careful not to create so much as eye contact with his players. He was too consumed with figuring out ways to win a ball game to care about the players' needs or feelings. Pitcher Jim Palmer, just to goad his intense manager, would blurt out as Weaver walked through the clubhouse, "Hey, how are you doing!"

"And it was like you shocked him, like you had just Tasered him," Palmer says. "Because he was busy thinking about the ball game."

A generation ago, managers did not care about being friends with their players. "A manager should stay as far away from his players as possible," Weaver once said. "I don't know if I said ten words to Frank Robinson when he played for me."

One day Pat Kelly, a pious outfielder for the Orioles, noticed Weaver fuming after Kelly struck out with the bases loaded.

"Earl, I hope you walk with the Lord one day," Kelly said.

"Pat," Weaver shot back, "I hope you walk with the bases loaded one day."

Gene Mauch used to ride opposing players relentlessly, and sometimes even his own. Few of his players liked him, and Mauch was just fine with the arrangement. One day in Milwaukee in the early 1960s, with Joe Torre of the Braves in the batter's box, he screamed at his Phillies pitcher, "Knock this guy down!" Torre got a base hit. When he reached first base, Torre turned toward the Phillies dugout and started screaming insults at Mauch. "He was an arrogant bastard," Torre says.

As Torre yelled at Mauch, Philadelphia first baseman John Herrnstein covered his mouth with his mitt and encouraged Torre to keep it up. "Give it to him!" said Herrnstein, choosing the opponent's side over his own manager.

Old-guard managers such as Weaver, Mauch, Sparky Anderson, and Billy Martin deployed top-down leadership, as in the military, with respect given to rank. The manager dictated the style, strategy, and personnel. Those days are over. As front offices and players gained power, managers lost it. Pay scales and hiring practices reflected the shift.

When the Cubs hired Maddon after the 2014 season, they paid him $25 million over five years, which was more than the $18.5 million over five years they were paying Theo Epstein as president of baseball operations. Within four years, the pay and the power nexus had flipped. Epstein was signed again after the 2016 season to a five-year deal worth $50 million. Maddon did not get another contract from the Cubs.

Change happened quickly. Baseball outsiders were behind the three most seismic managerial hires in this revolution. It began with Alderson, the San Francisco lawyer, hiring Art Howe to be A's manager in 1995 with instructions to implement the front office's philosophy, not his own.

The next leap came in 2003, when Boston Red Sox owner John Henry, who had made his fortune trusting data in a financial trading firm, with Epstein as his data-savvy general manager, hired Terry Francona to implement cutting-edge, front-office-generated analytics.

The third leap happened in 2005, when three Wall Streeters new to the Tampa Bay Devil Rays, Stuart Sternberg, Andrew Friedman, and Matthew Silverman, hired a first-time manager who had never played major league baseball, was comfortable around computers, craved information, and questioned the status quo: Maddon.

Since then, the size of front offices and their impact on how baseball is played have grown enormously. In 2012 the Tampa Bay Rays' staff directory listed thirty-six employees in core baseball operations jobs, including ten in analytics. In 2021 it listed eighty-one people in core baseball operations jobs, including thirty-one in analytics.

The computational brainpower of front offices made a club directory look like something out of the aerospace industry. Among the new titles in the Tampa Bay front office were director, baseball performance science; senior database architect, baseball systems; UI/UX developer II, baseball systems; product designer II, baseball systems, biomechanist; devops engineer; analyst, performance science; analyst and junior analyst, research & development; and junior data technician, baseball research & development. Those hired to such jobs by the Rays brought undergraduate, master's, and PhD degrees in disciplines such as philosophy, data science, exercise science, industrial engineering, statistics and machine learning, electrical engineering information systems management, atmospheric science, computer science, mathematics, statistics, and applied geospatial techniques. They came from schools such as Carnegie Mellon, MIT, Yale, Columbia, Colgate, Wisconsin, Pitt, Florida, East Carolina, and Santa Clara.

Teams scouted and acquired brainpower with as much verve as they did players. It was a quick buy-in by owners. Most owners had amassed their fortunes in business, often leveraging logistics, algorithms, and analytics in fields such as finance and consumer products. They were much more comfortable with the new front-office language of math and science than with the mysterious and often insular language of scouting, with its emphasis on "character," "makeup" and "five tools." The keys to the kingdom passed from *Scrappus* to data scientists, from Anderson to Zaidi.

The more information and front offices expand, the more Maddon goes back to a core philosophy that applies equally well to baseball and life: "Do simple better." It was the slogan Maddon chose to put on Cubs' T-shirts in spring training of 2015, his first year with the team, after it had suffered five straight losing seasons. On one level, it means winning baseball games by paying attention to the fundamentals, such as hustling, baserunning, hitting the cutoff man, playing good defense, and avoiding mental mistakes. On another, it means fighting the urge to believe that more must be better.

"I don't want extra work," he told them. "I don't want too much information."

The players bought in. Pitcher Jon Lester put his own spin on this quest to simplify by calling it "playing stupid." Catcher David Ross said in midseason of that transformational year that "Joe convinced us early in spring training, 'Let's do simple better.' I really think that has gone a long way with the younger players. People want to analyze this game to every detail. With all the stats and numbers, it can be really overbearing. Joe gives the players a chance to be just us, away from all the ancillary pressures of the game."

Mentored by Mauch and hired at the dawn of the information revolution, Maddon is a firsthand witness to how the game grew more complicated and changed the responsibilities of the manager. He defines the differences declaratively between the old guard of managers and the new guard:

The old guard did not want or get interference from the front office.

"General managers legitimately were kind of afraid to walk into the manager's office," Maddon says. "They only showed up on the rare occasion."

When Maddon was hired as interim manager in 1996, he told general manager Bill Bavasi, "I don't want anybody in my office between six and seven. I need that time to draw things together and get my game plan."

Bavasi replied, "Great. I'm with you."

"That was part of playing the game before it's played," Maddon says. "On my card I want to be aware of things that could happen in the game. Then you have the reality of the game, and you have to be flexible. After the game is the postmortem, when you really analyze what occurred and remember something to keep in your back pocket the next time you see this opponent. That's Gene's way of managing each game three times.

"With the Rays, the front office would come down on occasion before a game. It increased with the Cubs, where people were constantly coming in and out of the office, people with information who wanted to contribute and be a part of it. I get it. But that information should not be doled out or given right before the game."

The old guard had power over roster construction.

"How the team was made was based on what the manager wanted to do," Maddon says. "You have meetings, and everybody has an opinion. They could be devastating. Some guys did not want to speak up against the manager. When it came to roster construction, the GM had his say, but it came down to what the manager wanted.

"Major league managers are not necessarily good scouts. They might be good strategists or tacticians, but when it comes to scouting, it's not always their bailiwick. And that's one thing I'm grateful for with what I did in the minor leagues.

"I'm so grateful for the time I spent as a scout because I think that's what kind of set me apart with managers today. Managers today don't have that kind of experience. The experience teams want in managers today is primarily—I'm not saying this in a bad way—a lot of it has to do with media training via being on television or might be consultancy to the president or the GM. And again, I'm not criticizing. That just seems to be the route now."

The omnipotence of the manager in roster construction led to many mistakes, especially when it came to frivolous reasons why the manager liked a player or not. In his first organizational meeting with the Angels, Maddon listened as the minor league managers reviewed the players on their rosters and argued for promotion, demotion, or worse. He was taken aback when one of the managers used a vulgar epithet to describe pitcher Jeff Conner, a third-round pick out of a Phoenix high school.

"These guys had the right of last refusal," Maddon says. "If anybody did not want to cut somebody, the guy was saved. So that part of it I liked, but it was a personality contest, and there was not a lot of high-level intellect going into these decisions other than it was all based on what they had seen in a brief period of time.

"So when it got to Conner, and this guy is calling him a terrible name and saying he should actually have been released, I was like, really? I was expecting a lot more than that. But that was the way Jeff was described by one of the managers, which pretty much was the death knell for Jeffrey. There was no way he was going to be able to survive that, and I was astonished by the method incorporated right there."

The Angels kept Conner at Double A for three straight seasons despite a 3.65 ERA over almost five hundred innings. He left the organization to sign with Detroit as a minor league free agent. Conner did reach Triple A but never made the big leagues.

"I saw it with Gene, and Johnny McNamara, Cookie Rojas, Doug Rader, and Buck Rodgers," Maddon says. "For the most part, managers are only able to see what they like based on a good performance they're observing. It's really hard for these guys to look into the future and try to project players.

"On this subject, I like the way things are done today. There is much more involvement from the scouting department and general managers who have a much better feel and read for things. Plus, they get an opportunity to see other teams more often. The scouting scope is much greater, and thus they're able to make better decisions.

"I relied on that. I did. I relied on my own evaluation, yes. I felt very confident in it. But I always deferred in a situation where these guys had an opportunity to see more than I had a chance to see, and thus it's a much better process."

The old guard had power over trades.

"The managers and coaches are the worst talent evaluators because they only like what they see," Maddon says. "That's why a lot of bad trades were made. Few teams adhered to an organizational philosophical strategy like the Dodgers and Cardinals. A lot of it was left to the whims of the managers, and that's why teams changed constantly. They would tell the front office how they were going to play the game. They had limited experience in the process."

From 1987 to 2000, the Angels had eleven managers in fourteen seasons. "As a young coach I constantly had to alter things," Maddon says.

Maddon was running the minor leagues in 1991 when the Angels hired Rodgers. To establish a unified organizational strategy, Maddon compiled a handbook of bunt defenses, relays, baserunning techniques, and other fundamentals so players in the minors and majors would all be playing "the Angel way." He presented the packet to Rodgers.

"I wanted to get us on the same page and move this forward," Maddon says. "I never heard back from him. What I did hear was that he was galled by my nerve, that I would attempt to curry favor with him based on me putting this together, like a brownnosing attempt. When I heard that, I was so pissed I wouldn't even talk to him for a while."

The front office did not interfere with the old guard on pitching decisions.

"It was the manager's decision, based on how many days of rest or how many pitches," Maddon says. "That was common sense and your experience. My own experience with relief pitchers is that if a guy throws fifteen pitches, he is absolutely available the next day. Twenty-five in a game? I may be able to use him, but I have to check with him. Thirty plus, he was down for a day. If it's over thirty-five he's probably down two days.

"Of course, you have to know your guys, how they respond physically and emotionally. The old managers relied on their eyeballs. A big part of it was, Is he coming out of his delivery? Once he is, it definitely gets me thinking something different. It's usually right around one hundred pitches."

The front office did not influence the old guard's game decisions.

"I can't imagine what would have happened if a GM went downstairs and told any manager who to bat where," Maddon says. "That was left alone. The manager was able to make decisions independently, with input from his coaches, especially the one guy who was his drinking buddy after games.

"In-game decisions were not questioned by the front office. There were no GMs or minions coming down to ask specifically about moves and intimating what they would have done differently.

"The speed of the game is never fully understood by somebody sitting upstairs, with all the options available, right down to doing what's best for a player's confidence or what's best at the moment. There are all kinds of decisions to be thought through in this nanosecond, and even if they say they do understand, I just think it's different. Sitting upstairs as opposed to being on the top step of the dugout with this thing unfolding in front of you, it's warp speed. It's that moment when the Starship *Enterprise* takes off in a blur.

"In-game decisions were never questioned. They didn't have a lot of information to consider prior to the game. Everybody thinks the job they do is the most important job in the world. Absolutely we do. And you should think that way. Thing is, there is redundancy in these jobs. Analytics could be reduced to what is absolutely necessary to that opponent and that day.

"The poor coaches are just hammered with this stuff. A lot of people are coming downstairs a lot of times to confront a coach instead of the manager based on what happened in the game and whether the information was used properly or not. It's really incredible how that plays out."

The better the team, the more interference the new guard gets.

"The front office wants to be a part of it," Maddon says. "Once you get to the playoffs, they really want to interfere. They really want to take over. If your team is not in the race, that's when you probably have your quietest moments."

In 1886, three years after the Brooklyn Bridge opened to great awe and wonder, a raconteur named Steve Brodie took a hundred-dollar bet that he could jump off the bridge and survive. Seven people had tried the 120-foot leap. All had died. Brodie survived, though he was arrested for attempted suicide as soon as he reached shore in a friend's rowboat.

Great fame and fortune followed. Brodie played himself in a Broadway play. A beer company put him in charge of his own bar, the Steve Brodie Saloon. When Brodie died at age thirty-five in 1901, rumors persisted that the jump had been a hoax, that a dummy had been thrown off the bridge while Brodie jumped from the rowboat into the water.

The truth remains murky, but not the legend. *Taking a Brodie* entered the American vernacular as a colorful term for taking a dive, which became a popular baseball front-office strategy in the 2010s. Rather than invest in an unlikely chase for a playoff spot, teams accepted years of being noncompetitive while building their inventory of young (i.e., cheaper) players. Taking a Brodie became accepted baseball wisdom.

"The rebuild is nothing more than a safe haven for a lot of organizations where you have four years where you don't worry about the outcomes of games," Maddon says. "And the fans have to wait. It's just a safe haven for executives, that's all it is. I don't believe they are necessary. Fans want to be absorbed in this on an annual basis."

The old guard was free to explore its instincts.

"If you bring up instincts and feel today—based on what has happened in the past and how it applies tonight—and it doesn't have a calculus or percentages, these guys don't want to hear it," Maddon says. "They want to go big picture all the time. They are not into trends. They are into large sample size. This is where I really differ with a lot that goes on today.

"Gene and Earl, their mental hard drive was just filled with stuff they could recall in the moment. The really great managers always had the really big hard drive and severely big RAM. Instinct allows you to react to the moment. The blink moment, instinct, intuition…whatever you want to call it, these guys had it. That was during the game. That was part two from Gene. That was reality. Before? Theory. During? Reality. Postmortem? How do we build this hard drive to really access the information in the moment when it really gets hot?"

The old guard was free to create organizational identity on the field.

"With Gene," Maddon says, "you knew when you played his Angels, Expos, or Twins it was going to be a baseball war. When GMs hired Gene, they didn't know they were going to the World Series, but they knew they were going to have a very competent team that year that would play the game properly.

"If you played the Orioles, you knew Earl was going to play his platoons and really set things up for that three-run homer. You knew that. You knew the Orioles had great starting pitching.

"The Dodgers had a lot of hit-and-runs, loved to steal bases, were active on the bases, and had dominant pitching. Once you got to know Tommy Lasorda, you saw where that fearlessness came from. It was a big part of their identity.

"Their front offices were primarily there for acquisitions and running the business side and staying clear of actual operations on the field. I would love to see it return to that, where real baseball people are running the team with the help of the manager and his coaching staff and player development. I would love to see this front-office group in charge of molding the team and once they've done that, please stay out of the way, hand it over to the baseball ops on the field.

"Baseball operations should include an analytics department that provides information, not over-the-top information, just information that's necessary, such as coordinating video in a teaching sense and scouting sense. Organize this stuff, but once you get it together, dispense it in a manner that is not oppressing the baseball folks. It should be there as an aid, not in an adversarial sense whatsoever."

One of Maddon's favorite success stories of using analytics as a strategic aid is about how the Rays became a premier defensive team. Tampa Bay finished last in the league in defensive efficiency in each of his first two seasons there. Defensive efficiency measures how often a team turns batted balls into outs. But as Friedman built a solid analytics team, which included future lead baseball operations executives Chaim Bloom, James Click, and Erik Neander, and as premier defenders such as third base-man Evan Longoria and shortstop Jason Bartlett joined the roster, the Rays proved to be ahead of the curve in translating data into defensive efficiency. Starting in 2008, the Rays finished first, fourth, second, first, third, second, and fifth, respectively, in defensive efficiency.

In a memorable 2012 opening series against the Yankees, the Rays took away so many would-be hits from the Yankees that New York hitting coach Kevin Long scoffed, "They're not above the game by any means. They hit the jackpot against us in the first series. They were in the perfect spot. Come on, man, that's not going to happen all year."

But it did. The 2012 Rays held opponents to a .228 batting average, a record low at the time for any American League team since the introduction of the designated hitter in 1973.

The new guard welcomes information until it becomes interference.

"I'm going to say this straight up, because it's absolutely true," Maddon says. "This group has constant interference from the front office regardless of how long they played or managed. What is interference? Interference is when it goes beyond just giving us information to utilize. It's being hypercritical when things don't work your way.

"A big part of that is the front office has acquired these players, so they assume a disconnect between the player and the coaching staff if somebody's not performing well. What's part of it is based on factors such as exit velocity, launch angles, spin rates, things of this nature. When a player is experiencing results less than expected or projected, there has to be an underlying reason, and coaches are often the first to be blamed. And coaches can't say anything. Their job is way more tenuous than managers'. And they're getting fired way too haphazardly the last several years. Take for example, a defender's range..."

After the Cubs acquired outfielder Nicholas Castellanos at the 2019 trade deadline, the Cubs' analytics team told Maddon that he was not a good outfielder. Maddon asked them to explain why, figuring it had something to do with his technique. Instead they showed him a series of video clips of Castellanos not getting to balls hit to the spacious right field at Comerica Park in Detroit.

"There's a lot of territory to cover between the right fielder and the center fielder," Maddon says. "So I get this video with a couple of balls falling in front of him. This labeled him as not being a good outfielder. The metrics indicated he was a below-average outfielder. And all I wanted to know was, 'What's the technique involved here?'

"I relied on the history I had done with Dexter Fowler and back in the day with B. J. Upton. But what was coming from the front office was that they did not like his zone rating. That's how they calculate defense. The reality is it comes down to positioning and where we put people. That's how these zone ratings would work. So again, what is he doing wrong? I watched it. He actually was doing nothing wrong. He actually had a very good second half with us.

"On top of that, when we got him, the analytic guys didn't want me to play him at all because he chased sliders out of the zone. But what did he do with sliders in the zone and the fastball in the zone? There's always this assumption that the pitcher is going to make this pitch a hundred percent of the time and that Nick would swing at it a hundred percent of the time.

"These numbers, like a lot of things in life, have a bias. What does the Cubs' defensive cocktail indicate? The Tigers'? The Reds'? Just tell him where he can get better and get him out there to work on it. Just don't tell him his zone rating is bad and that he's a bad outfielder.

"I played him. We just acquired this guy to play and help us win, and now these people who are supposedly there to help you are telling you he's a bad outfielder who shouldn't be playing against pitchers who can expand the strike zone. So that's what I mean by interference."

The new guard gets influence about who plays.

"The front office gets the other teams' pitchers in advance," Maddon says. "If there's a bias and they want to see somebody play, they're just looking for the right moment and they'll say, 'What do you think about next Wednesday? Are you thinking about playing so-and-so?'

"Just say, 'We want you to play so-and-so.' When you come downstairs with that in mind, just say it. If the matchup is good, I probably would have played him anyway."

The new guard has limited input on trades.

"This I am all for," Maddon says. "When it comes to trades and acquisitions, managers who have never scouted only like guys they see have success against them. The people who should have the most valuable opinion are the people who are seeing the players the most. Real scouts. The front office should combine their analytics with good old boots on the ground, scouts doing their thing, going to talk to these guys."

The new guard must give players clear explanations.

"Back then, managers did it in a gruff manner, if at all," Maddon says. "Today we have to give the players a full explanation of what's going on in the moment. Back then, as a player you were afraid to ask. You just played hard, and hopefully you played better than somebody else. And maybe I didn't ask because I didn't want to hear that I stunk, that there was somebody better than me. If you said that now, you would absolutely crush somebody."

The new guard is not worried about what will be written the next day but about what is said postgame by the front office.

"Things go awry in the course of a game," Maddon says. "Whether it was something you wanted to do or if you went off script, the head guy or one of the minions will be in your office very quickly. Rare is the time they come down and say, 'Hey, bad luck, the other team is good, too.' It's normally the manager's fault.

"A manager these days is not worried about what is going to be written the next day. We're more worried about someone coming downstairs and ruining your night or your dinner plans."

During spring training in 2019, members of the Cubs' analytics department made a presentation to the staff in the Performance Center theater. Maddon remembers how the analysts struck the perfect balance between the power and the limitations of their information.

"The guys admitted, 'Listen, we're just giving you information,'" Maddon says. "'We don't know how the body works, but we can show you stick figures based on the technology we have to illustrate what we're seeing. We're not telling you how to coach the players. We're just saying, "This is what we're seeing."'

"That's it. Perfect. They're providing information that helps coaches become better coaches and players more efficient players. That's something that I think needs to be more prominent in how they are defined: good, hard-working people here to provide information to make the coaches better, not to coach."

Maddon did not always believe in "Do simple better." He was raised to believe blindly in more work, whether it was by Coach Sieminski making the Hazleton High football team run after losses or Larry Himes ordering his Angels minor league managers to make sure every player showed at least one inch of his stirrups or Mauch insisting on dress codes and daily batting practice. In the same stubborn manner, Maddon attacked his job as a minor league instructor and coordinator.

"I was a mule," he says. "I always felt my job was to get myself tired as much as I can and do the work for the manager when I was in town so that he gets kind of a break. We almost invented extra work back then in the eighties. In the seventies there wasn't a whole lot of that. There weren't enough coaches to cover it per team, per organization. But then it got to the point where organizations started hiring enough coaches to cover it. So you could actually do extra work, and the pitching machines became better and more portable."

One day in 1995, fellow Angels coach Rick Burleson changed Maddon's mind about all the mule work. Burleson had spent most of his playing career with the Boston Red Sox. He'd also coached two years with Boston. Burleson told Maddon he could not believe the Angels took batting practice every day, even in the blistering heat before

Sunday-afternoon games following night games. Four groups a day for an hour or so.

Every year, in a tradition that dated to Mauch, the Angels would stick to the daily grind of batting practice, and most every year, the Angels would fade in September as if exhausted. The Angels posted losing Septembers in twelve of the fourteen seasons from 1987 through 2001. In that span they played .495 baseball through August, only to play .406 baseball in the final month.

"Me, I do what I'm told," Maddon says. "I had nothing to compare it to. But Burley, he used to get mad. He was pissed. I just listened, but it absolutely stuck with me because as I got to move up further and have an eventual say with it, even as an interim manager, I would make sure we didn't hit every day for that length of a time and definitely not on a day game after a night game.

"As I became a manager with the Rays, even though we're playing inside, I started instituting days with no pregame hitting. And there were guys that didn't like it. We had some guys who would go watch the Yankees and see Jeter out there hitting every day, and I used to get some flak from the boys. 'If the Yankees can do it, if Jeter can do it, I can do it.'

"Jeter might have had a little bit of the Michael Jordan maniacal work ethic in him. I'm not sure, but I knew it wasn't good for us because I saw it didn't work. And so we wouldn't hit. Show up late, go out there and play, and win. I mean, just look at the records the latter part of the year that I was manager."

In his first fifteen seasons as a full-time manager, Maddon's teams played much better in the second half (.553 winning percentage) than in the first (.513), including a .526 winning percentage in September. From 2015 through 2018, the Cubs had the best second-half record in the majors (.647). The next-best second-half team, Cleveland, wasn't close (.608).

"One of the most overrated components of the game or pregame is batting practice on the field," he says. "Of course there are times I like it. Of course there are times it's necessary. And I do believe in the camaraderie that is derived from all of that. Absolutely.

"But we play so often, and it's so good in our game to get off routine.

For as much as I love routine, our game also absolutely mandates you to get off routine once in a while to make it all work, so your brains don't burn out."

At his Cubs introductory news conference, Maddon proudly noted, "I won't be there for a seven o'clock game at two o'clock or one o'clock in the afternoon. I promise you I won't. I have a life outside baseball. I don't like sitting in concrete bunkers drinking coffee and watching TV. I'm not into that. The players don't have to be the first one there and the last one to leave to impress me. Not at all. That has nothing to do with winning. Zero."

Each year Maddon held "American Legion Week," during which players were encouraged to show up later than normal without the usual hours of batting practice, extra hitting, cage work, and video study. Put on your spikes and go play, just like back in American Legion ball, when your passion for the game and desire to compete carried you. That's "Do simple better." It meant achieving an uncluttered mental state to perform a task better.

"Constantly reduce," Maddon says. "I wanted to keep players from overcomplicating their jobs. I didn't want extra work. I didn't want too much information. 'Do simple better' sums up my entire approach. I do not like convoluted—wordy or layered—when it comes to teaching and communicating. Straightforward works better. It permits the athlete to hold on to one nugget in a hot moment. 'Do simple better' means reduce, reduce, reduce.

"For example, our defenses were conceptually simple. We were very small on pickoffs. We would pick behind runners, but we didn't have pickoff plays where there was a lot of timing involved or a lot to think about. We were talking about being more intuitive and situational. What is the moment and what are we looking for?

"Our signs were simple. Everybody is worried about somebody on the other side getting signs. The worst part about signs is when your guys don't get them. Preston Gómez used to go through a signs meeting with the Angels, and he would start by saying, 'You guys have to be able to get the signs. Don't worry about everybody else.'"

In 1977, with the Salinas Angels, Maddon roomed on the road with Don Lyons, a first baseman from San Francisco who had been drafted in the fifteenth round out of Gonzaga, where he was an English major. Lyons, the Irish Catholic son of a firefighter, and Maddon, the Italian-Polish Catholic son of a plumber, clicked. They bonded over Jackson Browne, Bruce Springsteen, good books, the pasta Maddon would cook in their adjoining units when the team was home, and especially Lyons's sunny, sharp sense of humor. Teammates called Lyons "Doc" because of his wit.

When Maddon and Lyons would leave the hotel for the ballpark, Maddon would drop a dime and a nickel into the ashtray of their room.

"What are you doing that for?" Lyons asked.

"If I come back and either my dime or my nickel is gone, I'll know I can't trust them," Maddon replied.

Lyons's father had died from a heart attack at age forty-three, when Lyons was thirteen. Lyons had lost other relatives to heart conditions, prompting him to say when playing with Maddon for Salinas at age twenty-two, "I think you can laugh about anything. If somebody was dying, I would tell them that nobody is going to get out of here alive anyway.... I don't give myself a long life. I live from day to day and try to make the most of it."

After playing three minor league seasons, Lyons became a firefighter, an avid gardener, an English teacher who loved Shakespeare, and a high school baseball coach. Joe and Doc maintained their friendship over the years. Maddon marveled at Lyons's way with words in his letters and emails. When Lyons became head coach of Sonoma Valley High in 1999, he called his old roomie and asked for a piece of advice.

"Teach one process really well each day," Maddon told Doc. "Don't try two. Even guys who make millions of dollars are amazed when a jet flies overhead. Don't lose them."

Lyons coached at Sonoma for eighteen years, the last two while battling cancer. Doc Lyons died in 2017. He was sixty-three years old. The advice Maddon gave his good friend in 1999 remains a core part of his philosophy.

"It all comes down to 'Do simple better,'" Maddon says. "Everybody thinks convoluted and complicated must be right. They think, *It has to be right. It's just a really confusing thing to understand, so it has to be right.*

"The reality is that the more you reduce something and give people simple concepts to work with, they can nail it."

CHAPTER 17

"No Regurgitation. We Are All Originals"

Autumn of 1979 in Salinas, California, fell as slowly and heavily as a velvet mohair stage curtain on the playing career of Joe Maddon, the benchwarming, knuckleball-specialist catcher of the ragamuffin Santa Clara Padres. The previous fall the Angels had told him via a dagger of a letter that they no longer wanted him. This time it was cold silence from the rest of the baseball world that signaled to Maddon that he was done.

The silence broke one day with the ringing of the telephone in his rented room in Salinas. It was Pete Ciccarelli, who had been the general manager of the Salinas Angels the previous two seasons, when Maddon played there. On the final day of the 1978 season, manager Chuck Cottier had let Ciccarelli manage the team. Ciccarelli had signed the team's clubhouse manager, Frank Coppenbarger, to a one-day contract and started him at designated hitter, batting third, which is how, in his last game playing affiliated baseball, Joe Maddon came to bat behind the team clubbie.

Ciccarelli was calling from sunny Rancho Bernardo, a section of San Diego. He invited Maddon to visit him. The trip might do him some good, he said. Maddon agreed. He bought a bus ticket.

The bus trip from Salinas to San Diego took about ten hours down I-5. Maddon had plenty of time to stare out the window and to think— and to watch all the gleaming cars that belonged to everyone else purring past him in the California sun.

"I'm just thinking to myself, *One of these days*," Maddon says. "*One of these days, I'm going to drive my own new car down here. Someday...someday I'm going to drive the same Interstate 5 from Northern California down to LA in a new car of my own. It's going to happen someday.*"

The mileposts of our lives are many and familiar. Triumphs and defeats. Weddings and divorces. Births and deaths. Maddon's friend Ciccarelli, for instance, died in 2013 at age sixty after battling MS for three decades. But Maddon can mark the arc of his own professional life in a more unusual manner: with cars, not to mention trucks and the occasional monster recreational vehicle.

"They are the residue of where I grew up," he says. "It also definitely draws on a time gone by that was near and dear to me."

Still running strong in his mind's eye is his father's '53 Chrysler automatic with a clutch, and then the '57 Ford Country Squire wagon, which, with its round headlamps and streamlined fins, looked just as good coming and as it did going. There were the cool cars with killer sound systems that his friends drove around Hazleton. Dave "Cass" Cassarella drove a green '69 Chevelle with a black top, a Hurst shifter with four on the floor, and a 350 engine with cowl induction. When Cass tired of that, he picked up a '70 Chevelle in Olympia Gold.

When Maddon rode in these chariots of his friends', he was transported to another realm just out of his reach. The car-owning cool dudes had decent enough jobs to afford a ride. But Maddon wanted more than a decent job. He wanted a career in baseball. A car—especially a really cool car that invoked style and rattled your ears with seventies rock bands— became the proxy for the sacrifice to chase that dream.

"They had enough to afford vehicles, and I had a dream," Maddon says. "It was a vision, this mental conception that I wanted to be a baseball player, and nothing was going to hold me back. That led to me not being able to afford those kinds of things back then.

"Even as late as 2003, following a divorce, I was pretty much back to rock bottom financially. And I was picked up off the floor by the Devil Rays. And that's pretty much what got me going. A lot of this I owe to those guys. That interview in Houston with Andrew and Matthew and the fact that Stu trusted them and gave me a job . . . I loved those guys.

"I was fifty-two years old. And I am not ashamed to say I worked as hard if not harder than anybody I've ever met on the baseball field. And you can talk to a lot of folks that saw it, as a scout and a manager and a coach and instructor and a coordinator. And then you arrive at a point after all that work where you pretty much had nothing. You were just trying to put it together. There are no bank accounts. There are no savings. No stocks. There's nothing. You're trying to pick it back up and get it going back in the right direction.

"I hope people don't get the wrong impression. This is not old money that I inherited to get to this place. The point is that I might be a risk taker, but I was never a gambler in a sense I didn't gamble money. I felt I worked too hard for it. I think I gambled my ability more than I gambled my earnings.

"In other words, I had a lot of confidence in myself from day one. And I would gamble with that. I would put that on the line all the time. And I still do because I believe it.

"So I took chances. I took risks because I believed I was coming out on top. I believed in the work I put in and how my theories played out. And I have nothing to apologize for. It was pretty successful. That is not an arrogant statement. That is just a confidence based on my belief system.

"So that's the part of this journey that a lot of people don't understand. They will see people like myself in a high-profile position and pretty much think it's always been that way."

Maddon loves cars. As his wife, Jaye, says, he has "a sweet tooth" for cars, especially classic cars with a mélange of elegant design and nostalgia. The shape of a headlamp, the angle of a roofline, the curve of a chrome fender, and the audacity of fins all speak to his love for originality over conformity. It is the same aesthetic he wanted from his players. In the spirit of the '57 Country Squire, the most elegant wagon ever built with its bumper wing guards, cowl-mount spotlight mirrors, and headlamps that resemble inquisitive eyes with brows, Maddon encouraged his players to demonstrate original thought and a diversity of styles. A favorite aphorism Maddon shared with his teams, as he did in spring training with the 2016 Cubs, is "No regurgitation here. We are all originals."

"I get so annoyed when you get around baseball people and all they want to do is regurgitate previous thoughts," he says. "Tell me a better way. Be original."

To Maddon, classic cars represent this spirit of unique self. They are an art form as well as a narrative form. They transport the mind as well as the body. Cars tell his story of growing up in Hazleton, of working his way slowly up the professional baseball ladder without money or pedigree, and of making it in the big leagues. Each seized engine block is another job that went to somebody else. Each car passes a milepost that reminds him of the path that took him here. While not comprehensive, this is a car-by-car story of Maddon's rise in professional baseball:

1980, Boulder Collegians: 1969 Volvo 164

The car made it from Hazleton to Boulder, where Maddon was a player/coach for the Boulder Collegians and worked the counter at Bauldie Moschetti's Baseline Liquors. The trouble began once the blue Volvo made it there.

"It had a bad coil wire," Maddon says. "I'd be making a turn in the middle of a busy intersection, and it would just die. I'd have to get out in like this huge intersection, open the hood, jiggle the wire, and get it going again. But the most interesting part of that car was when it would not go in reverse all winter. All of a sudden, it decided not to go in reverse.

"I always had to be aware of where I was parking. I could go straight out, but there were times where I had no choice, like going into the bank parking lot. There were too many cars. I could not back into my spot. I had to choose one, go in there headfirst. I don't even know what I was doing at the bank anyway. Might have been depositing a check for Bauldie. So I came back out, had to push the car in reverse. I would put it in neutral, punch it on the snow and ice, and jump back in and be on my merry way. An entire winter like that."

1981, California Angels scout and minor league manager: 1981 Plymouth TC3

Maddon knew the Volvo would never make it from Boulder to Anaheim for the start of his job with the Angels. He traded it in toward a new Plymouth TC3, a perky two-door hatchback with square headlamps. No money down.

"Lee Iacocca of Chrysler was giving away cars when I started my scouting career," Maddon says. "Unbelievable. I had no money."

285

1981, Arizona Instructional League manager: 1979 Audi Fox

Maddon had a hankering for a compact station wagon. He traded in his TC3 for a Fox, a four-speed wagon with a slanted hatch and rear seats that folded down.

"I thought it was cool," Maddon says. "I thought it would provide more utility. Wrong.

"Not long after I got the Fox, I'm driving home to Mesa from Tucson. I think it had a slow oil leak, but I did not check it. All of a sudden it was a big oil leak. The engine seized right below Casa Grande and Picacho Peak.

"I traded in a brand-new car because I didn't like it—but it would have run forever—for a car that didn't last me a year. That's how smart I was."

1981, Arizona Instructional League manager: 1979 Chevy Caprice Classic

The Fox was towed to a Phoenix Chevrolet dealership run by Joe Sparks, a minor league manager. The car was pronounced dead. To replace it, Maddon picked out the '79 Caprice, an angular beauty that hit the sweet spot for people who wanted a full-size luxury sedan with clean lines and Chevy value. The model had not changed much since the redesigned 1977 version was named *Motor Trend*'s Car of the Year. There was one problem.

"I've got no money," Maddon says. "Had nothing in the bank. Nothing. So I said, 'Let me call home.'"

Maddon called People's Savings and Trust in Hazleton. One of his buddies, Lee Pilger, worked there. They'd played midget football together. They worked out a loan that was cosigned by Maddon's father. Maddon gladly reported to Sparks that he had the financing for the car. Sparks called the bank to verify the loan.

"He calls People's Bank in Hazleton and gets the manager," Maddon says. "I know my boy Lee is in the background. Joe Sparks tells whomever, 'Joe wants a '79 Chevy Caprice Classic. It costs...' whatever. And the response—and Sparks had never heard this before—was, 'Give the kid what he wants.' I should have asked for a Mercedes, right? How about that? That's because of my dad and my uncles and the kind of reputation that goes around town.

"'Give the kid what he wants.' Sparky laughed at that for so many years."

1985–1994, minor league instructor: 1985 Mitsubishi pickup truck and 1990 Dodge Ram pickup truck

"The Dodge Ram was a four-speed with no AC—in Arizona," Maddon says. "It was great on gas. That's all that mattered. No AC? Just roll the windows down, brother. That did not matter."

1995, major league coach: 1995 Dodge Ram pickup

"I got into the Dodge trucks, the beefy-looking Dodge trucks," Maddon says. "And I loved the original concept of those and still do. This one had AC.

"One day I went to New York and got back home at four in the morning. I go to work out the next day at the Rossmoor Athletic Club. I park the truck out front. I get done working out, come back to my locker, and there's a different lock on it. I thought, *Damn, I know I was out late last night, whatever, but I'm pretty sure this is it.* I went downstairs and had them come up, cut the lock off. I immediately said, 'Oh no.' I went outside, realized, yup, my truck was gone—'95 Dodge Ram, black. Gone. That led to other Dodge Rams. I rode those for a while."

2002, World Series champion Anaheim Angels coach: 1979 Chevy Corvette

"That's when I first started being able to buy somewhat classic cars," Maddon says. "These by no means were gorgeous, but that was my first step. Every long journey must begin with the first step: the '79 Corvette. Really nice shape. Bought it in Phoenix for twelve thousand bucks. Probably paid a little bit too much for it.

"Eventually I'm trying to drive this car from Phoenix to Anaheim after spring training, I get about fifty miles out of Phoenix and lost that engine, too. Something about Phoenix and highways. Anyhow, the engine is gone. I park on the side of the road. I had to have it towed to California.

"Listen, man, I had just gotten my World Series money, but most of that was gone anyhow. I did buy my mom a car. Bought her one of the first Mitsubishi Outlanders. My mom had never had a new car, so she was going to have a new car. I actually drove it all the way back from Huntington Beach to Hazleton. When I got there, I parked it outside of [my sister] Carmine's house and put a big red bow on it. And Beanie came out and was floored. Wow. That was the year my dad had passed away. We still have that vehicle, by the way.

"Later, the engine of the Corvette blew up again. Towed. A lot more money. I sent it to Troy Percival's dad. Mr. Percival had a four hundred cubic engine laying around, threw that bad boy in there and fixed it all up. It ran great for a while."

2003, Angels coach: 1969 Chevy Impala

"I found it parked outside my divorce attorney's office," Maddon says. "Three thousand bucks. Canary yellow with the black convertible top, three-fifty automatic. That thing ran well.

"When I went through my divorce, Arte Moreno offered to help by buying one of my cars to satisfy the settlement. He asked me which one do I want to sell? I should have said the Corvette, but I sold him the '69 Impala. Shoot. I think he still has it. Beautiful car. Loved it.

"I eventually sold the Corvette for nine thousand bucks. More accurately, I got nine thousand after I gave it to a kid for a test drive to see if he wanted to buy it. He totaled it. The insurance company gave me nine. You talk about fortuitous."

2006, Tampa Bay Devil Rays manager: 1994 BMW 740Li (Alan Shore)

"Every time Jaye came into town, we rented a car," Maddon says. "I said, 'This is nuts. Let's just buy something cool that will last and be fun.' We found a '94 BMW. Still have it. It was repainted by the Hillsborough county community college auto department class and redone a bit. That thing runs like a champ.

"Alan Shore is from the TV show *Boston Legal*. We were into it."

2009, American League champion Rays manager: 1972 Chevy Chevelle (Bobba Lou) and 1956 Chevy Bel Air (Bella)

"Fortunately, Jaye, my wife, is into it, too," Maddon says. "The Chevelle was actually in a dealer showroom in Chicago, which is unusual. We went to Chicago, ran it down, found it, paid twenty-eight thousand bucks. That was the first one. That's the one we named Bobba Lou.

"The second one, it's OK to reveal it now, was the result of a bonus payment on the Rays contract. I had never received a bonus. Ever, ever, ever. And I wasn't going to ask the Rays for money. So I asked them if I could have a vehicle, a nice vehicle. We're talking Mopar.

"Jaye and I were up around Oakland. We stopped at this consignment shop for old cars. And we saw an absolutely marvelous '57 Nomad with an LS engine. All red. All-red interior. I fell in love. I gave the guy a twenty-five-hundred-dollar deposit. We still hadn't worked through the contract. And I said, 'I'll finish it off when I come back. We're going to Europe.'

"We're walking through Venice, and I get a call. The dude with the Nomad says he's got a buyer. He needs me to step away from the deal. How about that? I'm in Europe, and this dude walks away from our deal on a gorgeous '57 red-on-red LS engine, four-wheel disc brake.

"We came back and set out to find another car. We ended up in Phoenix at another kind of an antique classic car dealership on Scottsdale Road. They've got a '56 Bel Air. It took the dude seven years to build it. Seventy-five thousand bucks. Still got it. It's a magnificent car. Magnificent build. Built on the Camaro platform, IROC, mid-eighties. The thing runs. It's got four bucket seats. Made out of a Chevy Blazer. The firewall is an old tailgate from a Chevy pickup. That car is magnificent."

2010, Rays manager: 1990 454 SS Chevy pickup
With its huge engine in a relatively small platform, the 454 SS paved the way for performance pickups. "Spring training in Punta Gorda," Maddon says. "We needed a truck because I really missed having the utility of a truck. I'm driving down the main drag there going into Punta Gorda, probably 41. Again, there's an antique or classic car dealership on the right. And I look in, I see in the back there's this pickup truck. And I get closer. It's a 1990 454 SS Chevy pickup, only six thousand or so made. Seven thousand bucks. Jumped on it. To this day one of my favorite vehicles. That's the vehicle with the 454."

2015, Chicago Cubs manager: 1985 Oldsmobile Custom Cruiser station wagon (T-shirt Ted)
Clark Griswold (Chevy Chase) drove a mustard-yellow 1970 model in *National Lampoon's Vacation*. Maddon's ride is Light Royal Blue with wood panels.

"God, do I love that vehicle," he says. "That vehicle runs like new. Fifty-five thousand original miles. I paid seventy-five hundred for that. The station wagon is named T-shirt Ted after Jaye's dad, who drove station wagons and always wore a T-shirt."

2015, Cubs manager: 1976 Dodge Tradesman van (the Cal State Fullerton or the Shaggin' Wagon)
"When I was playing in 1976, first year out of Lafayette, I came out to California for spring training at Cal State Fullerton," he says. "I'm staying at Aunt Ted and Uncle Rick's on 7922 East Garner in El Dorado Park in Long Beach. And a friend by the name of Doug Slevett would pick me up every day at Aunt Ted's in a '76 black Dodge Tradesman 200 van. I swore I was going to have one of those someday.

"It took me a while. I couldn't find it. Finally I found one on Craigslist in a little town outside of Pittsburgh.

"What a great vehicle that is. They're not big, brother. You can deal with that in a parking lot like a Jeep. The wheels are so far forward and back. Easy. Wonderful. Love that thing."

2016, World Series champion Cubs manager: 2016 Dodge Hellcat (the Purple Car)

"After the World Series, me and Jaye decide to give each other a gift," Maddon says, "and that gift was a Plum Crazy Hellcat with black carbon fiber stripes going down the middle, 707 horsepower with everything in it, six-speed TREMEC. What a great car. Not just from speed. They did a great job. Design. Engineering. Nothing brakes like that. Stereo system. Nav unit. Tremendous."

2017, Cubs manager: 2017 Winnebago Grand Tour (the Cousin Eddie)

Maddon cut a deal with Winnebago to serve as a spokesperson, which meant replacing his old RV, the one that had hosted his Cubs job interview with general manager Theo Epstein and assistant general manager Jed Hoyer at a campground near Pensacola, Florida, after the 2014 season. They sat around on beach chairs, drank from wide-mouthed Miller Lite beer bottles, and snacked on chips and salsa while discussing the Cubs job. The original RV and the newer model, a forty-five-footer, share the same name in honor of the Randy Quaid character in *National Lampoon's Christmas Vacation*.

2020, Los Angeles Angels manager: 1979 Lincoln Continental

The original press release touted this sharp-edged yacht on wheels as "the last traditionally full-size American car." No production car in the world would again be this big: a shade over nineteen feet long and weighing in at 4,763 pounds.

"Acquired for five thousand bucks," he says. "Some of my cars are very expensive, some are not. And I build into them a little bit. You got to know when you're wasting money, or if you're doing it just because you dig this car—which would be the Lincoln. That's Hazleton history. That's a time capsule right there."

Maddon has come miles from riding the bus on I-5 for ten hours or pushing a disobedient Volvo in the snow and ice of Colorado. The Cousin Eddie, for instance, is tricked out with four televisions, one of which is sixty inches, a washer and dryer, a full refrigerator, heated floors, and a fireplace.

The story his cars tell is one of the fearlessness required of leaders.

"All of these different things that I've done and all these different cars I've driven, all the different places I've lived, all the different influences I've had, permit me to take chances," Maddon says. "Fortune favors the bold. I have to tell you, man, I wasn't always like that. Of course I was afraid."

Maddon, for instance, did not do well with public speaking as a young man. He fretted over the preparation. He worried his discomfort with public speaking would cause him to bomb managerial interviews or that if he ever did get a big league managing job, he would fumble the many public appearances and media conferences that are a part of it. "It was a concern of mine—big-time," he says.

In the early 1990s Maddon took a Dale Carnegie Course to learn coping strategies. A line from a Carnegie graduate about public speaking stuck with him: "I would rather be whipped than start, but two minutes before I finish, I would rather be shot than stop."

"That's brilliant," he says. "So whenever I was having a hard time, I would think about that. It was very helpful."

Maddon was especially nervous before the news conference when he was introduced by the Devil Rays as their new manager, his first full-time managing job in the majors. He began with that Dale Carnegie line. Sure enough, he killed it. He enthralled the media with his bullpen philosophy ("You need to have four functional guys out there that you can pitch when you're even or ahead"), his musical tastes (Motown, Pavarotti, rock, but "Springsteen is always number one"), his favorite dish to cook ("Chicken Maddonni"), his lawn-mowing technique ("Stripe it out like a [baseball] field"), and his father, who hadn't lived to see his son become a full-time major league manager ("Dad never had a bad day. People are in such a hurry to grow up. I'm in no hurry. This is a dream job. But every day is a dream").

"Afterward my agent, Tommy Tanzer, came up to me," Maddon says. "He looked at me with those wide eyes, and he asked me, 'Where did that come from?' I said, 'What do you mean?' He says, 'I've never seen that person before.' And my response was, 'I've never been asked before. Never been in that position before.'

"Tommy had never heard me be the lead singer in the major leagues before, other than a little bit of interim work. The stuff that he heard, I had done so many times at Gene Autry Park in Instructional League, but, of course, nobody was there—'When the tree falls in the woods, does anybody hear it?' kind of a thing. When a manager speaks at Gene Autry Park on September eighteenth, with a hundred and five degrees screaming down the back of your neck, does anybody hear it other than the players? Of course not."

The Hazleton Maddon knew in his Kodachrome childhood, the one that inspires his car buying, changed dramatically about twenty years ago. As the coal industry dwindled, so did Hazleton. Pennsylvania offered tax breaks to attract new businesses. Many of the jobs created were low-wage, unskilled jobs that attracted immigrants. Hazleton was no longer just a subdivision of Europe with its many Poles and Italians. From 2000 to 2006, the Hispanic population in Hazleton grew from 5 percent to 30 percent. The city council and Hazleton's mayor, Lou Barletta, who'd attended school and played ball with Maddon, passed the Illegal Immigrant Relief Act, which targeted businesses that hired undocumented immigrants. The rapid demographic change cleaved the city.

"I came home in 2010, and I was really disappointed with how it felt," Maddon says. "The vibe was terrible. It was dark. We decided to do something about it."

In 2011 Joe and Jaye started the Hazleton Integration Project to build bridges between the established Eurocentric population and the emerging Latino population. Two years later, they opened the Hazleton Community One Center, which provides classes, computers, activities, and food services, largely for children from economically disadvantaged families. In 2015 they formed the Respect 90 Foundation with the mission of creating opportunities for children and families "to develop championship attitudes through sports, academics and community involvement." That, too, is leadership, and with a higher purpose: playing a part in helping create childhoods as happy as the one he holds so dear. Many of his cars honor the sweetness of his youth and the length of his journey. The story they tell is as original as it gets. He is glad that story is a long, difficult one.

"I know the cars sound frivolous sometimes," he says, "but to me, they are not. They are a big part of my past and how I've arrived at this point. That's why I enjoy them so much and that's why I take care of them so well.

"Those are my trophies. The championship rings are wonderful, and they indicated we were really good, and I was really good at what I did. But these cars...man, there's something deeper. I could just sit by them and stare at them forever, when they're all shined up, and take them out for a ride and everything is humming properly.

"Between cars and music, I could pretty much chronologically recap my existence. Vividly. And I can honestly say that all of it was earned. *Earned* is a really important word to me. That I've earned something is a really, really important concept.

"I have such a hard time when I'm given something because I have to feel like you have to repay somehow. I have this mental scorecard constantly that, weirdly, I just cannot be on the downside of this ledger because—probably a lot of folks that feel that way, but I'm telling you, I'm at the top of the list, man. I am. I'm really good at giving things away, and I'm really bad at getting things. And I'm grateful for that."

CHAPTER 18

"Embrace the Target"

The Lead Bulls stopped running in 2019. Theo Epstein stopped them. The Chicago Cubs president of baseball operations told Maddon his annual policy-setting meeting would be overhauled. There would be no more handpicked Lead Bulls, Epstein said, but rather a council of players picked by a vote of all members of the team. The council also would meet several times during the season. Furthermore, Epstein and his general manager, Jed Hoyer, would be a part of these meetings. Never had anyone from the front offices of the Rays or Cubs attended Maddon's Meeting of the Lead Bulls.

"All of a sudden, what we were doing wasn't right anymore," Maddon says. "Now the meeting has to be elected people where we have to have players vote upon it. They were no longer the Lead Bulls. They were now the executive council, something like that.

"I remember one time that meeting really went bad because they started talking about playoffs almost like it was a foregone conclusion, like that's going to happen. And God, I didn't like the tone of that meeting at all. I didn't like what was being said at the table. It was almost like the bats were already packed. 'We're in.'"

The death of the Lead Bulls was a symbolic start to the season. After the Cubs' Wild Card loss to Colorado the previous season, and with Maddon cast as a lame duck on the last year of his contract, the 2019 Cubs would be run day to day with more input from the front office.

"The year of interference," Maddon calls it.

"I totally disagreed with changing the Lead Bulls meeting, but at the same time I go back to Colin Powell: 'I'll give you my strongest advice and give you my strongest loyalty.'

"This is where you get to the point where you're talking and you look at the door to see who's walking in. When you arrive at the point where you can't talk without looking at the door, that's a bad place to be."

One day in the late 1970s, the musician Neil Young, then thirty-three years old, was jamming with Mark Mothersbaugh of the band Devo. Mothersbaugh had worked as a graphic artist for an advertising company. One of his clients made a rust inhibitor. As they were playing Young's "Hey Hey, My My," Mothersbaugh drew on the ad campaign from his daytime job and ad-libbed the lyrics "Rust never sleeps." Young immediately loved it. The phrase captured the essence of where Young was in his career. He was enormously successful but fearful of the danger of artistic complacency—the musician's version of rust. Young named his 1979 album *Rust Never Sleeps*. It went platinum, won *Rolling Stone*'s critics' poll for Album of the Year, and is often considered Young's best album because of his renewed boldness.

Complacency can corrode. Baseball is proof. Never in the history of baseball has defending a championship been more difficult than it is in this generation. Entering 2022, none of the previous twenty-one World Series champions had successfully defended their title. The past nineteen champions had averaged ten fewer wins in defense of their title than in their championship season, based on prorated winning percentage.

The reasons are many. Competitive balance never has been better. Analytics have leveled the playing field. The days are long gone when smart general managers such as Billy Beane and Epstein could pick the pockets of old-school general managers who still valued batting average and runs batted in. Fourteen franchises, nearly half the teams in baseball, reached the eleven World Series between 2011 and 2021. The expansion of the playoffs after 1995 added another potential hurdle to trip up even the best teams.

The 106-win 2021 Dodgers, for instance, beat the 107-win Giants in the Division Series but lost to the 88-win Braves in the National League Championship Series. The nineteen-win gap marked the third-biggest upset in postseason history based on win differential, behind the 1906 White Sox over the Cubs (–23) and the 2001 Yankees over the Mariners (–21). The "better" team can easily lose when a season is reduced to a short series, but when it takes three or four series to become champion, the odds increase of falling into such a trap.

Defending champions can also suffer a natural letdown from the intensity and rewards of a month of playoff baseball. When Cleveland began 2017 with a 24-25 record after the Cubs stopped the team one inning from a World Series title, manager Terry Francona noted the drop in emotional edge from playing in the postseason spotlight to playing in lousy early-season weather in front of sparse crowds. "It's just not the same environment to maintain that sharp focus," he said. "It's human nature."

Rust never sleeps. Maddon saw it firsthand himself. After winning the 2002 World Series, the Angels began the next year 13-17 and never recovered. They won twenty-two fewer games. His 2009 Rays had a losing record sixty games deep into their defense of their shocking AL pennant and won thirteen fewer games.

"Going back to camp in '17, I was very aware of this, very aware," Maddon says. "First of all, you have to address it. I always believe in talking about it. So I wanted to make sure we went to camp and when we opened the meeting that all my thoughts I would bring out to the front. 'This is my concern. This is what was going to get in the way of the repeat.' I was really concerned about that.

"The plan was to take it easy on the pitchers, take it easy on the starters. Build into that first part of the season knowing that there's going to be a little bit of a physical letdown, definitely an emotional letdown based on the previous year. These games, even if you're playing in Wrigley and it's jam-packed, they're just not the same. Think about it. You've just won for the first time in 108 years, and on top of that, you're the youngest team ever to win it. There's a lot of stuff going on there. A lot. So I was aware of not pushing too hard. I was aware of filling them up with my previous experiences as to what I think can happen that we have got to guard against."

The dynastic Yankees of Joe Torre conquered the rust of complacency. In doing so, they set an improbably high bar in this expanded playoff world. The Cubs were just one of many teams who could not live up to it. From 1996 until the 2001 World Series, Torre's teams won seventeen of eighteen postseason series and fifty-three of seventy-one postseason games, an astounding .746 winning percentage at a time when analytics mavens such as Beane were arguing the small sample size of October baseball made the postseason a glorified coin flip. The Yankees kept coming up heads series after series. Why?

Says Maddon about defending a championship, "It's a physical and emotional test that requires at least a couple of extraordinary guys that are able to just keep it moving forward, who can rise above the natural letdown and challenge themselves."

The Yankees were loaded with such players. They benefited from a core of level-five players who had grown up in the Yankees system, in which "All I want to do is win" was emphasized throughout the minor leagues—players such as Derek Jeter, Bernie Williams, Jorge Posada, Andy Pettitte, and Mariano Rivera. The front office supplemented the core with like-minded players such as Paul O'Neill, Tino Martinez, Scott Brosius, and David Cone.

"We won a World Series, and nobody was ever satisfied with that," Torre says. "I noticed that almost nobody wore their World Series ring. That told me something. The players never stopped to admire what they accomplished. You can't teach that. Derek was the one most responsible for that attitude right from the get-go."

From the start, Torre contributed mightily to the "never satisfied" environment around the Yankees. Fifty-five years old and fired three times, he was the right man at the right time to work for George Steinbrenner, the team's impetuous owner. "What's the worst that can happen to me? I get fired again?" he would say. In his first meeting as manager in 1996, Torre told his players he wanted to win not just one World Series but at least three, even though he had never been there as a player or manager.

"I just felt that if you won one, the real test came after that," Torre says. "You win once, now what am I thinking? Do you have the responsibility in you to go out there and drive yourself again to go further? I always had the feeling that you have to keep getting better in this game. Staying the same isn't enough. Everybody is shooting at you.

"One thing I preached to my daughter, because I managed all those years when we didn't win and I'd have to find something to motivate them, is that I told her failure is OK. You can't live there, but you learn from it. It's a tough lesson to learn because nobody wants to fail. And that's where Jeter stands out above anybody else. Paul O'Neill was the same way. If they failed, they did not change. They still went out there with reckless abandon. And they did the same thing when they won."

Torre provided another advantage that contributed to the Yankees' extending their success. With his calm temperament and communication skills, he made sure any smoldering issues did not ignite into brushfires the way they had in past Yankees teams under Steinbrenner.

"When I took over, I thought the most important job I had was communication," Torre says. "It wasn't always verbally, but it was also important to let the players know through my actions that sure, I had a boss, but I make all the baseball decisions. Nobody was going to play because he called down and said, 'Play this guy.' I thought that was important— to insulate the clubhouse from possible distractions."

As competitive balance grew, as the core New York players aged, and as teams became smarter about building a winner, especially the rival Boston Red Sox, the Yankees stopped winning postseason series at the same nearly impossible rate. It wasn't that they stopped winning games. Torre managed the Yankees for twelve years. They won at a better clip in his last six years (.609) than they had in the first six (.601). But they did not win as many of those small samples of October. The second half of the Torre era yielded two pennants, but no World Series titles. The strain of not winning titles in those second six years eventually led to a breakup between Torre and the Yankees' front office.

"The last few years with the Yankees, I felt there was an element that wanted to make a change," Torre says. "I don't think either one of us knew how to say goodbye."

At the end of his managerial career and into his tenure as a vice president with Major League Baseball, Torre saw the power balance in baseball tip toward the front office and away from managers. As an MLB executive, Torre spoke to every manager new to the job about the importance of honoring the unique leadership and decision-making skills that had carried him to the dugout.

"I talked to all of them one-on-one," Torre says. "And the one message I give that is consistent with all of them is, 'You've been in baseball a long time. Don't ever put yourself in a position not to use your instincts. You've earned that. You don't want to lose that sense of what you need to do. It might not work all the time, but you must remember that when you took this job, it was not to forget what you've learned.'

"It's disturbing for me to see it happen sometimes, because there is so much you learn from being in the dugout during the game where you have to make up your mind from all sorts of sources you are observing—sometimes even just from the body language of the players. It comes down to this: Are you going to do your job, or are you going to do it so that you don't lose your job?—which means doing something just because you have a sheet of paper to back it up."

The 2016 Cubs were the youngest team ever to win Game 7 of the World Series. Why should they not have been expected to rattle off more titles? Why couldn't they become the next version of Torre's Yankees, or even Bruce Bochy's San Francisco Giants, who had won the three previous even-year titles? The answer may be found in how difficult it was to win one.

The Cubs' run in 2016 began when Javy Báez hit the only possible automatic home run in baseball that does not clear an outfield wall—a fly ball into the overhanging basket at Wrigley Field—in NLDS Game 1 against a dominant Johnny Cueto of the Giants. San Francisco left fielder Ángel Pagán swore he would have caught it if only that wire basket had not been there since 1970, a response to rowdy bleacher bums interfering with the game by, for example, falling off the wall.

It took an act of God for Game 7 of the World Series to turn in the Cubs' favor: the seventeen-minute rain delay.

The Cubs never did return to the World Series under Maddon. It would take only two seasons without a pennant for the marriage between Epstein and Maddon to hit the rocks—two seasons in which the Cubs won 187 games, more than any team in the National League except the ascendent Dodgers. Winning one World Series had set internal expectations soaring. The question of whether the Cubs could ever win a World Series hardened into a declaration that they *should* win.

The expectations did not bother Maddon. Indeed, after the young Cubs reached the 2015 NLCS, where they were stopped by the New York Mets, Maddon built his 2016 spring training on the theme of embracing expectations. On his iPad, he drew a diagram for his players to get the point across. He began with a circle—a target—pierced by an arrow pointing up. At the top of the circle, also accompanied by arrows pointing up, were the words "Expectations" and "Pressure."

Next to "Expectations" he wrote, "Strong Belief. Something will happen in my favor."

Next to "Pressure" he wrote, "A motivator. A positive. An indication you are in the right place."

"If you hear the word *expectations*, run toward it," he told his team. "If you hear the word *pressure*, run toward it. That's where your goals are going to be met."

Inside the circle was his message to the 2016 Cubs:

SPRING TRAINING 2016
1. Embrace the target.
2. We all have to set aside our personal agendas.
3. All do our jobs (9 on 1).
4. Know we are not perfect but can be present = power.
5. We are our own little planet.
6. Rotate around the same goals.

The diagram provided the basis of the notes he used to deliver his spring training address. His marginalia included these pearls:

Do simple better. Constantly reduce.

The process is fearless.

"Change before you have to"...Jack Welch.

"Wisdom is the reward from a lifetime of listening when you
would have preferred to talk"...Doug Larson.

Communication creates collaboration. Big ears are better than
big egos.

"When you're not listening, ask good questions"...Bill Walsh.

Maddon defined the expectations: "Playoffs. Div. W.S. Play the last game of the year and win it."

He defined the process: "Embrace the target. Expectations are managed thru the relentless execution of the process."

He defined *pressure*. "Pressure is defined individually...is a motivator... is a positive...is attractive. Wanna be around it."

The 2016 Cubs responded. They stormed out of the gate with eight wins in nine games. It took them only fifty-three games to build a ten-game lead. They won 103 games. They played fast and loose. By the time October hit, veteran catcher David Ross had put his finger on how Maddon prepared his team so well. "It's a freedom," Ross said. "It's a freedom of be yourself.... He lets guys, their athleticism come out. He wants you to kind of just play the game. Almost like in Little League. When you make mistakes, which we have done all year, you learn from them, try to teach, and move on.... There's a continual growth, and that stems from Joe."

The 2016 Cubs had more home runs from players twenty-five and under, 101, than any world champions except the 1957 Milwaukee Braves, with Hank Aaron and Eddie Mathews hitting seventy-six of their 107. The young team thrived on the pressure. Now they would have to do it again in 2017, only this time as defending world champions, with the rust of complacency a real threat.

"We fought the hangover," Maddon says. "So '17, what was so bad about it? That's the part about all of this that, really, I have a hard time processing. The '17 group was actually pretty fabulous. The way we fought back and the way we competed."

Were the 2017 Cubs a failure because they did not win the World Series? They won ninety-two games even after reaching the All-Star break with a losing record, 43-45. They beat Washington in the Division Series with a rally so miraculous that it suggested divine intervention, like that seventeen-minute rain delay in Cleveland. There are four ways for a batter to reach base without putting the ball in play: a walk, a dropped third strike, catcher's interference, and a hit by pitch. The four methods occurred consecutively, for the first time in baseball history, in Game 5 of that series. It happened in the fifth inning against Nationals ace Max Scherzer. An inning that began with the Cubs trailing 4-3 ended with the Cubs winning 7-4. They never trailed again and won, 9-8.

And then the Cubs' luck turned. The decline of the Cubs, and Maddon's job security, began that night.

"What happened after that game is what nobody talks about, and that's a big reason why we had such a hard time in the LCS," Maddon says. "We had a hard time in Washington, but we win the game. It's late. We're leaving out of D.C. for LA. Who knows what time it is, but you're so happy you don't care. It was that tough of a game, that tough of a series against a really good team.

"So we're flying west and, all of a sudden, we have a medical emergency where we have to land in Albuquerque. What was it, three o'clock in the morning, four o'clock in the morning Albuquerque time? That's pretty late. Our body time is a couple hours ahead of that.

"We take care of the medical emergency. You always have to honor that, there's no question. That's not my complaint. And what happens after that? We sit on that tarmac until ten o'clock in the morning Albuquerque time because we had to wait on pilots and the pilots are coming out of Denver.

"So we're sitting on that plane. Again, we're not upset. You just won a tremendous game, but now you really run out of gas. Finally we take off at ten in the morning and land at LAX. The buses greet you. You go to the hotel, and they already have a breakfast/lunch set up for us upstairs in the hotel. And of course they want our players to show up for interviews. I'm pretty sure we didn't permit that, but I had to go out there to do my thing. Again, who cares? Who cares? You won, we're good. Let's go.

"We go out there to play the Dodgers, who had just gone back and forth between Phoenix and LA playing the Diamondbacks. They got them in three, relatively simply. So we had this knock-down, drag-out battle with the Nationals while they were rested. We had to show up and play that next day, arrive at noon that day.

"Our guys battled their balls off, but it's just not good. The one thing more than anything I want my guys to have on a daily basis or before they're playing any big game is rest, and we certainly didn't have that. For those that don't think that's a big deal, it is.

"So the Dodgers had their way with us. Beat us up pretty well."

The weary Cubs managed four hits in Game 1 in Los Angeles and lost 5–2. They never did hit much. The Dodgers were a loaded, 104-win team with the biggest payroll in baseball and a pitching staff that led the league in ERA and strikeouts and walked the fewest batters. Los Angeles held the Cubs to a .156 batting average and won in five games, three of them started by Clayton Kershaw and Yu Darvish, both of whom were fully rested. It was a matchup nightmare for the Cubs. They hit .070 off the Dodgers' breaking pitches, with just three hits in forty-three at bats. They did not score a run after the fifth inning.

"But from my perspective, we won it in 2016 with the youngest team ever, and the next year, in spite of a lot of difficulties, we got back to the LCS again and probably played a little more hungry Dodger team," Maddon says. "We had beaten them in '16, and so they came back and got their revenge.

"I mean, are we that narcissistic to believe that we're that good? That it can't be that these other teams are also very good, had a lot of dough, had some nice players? All of a sudden, it's got to be somebody's fault you lost to the Dodgers? Really? That's so lame. It just lacks total understanding not only how baseball works, but how the world works.

"I was so proud of our guys. Could not have been more proud of our guys."

Epstein was pragmatic about the series defeat, saying, "It's not about front offices or managers. It's about the players." He would not be so dismissive when the Cubs came up even shorter in 2018.

The 2018 Cubs won ninety-five games, an improvement of three wins, including the last scheduled game of the regular season, to force a tie-breaker game at Wrigley Field against Milwaukee. They lost, 3–1, while managing just three hits. The defeat put them in the Wild Card Game against Colorado. They lost that game, 2–1, with just six hits.

Because of rainouts, the Cubs played forty games in the final forty-two days. In one stretch in September, they played Wednesday in Chicago, Thursday in Washington, Friday in Chicago, and Monday in Arizona. In the Thursday game, Maddon allowed reliever Pedro Strop to bat with a one-run lead. Maddon wanted Strop back on the mound to protect the lead. But when Strop injured his hamstring running out a ground ball, Maddon absorbed withering criticism from the media for letting his relief pitcher bat. Epstein was upset, too, because he had considered sending a reduced roster to Washington just to conserve the energy of some players rather than having them travel for one game.

"When Stropy got hurt, I know Theo was upset about that to the point I think he made a comment he should have done what he thought and not sent him in the first place, which is just antithetical," Maddon says. "You're just trying to win the game and especially that one game. It was unforgivable—only because he got hurt. Of course, if he had either gotten a hit or was just out and didn't try to beat it out at the end, just being competitive, it would have been fine, but he didn't, and he pulled it, and it becomes my fault.

"That's the kind of stuff that really is very annoying when you're making decisions based on trying to win and something goes awry. But I knew it was a great victory, one that permitted us actually to tie in that one-game playoff. Maybe we would have been better off losing and having some rest going into the Wild Card, I don't know. Look at the schedule that occurred at the end of that year. There's so much to not apologize for. It was fabulous."

Epstein was bewildered that the Cubs had stopped hitting in the second half. After the All-Star break, they ranked twenty-third in OPS, twenty-fourth in home runs, and twenty-seventh in slugging. The offense, he said, "broke somewhere along the lines." The Cubs hit 7 percent more ground balls than any other team in the second half.

"That's unacceptable," Epstein said the day after the Wild Card loss. "We have to learn from it, and we have to get better. What's the cause of it? What are the contributing causes? We have some ideas, but that's why we're doing all these exit interviews."

Exit interviews? Epstein would interview his players before they went home. He was determined to find out why the offense had "broken." Some of the evidence, he decided, pointed to Maddon and his methods.

About three weeks later, Maddon was in Nashville for the grand opening of an intimates shop owned by his son, Joey, his daughter-in-law, Natalie, and his wife, Jaye. From there he and Jaye were leaving on a tenth-anniversary trip to Austria, Germany, and Italy. He was at the airport in Nashville when his phone rang. It was Epstein.

"I just wanted you to know we are not going to offer you a contract extension," Epstein told him. "I think at this point all of us should just focus on winning next year. Just concentrate on next year."

Epstein would announce the decision to the media on November 5, 2018, explaining, "We are not running away from Joe in the least, but given that we all have things that we're working on to get more out of this team and to be one game better than we were last year, this is the appropriate move."

Maddon was dumbfounded by the phone call. The news from Epstein caught him off guard.

"I played along," Maddon says. "I'm not one to create controversy, especially with the season over, we're in the airport, we're getting ready to go to Europe, our tenth anniversary, all that kind of stuff. I am not going to stop and say, 'What does that mean?'

"But afterwards, I thought, *What the hell does that mean?* It's executalk where guys make stuff up and they try to pass it along to everybody else like it matters and makes sense when it really doesn't.

"So I got on a plane going to Europe knowing that my Cub future is in doubt. There's going to be no extension in spite of averaging ninety-five or ninety-six wins a year, really developing a lot of young players, holding down the media fort, defending everybody, including the front office, and you're going to be left out in the wind like that without any support whatsoever. That's the part of that that really was not cool. That was not cool."

It was about to get much worse for Maddon.

CHAPTER 19

"Know We Are Not Perfect but Can Be Present"

The document ran three pages, single spaced. Across the top, in capital letters, it said, "EXIT INTERVIEW THEMES FOR JOE." This was Theo Epstein's white paper on Joe Maddon. Epstein had prepared it from the information he'd gleaned from the players' exit interviews. He summoned Maddon from Pennsylvania to Chicago to present him with his findings. Epstein had identified four issues for Maddon to fix in 2019. He'd headed them "Work/Structure," "Communication with Players," "Need to Reinforce That the Players Come First," and "Urgency Necessary to Replace Complacency." Epstein had included a total of fifteen solutions to fix these issues.

Under the "Work/Structure" topic, Epstein had written, "One clear takeaway from the exit interviews was that our young position players need more structure and more routine-oriented work." They'd admitted to Epstein that the freedom Maddon gave them "has been unintentionally taken advantage of." The solutions Epstein offered included more batting practice, more structure in the daily schedule, and more meetings.

Under the communication heading, Epstein had written, "There's no other way to say this other than the players still feel there is a communication deficit with you," and that the fact that "there were always people in your office" precluded conversations. The suggested solutions included Maddon's arriving earlier at the ballpark, keeping his office clear of visitors before games, walking the outfield during batting practice, and considering monthly individual player meetings—with Epstein or Hoyer sitting in.

The "Players Come First" issue, Epstein had written, resulted from players complaining that Maddon would mention one-on-one conversations with players in media interviews and that his forays into charitable artwork and T-shirts were "all about you." Epstein advised him to "strongly consider stopping the art and T-shirt programs" and replace them with "something clearly 'about the players.'"

The complacency issue referred to complaints by players that in the first five months of the season "there was a pervasive sense within the clubhouse that 'we would be fine.'" Epstein suggested "an enhanced sense of urgency," starting with a spring training that was "a bit more workmanlike."

The memo surprised Maddon.

"Theo needed to do something else," Maddon says. "He needed to become more involved. It started with those exit meetings, and he had me fly in from Pennsylvania to sit there with him and listen to the download they had received from players."

Maddon regarded the white paper as a repudiation of the same methods that had previously been lauded—the same ones he'd used over his four years as manager to guide the Cubs to three straight Championship Series, their first World Series title in 108 years, and the best record in baseball.

Hadn't he proudly announced at his introductory news conference that he would not be showing up early at the ballpark "sitting in concrete bunkers drinking coffee and watching TV" because such eyewash "has nothing to do with winning"? Now Epstein wanted him in early.

Hadn't David Ross said the key to the Cubs' winning in 2016 had been the "freedom" Maddon gave his players? Now such freedom needed to be curtailed.

Hadn't his teams' loose approach resulted in the best second-half record in baseball over his four years in Chicago? Maddon's Cubs had played .621 baseball in the second half, compared to .549 in the first half. Now taking the long view needed reappraisal and more season-long urgency.

Hadn't young players flourished under Maddon? In his four seasons as Cubs manager, no other team had had more plate appearances, hits, home runs, and RBIs from players twenty-five and under than had his

Cubs. And yet now Epstein heard such dissatisfaction from young players that Maddon came to refer to the white paper as "the millennial study." Maddon would even read *Managing Millennials for Dummies* that winter to appease his boss.

The 2018 season had forced Maddon into more difficult lineup decisions, especially with more level-two players entering the mix, just trying to survive. Three of Epstein's number one draft picks, Kyle Schwarber, Albert Almora, and Ian Happ, were competing for playing time in the outfield with veterans Jason Heyward and Ben Zobrist. As with most young players, their development happened in fits and starts. Shortstop Addison Russell lost his job, first because of nagging injuries, then with a violation of MLB's domestic violence policy.

"As opposed to veterans, where I did not interfere with their greatness, I would be more apt to interfere with an ascending player," Maddon says. "Kyle Schwarber. Albert Almora. Addison Russell. Willson Contreras. Ian Happ. Ascenders. Yeah, you interfere a little bit more. Not in the sense you're trying to change them, but you have to help them work through moments. And a lot of it has to do with conversations based on their usage, which they're never going to be happy with.

"Back in the day, the nineties Angels, we had Garret Anderson, Tim Salmon, Jimmy Edmonds, and Darin Erstad. They were the four before Jimmy got traded. All outfielders. All needed to play. And we thought, as a staff, that's great. We will be able to give one a day off as a DH, rest him up a little bit and should benefit all. Cool.

"I don't know if it was among the four of them or possibly conversation among the veteran players or it was purely media driven, but that turned into a little bit of a hot mess. It was very uncomfortable for Terry Collins. When you get into moments like that, it's not a leadership situation necessarily from the manager on down. It could be a perception problem from your guys.

"And they're young, don't forget. And they are easily influenced from a variety of different sources. So you're not just fighting the player himself. You're fighting maybe an agent, a father, a friend, a wife, a girlfriend, public opinion. You're fighting a lot of different things right there in an attempt to do the right thing for him and the group.

"When you have to work through Albert, Kyle, and Ian, and provide adequate at bats for them to develop and try to place them at their best possible moment, based on all the different factors I just mentioned, that could influence them walking into the door every day. Not easy.

"It's not a leadership thing. It's not like you don't know what the hell you're doing. It's trying to answer their questions while they're constantly trying to be a good teammate and pontificating that they are and, at the same time, having to answer them in closed-door meetings when they're upset for not playing often enough.

"So that's the balancing act. That's an ascending star. The superstar for me and just a veteran player in general, normally, has been easier. If it's a veteran player that is a role player, he knows it. He gets it. He knows when to be ready. He knows when he's probably going to play. He doesn't bitch and moan. He just comes ready. And if he has a question, it's very respectful, and it's normally an easy conversation."

It had been only eighteen months since Epstein spoke glowingly about Maddon at the Yale commencement, saying he was the right manager to lead a core of young players to the World Series title. "Thankfully, we hired a manager in Joe Maddon who agreed it was time to turn these conventions on their heads.... Unburdened and empowered, our young team flourished," Epstein said then.

What had changed in eighteen months?

At the field level, pitching changed. Hitting across baseball was entering a trough. The growth of technological aids, including super-slow-motion cameras and spin-tracking devices, changed pitch selection and pitch properties to make hitting more difficult. For instance, the percentage of breaking pitches and cut fastballs—pitches under the umbrella of "spin"—increased over eight consecutive seasons from 2013, when it was 22.1 percent, to 2021, when it was 36.2 percent. Just from 2016 to 2018, the spin percentage increased from 31.5 percent to 33.2 percent. The MLB batting average fell in that time from .255 to .248, a forty-eight-year low since the introduction of the designated hitter. Epstein employed different hitting coaches in 2017, 2018, and 2019, part of a stretch of changing hitting coaches six times in eight years.

The Cubs did increase their batting average and slugging slightly from 2016 to 2018, but the effects of the "spin revolution" showed in the second half of 2018, when Epstein said the offense "broke." Where the Cubs saw 29.5 percent spin in 2016 and 33.7 percent in the first half of 2018, that percentage rose to 35.2 percent in the second half of 2018.

What also changed Epstein's outlook on Maddon was that the Cubs' hitters went cold in two small-sample-size series. In 2017 they managed three hits in five games against spin from the Dodgers, the best pitching staff in baseball. In 2018 their postseason consisted of one game in which Colorado pitchers threw them 54.6 percent spin, against which they went 2 for 23.

Those two postseason ousters, followed by the exit interviews, caused Epstein to question Maddon's methods. In trying to determine why his offense had broken, Epstein valued the opinions of his young players, including level-two players in survival mode.

"I know you may disagree with this," Epstein wrote Maddon regarding how players complained he was not available enough. "I can only tell you that whether they are right or wrong about it, the players feel (and volunteer) that they aren't getting enough of you. If they feel that way, that means it's an issue and we should look for solutions."

Says Maddon, "They felt as though we needed more work, and that my office wasn't accessible. It is really a bunch of BS, quite frankly, for anybody that has ever known me before or after. It could have been something that was extrapolated from one conversation. It's really insulting, quite frankly, to hear all that because I just know it's not true. If you're going to listen to first- or second-year players who might be upset by the fact they didn't think they played enough, then it becomes even more disingenuous.

"But that's all I heard. That's all I heard in the off-season. But still, being the optimist, I thought, *OK, I'll put this back together for everybody.*

Then the more I thought about it, I really got more upset because I knew how disingenuous and incorrect it was.

"What we had done and how we had done it from the time I got there to the time this all came down, we had a great method in place, a great culture was established, the way we worked. There was less batting practice because I didn't want them on their feet all the time, especially with all the day games we played. How did that work out? Was it ninety-five, ninety-six wins? Come on. How do you somehow dissect all of that to indicate that there was a lack of leadership, lack of accountability?

"It's really execu-talk where they just have to make stuff up in order to promote the agenda that they want. For me it's easy. Just say, 'Listen, we just want to do something different next year. We need to get more involved again. We need more control of what's going on.' And that's it. And I'm good. Believe me, I'm good. That would have been such a much better way for me personally because I would have done anything.

"'Who do you want to break in? Who do you want next? Even if we win the World Series this year, good, I'm out. I'm good, I'll be fine. I'll land on my feet, whatever. Who do you want me to help nurture?' I'd have been so up for that if it was just straight up. But it wasn't.

"So that's it. That was the breakdown. The breakdown was this faux method developed based on what they wanted. I'm telling you, that's their right. If they choose to do that, absolutely, that's within their purview.

"That's fine if you don't want me to do what I'm doing anymore, but don't tear down what we've done, and don't tear down the way we've done it."

In addition to the white paper to Maddon, Epstein wrote a two-page letter addressed to "the Returning Players and Staff of the 2019 Chicago Cubs." He sent it to them weeks after the 2018 season ended and before the calendar turned. It began with a quote from Joe Torre, whose dynastic Yankees, with the way they won multiple titles, were becoming more of an outlier with every passing year.

In baseball, we never realize what we have until it is too late. Our time in this sport is borrowed. The time we have together goes incredibly fast. The chance to be part of a group that does special things can be gone before we know it. We owe it to ourselves and to each other to make sure we give absolutely everything that we have. We want to leave nothing undone in our quest to win together. We won't win every single time, but we will have no regrets.

—JOE TORRE (WORLD SERIES CHAMPIONS: 1996, 1998, 1999, 2000).

Epstein acknowledged in the letter that "in just a few short years, the certainty of losing has been replaced by the expectation of winning," which had made the 2018 Wild Card loss so painful.

He referred to the exit interviews in which "all of us admitted that our group suffered from periods of complacency this year. All of us admitted that a true sense of urgency failed to emerge until it was too late. Those who have been here a few years recognized that some things have slipped with how we go about our business and that it's time to clean things up."

He then detailed "some changes and new areas of emphasis for 2019." They were more batting practice and early defensive work; more structure to the workday; daily hitters' meetings; the hiring of a director of high performance and more testing and data tracking in training; the cleaning up of "important aspects of life in our clubhouse and on the road," from alcohol and fast food in the clubhouse to golf on the road before games; and more communication from Maddon, Epstein, and Hoyer, including five-minute sit-down meetings throughout the regular season.

"We were not at our best in 2018 and we won 95 games," Epstein wrote. "To use Torre's words, we are all lucky to be part of a group that is capable of doing some special things next year and beyond. But this is baseball, and we cannot take anything for granted—not winning, not even our time together."

Urgency became the operative word for the Cubs that off-season and through spring training. Epstein had used it five times in his white paper, and he'd used it again in his letter to the players and staff. Epstein suggested in that white paper that Maddon "use the final 7-10 days in spring training to mimic the regular season and ramp up intensity for opening day." And so Maddon did. He held his start-of-season meeting, the one he normally holds on the eve of Opening Day, a week earlier.

"The point is I want us to play the first seven games of the season before the first seven so that the first game becomes game number eight," Maddon said then. "I think it's important that we get off to a great start in order to accomplish what we want to this year. Great starts make things easier. You're going to go through a bad moment, and when you have a good start, the bad moment is more easily absorbed."

Maddon's theme for his address was "energy and enthusiasm." Of course, he gave it a Maddonian, T-shirt-ready shorthand: "E2=W."

"I really spoke from the heart," Maddon says. "Cut open a wrist and let myself bleed a little bit. Everything has been said, but it really comes down to energy and enthusiasm. I've talked about that in the past, too. It matters. That's running hard to first base, making good turns, totally hustling, and not getting frustrated in a negative moment. These are the kind of things that are separators when you get all twenty-five players and all the coaches to buy in. We've got to play the game properly and got to play the game with energy—at a greater level of energy than the other team does. It's that simple."

The plan for a more "workmanlike" spring training and to have the Cubs game ready a week in advance did not work so well. After a win on Opening Day, they lost six in a row. The bullpen was a mess.

Said Maddon then, "That's my concern going forward, having a functional bullpen that permits you to hold on to leads and win games you're supposed to win. More devastating than anything is losing those games you're supposed to win based on playing well, getting enough runs, being on top in the latter part of the game. There is nothing more demoralizing to a group than that in our game.

"The only time I get angry is through lack of effort or missed signs or just not carrying out a game plan that you had talked about. When people go rogue for no real good reason, that upsets me."

The bullpen did stabilize. It finished with the fourth-best ERA in the league. By the middle of May the Cubs were in first place. They were in first place as late as August 22.

But the job did not feel right for Maddon. He realized he was compromising himself and his methods. He was playing a part. He was acting like the manager Epstein wanted him to be, not being true to himself and his thirty-eight years in professional baseball. Theme trips, artwork, T-shirts, a loose atmosphere, and lively banter had all been quashed.

Gone was the Maddon who in 2011 stunned Tampa Bay reliever Joel Peralta with his reaction to the Rays losing their first five games of the season, all at home before a trip to Chicago. It was Peralta's first season with the team. On the plane to Chicago, Maddon passed out shots of liquor, walked to the front of the cabin, grabbed the microphone, and announced, "Here's a toast to the best 0-for-5 team in the history of baseball!"

"I knew then," Peralta said, "I was in a different place."

The Rays would lose three of their next four games. But they finished with ninety-one wins to win a wild card. That version of Maddon was stifled in 2019.

"I did lighten up with the Cubs in the last year," Maddon says. "I got less aggressive with this stuff. When I first got to the Cubs, as soon as I saw Travis Wood, he goes, 'What's our first theme trip? What are we wearing? Come on. Let's go!' Beautiful. Woody was one of the team leaders, so that made me go, 'OK, let's go.'

"But going back to the last year in Chicago, I was reticent to do different things because I didn't feel the same kind of support. When I first got into it with the Rays, I went back to how I used to always be the T-shirt king in the Angels' minor league system. 'Every Day Counts.' 'I Got Loud.' Two of my first.

"When you're doing things that are slightly different, it's really helpful when you feel support from above, when one of your superiors just checks in and indicates, 'Hey, that's pretty cool. Go for it. I like it. Give it a try.' Or 'I don't even know what I think, but go ahead and do it. See what happens.' That's sage advice. Same thing I have to do with a player. 'Go ahead. Give it a try. Yeah, move your hands. I'm OK. Let's see how it plays out.'

"You give support, and then you come to the right conclusions. But if you don't feel that support, then you will become gun-shy and, quite frankly, I did. I can't deny that.

"It just was another grouping of questions to be answered. If, in fact, the team didn't play well, then, of course, somehow it would be related to that. And then it's just not worth my time, and I don't want to put the players in that position, either. So the last year, I did feel reticent. I did not want to leave the throttle wide open because I didn't feel the same support I had prior to that. Again, this is not being upset. Just as a matter of fact.

"That and it was brought to my attention that the players thought I was self-promoting with the paintings. That hurt. That did hurt because that's the farthest thing from the truth and that did bother me. And those are the kinds of things that take a little nick out of your self-confidence. And when you're working with players, be careful what you say and how you say it.

"I wasn't as full throttle doing those things. I was basically more concerned with following the game plan from the previous off-season. Being more available. Getting there a little bit earlier."

Maddon would leave for the ballpark at one or two in the afternoon for a 7:00 p.m. game.

"You don't need to spend this much time at the ballpark," he says. "You need to relax, clear your mind, work the process, and enjoy the moment tension-free as opposed to creating tension in an artificial manner.

"On the road, we started taking a team bus at like two o'clock for a seven o'clock game because a couple guys said they wanted that. By the end of the year, of course, they didn't want that anymore. But that became part of the fabric also. I'm a big believer [in] don't get to the ballpark too early. Don't need to. It's primarily sitting around on the couches, drinking coffee, eating food, and going to check your video out and then go take a couple swings. That's pretty much what it is. Don't be deceived. That's all it is.

"When you sit in a room or stare at a screen, concrete wall, block wall, and don't get an opportunity to get outside, and you're there too long, there's a certain amount of fatigue that sets in. There's no doubt. Paralysis through analysis. Do this too often. Do it every day. You got one hundred and sixty-two games, folks. By the end of the year, you don't even realize what kind of a toll that took on you until you finally sit on your couch and the season is over and you can't move. You literally cannot move."

While surprised by Epstein's evaluation, Maddon also saw merit in it. He took the critical feedback as an opportunity to sharpen some of his methods and to remember advice he gave his players. In the "Embrace the Target" speech he gave the Cubs in spring training 2016—the one represented by a circle with an arrow pointing upward through it—the fourth of the six goals acknowledged what it means to be human: "Know we are not perfect but can be present."

Mistakes happen, especially in baseball. What other sport keeps a running tab of errors on the scoreboard? But Maddon did not want his players worried about physical errors because such outcome-based thinking leads to mental errors.

"Stay in the moment. It means be present, not perfect," Maddon says. "Worry about the process, not the outcome. If you're focused only on winning, I promise you that you're going to screw up a lot more often."

One Christmas break while he was at Lafayette, Maddon and three buddies, Willy Forte, Jeff Jones, and Ralphie Ferdinand, piled into his 1965 Thunderbird and drove from Hazleton to Fort Lauderdale. The car was a curvaceous beauty with its leather seats, sequential turn signal, and dashboard controls that resembled the levers of an airplane cockpit. Richie Tombasco had traded the T-Bird straight up for Maddon's 1965 Ford Galaxie, which Maddon had purchased for fifty dollars. Richie knew the T-Bird leaked oil prodigiously. The boys somehow made it there and back. In between they roasted in the sun until their tans peeled like old wallpaper, and they prowled the bars like alley cats by night. That was the same trip in which Maddon discovered Kurt Vonnegut. With *Slaughterhouse-Five* and *Breakfast of Champions*, Vonnegut joined Joseph Heller and Jerzy Kosinski as authors who spoke to this young man just discovering the breadth of the world.

"I start reading this, and I'm telling you, man, I was good," Maddon says. "Because the meaning of life was that nothing mattered—that you just go through it. Maybe that's my present attitude because there is a lot out of your control, and you just have to be you and do what you think is the right thing to do in the moment. Let her fly. That's the kind of stuff I read. I think it contributed to my method."

Meditating almost every morning keeps Maddon present. He will meditate on what the day will bring, on words like *joy, courage, fearlessness*, and *purpose*, and on the blessings of his family and the loved ones he has lost. He believes so strongly in the practice, he believes meditation should be taught in schools, just as are math and literature.

"It is amazing that whatever you meditate on in the morning transpires throughout the day in a positive way," he says.

To Epstein, Maddon needed to be more "present" for his players. Maddon agreed he should spend more time walking the outfield during batting practice. Ken Ravizza had told him years before how important it was to casually check with players during pregame work. It was how Maddon knew a rookie named David Price could handle the pressure of closing 2008 ALCS Game 7. It was what Jim Leyland did as a matter of routine, as well as Dave Roberts, whose goal was to touch every one of his players during pregame work.

To make sure he returned to that daily practice, Maddon had Peter Chase, the team's director of media relations, be more precise in carving out time for the media.

"With the Rays and Cubs, I would always speak up if I thought it was getting a little bit too overbearing," Maddon says, "or when it got to August and September, I used to spend less time with the media so I could spend more time with the team. It was all thought out. It was all planned. It was all plotted. But I had this all written out for me.

"In 2019 I got totally away from my personal script. This led to an entirely different routine that was not my bag, baby. But I'm telling you, I absorb what was told to me. I said, 'OK, I'll do something about it.'"

About halfway through the season, worn from the interference and feeling compromised in his methods, which made being present a difficult state to reach, Maddon decided he did not want to manage like this.

"I don't know exactly when it happened, probably the middle part of the year," he says. "But there was that moment when I said, 'Screw this. This is bullshit.' Most of what was laid on me in the off-season was absolutely a crock. And that's when I did get a little angry because I permitted interference with my methods, which were tried and true, things I knew that worked for people.

"So I did. I got upset, and I wish I could give you a line of demarcation, but that was kind of a moment. From that moment on I knew that was it—that I can't work under these circumstances anymore."

The Cubs were two games out of first place with twelve games to play. But injuries were decimating the roster. Javy Báez missed the final month with a broken thumb. Kris Bryant played through knee soreness and then sprained his ankle. Anthony Rizzo played with a bad back and a severe ankle sprain. Willson Contreras missed five weeks with a pulled hamstring. Addison Russell was hit in the head by a pitch. The Cubs lost nine games in a row, which eliminated them from playoff contention before a season-ending series in St. Louis. Maddon knew what he had to do.

He told Vijay Tekchandani, the director of travel, to book a party room by the pool of the team hotel in St. Louis, the Four Seasons, after the game Friday night. Maddon had booked a team function there earlier in the year, just to have guys hang out together and bond on the road, to get them out of their rooms and the video games that insulated them from one another. This time he had something to tell them, something he damn sure wasn't going to say in the visiting clubhouse at Busch Stadium.

"I did know one thing for sure: I was not going to permit that ballpark to hear me say goodbye to my guys," Maddon says. "It's like not having team meetings in the home clubhouse, not to sully the place. Here I did not want to give that Cardinal clubhouse, inside those walls in that building, the satisfaction of talking to my team in that manner. I did not want to get that message out in the St. Louis locker room where I stood in 2009 as the manager of the American League All-Star team greeting President Obama as he walked in the door."

Maddon wanted his players to hear the news even before he told Epstein.

"I waited for everybody to show up," Maddon says. "And then I just extemporaneously spoke to them for about fifteen minutes. And I wanted to thank them for all that they had done for me and my family, congratulate them on all they had done individually and as an organization.

"Just wanted them to know how much I loved them and how much I appreciated them."

And then Maddon told them, "I'm not coming back. I just want you to know that Sunday is going to be my last game. There are two more games left, Saturday and Sunday. I wanted you to know that so that we can say our goodbyes properly at the ballpark without any team meeting, without anybody smelling the fact that the Cubs have gotten together and wonder what they're talking about. The kind of stuff you don't need."

Maddon explained to them, "It's time for change. It's just right for the organization and for me."

"So that was it," Maddon says. "I wanted the boys to know from me in advance, away from the ballpark, no BS. And that gave us the time to exchange our appropriate goodbyes."

After the meeting, players visited Maddon in his room throughout the night, enjoying memories and drinks until five in the morning. Lester, Rizzo, Báez, and many more came by.

"It was very heartwarming to me to see them there," Maddon says. "And a lot of them had some very personal messages to give to me that I would never share, but it was pretty cool. It was very cool."

Was he quitting? Was he being fired? To Maddon, it did not matter.

"If you want to call it that I was fired, that it was a mutual understanding, that I left...pick whatever one you want," Maddon says. "They weren't going to offer me a contract. I wouldn't have accepted it, either. If they got the right of first refusal, I guess you'd have to say they fired me, although my contract had run out.

"But it's all semantics anyway. I pretty much knew into that season I wasn't coming back. I talked to my agent Alan Nero a lot and Tommy Tanzer and my wife, Jaye. And they all knew where I was coming from. They all knew that I had enough and that it wasn't going to work regardless, whatever we did, however we pulled it out. It just was time.

"Listen, I'm not the boss. I wasn't running it. But the one line that really stood out to me was that a different voice was needed. And I guess if you're in charge, you get to choose.

"But I really believe, if you were to take an honest poll among those that were still there and asked them which voice they wanted to remain—this is not an egotistical message, either, I'm just telling you—truth be told, I know the guys wanted me to stay."

The next night, after the game, Maddon sat with Epstein in Epstein's room. They shared a bottle of wine. Knowing Maddon so well, Epstein ordered a charcuterie board.

"My salamis and cheeses at a kitchen table always puts me in a relaxed, great mood to this day," Maddon says. "We sat there and talked. We pretty much went over everything."

Maddon told Epstein, "You and I know I'm not coming back."

Said Epstein, "Yes. Thank you for everything."

"Quite frankly, I get it," Maddon said. "I know you need to do this and, believe me, there's no hard feelings. This is good for both of us, to be able to move on from here. Change is good. I mean it."

Epstein mentioned he needed to contact Peter Chase to figure out how to schedule two news conferences, one for Epstein and one for Maddon.

"Who should go first?" Epstein said.

"Why can't we do it together?" Maddon said. "I'm fine with it. There's no animosity here whatsoever. What do you think?"

Epstein liked the idea. The next day Epstein and Maddon would announce their breakup standing side by side.

"A lot of people couldn't believe it," Maddon says. "We stood in front of everybody, went back and forth. It was very congenial, and I thought it was received very well, and I felt good about it, actually."

Epstein and Maddon continued to chat that night at the Four Seasons while making more than a dent in the wine and the charcuterie board. Two of Epstein's top assistants, Scott Harris and Jason McLeod, joined them.

"One thing about this has to be known," Maddon says. "I do not dislike any of these people. I like these guys a lot. Sometimes I don't like the methods. And the biggest part of the methods I don't like is the need for control and the need to manipulate conversation. Those are the two components I don't like, and that really rubs totally counterintuitively to who I am and what I think. I just can't work that way. Then the infamous line—'the sense of urgency.' That line has always bothered me because it always indicates you're not always urgent in what you do. I always had an issue with that.

"The differences come in differences of opinion, differences in philosophy. So please, don't be confused. I loved everything about the Cubs and Chicago. I am totally appreciative. I loved the guys. I loved Theo. I just don't like the methods. That's just the truth.

"We had a nice chat that night. There was no animosity either way. None. That is absolutely true. Theo was great to me that night. He said a lot of nice things."

Before Maddon left, Epstein handed him a letter.

"I still have it," Maddon says. "I shall always keep it. It was very sweet, very sincere.

"And it's something I will always cherish and hold near and dear to me. I believe it to be true. Once you write something down, it pretty much has to be accurate. Sometimes when you say things, not so much, but when you write it down, that's different. So he wrote it down and I got it. That letter really cements our friendship."

In five years as manager of the Cubs, Maddon won 471 games, an average of 94.2 wins per year. The only manager to win more games when Maddon was in Chicago was A. J. Hinch with the Houston Astros. Since

1903, when the World Series began, sixty-one men have managed the Cubs. Only twelve led them to the postseason. Only two won the World Series: Frank Chance in 1907 and 1908 and Joe Maddon in 2016.

Saying goodbye can be difficult, especially after so much success. This goodbye was not difficult. The reason was described metaphorically in 2000 by Los Angeles Dodgers pitcher Orel Hershiser. He was forty-one years old when one ugly day he gave up eight runs in the second inning against the San Diego Padres. His ERA was 13.14. That was the day he decided to retire.

"The best thing to happen to me," Hershiser said, "is that I got hit with a sharp knife and not a dull knife."

The dull knife leaves a wound that can be dismissed or minimized. The sharp knife leaves no doubt. Maddon was hit by a sharp knife. The job he was leaving was not the job he'd had for four sweet seasons. That was why, just three years after winning the World Series with the Cubs, Maddon walked out of Epstein's room at the Four Seasons in St. Louis a happy man.

"At that point I was kind of euphoric that it was going to be over," Maddon says. "I felt good about it. And I felt good about my possibility of getting another job somewhere."

On December 23, 2019, Maddon took out an ad in the *Chicago Tribune*. It began with his foundational concept for every one of his managing jobs:

Dear Chicago,
We have built relationships, established trust, and exchanged ideas.

What followed was the Nicene Creed of Maddonisms:

We embraced the target...Never permitting the pressure to exceed the pleasure...We knew/know the importance of telling me what you think, not what you've heard...Never forget the heartbeat...Do simple better...

It ended as Maddon's days of light in Chicago had begun.

Finally, let's raise our glasses in a toast...With a shot and a beer...

Like our parents and grandparents celebrated special occasions, or just a hard day's work...Thank you for the past five years, for your passion, for your open hearts and minds, for forging everlasting relationships and for sharing your beautiful city with Jaye and me.

Cheers and Happy Holidays.

CHAPTER 20

"Write One True Sentence"

It was September 20, 1998, before a game against the Seattle Mariners, when Joe Maddon, then the Angels bench coach, walked into the office of manager Terry Collins with his stack of his spray charts on Ken Griffey Jr. Collins was chatting with Sparky Anderson, the former manager who was broadcasting Angels games. Maddon put the charts on Collins's desk and pointed to them.

"What do you think about us shifting on Griffey today?" Maddon asked.

Teams rarely shifted defenders in those days. Eleven years earlier, Gene Mauch had created a stir when he ordered a shift against Minnesota Twins left-handed hitter Kent Hrbek with two outs and two on in the ninth inning with a 5–1 lead and DeWayne Buice pitching. It was based on nothing but intuition. Mauch anticipated Hrbek pulling Buice's forkball. Hrbek did. He grounded a forkball to second baseman Mark McLemore, who was playing short right field in the shift.

Maddon's idea derived from the data he kept on opposing hitters, as well as Griffey's prowess. Griffey had fifty-three home runs. Collins so feared Griffey that in July he intentionally walked him leading off the ninth inning of a tie game. Collins also used a shift against Griffey in one at bat in that series.

"Let's do it," Collins said.

The Mariners had runners at first and second with no outs in the first inning when Griffey came to bat. The Angels moved shortstop Gary DiSarcina toward second base and third baseman Troy Glaus away from the third-base line.

"I remember Griffey looking into our dugout," Maddon says, "kind of like, 'What's going on here?'"

Griffey had not bunted for a hit in four years. But on a 1-and-0 pitch, and with the third-base position vacant, the temptation was too great. Griffey tried to bunt. He popped out to catcher Matt Walbeck. Omar Olivares pitched out of the inning. The Angels won, 3–1.

When Mariners manager Lou Piniella was asked after the game if Griffey had bunted on his own, Piniella said, "The sign didn't come from me, that's for sure."

"Mission accomplished," Maddon says. "He saw the shift. It got in his head. My primary objective with all the shifting back then was to have people see it, have people notice it, get in their heads a bit and see how they would react to it. That's where I was coming from."

Four years later, Gary Sutherland, an advance scout for the Angels, spoke with Maddon about the possibility of using a four-man outfield in the World Series against Barry Bonds, the San Francisco Giants slugger. A third baseman against Bonds was superfluous. In 612 plate appearances that season, Bonds hit five ground balls that had been fielded by third basemen. Five—as opposed to 183 balls that had been fielded by outfielders. Maddon liked the idea but did not push manager Mike Scioscia to implement it.

"You're talking about a possible really big moment in baseball that takes getting to the point where you're willing to take chances," Maddon says. "But I'm not the manager, so I can't push or promote. I thought it was interesting. I could only say, 'I kind of like that, Gary.' But that was up to Mike Scioscia to make that call. Nobody was really comfortable doing it, although retrospectively, why wouldn't you, right?

"But at that time those mental leaps of trying things differently were only just getting there. And that's really why I needed to become a manager—so I could try these different things."

It took only fifteen games as a full-time manager for Maddon to take one of those mental leaps. Albert Einstein is credited with observing, "Logic will get you from A to Z. Imagination will get you anywhere." Maddon's Devil Rays were playing in Boston against the Red Sox on April 18, 2006, the opener of a three-game series. In the visiting manager's office at Fenway Park, Maddon studied the spray charts provided to him by the Devil Rays' front office. The chart for Ortiz grabbed his attention.

"I'm saying, 'Wow, there is nothing between third and short on the ground,'" Maddon says. "There is stuff in the air to the opposite side, but nothing at all on the ground to that side. I thought, *Four-man outfield.* And I went to Andrew Friedman and the guys because that's something you just don't spring on people without talking about in advance."

Friedman was on board. When Ortiz came to bat in the first inning, the Rays went in motion like a football team shifting into formation. Third baseman Ty Wigginton went to left field, joining Carl Crawford, Joey Gathright, and Russell Branyan in the outfield. Shortstop Tomás Peréz moved to the right side of second base. Second baseman Jorge Cantú played such a deep second base he stood on the outfield grass. The Rays defended Ortiz with four outfielders. No one stood on the left side of the infield.

Said Rays pitcher Casey Fossum, "It looked like they were spelling out something in the outfield."

Reporters had never seen anything like it. They peppered the rookie manager after the game about thumbing his nose at conventional wisdom.

"Who came up with conventional wisdom in the first place?" Maddon told them. "It's just something we've been doing for a long period of time.

"The game is the same game, but it's changed in other ways. And if you have enough information, you might be able to take certain chances based on information. This is the age of information. We've gone way beyond the industrial revolution. So let's try and see if we can come up with some new thoughts every once in a while."

Purists snickered that Maddon was trying to "reinvent the game."

"If we all thought that way, we wouldn't be watching color TV," he said. "You wouldn't have air-conditioning in your car. You wouldn't be writing your story on a computer. Whatever's present to us at this given moment, we try to utilize and get better with it. It's just growth.

"It doesn't mean we're right. We're taking a chance. It's a risk. So what? We'll see if it works. You never know unless you try something sometimes."

What some mistook as an attention-grabbing gimmick had been built on deliberation and information. Maddon first thought of a four-man outfield on a bike ride days before the game in Boston. The Ortiz spray chart convinced him. It showed that in the first thirteen games of the season Ortiz hit only two ground balls to the left side and twenty-three balls to the outfield, including six home runs.

"The four-three defense, as I called it at that time," Maddon says. "I wanted to borrow something from football. And I did it for two reasons. Listen, he's not hitting any ground balls over to the left side, and if he's hitting more fly balls, we have a better chance of catching them. If he hits them well, nobody catches them anyway. They're homers.

"The other reason was to make him think. Make him look out in the field and see a different field. Make him try to do something differently or just doubt himself. When you see that defense, it's not the field you grew up with. It can be impactful. I was trying to mentally bother him to the point where it could benefit us. That was another part of that for me.

"I know it bothered him, based on conversations with other guys that played with him at that time. He did see it. But he got over it. And by the next year or two, we had to get out of that because he was hitting hard ground balls and low line drives on the shortstop side of the field again.

"So organically, he made the adjustment to the shift, which is how I think everybody should do this. When you're seeing a defense you don't like, do something about it—whether it's a bunt or staying inside the ball, getting your hands closer to your chest, trying to drive it that way. When a guy gets to the big leagues and he hasn't done this to that point, it's really, really hard for him to try to do something differently like that."

Ortiz grounded out to Peréz in that first-inning at bat. When the Rays deployed the four-three defense again in the third inning—Maddon used it only with the bases empty—Ortiz smashed a double off the Green Monster. He scored on a double by Manny Ramirez. The Devil Rays lost, 7-4, one of their 101 defeats that year.

Maddon was an early adopter of data. It was why Friedman had hired him. It was how Tampa Bay turned around its franchise fortunes, especially as it related to the edge the Rays created on defense. Friedman had an uncanny knack for collecting and interpreting data to have defenders consistently positioned in optimum spots. Maddon's motto in Tampa Bay became "We catch line drives." From 2008 through 2014, after which Friedman left to run the Dodgers, the Rays allowed the lowest batting average on balls in play, .282—16 points better than league average and at least 3 points better than any other team, a significant advantage. Friedman continued his magic in Los Angeles. From 2015 through 2021, his Dodgers allowed the lowest batting average on balls in play, .281.

The early advances in defensive positioning led to more shifts, which especially siphoned offense away from left-handed hitters. In 2013 a left-handed hitter who hit a ground ball or line drive up the middle or to the pull side batted .366. By 2021 those same hits by left-handers lost 31 points, down to .335.

Data also led to more detailed scouting reports as pitch-tracking systems proliferated, even in the minor leagues. When Robel García made his debut for the Cubs in 2019, the first pitch he saw from the Pirates was a curveball—as were his second and fourth. He hit none of them and struck out.

"He can hit anyone's fastball, but they already knew that," Maddon says. "That stood out to me. This method takes away that three-to-four-week period of when a guy comes to the big leagues and he tears it up until advance scouting and word of mouth reveals the weakness that needs to be exploited."

The early foothold of analytics was as an evaluative tool, most notably by Billy Beane's Athletics and Epstein's Red Sox. Its impact expanded to Friedman's Rays changing the game on defense, which expanded to Friedman's Dodgers, Jeff Luhnow's Astros, and Erik Neander's Rays mining spin rates and attack angles to build deep pitching staffs with high velocity and high spin. Today, analytics' influence is everywhere. It dictates strategy, techniques, and hiring practices.

In 2022, thirteen presidents of baseball operations or general managers played or worked under Epstein or Friedman. Seven general managers held Ivy League degrees, with others hailing from Haverford, Amherst, the University of Chicago, Tufts, and Stanford. They have hired young pitching and hitting coaches out of private labs and college campuses, where they spoke analytics and technology as a first language. The analytical advances mostly favor the run-prevention side of the game, which is more static than the run-production side, which is more reactive and thus has more variables.

Analytics primarily define and reduce risk. The universal adoption of those methods has led to a homogenous, risk-averse game. Its marks are seen on every team every night. Spin the ball more. Elevate fastballs. Change pitchers. Keep the ball out of play on defense. Paradoxically, accept strikeouts on offense as the tariff for trying to hit home runs. The bunt, stolen base and hit-and-run become less purposeful, even ill-advised, when the game pivots so much on home runs. The style promotes more one-dimensional players with "showcase skills," a reflection of how fastball velocity or exit velocity off the bat are valued at amateur showcase events.

Mauch used to say, "The home run is a thought remover. I can't manage against a home run." Home runs accounted for 47 percent of runs in 2021, up from 33 percent in 2014. In 2021, the teams that won the most games and won the World Series relied the most on home runs: the Giants (53.5 percent of runs) and Braves (52.4 percent of runs).

Analytics have made for a brutally efficient game. Little wasted. Little risked. Little room for creativity. To watch a baseball game is to observe Firestone Library at Princeton University during finals week. Everybody is reading. The catcher is reading a wristband bearing a scouting report and sign sequences. The pitcher is reading a card with similar information. The fielders are reading a card that tells them where to play depending on the hitter and the pitcher. The hitters are reading a tablet with video of the opposing pitchers. The manager is reading a binder with recipes cooked up from the analytics department. Information is everywhere. Processing it takes time.

Never has baseball taken so long to play with so little action as today. The descent into careful baseball has been remarkably fast. In 2021, the average game took eleven more minutes than in 2013, from three hours to three hours and eleven minutes, a record. It was eleven minutes of nothingness that was added. The real story is not the length of the game but how little is happening. In 2013 a ball was put into play every three minutes and thirty-one seconds. In 2021 the wait was four minutes and two seconds, a 15 percent increase in dead time within eight years. Go back to 2002, when the Angels won the World Series, and the wait time for a ball in play was two minutes and fifty seconds. In twenty seasons the dead time in a baseball game increased 42 percent.

Baseball devolved into a game of keep-away. The percentage of plate appearances without the ball in play (home runs, strikeouts, walks, and hit by pitches) grew from 31.6 percent in 2013 to 36.3 percent in 2021. That means that for one of every three plate appearances the game is inert, with no need for players on the field except the pitcher, batter, and catcher.

Throughout history, fans could always expect to see more hits than strikeouts in a major league game. That changed in 2016, and the game's historic balance shows no sign of returning. Whereas in 2015 there were more than four thousand more hits than strikeouts, in 2021 there were more than 2,500 more strikeouts than hits.

"The original intent of data was acquisitions by the front office," Maddon says. "Why have they gained so much power over methods utilized in the game right down to mechanics, strategy, how the game is played, and what should be compensated? The pecking order of importance is power on both sides of the ball, walks and no concern for strikeouts for hitters, and pitchers who can record outs without the ball being put in play."

When Maddon began managing the Rays, he kept a small notebook with observations and reminders that went back to his years as a bench coach with the Angels. On his lineup card he would write notations relevant to that game, such as batter-pitcher matchups that were favorable or not. Over the years he developed his own analytical shorthand that he called his "matrix," which reduced information on such matchups to one number each.

"I wanted more involvement. I wanted good information," he says. "And I've never turned my nose to the information, ever. All of a sudden, this information started to become more and more important to the people upstairs, more vital to what we're doing to the point, and I think this is where my real big rub is, they start eliminating jobs. Guys that had put in their time were not wanted anymore. The newer front-office guys really did not want to hear from the old baseball guys. And they especially did not want to hear their evaluations because the new method evaluation had to be done in an analytical perspective. It was, in their mind's eye, more precise. It subtracted feel. It subtracted experience. It was more unaffected. It was 'purer' because the numbers lacked emotion. Their process lacked emotion.

"I always talk about the process as being fearless. Maybe that's part of what their aspirations were, to have this fearless method. I admit I kind of agreed with it sometimes."

On November 17, 2020, thirteen months after Maddon and Epstein agreed on their breakup at the Four Seasons in St. Louis, Epstein was gone, too. He resigned as president of baseball operations of the Cubs with a year left on his contract. Epstein explained he wanted to give Hoyer, his friend and replacement, the proper runway to deal with long-term decisions facing the team as the contracts of Bryant, Rizzo, and Báez were running out. Epstein also admitted he needed a new challenge after nine years with the team. Epstein was a builder, having busted droughts with the Red Sox and Cubs, but by his own admission he had proved less adept at sustaining a championship team.

"We did some pretty epic things," Epstein said upon announcing his departure. "And then the last couple of years weren't as impressive. And maybe what that tells me is what I think I'm great at and really enjoy is building and transformation and triumphing. Maybe I'm not as good and not as motivated by maintenance, so to speak."

If that was his shortcoming, he shared it with his peers. The edges that could be found in acquisitions and development through data no longer were as robust or easily found. Nobody was repeating. The sameness of philosophy and style adopted by those inspired by Epstein made for a crowded highway. Blowing up that very style he'd helped create would become his next challenge.

Within months of leaving the Cubs, Epstein signed on as an adviser to Commissioner Rob Manfred with the express mission of finding ways to make baseball more appealing. Epstein was one of the major stars of an era when owners had turned over the keys to their kingdom to front-office executives, usurping style and strategy from managers and players. As he left, Epstein had realized the result of this revolution was a more efficient game but a less entertaining one. He set out to fix what he'd helped create.

"The executives like me who have spent a lot of time using analytics and other measures to try to optimize individual and team performance have unwittingly had a negative impact on the aesthetic value of the game and the entertainment value of the game in some respects," Epstein said. "I mean, clearly the strikeout rate's a little bit out of control, and we need to find a way to get more action in the game, get the ball in play more often, allow players to show their athleticism some more, and give the fans more of what they want."

A more fan-friendly game, he said, begins with this objective: "Put the game back in the hands of players and let them do their thing on the field."

Sandy Alderson, whose hiring of Art Howe as Oakland manager in 1995 began the power shift from the dugout to the front office, agrees the pendulum has swung too far.

"Basically, organizations solve competitive issues in favor of efficiency and probability. They don't solve them for entertainment value," says Alderson, the New York Mets president. "Over time what happens is the decisions to operate based on efficiency drain the life out of the game. We need a more scriptless, unpredictable game. Change it up. Take some of this intellectual capacity to drive more efficiency and higher probability and force it to reset."

One way toward a more entertaining game, Alderson says, is to require two infielders on each side of second base. MLB plans to adopt such a rule in 2023.

"I'm very much in favor of eliminating the shift," Alderson says. "The shift screams efficiency. We've replaced singles with walks because of the shift. It's the perfect example of solving a problem for efficiency's sake. It creates a competitive advantage at first. Over time, as more teams buy in, the competitive advantage has gone away, but the game has changed significantly.

"If we end up with more players who are power oriented, that means fewer players are speed oriented, and ultimately that means the single to left is not going to score that guy from second.

"To me it's not even debatable. It has to go. To me the shift is symbolic of the complete intrusion of the front office onto the field. Symbolically, if you get rid of the shift, you push back on that notion.

"You just can't eliminate all of the learning that's taken place over the last forty years. You have to figure out how to accommodate it in a broader sense with a more entertaining game. You can't put the genie back in the bottle. One of the things I hope the commissioner does is look hard at the rules and not allow general managers to dictate the direction of the game.

"I actually think front offices are more conservative than players. It's almost become too comfortable in front offices—too efficient, too reliant on probability and sustainability. Risk aversion is big.

"Whatever the solution is, you have to look at the owners around the game. Most of the people who own teams think the same way as general managers. Why? Owners hire search firms to find general managers who are cut from the same mold. Then the managers the general managers hire are an extension of the front office. And the players become an extension of the front office because of the analytics they use to construct a roster.

"The problem is the front office. Front offices have influence that not only extends down to manager but also up to the owner. It's all connected. Rather than bleed every last ounce of efficiency out of the system, change the rules and turn them loose. 'You're so smart? Here's a new set of facts. You're great at poker? Let's play blackjack.' Front offices have a lot more influence on owners than they used to."

To Maddon, changes begin with the baseball itself. He favors a less lively baseball, which reduces the craving for power, which incentivizes more balls in play and diverse styles.

"By taking some of the flight out of the ball, we then have a better chance to create a game that resembles the past, while permitting the newer front offices an opportunity to stay connected with the field," Maddon says. "Let's bring the game back to where it had been, and now the baseball lifers and newbies can agree on methods. And you may see a resurgence of the 'Art of the Game,' and less on the 'Best in Show.'"

The primary T-shirt-worthy Maddonism he crafted for the 2021 Angels was "Play like it's 1985." Maddon wanted an offense that could put the ball in play, hit behind runners, choke up on the bat with two strikes, and run the bases aggressively. Injuries limited Shohei Ohtani, Mike Trout, and Anthony Rendon, his best hitters, to just seventeen games in the same lineup. The Angels finished 77-85. Despite Maddon's intentions, and most unlike in 1985, home runs remained king. Of the ten teams who hit the most home runs, seven made the postseason. Of the ten teams who hit the fewest home runs, none made the playoffs. The Angels finished in the middle third, tied for nineteenth.

But like most Maddonisms, "Play like it's 1985" also held a deeper meaning. The game in 1985 was not predicated so much on information. There were fewer Firestone Library reading sessions happening on the ballfield. Yes, Maddon wanted his players to use information for their betterment and to gain competitive edges, just as he did with the four-man outfield back in 2006. But the information was used as a supplement to trusting instincts in the moment, not as a replacement. That's the hidden meaning behind *1985*.

"It's playing with your heart and your head," Maddon says. "It means trusting your experience and talents. You know what the analytics call for, but you keep your mind uncluttered by ignoring the overwhelming information and picking out the usable nugget or two."

The 1985 season also marked Mauch's return to managing the Angels. After two years in exile, he could not resist the siren call of the ballfield. He pulled on his Angels uniform again for spring training in Arizona, complete with a pack of cigarettes in his back pocket, and returned to the pleasure and the pain of competing.

"People say I'm gruff; they ask why I frown all the time," Mauch said at that camp. "That's not a frown. That's concentration."

Such absolute certainty did Mauch project that Reggie Jackson, one of his players, liked to say that if Mauch lost his wallet in the desert and you watched him walk back to find it, you would be convinced he knew exactly where he had lost it.

"You believe what he says," Jackson said then, "because the image he projects doesn't give you reason to doubt it."

Like Mauch in 1985, Maddon returned to the Angels in 2020 with absolute certainty, having lost it in his compromised year of 2019. Beyond the Maddonisms, the T-shirts, the art, the theme trips, the four-man outfields, and the glasses, there is one basic concept Maddon holds at the root of how to manage a ball game and how to navigate life: pure intentions.

The organization and the person succeed only when the agenda is no agenda, when altruism is the guide, when meetings are driven by such honesty that there is no need for those meetings after the meetings, the ones by the water cooler or via encrypted text, when the real truths are spoken. It took the discomfort of 2019 for Maddon to fully appreciate the power of pure intentions.

"When I was looking for another job that winter, I was looking for somebody to work with as a partner, somebody to work together with and not pretend, not go into leadership-speak," he says. "I wanted sincerity, where I felt just like I am one of the guys, a place where I can be myself. Because the one thing I hate is that I probably did sell out in 2019. I did. I played along. I didn't fight. I didn't challenge different things because I thought, *Maybe I am wrong*. But then when I found out that I wasn't, yeah, it bothered me a little bit.

"The more freedom given, the greater respect and discipline returned. I'm talking about professionals. I'm talking about people who are able to think and discipline themselves. There is the great line from John Wooden: 'Discipline yourself so nobody else has to.'

"And there is the great lesson I learned long ago: 'Whatever you put out there comes back to you.' These are my go-tos. And they are interconnected."

In Maddon's first season managing the Angels, 2020, the pandemic shut down baseball for five months. Maddon took online his work of establishing culture there. He held regular Zoom meetings with his players. The sessions included free-flowing discussions about the pandemic, Black Lives Matter, national anthem protocols, Lead Bulls policy, and minor leaguers and club employees who were furloughed. He even held virtual cocktail parties. Maddon encouraged his players to speak freely. He wanted them to be as unencumbered as he felt. The culture he wanted was one in which pure intentions flourished.

"I gave them the line from Hemingway: 'Write the truest sentence you know,'" Maddon says. "Write one true sentence, the truest sentence that you know, and then follow with the next one and then the next one and then the next one."

In *A Moveable Feast*, Ernest Hemingway described what he did when writer's block stalled his creative process:

> I would sit in front of the fire and squeeze the peel of the little oranges into the edge of the flame and watch the sputter of blue that they made. I would stand and look out over the roofs of Paris and think, "Do not worry. You have always written before and you will write now. All you have to do is write one true sentence. Write the truest sentence you know."
>
> So finally I would write one true sentence, and then go on from there. It was easy then because there was always one true sentence that I knew or had seen or had heard someone say. If I started to write elaborately, or like someone introducing or presenting something, I found that I could cut the scrollwork or ornament out and throw it away and start with the first true simple declarative sentence I had written.

Says Maddon, "That has had such an impact on me. And my take on that is, and then do it again. Write another one. For what I do, I speak one true sentence, the truest sentence that I know, and then move on to the next one."

Maddon interpreted the Hemingway method as "pure intentions" meets "Do simple better."

"As a manager you have to understand that failure is temporary. It should be, anyway. It will remain temporary as long as you don't give it enough power. That means staying in the moment.

"I had a rule with my team: win hard for thirty minutes or lose hard for thirty minutes. After that, move on. The mistake we make is to dwell on those down moments too long. When you do that, they are more likely to carry over. So don't give it any more energy. How do you do that? It's all about staying in the present tense. It's all about humility. Your ego lives in the past. Your anxiety lives in the future. Stay in the present."

With one true sentence at a time, the joy of managing returned—at least until Perry Minasian and the reality of a front-office driven game showed up one morning on his doorstep. Maddon believes there is still a place in the game—a *need* even—for the veteran manager who can deploy instinct and trust to complement the data. He knows such opportunities are dying out. But he still loves the job and what it can be. Ask Maddon to identify his favorite part of managing, and it has nothing to do with outcome.

"The day," Maddon says. "The day inspires me."

His ideal day begins with coffee. At home in his beach neighborhood of Long Beach, he brews a cup of bulletproof coffee (the kind with butter in it) and settles into a low-slung chair with a firm backrest by a large front window. On the road, he sets up a work space in a coffee shop and orders an Americano or French press coffee. The soundtrack to his mornings is softer rock delivered by a killer sound system at home or headphones on the road. The likes of Simon and Garfunkel, the Beatles, Eddie Vedder, the Hollies, and Bread start the day. The rock grows louder as the day unfolds.

He reads newspapers on his iPad, including the *New York Post*, the *New York Daily News*, the *New York Times*, the *Wall Street Journal*, and Hazleton's *Standard-Speaker*. Then he digs into a PDF file sent by the team's analytics department, a scouting report specifically tailored by

Maddon to help him build his lineup for the game that night. The information he wants on opponents includes pitchers' pitch types and usage, third-time-through-the-order data, bullpen usage, and managerial tendencies. The report also includes the Maddon Matrix, his home-brewed metric that reduces each batter-pitcher matchup to one number that in scale most closely resembles batting average. A .300 matrix, for instance, favors the hitter over the pitcher. A .200 matrix means the pitcher has the advantage.

If he needs video, he opens the team's proprietary video application. With the Angels it was Halo. With the Cubs it was Ivy. Both worked in similar ways. The video helps him study such areas as pitch framing by catchers, hitters just up from the minors, and hitting mechanics. After discussions with his hitting coaches, Maddon might build a photo file to send to a player if he wants to suggest an adjustment.

"All my information is there," Maddon says. "Who in the hell needs more than that? And why do you need to spend more time in a concrete room at the ballpark when you can study away from the ballpark via devices? It's so adept. It's beautiful. It's great.

"I'm able to look for exactly what I need to be paying attention to during the game. So why can't the hitting and pitching coaches be able to do the same? The video is pretty much point and click on exactly what you want. Outstanding. Great setup. Really intuitive. Interactive. Anything you want, brother, is right there.

"I could be in a Starbucks, could be in my room, could be in my Four Seasons room in St. Louis looking out over the arch. So many more creative places where I'm not just in a room with a bunch of walls getting a headache, repeating over the same things, looking for something that's not there and looking for something that's not necessary. That's what's happening a lot around the game.

"I know what I need during the game. If there's something that pops up that caught me off guard, easy. Call upstairs after the game: 'Hey, listen, by the way, from now on could you please include this in my series prep?' And that's all I need. There has been so much oversell and overkill, again, based on whomever is in charge, based on where they come from. And this is not Wall Street, ladies and gentlemen."

Maddon typically will decide lineups on a series-by-series basis. The day before a series, players generally know who is playing when. Game-day decisions can be based on the matrix number and what he sees on video.

"I want to know where the opposing pitcher gets his strikeouts and how does that play against my hitters because I know my hitters' swings," he says. "I know what they can cover. I know what their angle looks like. I know it's supposed to be reflected in the matrix and give full faith and don't even worry about it, but I do. So I'm really big on that. I'm always matching up numbers with videos."

He distributes the lineup to staff and players via a text chain.

Next Maddon makes note of the availability of his relief pitchers, based largely on recent use but also on confidence levels. When Maddon first arrived in the big leagues as a bullpen coach with the 1994 Angels, he was struck by the pressure and difficulty of relief pitching. He still carries the image of Craig Lefferts running from the bullpen to the mound with runners on base in a hot situation. He thought, *These guys are always running into the danger, and then they have to be perfect.* The intensity of the job has increased as relievers are asked to pick up more innings.

"Relief pitching is a perfect example of something in our game, if you've never done it, it's really hard to understand it," Maddon says. "You know which way your guy's confidence is, up or down. So much criticism is directed to the latter part of the game when a relief pitcher fails. They're held to an impossible standard. They are held to a standard of perfection. It's really not fair to them.

"As a manager before the game, it's about trying to realize who is the right guy to put in that situation. And then if it doesn't work, it doesn't work. That's the part of our game not many people understand. You can make all the right decisions in the world, and it can come out wrong. Doesn't mean what you do is wrong. Just means it didn't work. Also means the other team's good, too.

"Those guys hold the key to winning and losing. They are the keepers of the gate. For me, they're the most important dudes every night."

When the game prep is done, Maddon has time for a workout and a meditation of fifteen to twenty minutes. He will arrive at the ballpark around 3:00 p.m. He first will take care of any conversations he needs to have with players, staff, trainers, or the front office. A charcuterie board with Italian meats and cheeses is a typical accompaniment. Around 4:00 p.m. he holds a scheduled session with the media.

"With the Cubs, before the pandemic, that was a lot," he says. "There's more press, more controversy to be created, more false narratives. It was just part of the landscape. You had to be on your toes, and the best way to be on your toes is to be straight up because if you try to dissemble it all, it will bite you in the ass. My communication with these people was always straight up, and you would have to wait to see how they would want to spin it. Honestly, it did not bother me. I really enjoy that, actually. And I've often complimented them because if you work with a real fair-minded group of press, a lot of times they're going to say stuff to you that you haven't even thought about that's actually really helpful. And I've actually told reporters that."

Batting practice is next. Before he hurt his shoulder, Maddon took pride in throwing batting practice.

"When I went to spring training in the 1980s as a grunt," Maddon says, "if Gene Mauch caught me throwing to anybody but his varsity, he'd come up and he would bark at my ass. 'I didn't bring you here to throw to your guys. I brought you here to throw to my guys.' Swear to God."

After batting practice, Maddon prefers an hour of solitude before the game, though inevitably there are meetings with players or the front office that become necessary.

Then arrives what former Angels manager John McNamara once told him was "my favorite time of the day": the walk through the tunnel from the clubhouse to the dugout.

"I never knew what he was talking about, but now I know that it is," Maddon says. "It's the most fun, based on everything you've put together.

It's the whole core philosophy of the organization, the group, the culture you've created, the identity that is beginning to take shape, going on display. It is so good. When you're going down that tunnel and you've got a good group that plays hard and is playing it right, wow, it's stimulating, man."

And then game time. Maddon will stand the entire game at the dugout rail in that great horned owl pose, picking up the faintest sights and scents of the game. He needs to feel the game as much as see it.

"When you play a game deep into the night," he says, "with a lot going on, and eventually you win a tight game at the end . . . wow, what a great, great feeling that is. It's like you played. I swear to God, you're exhausted. I can't get that feeling as a bench coach or a third-base coach. You have to be a manager to get that feeling. And that's also why I think managers lose harder than anybody. You just do.

"You revel in victory, briefly. I do, as I'm walking out to the mound. There is nothing more fun than walking out to the mound in Yankee Stadium with 'New York, New York' playing, or Boston, going out to the mound and really being jacked up about walking out toward their mound victorious. Three minutes of absolute euphoria. Baseball euphoria."

There is another media session after the game.

"I admit, you will protect your team," Maddon says. "You will protect your team and your players at all costs. The thing you try not to do is protect yourself. At least that's my perception.

"I'll give you the answer. I'll tell you what I thought. If you don't agree with it, nothing I can do about it, but I'm going to give you what I thought. It's that simple. And I think when you work or deal from that methodology, all this stuff becomes a lot easier. If you tell the truth, then you never have to remember what you say. And that's pretty cool."

The media session, a bite to eat, a shower, and a change of clothes provide thirty minutes or so of mental decompressing.

"When you walk out after a loss, any kind of loss, it's different," he says. "Could have been the night you had to make a tough decision that didn't go your way. Could have been a player had a tough night and you feel for him. It's just different. The emotions attached to the win are, of course, easy to absorb. The ones attached to a loss are much more difficult."

The coda to the day is the drive home. A win inspires rock 'n roll, usually Springsteen or the Stones, played very loudly on his Focal car speakers. In Tampa Bay the drive home took him over the Gandy Bridge or Howard Frankland Bridge. In Chicago it was Lake Shore Drive. In Anaheim it was the 22 toward the Seal Beach Boulevard exit, where the familiar smokestack sentries in their golden glow reminded Maddon not just of Uncle Rick but also of where he came from and how lucky he is to have traveled this far and in this circuitous way.

"That's the day," Maddon says. "It inspires me."

On January 1, 1981, with a hundred dollars in his pocket, Joe Maddon pulled out of Denver in a Plymouth TC3 purchased with no money down and pointed it toward California and a life as a scout and a rookie league manager. At twenty-six in Idaho Falls, he was the youngest manager in professional baseball, which caused him to observe two years later, "Managing is something I've always wanted to do. Managing is as satisfying as playing. It's ironic that I'm getting into this fairly young, while I got into playing when I was fairly old. I have a much brighter future as a manager than a player."

Entering the Angels system as an undrafted player out of Lafayette at age twenty-two, Maddon, like all players, was asked to fill out a questionnaire. One of the questions asked the players to name their hero and explain their choice. Most of the responders named the great major league players they had grown up watching, such as Hank Aaron, Roberto Clemente, and Sandy Koufax. Not Maddon. He wrote, "My father, Joe. He's a plumber. He takes pride in it, so he's the best there is."

One day as a child Joe broke a window with a baseball on an errant throw. First on the scene was one of his uncles, part of C. Maddon & Sons Plumbing and Heating. He grew angry at the boy's carelessness. Then Joe's father arrived. He took stock of what had happened, looked at his son, and said, "Nice arm, Joey."

That was Joseph Anthony Maddon. He taught the boy more than how to handle a difficult moment. Above all, simply by the way he lived his life, he taught him that working hard and having fun should go hand in hand.

It is why the best part of managing for Maddon is the day. It is not the outcome. It is the opportunity. And that is why in the dawning of the day, as the coffee brews and the comforts and challenges of managing await, he is never more his father's son, honoring his example of working hard and having fun.

CHAPTER 21

"Meetings Are for Presenters. Conversations Are for Teachers"

Billy Martin was fired nine times. The first time he was dismissed, in 1969 by the Minnesota Twins, he was fired by appointment. One Sunday night shortly after the season, the brother of Twins president Calvin Griffith told Martin to expect a call from Griffith at precisely ten thirty the next morning. Martin deduced his boss was not arranging the call to extend his contract. He was correct.

Yogi Berra was fired by proxy in 1985. New York Yankees owner George Steinbrenner sent his general manager, Clyde King, to fire Berra after a win in Chicago, just sixteen games into a season in which Steinbrenner vowed Berra would manage the full year. So upset was Berra about Steinbrenner firing him through an intermediary that Berra did not set foot in Yankee Stadium or speak to Steinbrenner for the next fourteen years.

Willie Randolph was fired by the New York Mets in 2008 in his Anaheim hotel room after a win over the Angels. The press release of his sacking went out at 3:14 in the morning New York time.

The Philadelphia Phillies fired Gene Mauch by telephone in 1965 after he had flown from Philadelphia to Los Angeles to attend to his wife, who was hospitalized with a stomach ailment. Asked when it dawned on him that he might be fired, Mauch, the franchise's longest tenured manager since 1893, snapped, "Eight years and two months ago." That's when Philadelphia had hired Mauch.

Joe Maddon was fired in his living room, in a freshly cut mohawk. On the morning of June 7, 2022, the Angels had lost twelve games in a row in a cavalcade of oddities and disasters, including the worst two weeks of Mike Trout's baseball life (he hit .114 and struck out seventeen times in those twelve games), a simultaneous slump by Shohei Ohtani (.180, fifteen strikeouts), injuries to key hitters Anthony Rendon and Taylor Ward, and epic failures by whatever relievers emerged from the bullpen. The Angels held ten leads in those dozen games and lost them all.

Maddon had figured it was time to pull a page from his old Rays winning playbook. On September 15, 2008, the Red Sox had pummeled his Rays, 13–5, to create a virtual tie atop the American League East between the two teams. It was the first time in fifty-two days Tampa Bay did not hold the outright lead. The upstart Rays had lost three games in a row. They were fading, and so, too, was the amazing story of their rise from the worst record in baseball one year to the playoffs the next.

Foreboding in the air, Maddon showed up at Tropicana Field the next day with a mohawk, a bold move if only because Jaye and Joe were to be married the next month. Jaye had reminded him that wedding portraits last forever. Vanity be damned, Maddon figured the haircut was a good way to loosen his team in the heat of the pennant race. Earlier that month, Rays center fielder B. J. Upton had sported a mohawk. The sight of their manager also rocking the 'do raised the silliness factor. Soon other players, and it seemed half the Rays' fans, were sporting mohawks.

The night of the Maddon Mohawk, the Rays won, 2–1, on a walk-off single by Dioner Navarro. They won the next night, too, 10–3. They won eight of their next ten games after the Maddon Mohawk, to pull away from the Red Sox and win the division by two games.

This time, Maddon never made it to the ballpark with his mohawk. Angels general manager Perry Minasian arrived at Maddon's front door and rang the bell. Maddon answered it and invited him in. Minasian did not immediately notice the mohawk. If he did, he said nothing about it. He appeared uncomfortable.

Maddon had a good idea of why Minasian was there. Over the previous few days Minasian had told Maddon over the telephone he was considering firing some coaches.

"You can't do that," Maddon had told him. "They're very good at what they do. No, that's not the answer."

That's why Maddon took Minasian's appearance on his doorstep as a bad sign for his coaches.

"We were struggling in the bullpen, struggling at the plate, and in the front office's perception our defense was struggling," Maddon says. "When you're going badly you really rely on people to break it down properly. But sometimes it just gets emotional. So I thought he was coming to my house to talk about firing a coach or coaches."

They sat down in the living room. Minasian made a quick comment about Maddon getting "a haircut." The words lacked the lilt of humor. Quickly it was apparent why. Minasian told Maddon he was "making a change" and removing him as manager.

"I've got to do something, Joe," Minasian told him.

Says Maddon, "I did not overreact at all. I just said, 'Okay.' Quite frankly, I was happy he chose me and not the coaches. I was very happy he chose me over them. No one on that staff deserved to be fired.

"What was needed at that juncture was support more than anything. We all needed support and not another version of the blame game. We all needed support from the bosses. That includes ownership. It would have been very easy for Arte Moreno to get on an airplane, walk through the clubhouse, talk to us, see what was going on, and I believe he would have come to a different conclusion."

Moreno and Maddon had known one another for two decades. During spring training Joe and Jaye had hosted a party at their Arizona home for the entire staff and their spouses to foster organizational unity. Moreno and his wife, Carole, attended. Moreno did not speak to Maddon after the firing.

Maddon's firing had not been Moreno's idea, anyway. It was Minasian's idea. Minasian spoke with Moreno just that morning and told the owner what he had in mind. The decision came four days after the Phillies had fired Joe Girardi, after which the team responded by sweeping three games from the Angels. A seal had been broken. Moreno did not stop Minasian.

"If this is what you decide is needed to right the ship, go ahead," Moreno told him, according to a team source familiar with the conversation. "It's totally your call."

"If he really wanted Joe, Joe would still be there," the source said about Moreno. "At the time it was easy to agree with it. The team is on a twelve-game losing streak when he's presented with the idea of making a change."

The firing was not about Maddon losing the clubhouse. Minasian later said he did not consult with any players or coaches about the change. It was not about effort. Minasian said at his news conference later that day "the effort has been great." He did not give Maddon any specific reasons for why he was firing him. He kept telling him, "I've got to do something." Nor did Minasian provide specificity at his news conference. It was filled with boilerplate material such as, "It was time for a new voice."

Why, then, was Maddon fired? Before the losing streak, only the New York Yankees and Houston Astros had won more games than the Angels in the American League. The team was improving under Maddon in his third year, just as it had in his second year, just as his teams did with the Rays and Cubs. How could a World Series–winning manager with nineteen years and 2,599 games of experience lose his job over a twelve-game sample? The answer is that the firing had been in the works long before those dozen games, even if both men could not or did not want to see it that way. The losing streak simply provided the convenience of an exit ramp for a relationship that was going nowhere—not because of any personal animosity but because of philosophical differences. They looked at baseball, and especially its power nexus, very differently.

What happened between Minasian and Maddon tells a familiar story of what has happened to the role of the manager—and baseball itself—ever since Sandy Alderson told Art Howe in 1995 he was not hiring him for his baseball acumen but to implement Alderson's philosophy. The power shift from the dugout to the front office over more than a quarter of a century has changed how the game is played and its value system. Knowledge over wisdom. Technology over teaching. Data over art. Efficiency over entertainment.

As front offices seized control, games grew longer with less action and there were more pitching changes, more fungibility of personnel, and fewer fans. Attendance has declined slowly but steadily since the all-time per-game high in 2007, down 14 percent in 2019, the last pre-pandemic season. At that 2007 crest, the World Series drew 85 percent more viewers than the NBA Finals. In ten of the fourteen years since then, the Finals have drawn the bigger audience.

Meanwhile, as another consequence of the game growing more clinical, baseball managers ceased being celebrities. It happened in part because the replay challenge system reduced colorful arguments with umpires to almost nothing, but mostly because they operated with less power and job security than general managers, and to survive they adopted the bland, corporate-speak of their bosses.

The shift happened over the arc of Maddon's career in the major leagues. He was trying to hold on to the soul of baseball as he knew it, relying on trust, relationships, and his coaches. Minasian, mentored by Braves general manager Alex Anthopoulos, who was in turn mentored by Andrew Friedman and Farhan Zaidi, was part of the second generation of power brokers—no longer disrupters, but mainstream—who dove even deeper into data and process for the answers and, even as minor league teams were being culled, built out enormous front-office staffs. Depending on how you were raised in the game, a sixty-eight-year-old man in a mohawk was either a colorful master motivator or an unfunny gimmick that had no bearing on the win probability of the game that night.

If there was one physical space where this dynamic openly played out it was in the coaches' room at Angel Stadium. Minasian and his top assistant, Alex Tamin, maintained lockers in the same room as the coaches, using the room as they changed between front-office attire and workout or game-day attire. They used the small adjacent coaches' meeting room as a workplace to crunch their numbers.

In the game in which Maddon was raised, general managers stayed out of the clubhouse altogether, unless they had specific business to attend there, such as consulting with trainers or delivering news to a player. The clubhouse and its immediate environs belonged to uniformed personnel, the proud foot soldiers doing battle.

But Minasian and Tamin found it perfectly normal to share space with coaches on an everyday basis because it had become perfectly normal for executives to dictate game strategy as much as coaches. What Maddon regarded as interference was what Minasian regarded as standard operating procedure.

Minasian was born one year before Maddon began managing. Minasian was forty years old when the Angels hired him to replace Billy Eppler, the general manager during Maddon's first year with the Angels. The son of Texas Rangers clubhouse manager Zack Minasian, Perry began in baseball as a clubhouse attendant and batboy before becoming a scout in 2003. He spent nine years with the Blue Jays before joining the Braves in 2018 as assistant general manager.

One of his first hires with the Angels was Tamin, a 1995 UCLA Law graduate who worked with clubs on salary arbitration cases before he was hired in 2011 by the Dodgers during their nascent analytics period as director of contracts, research, and operations. He rose to director of major league operations before Anthopoulos hired him with the Braves in December of 2017 to handle rules and transactions and to help run the team's advanced scouting process.

"My first year was a totally different management style with Billy," says Maddon. Also, all teams operated under COVID protocols in 2020 that limited interactions and time at the ballpark. "He was very much into the numbers, too, right down to how often guys played was based on the exertion they demonstrated in a game, such as running the bases or going after fly balls. All this stuff was part of an equation that needed to be followed. Guys were peeing in a cup to see where they were as far as hydration."

In 2021, the first year under Minasian, the Angels won seventy-seven games even though a massive number of injuries caused them to cycle through sixty-four players, including forty-one pitchers—both franchise records. Under Maddon's Law about front-office interference—the better your team, the more interference—he did not endure much intrusion from above.

"We were just trying to get our footing," Maddon says. "Seventy-seven wins with all the turmoil was actually pretty good. The biggest thing that occurred and what I thought got Perry and I on the same page was the Shohei situation. There was no interference at all. It was me and Shohei the whole way. Nobody else got involved."

Freed from playing time restraints to pitch and hit at will, Ohtani won the MVP. But trouble was taking root. Minasian and Tamin had begun dressing and working in the coaches' room in 2021. Brian Butterfield, one of Maddon's coaches and one of the most respected longtime coaches in the game, indicated to Maddon that their constant presence was a problem with the coaches.

"He complained to me about too many people in the coaches' room and the coaches could not speak freely because they were always there," Maddon says. "And I probably should have paid more attention to him. I love Butter. I think he is one of the better coaches *ever*. He's that good. He would tell me, 'There's too much going on in the coaches' room, too many people that don't belong in there.'

"We talked as coaches in the off-season and one of the subjects was that. I told them I would talk to Perry and Alex about it before the season began and tell them we wanted more autonomy with that. But I'm certain I failed to have that discussion. I doubt any changes would have been made.

"There's a little conference room where these guys are always plotting and planning, and the coaches never have a chance to take a breath and they always feel under the gun. Always. Bad method. GMs and assistant GMs should never dress among the coaches on a daily basis. They should absolutely be involved and come in and out but not to the point where nobody has a chance to breathe. Everybody was watching what they said. You should never have to worry about who's going to walk in and have to change your conversation. And that became a big part of the landscape there."

Maddon did bring one complaint to Minasian and Tamin that off-season. A certain intramural competition exists among this second generation of executives, a kind of Silicon Valley cutting-edge war as to who can hire the smartest experts and install the latest technology, whether it's $15,000 whole-body-vibration "power plates" for training or $24,000 air and surface purifiers that convert ambient oxygen and humidity into dry hydrogen peroxide to reduce the presence of microbes. (The Dodgers travel with at least four of them to make sure their air-quality advantage is not limited to home games.)

Under Zaidi and manager Gabe Kapler, who both worked for the Dodgers, the Giants have become one of those trendy, savvy model franchises. Last season they plowed new ground by employing thirteen coaches—one for every two players—including three hitting coaches and three pitching coaches. The number does not include their "breathing coach." Listed, perhaps redundantly, as a "human performance specialist," Harvey Martin, thirty-two, is a former minor league pitcher who earned a master's degree in sports performance and is a certified "Neuro-Linguistic Master Practitioner." Among the many other job titles in the Giants front office are Director of Performance Nutrition, Performance Research Scientist, and Vice President, Player Performance and Wellness. At least twenty-two people work as analysts, software engineers, or video engineers. The vice president of pro scouting is Zack Minasian, Perry's brother.

"The GM can be influenced by his right-hand man who always, always, always talked about doing things the way other teams do it," Maddon says. "Last year after the season was over, we had our meetings and it was just me, Tam, and Perry and I said, 'Quite frankly, I'm tired of this. Fuck everybody else and let's do things our way. It doesn't fucking matter what everybody else does.'

"Uh...that didn't go over that well."

The Giants, Dodgers, and Braves especially served as references for Minasian and Perry. In 2022 Minasian instituted daily meetings with players, primarily the hitters, rather than just the traditional first-game-of-a-series meeting.

"That was something Perry wanted," Maddon says. "I just think it's way too over the top. He kept reminding, 'The Braves did it. The Braves did it.' Fine. A lot of things were related to 'We did it this way with the Braves' or 'This is how the Giants did it,' because Alex is a big fan of the GM there. We were all over trying to do things like somebody else.

"On top of that he had Ray Montgomery run the daily meetings."

After last season, Minasian replaced Maddon's bench coach, Mike Gallego, with Montgomery, a fifty-two-year-old former player making the rare jump from the front office to the field. Montgomery, who had been director of player personnel, was working in uniform for the first time after spending most of his career in scouting. Montgomery helped run the daily meetings.

"My method is I talk to the players individually and let the coaches handle [the previous game's items] and not have one person speak for everybody," Maddon says. "Didn't like that, either. And the daily schedule was made up with Ray and the front office, independent of many of my suggestions.

"We play 162 games. The more I talk to them as a group the greater the threat they would stop listening. They would be there physically but not mentally.

"It is obvious to me now that they did not want to include me in either meetings or planned practice because they knew I would not agree with their methods. I did tell Perry once that I did want to implement his vision and supported him on it. But I believe my disagreements wore thin and did not indicate support in a classic sense to him. The disagreements weren't like the disagreements Bobba Lou and I had back in Instructional League. Many of those got loud, but we always left having each other's back. I can assure you I always had the backs of these guys, even though I privately disagreed with different methods."

Maddon's method is built on trust, so he did not see the warning signs. In 2022 he was in the last guaranteed year of his three-year contract. Minasian was signed through 2024; he had the longer contract and more organizational power. Butterfield and Gallego, two of Maddon's top lieutenants, were replaced. Montgomery had come down from the front office to be his bench coach. Moreover, what Maddon calls a pregame "choreography" took root, spearheaded by Minasian and Tamin.

"They see what other groups do and try to emulate," Maddon says. "As an example, the backdoor slider, pushing its use because another team did. They wanted a more choreographed pregame. Believe me, I am the king of choreographed pregame, but there are times to back off and just let the guys show up and play baseball."

Minasian and Tamin, not Maddon and his coaches, would decide which relief pitchers were not available for the game that night. It was based on a proprietary algorithm developed by Tamin that kept track of pitchers' work in rolling thirty-day increments. In recent years it had become common for front offices to usurp control of the bullpen from managers. So-and-so "is down tonight" entered baseball daily parlance, and it came from upstairs.

"The previous year Matt Wise and Dominic Chiti would be the bearers of bad news," Maddon says, referring to the pitching coach and bullpen coach. "Matt would walk in and tell me who was not available. That was really wrong, laying it on Matt to tell me based on their charts. But I knew they were just messengers. And I could tell Matt was not loving being the messenger. But he had to be."

In 2022 Minasian and Tamin dispensed with the messenger.

"Perry and Alex felt it was necessary to be with me in the room to discuss it," Maddon says. "That's the one part that was a big sticking point. Every day the last meeting I like to have before the game is with the pitching coach and bullpen coach. Perry and Alex would be in there telling us who was down, who we were not able to use, and then on top of that suggesting where to use the ones who were available.

"You're going to hear I was never told what to do. If that's the case, they should never have been in the room unless I asked for a specific reason. Because it just gets cloudy and there's too much doubt created.

"In that losing stretch that led to my demise a lot of relievers were made unavailable. I couldn't use them. A lot of that quite frankly is based on the size of the contract and the perception that somebody's going to get hurt.

"Tam had the thirty-day matrix built on how to use relief pitchers, how often and how much rest they needed. Honestly, that's insulting. I know. We know. Wise and Chiti know. And the most important component is the player himself, where you ask relief pitchers, especially veterans, are they good or not today."

Maddon read body language, mechanics, clues in how they answered his questions…all the insights gleaned from forty-two seasons in professional baseball. For instance, Maddon had a reliever with the 2010 Rays, Rafael Soriano, who told him his arm felt better the more he pitched. He encouraged Maddon to use him three days in a row, a taboo among the analytical set. Soriano pitched five times on a third straight day and pitched scoreless ball each time. He made the only All-Star team of his career and finished the season with forty-five saves and a 1.73 ERA.

The modern front office, however, has too much access to data and science to rely on the instincts of a veteran manager. This second generation is too familiar with process, having grown up with it as a first language and used it as entry or advancement in the game, to defer to life experience. Minasian and Tamin were not revolutionaries. They were deploying methodologies that had become mainstream.

Maddon found himself deploying relievers with Tamin's matrix in mind. In one game during the losing streak, the Angels gave up runs to Texas in the sixth, seventh, eighth, and tenth innings while veteran relievers Aaron Loup and Ryan Tepera were off-limits.

"That one really stands out," Maddon says. "What people don't understand is momentum. There is such a thing. When you are giving up games you're supposed to win the momentum is lost and the vibe in the clubhouse is different. You can't overlook one game.

"I had to go to pitchers, or Dominic or Matt did, and tell them they were down today, and they'd go, 'Why?' I even took guys out of games and they'd say, 'I can go back out there again.' And I'd have to say, 'No, I want to be able to use you tomorrow. If you throw ten more pitches you might be down for two days.' I would actually have that conversation with pitchers in the dugout after I took them out.

"If you've grown up in an era of understanding the game and how important it is beyond the numbers to connect with people and establish patience and relationship with your players in order to have success, it's hard to get on the same page with front offices today.

"Of course, I'm into the numbers and any kind of information that helps your team play better. But when it comes to people that really never have done this before and are coming from an outside industry and primarily know how to work up a spreadsheet or take information and create their own little cocktail and then try to argue in favor of it, that's when I have a hard time.

"I know other managers that I've spoken with, guys with experience, feel the same way and they are encouraging me to speak up. This is not an attempt by me to 'get even' or anything like that. I'm not trying to protect myself. It's exposure. If you're a baseball fan, if you love the game and care about the game, you should know what is behind how the game is being played today and how it's run. And the group that's in power now is a little heavy-handed and creates tension instead of cooperation.

"Meetings are for presenters. Conversations are for teachers."

As the Angels played well at the start of the season, the input from the front office intensified. Coaches were told to make sure players did not freelance from the defensive positioning charts created by the front office.

"The dots. 'Play the dots.' That was said more than once," Maddon says, referring to defensive positioning charts players must carry in their back pocket. "It was said so many times, 'Don't permit your defensive player to make adjustments.' It's hard when you're a professional and you've been doing this a long time and people want to dictate to you what to do.

"From a pitching perspective, our pitching coaches really didn't have a game plan. The game plan is instituted by the analytical approach. For the most part, it's macro. Big picture stuff. And it doesn't address enough what the pitcher does well. It's more about what the hitters on the other side do poorly. And what happens is in the game if it's not done properly or something goes awry, the coach will get blamed."

Minasian got involved in a heated discussion with the hitting coaches about how outfielder Brandon Marsh should start his bat when he swung. Some pitchers were told not to shake off the catcher's signs. Maddon was quizzed on his pitching scripts going into a game.

"Don't say, 'You really have to be careful after this guy faces eighteen batters,'" Maddon says. "Please don't say that to me. Or, 'If it's the fifth inning and it's a left-on-left situation, what are you going to do?'

"What do you mean, what am I going to do? I don't know. You have to watch the entire context play out. Are we leading? Are we behind? Is their closer right-handed or left-handed? Please get out of the way and rely on me to make that particular decision.

"They are really into the pinch-hitting situation. There's a phrase they utilize: 'Win the platoon matchups.' It's like a badge of honor, like the team that has the most platoon matchups in their favor wins the analytical wars. You have to understand there's a sort of competition between front offices to look good statistically, sometimes even more than what happens on the field. It bothers the crap out of me. Anybody who puts a thought in your head before you manage the game mostly only serves to confuse and make things worse.

"Even if you're strong-minded, as I think I am, 'here is the situation that's going to come' is more complex than the sterile version before the game. The part they don't understand is establishing confidence, particularly with a young player. 'What do you mean he can't hit a left-hander? Let's give him an opportunity before we say he cannot.'

"Then the counterargument is, 'We have to win games. We can't give up games by permitting this left on left.' And then my argument would be, 'We can't lose games by not permitting our relief pitchers to pitch.'"

The divide between old and new, between manager and front office, between data and art, between Maddon and Minasian, reached a boiling point on May 9. The Angels had just scored five runs in the seventh inning against Tampa Bay to turn a 6–3 lead into an 11–3 blowout. Ohtani hit a grand slam. The dugout was lively. Suddenly, head athletic trainer Mike Frostad walked up to Maddon at his usual perch on the top step of the dugout and said, "Perry just called down. He said get Trout out of the game."

Says Maddon, "I went apeshit. That really might have been the first little break in the marriage right there. I was pissed."

Earlier in the day Trout had complained about a bit of soreness in his groin. But later he told Maddon that the soreness dissipated, and he was fine.

To Maddon, Minasian broke a sacred code. The general manager had called the dugout during a game to dictate strategy to the manager—and to a proven, veteran manager at that. To Minasian, he simply was deploying the power given to this generation of executives. Nothing was sacred. Nothing was out of bounds. Not dressing and working in the coaches' room. Not telling the manager which pitchers not to use. Not ordering backdoor sliders. Not calling the dugout during a game to order a lineup move.

The next day Maddon blew up at Minasian in Maddon's office.

"Listen, don't you *ever* fucking call down to the dugout again!" Maddon said.

"He didn't like that," Maddon says. "We went back and forth on it. I eventually told him, 'If you need something like that, you need to work it better. You can have the trainer talk to the player and have the trainer recommend to me that you think we should take him out of the game.' I would have been fine with that. But to call downstairs and get involved in the game . . . I would never call upstairs and tell anybody who to acquire or release."

Twenty-six days later, Maddon was gone. When Minasian fired him, Maddon offered him advice. He suggested that Minasian not bring Tamin on road trips. He wanted to give coaches more room to breathe and work freely.

"Don't bring everybody with you," Maddon told him. "Give people a break from other people."

He did not tell Minasian to leave the coaches' room to the coaches.

"I was going to text him the next day to bring it up, but I chose not to," Maddon says. "I didn't want to keep coming back to it. It was over. I should have mentioned that to him because I did talk to him about Ray and his role and Alex and his role, but I really should have mentioned I really believe they should not dress in the coaches' locker room. And the coaches' little meeting room should not be theirs, either. That should be for the coaches and not what the front office did."

Coaches and coaching are at the heart of Maddon's belief system in baseball. To him they are to baseball what teachers are to education. Underpaid and underappreciated, but indispensable. Keepers of the flame. The epitome of pure intentions. When you attack Maddon's methods you are attacking Coach Rute and Bobba Lou and Gig and Monty and the Little General and Richie and Jack and loose-toothed Sieminski. It is no different from attacking family.

The new front offices prefer hiring coaches from hitting and pitching labs or college programs raised on data-based doctrine. It dovetails with the executives' viewpoint that baseball could be mastered from a mathematical approach more so than a liberal arts one. Jeff Luhnow, the architect behind the Astros team that won a 2017 championship with the help of using monitors to steal signs, did not enter baseball because he loved it. "At no point was I planning to go into sports or baseball," Luhnow once told the *Daily Pennsylvanian*. For fourteen years he worked as an engineer, a McKinsey consultant, and a tech entrepreneur. His only connection to baseball was playing in a fantasy league. Then in 2003 a McKinsey colleague helped him land a job with the Cardinals.

Doors opened for Luhnow and outsiders like him as owners realized the ideas of logistics, algorithms, and efficiency that worked in the businesses where they made their money should work in baseball, too. It was their language, not the mysterious, exclusive world of scout-speak. The Astros hired Luhnow in December 2011. When Luhnow wanted someone to run his baseball operations department, he specified he wanted someone not from within the game but from banking. He hired a derivatives valuations expert, Brandon Taubman. It wasn't long before their statistical analysts were setting up shop in the clubhouse and using video and algorithms to decode opposing team's signs. It wasn't a far leap to players stealing signs off live feeds and banging on a trash can to alert the batter what was coming.

The biggest scandals in baseball in recent years all have roots of outsiders not raised in the established codes of the game: Luhnow and the sign stealing; Chris Correa, who was working on a doctoral project when the Cardinals hired him as a quantitative analyst and who hacked the Astros' computer system; and John Cappolella, a business management graduate who initially accepted a job at a semiconductor company, and who has been banned for life from baseball for international signing violations as general manager of the Braves.

"Who is teaching the next generation of coaches and what are they teaching?" Maddon says. "Is the game being taught or is it more reliant on studying feedback from technology? Best in show. The players want to hear more and more about exit velocity and spin rates from coaches as opposed to absolute mechanical information that only a well-trained pitching coach or hitting coach could pass along.

"Who is mentoring these groups? How is the game being passed on with the eradication of minor league teams? There is a lot of tearing of the fabric right now.

"With the Angels, everything was controlled through the coaches' room through the analytical department, accumulating information and then being there to present it to or question the coaching staff. The coaches in a traditional sense never felt really free to coach, because they only feel free when it came to the acquiescence to those handing them the stuff. Once you get acceptance from the front office, you're good to go. But if you don't have their blessing it becomes a lot more difficult, and you'd better be right. It's no different than third time around the batting order.

"The front office mostly stays away from the hitting side because it's more difficult. They want to get more involved in where pitchers should throw the ball and where the defense should stand. I would want that. Large sample plays out on defense. But not in a vacuum and not without input from the coaches. Get the coaches involved and you get better buy-in.

"Imagine you've coached for twenty, thirty years and all of a sudden you're castrated when it comes to organizational game plan implementation."

The most successful period in Angels history was marked by stability and an all-star coaching staff. From 2000 through 2007 they were run by the same general manager, Bill Stoneman, a former major league pitcher; the same manager, Mike Scioscia; and a coaching staff that had remained largely intact before other teams began hiring some of them to manage: Maddon, Bud Black, Ron Roenicke, Alfredo Griffin, and Mickey Hatcher. Stoneman, raised knowing the sacredness of the locker room, stayed out of their physical space. At their height the Angels made the playoffs six times in an eight-year window, including the franchise's only world championship in 2002. Such a model is dead.

Entering 2022, the Angels had not made the playoffs in seven years and had not won a playoff game in twelve years. Moreno has changed general managers five times in his nineteen years of ownership. He changed the manager or general manager every year for four straight years: a new manager in 2019 (Brad Ausmus), a new manager in 2020 (Maddon), a new general manager in 2021 (Minasian), and a new manager in 2022 (Phil Nevin). Ohtani played for four managers in his first five years with the team. In six seasons from 2017 to 2022, the Angels also chewed through four bench coaches, four pitching coaches, and six third-base coaches.

Maddon was given a three-year contract with a club option when Moreno hired him. It was a fractured run. The first season included only sixty games because of the pandemic. The second season was marked by a record number of injuries, especially to Trout, who played in only thirty-six games. The third season lasted only fifty-six games for him. Two of his three spring trainings were abbreviated, once because of the pandemic and in 2022 by a lockout.

The end came suddenly. The Angels were 27-17 on May 24. It was the fifth best start in Angels history, and the franchise's best start in eighteen years. Twelve games later Maddon was gone.

"I felt good about where we were headed," Maddon says. "I've been through some tough moments like that and always figured out a way to work through them. One of my strong suits is in difficult moments you stand tall and don't change. You don't get upset. You don't start blaming people. That's when you need support.

"Relationships have to be built. Trust has to be established in order to survive these kinds of moments. I thought we had done it. Apparently not. The trust, the exchange of ideas, the constructive criticism... absolutely that was established between me and the coaching staff and between me and the players.

"But apparently not all the way to the top."

At the top of a major league organizational chart today is a triangle. The owner, lead baseball operations person (traditionally the general manager, though title inflation has wrought fancier designations), and manager form the corners of the triangle. But the triangle is inverted. The manager is at the bottom. The owner and general manager hold power over the manager, even as it relates to game strategy and coaching. The triangle works best only when all three positions buy in completely to the structure and philosophy.

The New York Yankees, for instance, arrived at this triangular balance after the 2017 season, when general manager Brian Cashman decided not to rehire Girardi, even though the veteran manager had been successful, and the team came within one win of the World Series. The Yankees brimmed with rising young stars. Cashman, given autonomy in baseball operations from owner Hal Steinbrenner, had to decide who the best manager would be for the next five years or so, not just for the moment. Girardi had difficulty connecting to the younger players.

Cashman interviewed Carlos Beltran, Aaron Boone, Hensley Meulens, Rob Thomson, and Chris Woodward—none of whom had managed before in the majors—and Eric Wedge, who had not managed in four years and could have been another version of Howe in Oakland. He swapped out Girardi's experience for the newness of Boone, who was a managerial blank slate. Boone got along well with Cashman personally and professionally. The inverted triangle of Steinbrenner-Cashman-Boone has been a model of stability. The Yankees produced a .601 winning percentage in the trio's first four seasons together.

General managers increasingly prefer such managerial blank slates; there are no established managerial philosophies or norms to clash with how they want the job done. In thirty-two managerial changes from the 2017 to 2018 off-season through Maddon's firing by the Angels, general managers picked a first-time manager nineteen times, indicating a preference for a blank slate almost 60 percent of the time.

The Angels' inverted triangle for years has lacked seamless philosophy and stability, including the Moreno-Minasian-Maddon triangle. Deep down, and on occasions painfully obvious, Minasian and Maddon knew this. Both knew the makings of a long-term marriage were difficult to find. Twelve straight losses forced Minasian to confront that reality. He replaced Maddon with Angels third-base coach Phil Nevin, another first-time MLB manager.

"The only reason you fire the manager," Maddon says, "is there is a total disconnect between the manager and players, or there is a philosophical disconnect between the manager and either the GM or the owner—primarily the GM. I plead guilty to having philosophical differences with Perry. You don't take it personally. It's business.

"I enjoyed working with him, laughing with him. I guess philosophically it wasn't going to work. If you put a match to his foot, I'd have to believe it came down to philosophical differences more than anything. Getting me out of the way permits them to have total control without having to be concerned with any pushback from me, which they did get and would have continued to get as we continued to ascend, which we would do."

Hurt by how his run with the Cubs fizzled, Maddon had returned home to the Angels with optimism and energy. In a way, he never shook the infield dirt from his shoes from those sweat-soaked, 100-degree days in Arizona Instructional League, when in front of no crowds but the occasional approving nod from Mauch and the prideful gaze of Gene and Jackie Autry, he helped players such as Tim Salmon, Devon White, Damion Easley, Jack Howell, Dante Bichette, and Troy Percival on their path to the big leagues.

"When I came back here, all I wanted was somebody to work with," Maddon says. "That was my only intent."

It didn't happen. He still has that intent. He wants to manage again. But the game has changed over the arc of a major league managerial career that began with the 2006 Devil Rays. It doesn't value in a manager nearly as much as he does the dirt in your shoes or a pedagogical approach. If he has a place in the game again, it will be for someone else who also honors the soul of the game, who believes data enhances and complements art and instinct, not depreciates them.

"Going into the game right now as a manager you need to understand you are going to be controlled," Maddon says. "There is a need to control you. Personal thoughts, feeling, instinct . . . they're going to be not wanted.

"You're really going to be required or asked to do exactly what the front office wants you to do. The trick then would be to somehow be able to build relationships but even then, your ability to freely think, work, and suggest with these players can be constricted by methods coming from the front office to you. It's just the way of the world right now.

"It's a big part of the landscape. For those wanting to manage today, if you've never done it before, yes, you're not going to have the same methods or freewheeling ways we utilized in the minor leagues, which I loved, from Idaho Falls to Midland, which wasn't great. That was a perfect example of when it's yours and you stink, it's much easier to put up with and say, 'Yep, I screwed up. It's my fault.'"

Acknowledgments

Every book has a story behind the story. This one made it through a global pandemic and two dismissals only with the help of many dedicated people whose names do not appear on the cover.

Sean Desmond, publisher of Twelve, was our guiding light. Providing the vision, encouragement, support, commitment, and a deft editing hand, Sean defined great leadership. He was our Manager of the Year a few times over.

Editorial assistant Zohal Karimy was our quality control coach, pulling the project together with diligence and enthusiasm. Senior production editor Mari C. Okuda and copy editor S. B. Kleinman did an amazing job treating every word, sentence, fact, and name with utmost care and thoroughness. If there is a polish that shines from these pages, it is from their hands.

David Black of David Black Literary Agency was more than the invaluable sounding board all authors need to navigate the changing seas of a project. He was an editor, an idea person, a fighter and, above all, a friend.

Our unsung MVP is Louise Sousoures, who turned around impeccable transcripts with astounding speed. Joe huffing and puffing into his microphone while biking or the occasional mechanical blip of his ancient reel-to-reel tape recorder bothered her none.

Nearly every current manager and many past ones contributed to this material in some way. They are the keepers of the game and its primary spokespeople. No person represents their club and the sport more often in front of cameras, microphones, and notepads than the manager. Joe Torre, Bruce Bochy, Dave Roberts, A. J. Hinch, David Ross, Dusty Baker, Alex Cora, and Brian Snitker are among those deserving special

367

mention for their acuity and cooperation. Likewise, from a front-office perspective, Sandy Alderson and Theo Epstein, as usual, were particularly gracious with their time and insights.

Because memory is wonderful but facts rule, BaseballReference.com and Newspapers.com were vital and frequent resources. The writing life before them was much harder.

Every winning team is the sum of many parts who share in the glory, though in unequal measures. A tip of the cap to the scouting and player development staffs of the world champion 2002 Angels and 2016 Cubs and American League champion 2008 Rays, as well as all the "baseball lifers" whose dedication comes from passion for the sport and helping others, not individual agendas.

When the pandemic first hit in 2020, many teams furloughed staff or released minor league players rather than pay them for a season that never was played. However, Kansas City general manager Dayton Moore pledged the Royals would not only keep all its minor leaguers but also would pay them a $400 weekly stipend. They can impact the game, he said, as much as a ten-year major league veteran.

"Those individuals go back into their communities and teach the game, work in academies, are JUCO coaches, college coaches, scouts, coaches in pro baseball," Moore said. "They're growing the game constantly because they're so passionate about it."

Some could even go on to manage nineteen years in the big leagues and win a World Series.

This book reflects that spirit of passion and pure intentions. Most important, it would not be possible without the love and support of our families. Nothing matters more.

J.M.
T.V.

About the Authors

JOE MADDON is the former manager of the Los Angeles Angels.

TOM VERDUCCI is the lead baseball writer for *Sports Illustrated* and a lead analyst and reporter for MLB Network and Fox Sports.